UNEMPLOY

ECONOMIC PROMISE AND POLITICAL WILL

EDITED BY ED CARSON, ADAM JAMROZIK, AND TONY WINEFIELD

First published on behalf of the Social Policy Research Group,
University of South Australia in 1998 by Australian Academic Press, Brisbane.

Distributed by
Social Policy Research Group, University of South Australia
St Bernards Road, Magill SA 5072, Australia.

National Library of Australia Cataloguing-in-Publication entry

Unemployment: Economic promise and political will.

ISBN 1 875378 23 5

1. Unemployment — Congresses. 2. Unemployment — Australia —
Congresses. 3. Labor Market — Congresses. 4. Labor
market — Australia — Congresses. I. Carson, Edgar. II.
Jamrozik, Adam. III. Winefield, Anthony H. (Anthony
Harold). IV. National Conference on Unemployment
(4th : 1997 : Adelaide, S. Aust.).

331.137994

Designed and typeset in Goudy 10/11.5 pt by Australian Academic Press, Brisbane

CONTENTS

2 CHANGING NATURE OF WORK

3 LABOUR MARKET PROGRAMS

4 POLITICAL WILL

ACKNOWLEDGMENTS

Many people made the Conference and this book possible and the Editorial Committee is indebted to all of them.

Special thanks to Elizabeth Hoon and Anne Braybon for tireless work both before and during the Conference. We are also grateful to Deirdre Tedmanson for assisting with negotiations and linkages.

The Editorial Committee would like to acknowledge Sal Humphries, Amanda-Jane Lambden, and Bev O'Brien for their editorial work in the preparation of this book. Thanks also to the (anonymous) referees.

PREFACE

The Fourth National Conference on Unemployment, held in Adelaide in June 1997, brought together key researchers and practitioners in the field. The theme of the conference, Economic Promise and Political Will, turned our attention to the fact that unemployment is not only an economic problem but also a political problem. We have now experienced high levels of unemployment for at least 20 years, and there are no signs on the horizon of any change for the better. Unemployment has become entrenched in certain sections of the population, despite repeated promises of reducing it coming from each newly elected government, later followed by explanations why the promise had not been fulfilled. In the media and in the community, comments about a growing marginalised 'underclass' in our society are now frequently heard. Serious doubts must be raised as to the likelihood of a solution being found within the current economic theories and policies adapted from these theories.

High levels of unemployment are not confined to Australia; they are experienced in most industrialised countries. Free market economies seem to function well but at the price of excluding a high proportion of their populations from employment. With each passing year, an impression grows stronger that unemployment might be an unavoidable by-product of economies which follow free market policies. If this is so, as it seems to be, then the search for solutions to unemployment has to extend beyond current economic policies and theories that guide them, into different thinking and new perspectives on the problem and new policies. In the final analysis, the solution to unemployment may indeed come down to political will. The economic will have to become the political.

The Conference contributed to such new thinking and new perspectives and attracted a wide range of contributions. It received national attention and was deemed to be critical in advancing understanding of the issues and furthering policy development in the area. In addition to keynote addresses presented in the plenary sessions, there were approximately fifty papers, workshops and panel presentations in the concurrent sessions, arranged in eight sections: Youth; Aboriginal Employment; Women; Politics, Policies, Theory; Psychology; Economic Change and Solutions; Ethnicity; and Labour Market Programs.

A rigorous process of peer revision and refereeing has resulted in the selection of thirty papers covering the major themes that emerged from the Conference. This text presents the views and research of some of today's leading scholars and practitioners and in the fields of sociology, psychology, both nationally and internationally. The Editorial Committee, after completing the referee and selection process on the papers has grouped them under four general categories. They are as follows:

1. Economic Promise

Themes which emerge from the papers in this section include a questioning of the veracity of recent economic policy, identifying its undesirable consequences on unemployment levels, and the impact of anti-inflationary policies on unemployment. Throughout the articles, alternative sets of policies are proposed for maximising employment growth and reducing unemployment.

2. The Changing Nature of Work

The key themes to emerge from this section address the increasingly precarious nature of work (for example, part time, casual and temporary work), the disjuncture between people's expectations of future work and the likely outcomes for them in view of this trend. The section also identifies the consequences of this for patterns of recruitment, and highlights the impact of these recruitment changes on particular groups within the labour market.

3. Labour Market Programs

This section examines the impact and effectiveness of a range of labour market programs. The themes that emerge include the merits of 'work for the dole' schemes, the difficulties of case management strategies at the heart of new labour market provisions, and the impact of new employment assistance policies on workers who have to implement them.

4. Political Will

The final section identifies political strategies for addressing the problems of the labour market and unemployment most importantly strategies for achieving full employment. The section also addresses the links between poverty and unemployment, and the importance of new political alliances, particularly the Green movement, in confronting concerns about jobs and unemployment.

Although the papers come from various disciplines, including economics and the social sciences, the language used has been edited for accessibility. This book will have a broad appeal to academics and students, in particular, second, third and fourth year undergraduates in Economics, Politics, Sociology, Psychology, Social Work and related disciplines. Academic staff and graduate students researching in this area will also find this an important resource, in that it is topical and reports on a range of current Australian research by established authors in the field.

Moreover, since the conference brought together researchers and practitioners in productive dialogue, the appeal of the book will extend to practitioners, field workers and policy makers.

Finally, we hope that the ideas presented in these papers will generate lively and fruitful discussions that will lead to some imaginative and constructive suggestions for possible solutions to unemployment. We should then be able to take these suggestions to develop the ideas further, and disseminate them in our communities by whatever means are at our disposal. We are confident that the book is a major contribution to debates in the areas of employment, unemployment and labour market policy.

On behalf of the Editorial Committee
Ed Carson

Editorial Committee:
Associate Professor Ed Carson (University of South Australia)
Associate Professor Adam Jamrozik (University of South Australia)
Dr Tony Winefield (University of Adelaide)

CONTRIBUTORS

Alphabetical List of Contributors

ARMSTRONG, *Bruce*, School of Business, Southern Cross University, Coffs Harbour Education Campus, Hogbin Drive, Coffs Harbour NSW 2457

BELL, *Stephen*, Department of Political Science, University of Tasmania, PO Box 252C, Hobart Tas 7000

BURGESS, *John*, Employment Studies Centre, University of Newcastle, Newcastle NSW 2308

CAMERON, *Michael*, Department of Employment, Education, Training and Youth Affairs (DEETYA), PO Box 9880, Canberra City ACT 2601

CARSON, *Ed*, Social Policy Research Group, University of South Australia, St Bernards Road, Magill SA 5072

COLLINS, *Jock*, School of Finance and Economics, University of Technology, Sydney, PO Box 123, Broadway NSW 2007

CREED, *Peter*, Gold Coast Campus, Griffith University, PMB 50, Gold Coast QLD 9726

CROWLEY, *Kate*, Department of Government, University of Tasmania, PO Box 252-22, Hobart TAS 7001

DOW, *Geoff*, Department of Government, University of Queensland, Brisbane QLD

DREVER, *Margaret*, School of Business, Southern Cross University, Coffs Harbour Education Campus, Hogbin Drive, Coffs Harbour NSW 2457

DRURY, *Brian*, Gold Coast Campus, Griffith University, PMB 50, Gold Coast QLD 9726

DUNSTAN, *Don*, Centre for Labour Studies, University of Adelaide, Adelaide, SA 5000

DWYER, *Peter*, Youth Research Centre, University of Melbourne, Parkville VIC 3052

EARDLEY, *Tony*, Social Policy Research Centre, University of New South Wales, Kensington NSW 2052

FITZGERALD, *Robert*, Australian Council of Social Service, Locked Bag 11, Darlinghurst, NSW 2010

FORAN, *Angelica*, Bond University, Gold Coast QLD 4229

GEORGE, *Jennie*, ACTU, 6th Floor, ACTU House, 393–397 Swanston St, Melbourne, VIC 3000

GODDARD, *Richard*, School of Learning and Development, Queensland University of Technology, Kelvin Grove Campus, QLD 4059

GREEN, *Roy*, Employment Studies Centre, University of Newcastle, Newcastle NSW 2308

JAMROZIK, *Adam*, School of Social Work and Social Policy, University of South Australia, St Bernards Road, Magill SA 5072

JUNIPER, *James*, School of Economics, Finance and Property, City West Campus,

University of South Australia, North Terrace, Adelaide SA 5000

KERR, *Lorraine*, School of Arts, Community Development and International Studies, University of South Australia, St Bernards Road, Magill SA 5072

LI, *Simon Chi Fai*, Department of Public and Social Administration, City University of Hong Kong, 83 tat Chee Avenue, Kowloon HONG KONG

MACDONALD, *Helen*, Brotherhood of St Laurence, 67 Brunswick Street, Fitzroy VIC 3065

MISHRA, *Gita*, Research Institute for Gender and Health, University of Newcastle, Newcastle NSW 2308

MULLER, *Juanita*, Bond University, Gold Coast QLD 4229

NOHILLY, *Helen*, School of Business, Southern Cross University, Coffs Harbour Education Campus, Hogbin Drive, Coffs Harbour NSW 2457

PARKER, *Rachel*, School of Management, Queensland University of Technology, PO Box 2434, Brisbane QLD 4001

PATTON, *Wendy*, School of Learning and Development, Queensland University of Technology, Kelvin Grove Campus, QLD 4059

PIGRAM, *Derek*, Department of Employment, Education, Training and Youth Affairs (DEETYA), PO Box 9880, Canberra City ACT 2601

PROBERT, *Belinda*, Social Sciences, Royal Melbourne Institute of Technology, 124 Latrobe Street, Melbourne VIC 3000

SAVELSBERG, *Harry*, School of Social Work and Social Policy, University of South Australia, St Bernards Road, Magill SA 5072

STILWELL, *Frank*, Department of Economics, The University of Sydney, Sydney NSW 2006

SWEENEY, *Stewart*, Elton Mayo School of Management, City West Campus, University of South Australia, North Terrace, Adelaide SA 5000

THOMSON, *Pat*, Department of Education & Children's Services, 31 Flinders Street, Adelaide, 5000

TOMLINSON, *John*, School of Social Science, Queensland University of Technology, Beams Road, Carseldine QLD 4034

VANDENHEUVEL, *Audrey*, National Institute of Labour Studies, Flinders University, Bedford Park, SA 5042

WATTS, *Rob*, Social Science and Social Work, Royal Melbourne Institute of Technology, Melbourne VIC 3000

WICKS, *Deidre*, Research Institute for Gender and Health, University of Newcastle, Newcastle NSW 2308

WILSON, *Lou*, School of Social Work and Social Policy, University of South Australia, St Bernards Road, Magill SA 5072

WINEFIELD, *Anthony*, Department of Psychology, University of Adelaide, Adelaide, SA 5000

ECONOMIC PROMISE

Political Will and State Capacity: The Post Liberal Implications of Post Keynesian Political Economy

Geoff Dow

Satisfactory political resolution of the problem of contemporary unemployment requires that we embrace the political possibility of subjecting structural economic change to the policy process, even in the face of globalization. Despite longstanding intellectual scepticism, especially from economists, recent developments in the theory of state capacity suggest that such a politicization of the economy is possible.

In political theory, three major traditions of analysis — liberalism, marxism and a conservative, statist approach — have attempted to deal with the dilemma posed by extra-political constraints on political possibilities. Each offers a distinctive resolution to the dilemma.

Corporatist critiques of liberalism and post keynesian critiques of economic orthodoxy suggest that it is desirable and also indicate the institutional mechanisms by which the political project might be effected. So, together, statist political theory, corporatist theory and post keynesian political economy offer a basis for charting a route — in terms of conceptual understanding and institution-building — from unemployment.

This is the task of a post-liberal politics. In an age of generalized disillusion with mainstream politics, declining evidence of political will, increasing costs of state capacity and supercilious indifference to the possibilities of politics, we need to be very sure we know what the political process is being asked to do.

Politics exists because there is inevitably a realm of collective needs, objectives and responses to problems. Political decision making is decision making concerning ends whose achievement is reasonably imaginable but nonetheless beyond the immediate competences of individuals. Quite often, though not invariably, politics involves authoritative direction or allocation which might be opposed or resisted. For these reasons, the assertion of political possibilities embodies fundamentally anti-liberal characteristics; hence the liberal preference for small and constitutionally limited government prioritizing procedural rather than substantive goals.

Activation of political activity presumes political or collective possibilities. That is, the development of a political realm implies a belief in a distinctive sphere of political action relatively unconstrained by external or structural determination. In the modern world, this involves assertion of at least some national political autonomy and capacity over the national impact of market-driven economic and structural change, often emanating from extra-national conditions. Political will implies at least some degree of volitional, and effective, political autonomy. Statecraft and strategy and guile matter.

Of course, there are also limits to state capacity. Not all that is desirable is immediately achievable; political outcomes are constrained by levels of material development, by past political developments, by the extent and effectiveness of opposition, by the competence or otherwise of activists and by the position of the political terrain in wider contexts of national and international forces. Furthermore, political achievements can readily be reversed. Academic analysis of politics, both mainstream and critical, has tended to be sceptical of the likelihood of political development that can achieve objectives that would not occur spontaneously. However, comparative analysis of the advanced societies during the period of recession and structural adjustment (since 1974) shows that politics does matter, that unorthodox policy experiments can be effective. Is has been possible, for example, to defend moral or communitarian aspirations, to delimit market outcomes, particularly with respect to unemployment. What follows in this essay therefore concentrates more on the possibilities than on the limits to politics.

In political theory, the three major traditions of analysis — liberalism, marxism and a conservative, statist approach — have dealt with the question of how political possibilities might be expanded. Each offers a distinctive resolution; but each contains weaknesses that can be largely redressed by exposure to the political theory of corporatism and the political implications of post keynesian political economy.

Liberal politics

Liberal theories of the state, those emphasising the desirability of limited government, provide the approach to political development most compatible with current policy preferences for international (and competitive) considerations to frame government activity. Liberal theories have been most influential in the anglosaxon polities which are typically characterized by small government and poor economic performance. The liberal polity has but few capacities to deal with unemployment, mainly because unemployment is seen as either a sign of success — necessary and desirable structural change — or self-correcting. A significant paradox for liberal theory is its co-existence with a century-long growth in political influence, registered through levels of state expenditure, the development of corporatist forms of policy making and general 'decommodification' of social life as a result of the expansion of the welfare state. In other words, liberal governance produces outcomes that societies often find repugnant enough to warrant the construction of anti-liberal responses. There are recurrent suggestions that liberal regimes undervalue the contribution of 'social investment' to societal development.

Though liberal theories do not satisfactorily account for what is happening in the mature capitalist economies at the moment, and may even be said to contribute to economic and social dislocation when used as the rationale for policy abrogations, liberalism as a movement has nonetheless left some important legacies which political development in any circumstances will probably feel obliged to respect. The achievements of liberalism, acknowledged even by its critics, include the ending of arbitrary political rule, the elevation of the principle of individual freedom and the establishment of legal guarantees of (and respect for) private property. Even where these are eroded by the encroachment of taxation and business regulation, or supplemented by more extensive infusion of moral or communitarian or democratic codes of conduct, the threshold of liberal proscriptions and protocols has been an important part of the emergence of civilized governance. The creation of state capacity beyond the boundaries of liberal tolerance will need to respect many of the caveats about the risk of government that liberalism has voiced (Hintze 1897; Janicke 1990).

Marxist politics

Marxian theories of the state are generally sceptical of the possibility that states (public sectors) can or ought to act in a progressive manner. But marxism's common conclusions (concerning the omnipotence or oppressiveness or functionality of politics) are not entirely convincing. There is a reformist theory of the state and politics. Marxian political economy does not imply the impossibility of progressive political interventions to undermine the logic of accumulation under capitalism. It is not Marx's view that the social relations established two centuries ago to facilitate the bourgeois 'mission' were likely to stay in place forever. An authentic marxian theory of the state would proclaim that, as capital accumulation can not be secured indefinitely by capitalist social relations, political activity by labour to democratize and decommodify the economy is inevitable, part of labour's 'anti-bourgeois mission'. In this reformist view, the state would not have 'a role'; it would be an arena of conflict, a terrain on which pre-existing conflicts are played out, a 'strategic field' whereon the economy can become politicized, through negotiation or institution-building or the insertion of macro-political principles concerning decommodification or public investment or equity or balanced national development. It is too cynical and pre-emptive of history to insist that state activity necessarily secures the conditions for ongoing capital accumulation, determined outside the realm of politics. From marxian political economy there are just as valid reasons for expecting the state's role in capital accumulation to increase (and to generate good macroeconomic outcomes) as there are reasons to expect it to be class-biased (against labour) or biased against particular national interests in favour of international imperatives (Das 1996).

The marxist theory of political reformism therefore depends on views of what politics generally and labour-led anti-market use of the state in particular can do to modify the effects of the capitalist economy. More specifically, it envisages ongoing political conflict over the institutional interventions required to effect full employment, equality, a stable macroeconomy and more democratic or principled economic decision making. To this extent, the distinction often drawn between social democratic and socialist strategies is often over-drawn. The retractions of social democratic principle that frequently occur ought to be seen as essentially failures of the socialist impulse rather than as betrayals from which authentic socialism is entitled to haughtily distance itself.

To postulate social democratic political possibilities is not to deny the pervasiveness of class conflict or the continuing exploitation that underlies capitalism or its recurrent crisis tendencies or its constraining social relations (market allocation, profitability as the criterion for investment, commodity production and hierarchical control of the labour process). Social democratic reformism is merely the assertion that 'the chase across the globe' after profitability is not the sole factor determining economic activity, that the scope of the market impulse has been declining throughout this century and that the political process is entitled to assert, as it always has, principles which violate the mechanical ascription of the rise and decline of industry to the logic of capital. There is no suggestion that such a social democratic project will ever be complete, or contradiction-less, or exempt from reversal and defeat, or even that its institutional practitioners necessarily have the competence to see the project through. Politicization of the economy will never free itself from the force of markets, the political organizations of business, the resistance implied by liberal institutions and traditions, underdeveloped (or historically discredited) statist apparatuses, the labourist compromises of the past, the sheer difficulty of the task (of invoking new economic activities, particularly during recession), or, in Australia, the shabby behaviour (including flights from principle) of the ALP's own apparatchiks (which the leninists want to include as a defining feature of social democracy).

The conservative or statist critique of liberalism

There is a second, increasingly influential, body of political doctrine and analysis opposed to market outcomes. The conservative critique of liberalism has become an important basis for statist theories of politics, those deriving from a weberian (or so-called 'society-centred') perspective. Here, the autonomy of political processes (from both external and internal influence) and the capacity of governments, especially through bureaucratic organization and the development of 'rational' procedures, to expand their capacities for effective governance (or to reduce impediments to governability) is postulated. There is in this tradition an implicit acceptance of a logic of political development, that is, an argument that political competence, governability and the legitimate scope of state activity are all prone to increase (as in the 'law of expanding state activity'). Much of the statist literature derives from conservative strands of political thought advocating the need for a national polity to maintain social solidarity in the face of market-induced uncertainties. The tradition emphasizes the potential countries still have to resist globalization and to retain national peculiarities (Levi-Faur 1997). It is often claimed that the economic success of the non-liberal Asian industrializers owes much to the influence of this conception of statism. There is much in this theorizing (including the work of nineteenth century German writers like Adolph Wagner and Friedrich List) which deserves to be re-integrated into a contemporary state theory. What is lacking from much of this work, however, is a well-developed sense of the resistances to statist activity, not only internal objections but also those from the international institutions that have been persuading individual countries' governments to adopt free trade or deregulatory stances (Bell 1994; Evans 1992; Weiss & Hobson 1995).

Corporatist political arrangements

The literature on corporatism is now well known. Despite the surge of academic interest in the many unorthodox policy-making arrangements that have been labelled 'corporatist' since the mid-1970s, there has not emerged any generally convincing definition of the purposes or effects of corporatism. Initially the analytical reception was hostile because the principles of liberal pluralism appeared to have been violated by the large role ceded to organizations such as peak councils of labour and capital that pluralists thought should not have been such active participants in or beneficiaries of direct public decision-making (Schmitter, Lehmbruch). In addition, the marxist tradition was concerned about the potential co-optation of labour, about the class biases of the state, about the partial or unstable nature of the political system thus created and about the 'statization' of society and the 'economization' of politics (Panitch, Jessop, Offe, Bauman). Nonetheless, though there was no single doctrinal advocacy of corporatism, many commentators saw the advantage of imposing public control on private ownership, particularly in an era of inflation-inducing class conflict, declining corporate competitiveness and the apparent need to respond to problems of structural adjustment with less ineffective and more innovative institutions (Winkler, Cawson, Cameron, Schmidt, Crouch, Katzenstein).

Though corporatist solutions had been advanced (in response to a diversity of real or imagined problems) by romantics, reactionaries, communitarians, fascists, authoritarians, technocrats, functionalists, socialists, modernizers, nationalists and liberal reformers, the main potential impropriators of contemporary corporatism appear to be labour movements (for reasons anticipated by, for example, Durkheim, Weber and Polanyi). Both labour's functional role in production and the ineliminable nature of its conflict with liberal protocols, especially concerning attempts to establish a 'labour market', are recognized and accommodated by incomes policy, tripartite decision-making institutions and other crisis-management arrangements that are incompatible with liberal modes of macro-economic management (Korpi, Regini, Meidner). Further, not only have corporatist modes of economic governance produced better outcomes than liberal regulation, but performance has deteriorated when the former have been dismantled. Social democratic corporatism in particular, then, seems well suited to the problems of economic maturity, neither dependent upon consensus nor supine in the face of administrative overload.

The post keynesianism foundations of post liberal politics

Post keynesianism is that body of analysis which, based on the protestations of Michal Kalecki and Joan Robinson that the lessons of the keynesian revolution had been bastardized in the 1950s, resuscitates Keynes's message — that control of economic recession (including those aspects of recession attendant upon global restructuring) requires institutional control of investment, control of inflation (at full employment and during periods of unemployment) by institutional control of conflicts over the distribution of income, and control of 'the labour market' (which can never really be a market) by institutionalized labour market policies. The most important rationale for state intervention into the operations of the market economy has been Keynes' call for 'a somewhat comprehensive socialization of investment' — in order to moderate the cycles of employment, income and living standards. The development of effective economic policy is an instance of the political and class conflicts in which labour as a class has recurrently been involved.

The important congruence between marxian and post keynesian viewpoints, however, is that 'economic management' — the attempt to have policy rather than market mechanisms determine the pace and direction of structural change will be resisted (Kalecki 1943). The class dimension of the conflict includes not only the conflict between labour and capital over their respective prerogatives in production, but the internal conflicts between sectors oriented to global and national, urban and rural, export and import, manufacturing and finance activities. How these divisions are reconciled historically determines the pattern of accumulation, the structure of industry, the preferred forms of regulation and, in turn, the opportunities the polity has to challenge the market logic sui generis.

The entire postwar period has seen significant class-based struggles, particularly extra-parliamentary, involving the organizations of labour and left political parties, to increase the level of economic activity and employment, to eliminate or mollify recession, to create and to maintain high levels of high quality employment, to guarantee living standards outside market social relations, to decommodify labour and to extend the force of democracy and civility. Social democracy does have to bear considerable opprobrium as a result of its functionaries' decisions and behaviour; but it ought not number among its political failures the continual striving to maximize rates of capital accumulation (Kalecki 1971).

Conclusion

To argue that full employment is possible is to affirm the possibilities of politics. And for political possibilities to be activated, we require political capacities as well as political will.

The following components of state capacity can be identified:

- developmental aspects of state provision involve infrastructure provision by the state; they were crucial at early stages of nation-building and state-building but remain important later when sectoral transformation of industry again becomes necessary;

- keynesian, or managerial, aspects of state activity involve economic management and counter-cyclical policy interventions; they can provide useful underpinnings for stable economic development but also invoke serious resistances from liberals;

- social democratic aspects of public policy involve explicitly anti-liberal policy developments such as cross-subsidization, decommodification, democratization, and politicization of the economy; they increasingly require extra-parliamentary institutions and incur both costs and difficulties which may be resisted.

The conception of state capacity developed here has postulated the ability of the society or economy or polity to achieve politically determined objectives, to develop political principles and criteria, to initiate public activity, to implement public policy (by creating appropriate extra-parliamentary institutions or arrangements, with labour and capital, with a permanent charter to develop pre-emptive policy competences, by 'embedding' policy autonomy, the legitimacy of collective demands and citizenship entitlements), to resist pressures from outside the polity (and to overcome objections from within), oriented towards outcomes, affecting people generally, which would not otherwise have been possible.

The task of a post-liberal politics is to create the new political institutions that are needed for full employment. Liberal polities have neither the political will nor the political capacity for full employment. The development of state capacity, while effective, is likely to be increasingly difficult, costly and contentious as societies and economies become more mature. It remains nonetheless, the challenge that the political process ought to accept. In an age of generalized disillusion with mainstream politics and supercilious indifference to the possibilities of politics, we need to be very sure we know what battles the political process is being asked to engage.

References

Bell, Stephen 1994, 'Statist analysis' in *Government, politics, power and policy in Australia* 5th edition, eds. Andrew Parkin, John Summers & Dennis Woodward, Longman, Melbourne pp 294–309.

Boyer, Robert & Daniel Drache eds. 1996, *States against markets: the limits of globalization.*, Routledge, London.

Das, Raju J. 1996, 'State theories: a critical analysis' *Science & Society* , V60(1), Spring: 27–57.

Dow, Geoff 1996, 'Full employment and social democratic institutions: the reconstruction of political possibilities' in *Socialism in contemporary Australia* eds. Tim Battin & Graham Maddox, Longman, Melbourne, pp 149–177.

Evans, Peter 1992, 'The state as problem and solution: predation, embedded autonomy and structural change' in *The politics of economic adjustment*, eds. Stephan Haggard & Robert R. Kaufman, Princeton University Press, Princeton, pp 139–181.

Gills, Barry ed. 1997, 'Globalization and the politics of resistance: Special issue' *New Political Economy* , V2 (1), March.

Hintze, Otto 1897, 'The state in historical perspective' in *State and society,* ed.: University of California Press, [1968] Reinhard Bendix Berkeley pp 154–169.

Janicke, Martin 1990, *State failure: the impotence of politics in industrial society.* Polity Press, Cambridge.

Jones, Evan 1994, 'Economists and the state', *Journal of Australian Political Economy* N33, June, pp 36–64.

Jones, Evan 1995, 'Economists and the neglected spirit of reform' *Journal of Australian Political Economy* N.35, June, pp 62–86.

Kalecki, Michal 1943, 'Political aspects of full employment' *The Political Quarterly* V14 (4), Oct, pp 322–331.

Kalecki, Michal 1971, 'Class struggle and the distribution of national income' in *Selected essays on the dynamics of the capitalist economy 1933–1971.* Cambridge University Press, Cambridge, pp 156–164.

Keohane, Robert O. & Helen V. Milner eds. 1996. *Internationalization and domestic politics.*, Cambridge University Press, Cambridge.

Keynes, John Maynard 1933, 'National self-sufficiency' in *The collected writings of John Maynard Keynes — vol.21: Activities 1931–1939 — world crises and policies in Britain and America* , ed. Donald Moggeridge, Macmillan, London, pp 233–247.

Levi-Faur, David 1997, 'Friedrich List and the political economy of the nation-state' *Review of International Political Economy* , V4(1), Spring, pp 154–178.

Weiss, Linda and John Hobson 1995, *States and economic development: a comparative and historical analysis.*, Polity Press, Cambridge.

Youth Unemployment: The Never-Ending Charade of Good Intentions

Adam Jamrozik

Youth unemployment in Australia has been a topic of public concern for about 25 years. The vast number of remedial programs, national and state, has produced no tangible results. Policy initiatives, volumes of research reports and the ongoing rhetoric of concern and good intentions have turned into a rather meaningless ritual, and there is nothing on the horizon to suggest that the situation might change. The paper addresses this issue, suggesting that it is rather naive to think that the problem is beyond governments' power to solve, and then advances certain political reasons and priorities why no successful programs have been implemented to reduce the level of unemployment. Unless these reasons are made explicit, the charade of good intentions and political platitudes is likely to continue.

I never start a paper with a story, but in this paper I will break the habit and will start with two stories, so that I can put my argument about youth unemployment in a proper perspective.

The first story concerns twin brothers, not very bright, who each received a horse for their eighteenth birthday. The horses apparently looked very similar and the brothers had great difficulties in recognising which horse belonged to which brother. They kept quarrelling about it, and finally a friend suggested that if they measured the horses, they would surely find a difference between them. They did so, and found that the black horse was ten centimetres taller than the white horse.

The second story concerns an economist who attended an evening seminar on youth unemployment, and when he came to his car, he dropped his keys in the gutter and could not find them because this part of the street was dark. So, he went a hundred metres up the street, to look for the keys under a street light, because there he could see better.

My argument is that the multitude of programs devised by Australian governments over the past two or even three decades has been one big failure after another, and the failures have been predictable because the obvious causes of youth unemployment have been deliberately ignored. Remedial programs have been introduced mainly for political effects, to demonstrate that the government cared and was doing something about the problem. I have been talking and writing along these lines for the past 30 years, so I will not go into details. Russell Ross identified 54 job creation programs introduced by the Commonwealth government between 1974 and 1988, and most of them were either directed specifically at youth unemployment or had a youth unemployment component. The total expenditure on these programs, at current prices, amounted to $6 339.2 million, and a significant proportion of this amount went for subsidies to employers (Ross 1989:23–47). Indeed, the main identifiable benefit of these programs was in the supply of cheap labour to employers. This process certainly did not stop in 1988 and has continued throughout the 13 years of Labor government. However, as I will show later, by 1996 the Labor government seemed to show some positive results. Now we are back, again, into the old habit of uttering meaningless statements of intention, with some added elements which indicate that the situation is likely to become worse. For example, what is to be achieved by the 'work for the dole' scheme?

Unemployment in the 'Free' Market Economy

Unemployment is an unavoidable logical outcome of the 'free' market economy, especially in periods of rapid technological innovation and corresponding changes in the mode of production and restructuring of industry. The productive capacity of advanced economies has been exceeding the capacity to consume for some years, despite the pressures of advertising, manufactured obsolescence, easy access to credit, and continuous invention of new needs and wants. Unemployment is further aggravated by the globalisation of the economy, because whatever is produced in one country can feasibly be produced more cheaply in another country. The mobility of capital takes place at the rate of the speed of light; for large transnational firms a closure of a plant in one country and opening a new plant in another is a very simple matter.

In discussions on the problems of economy it is customary to speak of 'efficiency versus equity'. However, in the business world this issue no longer holds such currency, and efficiency is the sole criterion. Also, efficiency is measured almost solely in regard to labour: the fewer persons a firm might employ, the more efficient it is regarded in the business world. Whenever a large firm sheds labour (or 'downsizes', as shedding labour is euphemistically called), or whenever unemployment figures go up, so do the prices in the stock market, because shedding labour is seen as a sign of efficiency.

Unemployment is also a good thing for a government which believes that the owners of capital should have unlimited power over labour. If we did not have such high level of unemployment, the current government would not have been able to pass its coercive industrial legislation. Unemployment, therefore, tends to be exacerbated through the mutually reinforcing interests of capitalism and certain government policies. Capitalism, or the 'free' market system as it is euphemistically called, works well but at the price of creating a larger and larger 'human residue.' As an example, in Australia, in 1966, about 10 per cent of the population of 16 years and over relied on public income support (pensions, benefits, etc.) as the main source of income; in 1996 the proportion was 28.8 per cent. In 1966, August, Australian Bureau of Statistics (ABS) recorded 78 600 unemployed, or 1.6 per cent of the labour force, and the average weekly number of persons receiving unemployment benefits was 14 927. In 1996, August, ABS recorded 771 100 unemployed (68 000 in South Australia) (I do not have the data on the payment of unemployment benefits for 1996, but in 1990–91, the average was 535 446 persons. For Tasmania alone the average was 19 357, that is, higher than for the whole of Australia in 1966 — and Tasmania accounts for 2.5 per cent of Australian population).

Youth Unemployment

Young persons in the 15–19 years group have been recording levels of unemployment higher than the rest of the labour force, for at least three decades. As an example, in 1966, August, the rate was 3.2 per cent (compared with 1.6 for the total labour force — see above). However, even this level concealed the extent of vulnerability of young people who left school early. For example, in 1966, of all young persons who appeared in the Adelaide Juvenile Court, those who had left school 30 per cent were unemployed; in 1971 the proportion of unemployed rose to 39 per cent (Jamrozik 1973). In 1991, the proportion of unemployed before the same Court was 42.6 per cent (Nocella 1994).

From the mid-1960s on, it became increasingly clear that structural changes in the labour market posed serious questions about jobs for young persons. The levelling of and subsequent decrease of employment in manufacturing industries, professionalisation of white-collar jobs, and employers' preferences for employing married women rather than young persons were some of the reasons for disappearing opportunities for young people in the labour market. Employers also reacted negatively to the adjustment of youth wages upwards in the early 1970s; they claimed that young people did not have work experience to warrant higher wages and were 'pricing themselves out of the labour market'. However, employers' most frequent complaint was about young people's poor attitude towards work conditions and employers' authority, lack of stability and punctuality, appearance (eg, long hair) and general behavioural 'problems' (Sungalia 1981).

It has to be noted that, from the outset, remedial measures introduced by governments for the purpose of solving growing unemployment among young people have focused almost elusively on young people themselves. Young people were tested by psychologists, encourage or forced to participate in remedial programs, and openly accused of that old affliction referred to as 'unwillingness to work'. While it was increasingly evident that leaving school early meant a likelihood of unemployment, some schools in working-class area were openly discouraging young people to continue with their education. Some teachers openly talked about preparing young people for unemployment, advocating the development of such skills as vegetable growing for survival.

The problem of youth unemployment deteriorated quickly during the period of the Coalition government from 1975 to 1983, along with the deterioration in the labour market as a whole. The government's policy was based on the belief that the world energy crisis which emerged in 1974 presented Australia with an opportunity to become the supplier of energy by extracting and exporting coal, oil, and later shale. Manufacturing industry was deliberately neglected, leading to a complete breakdown in 1982, where unemployment doubled in the space of two years. Other policy decisions worsened the problem. Among these was the shift of funds from public schools to private schools and restricting the growth of tertiary education. Retention rates in public schools began to deteriorate, as did participation rates in the labour force. Had the participation rates remained the same as they were when the Coalition came to power, unemployment rates in 1983 would have exceeded 12 per cent of he labour force. As I demonstrated in my address to the 1996 Conference in Brisbane, by comparative data of various periods since 1966, the period of the Coalition government from 1975 to 1983 was indeed a period of 'dark years' in the Australian economy. The problem we are facing now is that the same people who contributed to that deterioration of Australian economy in the late 1970s and early 1980s are in power again and seem to be reintroducing the same thinking and the same social, educational and economic policies. One is tempted to ask: do they now want to complete the job which they were prevented from completion when they lost office in 1983?

I have mentioned earlier that some positive results in reducing unemployment have been achieved by the Labor government during its period in office from 1983 to 1996. These results took a long time to appear, but the policies introduced under the *Working Nation* program, together with educational and social policies of those years held the best promise for many years of achieving success. Some significant effects of these policies are shown in the data in Tables 1,2 and 3.

The position of young people 15–19 years in the labour market in 1983 is shown in Table 1. In August of that year, ABS recorded 165 100 young persons unemployed, and most of them (136 400, or 82.6%) had left school. Indeed, close to 60 per cent (58.1%) in that age group were no longer in education.

The situation in 1996 was significantly different (Table 2). The number of unemployed young people decreased to 141 900, and the number of those unemployed who were no longer in education decreased by 42.4 per cent to 78 500. Of all recorded unemployed in that age group, 44.7 per cent were young people who were in full time education and were looking mainly for part-time work. Of all employed young people in that age group, slightly more than one-half were young people who were in full-time education. The increase in the number of young people staying in full-time education between 1983 and 1996 was the most promising sign of a shift towards reducing unemployment in general, and unemployment among young people in particular. Unfortunately, since the Coalition government took office this trend appears to have been again reversed.

How important education has become as the key to the entry into employment is shown in Table 3. The differences which occurred in the

TABLE 1

Labour Force Status: Persons 15–19 Years: August 1983, (N = '000)

Labour force status	(1) All persons 15–19 years N	(2) In full-time education N % of (1)		(3) Not in in education N % of (1)	
Population	1261.5	528.7	41.9	732.8	58.1
Not in labour force	531.5	415.1	78.1	116.4	21.9
In labour force	730.0	113.6	15.6	616.4	84.4
Employed	564.9	84.8	15.0	480.0	85.0
Full-time	406.7	0.7	0.2	406.0	99.8
Part-time	158.2	84.2	53.2	74.0	46.8
Unemployed	165.1	28.8	17.4	136.4	82.6
Looking for FT work	139.4	9.5	6.8	129.9	93.2
Looking for PT work	25.7	19.3	75.1	6.4	24.9
Participation rate (%)	57.9	21.5		84.1	
Unemployment rate (%)	22.6	25.3		22.1	

ABS (1983) *The Labour Force, Australia, August 1983*, Catalogue No. 6203.0

TABLE 2

Labour Force Status: Persons 15–19 Years: August 1996, (N = '000)

Labour force Status	(1) All persons 15–19 years N	(2) In full-time education N % of (1)		(3) Not in education N % of (1)	
Population	1276.3	864.6	67.8	411.6	32.2
Not in labour force	547.3	502.3	91.8	45.0	8.2
In labour force	729.0	362.3	49.7	366.0	50.3
Employed	587.1	299.0	50.9	288.1	49.1
Full-time	221.0	7.1	3.2	213.9	96.8
Part-time	366.1	291.9	79.7	74.2	20.3
Unemployed	141.9	63.4	44.7	78.5	55.3
Looking for FT work	82.5	9.0	10.9	73.5	89.1
Looking for PT work	59.4	54.4	91.6	5.1	8.6
Participation rate (%)	57.1	41.9		89.1	
Unemployment rate (%)	19.5	17.5		21.4	

Source: ABS (1996) *Labour Force, Australia, August 1996*, Catalogue No. 6203.0

labour market and in education over the 13 years of Labor government were quite spectacular. The number of employed persons increased above the increase in population, and the largest numerical and percentage increase was among persons with post-school education, especially among those with tertiary degrees. The unemployment rate was lower in 1996 than in 1983, and the real improvement in that area was masked by a substantial increase in participation rates, from 59.8 percent to 63.2 per cent, a rise of 3.4 percentage points. Had the participation rates remained at the level of 1983, unemployment in 1996 would have been reduced by nearly half a million persons (14 384.3 thousand x 3.4% = 489 066).

In examining the developments in Australian social and economic policies over the past two or three decades, I find two interesting mysteries: why the destructive policies of the Coalition government from 1975 to 1983 received so little attention from economic analysts; and why have the relative successes of the Labor government from 1983 to 1996 received so little recognition. These questions are important, as the present Coalition government

TABLE 3

Labour Force Comparisons, Australia, 1983–1996 *, (N = '000)

	1983	1996	Change (%)
Labour force status			
Population 15 years+	11569.6	14384.3	24.3
In labour force	6916.7	9090.8	31.4
Participation rate (%)	59.8	63.2	3.4 **
Employed	6232.7	8319.7	33.5
FT	5146.2	6236.2	21.1
PT	1086.5	2083.5	91.8
Unemployed	684.1	771.1	12.7
Rate	*9.9*	*8.5*	*−1.4* **
Educational Attainment Of Employed Persons *			
All employed persons	6255.0	8210.9	31.3
With postschool qualifications	2654.2	4095.9	54.3
With Degrees	557.6	1307.2	134.4
W/out postschool qualifications	3537.4	3921.6	10.9
Still at school	63.3	193.4	205.5
All unemployed persons	746.7	756.2	1.3
Rate (%)	*10.7*	*8.4*	*−2.3* *
With postschool qualifications	212.0	230.6	8.8
Rate (%)	*7.4*	*5.3*	*−2.1* *
With degrees	29.5	51.7	75.3
Rate (%)	*5.0*	*3.8*	*−1.2* *
W/out postschool qualifications	509.7	477.4	−6.3
Rate (%)	*12.6*	*10.9*	*−1.7* *
Still at school	25.1	48.2	92.0
Rate (%)	*28.4*	*20.0*	*−8.4* *

Source: ABS Labour Force data for 1983 and 1996
* Employment data for August; population 15 years and over
Educational qualifications data for February; population 15–64 years

has been taking credit for the achievements of its Labor predecessor and now it seems to be doing its best to destroy these achievements. It seems to me that it is an equally bad thing to ignore destructive policies as it is to ignore positive achievements, however limited those achievements might have been.

Are There any Solutions to Unemployment?

It would be presumptuous of me to suggest that I have some ready-made solutions to unemployment, or specific solutions to unemployment among young people. I want to say, however, that unemployment among young people is one aspect of unemployment in the 'free' market economies and any solutions have to be explored in that context. Therefore, I want to suggest some of the things that need to be done, if the problem of unemployment is to be solved, or at least reduced to a more acceptable level. I expect, my suggestions will be regarded as inappropriate, perhaps naive or utopian. However, in view of the past complete failure of policies which are currently again pursued, some new perspectives are definitely needed.

Current government initiatives suggest that the government does not regard youth unemployment as a problem that needs to be addressed with some urgency. One of the measures the government seems to be taking is to make funds available to non-government welfare agencies for them to assist young unemployed people. It is difficult to see what some social workers and youth workers can do in this area, except to show government's 'concern' and 'keep the lid' on discontent. It seems, this is yet another area in which welfare agencies accept the role of social control as peacekeepers of marginalised sections of the populations. If current trends in the 'free' market economies continue in the direction of greater 'efficiency', controlling discontent will be come an increasingly important function. However, there are some promising signs in Europe of changing attitudes towards unemployment, but, unfortunately, here the policies seem to be going backwards.

Solving unemployment among young people in itself can be solved by relatively simple measures, such as making it compulsory for large industries to employ a certain number of young people. The public sector alone could absorb a significant proportion of young people. This was suggested by the Manpower Committee of the OECD in 1986, which the Australian government invited to examine the problem of youth unemployment, but then ignored the Committee's recommendations. This measure alone would not change the underlying causes of unemployment as a whole, but it would give some young people a good start in the labour market. To address purposefully the problem of unemployment, some of the following measures may therefore be considered.

First, we need to start looking at the economy in terms of human resources, not simply in terms of material resources. Australia does not have, and has never had, a well-considered policy on human resources. There is much talk about a high technology industry and economy but the current government is again pursuing a deliberate policy of reducing the numbers in tertiary education. Retention rates in high schools are again declining, and public schools are deprived of funds. We decry the depopulation in rural areas, but we have never had a rural policy that gave priority consideration to people, rather than to hectares. Restoring free tertiary education and increasing the allocation of resources to tertiary education should have top priority. The fear of an 'over-educated' population should finally be put to rest.

Second, emphasis in the perspective on unemployment has to be shifted from the unemployed to the providers of employment, that is, business and industry. We need to examine what kind of changes have taken place in the utilisation of human labour, and why certain changes have occurred. How have employers responded to government initiatives? This shift in focus would give us some indication on how employers are likely to respond to certain initiatives, and devise policies which would provide employment career structures for young people.

Third, there is also great and urgent need to critically re-examine the concept of efficiency. Under the influence of managerialist ideology, the concept of efficiency seems to be translated to two dimensions, namely, pressure on the employees to produce greater effort, and reduction of the labour force wherever possible. Other measures, such as changes in organi-sational structures, a more efficient use of material resources, and more attention to the processing of products rather than focusing on the extract-ing industries have received little attention.

Fourth, immigration levels need to be increased to at least 150 000 a year and sustained at that level for at least ten years. Immigration has been the most important factor in the Australian economic development since World War II. With an increasing immigration intake, we need to re-orien-tate our thinking from extraction of resources to production of resources. We really need to become a true industrialised society.

One project that would play a very important role would be the establish-ment of a residential university specialising in the development of knowledge and technology of re-afforestation and dry-land farming. It would be a 'hands on' university where young people would learn and practice their knowledge at the same time. Furthermore, by offering free places for students from countries with dry climate, we would not only contribute to the economic well-being in developing countries but we would enhance our position in international trade.

To do some of these things the government would have to raise more revenue than it now does. I do not thin that an overall increase in taxation would be necessary to achieve the necessary increase. A good start would be to remove the option of not paying income tax which has been, and con-tinues to be, enjoyed by high income earners. Even by ABS data obtained from a survey of income distribution in 1995–96, there were 210 000 indi-viduals and other income units in Australia earning $100 000 or more per annum. A levy of five per cent would raise at least $1billion, and probably much more, as ABS surveys always underestimate the levels of people's incomes, especially the incomes of high income earners.

If the measures I suggest are regarded as inappropriate or not feasible, or as unlikely to achieve the intended results, I want to ask: how long do we continue with policies and measures which have repeatedly and utterly failed for the past two decades or more?

References

Australian Bureau of Statistics

(1983, 1996) *Labour Force, Australia, August*, Catalogue No. 6203.0

(1997) *Income Distribution, Australia, 1995–96*, Catalogue No. 6523.0

(1996) *Transition from Education to Work, Australia, May 1996*, Catalogue No. 6227.0

Jamrozik, A. (1973) *The Delinquent and the Law: Trends and Patterns in Juvenile Delinquency: South Australia: 1954–71*, Adelaide: Flinders University of South Australia

Nocella, L. (1994) *The Changing Nature of Juvenile Justice in South Australia: Is There a Place for Social Work?* unpublished BSW Thesis, Adelaide: University of South Australia

Organisation for Economic Co-operation and Development (1986) *Youth and Work in Australia: Comprehensive Policy Agenda*, Paris: OECD

Ross, R.T. (1989) 'Labour Market Programs and Income Support: The Australian Experience', in P. Saunders and A. Jamrozik (eds) *Social Policy and Inequality in Australia and New Zealand*; SWRC Reports and Proceedings No. 78, Sydney: University of New South Wales

Sungaila, N. (1981) 'Continuing Education for Work: The Employers' Viewpoint', *Unicorn*, 7(4)

How to Cure Unemployment

Frank Stilwell

The personal, social and economic costs of unemployment are enormous. Rational economic policy (not to be confused with 'economic rationalism') must provide a solution.

An effective alternative policy package would have the following elements:

1. Rolling back the constraints on employment growth arising from: (a) the current account deficit, (b) inflationary pressures, (c) inadequate capital investment and (d) skills mismatch;
2. Redistribution of work: shorter hours, changed working arrangements, flexibility in working hours and periods of leave;
3. Restructuring the economy for ecological sustainability: job growth through the development of more environmentally-appropriate industries;
4. Restoring the public sector: productive public sector employment as an element of Keynesian economic policy;
5. Fostering the conditions for long-term economic development; building cooperative relationships in economic institutions rather than relying on the individualistic competition associated with 'economic rationalism'.

It is a measure of the society's collective purpose to take on difficult problems. These policies, working together and developed more thoroughly, would make a major contribution. The unemployment problem can be solved.

Our political leaders have given up on the goal of full employment. The 'Working Nation' statement, produced by the ALP towards the end of its period of Federal government, set the modest goal of reducing the unemployment rate to 5% by the end of the century. The current Liberal government has avoided making any such specific commitment. It is relying mainly on labour market deregulation to provide an economic climate more conducive to business investment, in the hope that some of the benefits of faster economic growth will 'trickle down' to the workforce. Expenditure on labour market programs has been cut. The recent Federal budget projects a fall in the unemployment rate from 8.9% to 8.0% over the year ahead but does nothing to contribute to any such fall. Meanwhile, the 'work for the dole' scheme is being developed for primarily political purposes — as a punitive measure to show that the government is capable of being tough with the economically weak. Current estimates indicate that 'work for the dole' is unlikely to extend beyond about 10,000 young people, which is only 1.2% of the total number of people out of work.

Must we accept the indefinite continuation of widespread unemployment as inevitable? The current situation is one in which the unemployment suffer demoralisation while society as a whole bears the costs — the financial costs of providing social security, the social costs of the breakdown in social cohesion, and the economic costs of the outputs foregone because so many people are not working. There has to be a better way.

A starting point is to recognise the structural roots of the problem, rather than blaming the victims. The causes of unemployment are deeply embedded in the nature of the modern capitalist economy. It is a system geared to production for profit which treats labour merely as an increasingly dispensable 'factor of production'. The existence of a 'reserve army of labour' has long been a recurrent feature and has now seemingly become a permanent fixture.

The problem of unemployment in Australia is also compounded by some particular structural characteristics of the nation's economy. There is an over-reliance on capital-intensive primary industries and a corresponding weakness of the manufacturing sector. The public sector has also been slimmed to the extent of impairing its capacity to act as an engine of economic growth and an effective means of social redistribution.

The dominant economic orthodoxy offers no effective solution. Rather, that orthodoxy has itself become part of the problem. The 'economic rationalists' have run rampant in the key sectors of the Federal bureaucracy over the last decade, chanting the mantras of privatisation, deregulation and the 'level playing field', seemingly oblivious to the social costs of a simplistic free-market economics. This is the TINA syndrome ('there is no alternative') in action.

Of course, there is an alternative. In politics and economics there are always alternatives! A coherent alternative set of policies for dealing with unemployment would involve applying the principles of 'nurturing, building and sharing' in the economic system, rather than the prevailing 'slash and burn' approach to economic management (Stilwell 1995). It would constitute 'rational economics', not to be confused with the free market ideology of 'economic rationalism'. It would mobilise society's resources to satisfy social needs. It is not an alternative which is reducible to a simple formula or a political slogan, but a multi-faceted approach. Its principal components are as follows, moving from its most conservative to its more radical features.

Rolling back the constraints on employment growth

The Australian economy cannot currently sustain more than a modest rate of economic growth because it is constrained by (a) the current account deficit, (b) a possible resurgence of inflationary pressures, (c) inadequate levels of capital investment and (d) mismatch between the skills requirements of a growing workforce and the characteristics of the unemployed. There are no short-cuts in dealing with these problems: each needs to be addressed via specific policy initiatives which roll back the constraints on growth. Significant institutional change is required in each case.

For example, the constraint on economic growth recurrently caused by the current account deficit can only be rolled back if interventionist industry policy improves the capacity of Australian industries for import-substitution or export-promotion. That requires partnerships between government, business and unions, focussed on specific industry sectors on a case-by-case basis.

The constraint imposed by the possible resurgence of inflation requires an incomes policy which encompasses income from capital as well as labour. Wage increases are not the only cause of inflation: indeed, the current situation is one in which executive salaries, housing markets are income from speculative activities are the more important focal points for inflationary pressures.

The constraint imposed by inadequate productive capacity requires other policies for what Keynes called 'the socialisation of investment'. An obvious example would be setting up a National Investment Fund to channel the savings held in superannuation schemes more systematically into financing key Australian industry sectors.

Finally the constraint of skills mismatch requires extensive labour market programs for training and retraining the workforce. This is a policy area in which there were significant initiatives under the previous government, but it has remained poorly integrated with any policies for industry development.

Each of these policy areas requires attention if there is to be an end to the experience of 'stop-go' economics, whereby every resurgence of growth has to be aborted because it butts up against one or more of these four constraints. An extensive program of economic reform is indicated. None of these things will happen spontaneously on the 'level playing field' of a free-market economy.

Redistributing the work

'Working Nation' explicitly rejected job-sharing as an important ingredient in dealing with unemployment. The current Federal government evidently has no policy to promote the redistribution of work. In this regard, as in others, it is evidently bowing to the opposition to such proposals which comes from employers' organisations such as the Business Council of Australia. Yet the redistribution of work must be a central element in any long-term solution to unemployment. The nature of modern technology is such that the expansion in production of goods and services typically brings no corresponding increase in employment. This is the phenomenon of 'jobless growth' which some economists are now belatedly recognising.

The case for redistributing work in these circumstances is partly an arithmetical necessity and partly a moral imperative. If the potential labour force is growing annually by about 1% and productivity growth (output per person) averages 2%, then a 3% growth in the output of goods and services does not lower unemployment at all. If technological progress were to accelerate, as is commonly advocated in order to 'modernise' the Australian economy, then the 'break-even' figure for the economic growth rate is higher still. So economic growth is not enough to eradicate unemployment. And morally, it is quite unjustifiable that some people are working very long hours while others are denied work altogether. Indeed, there is significant evidence of the health problems associated with such disparities: the higher incidence of health problems among the unemployed and the unhealthy behavioural patterns associated with the stresses of long working hours (Scholfield 1996).

A more equitable redistribution of work must be on the agenda in these circumstances. Opponents of job sharing commonly cite the difficulties of implementing such policies, but there are some quite practical mechanisms for effecting change. Possibilities include (i) taking the benefits of productivity improvements as shorter hours rather than higher wages, and (ii) changed working-time arrangements such as a four-day week or (iii) allowing workers to take long periods of leave without pay with income spread over the whole period (Australia Institute 1996). Overseas experience indicates that there is considerably more scope for flexibility in these working-time arrangements than Australian employers (or trade unions) have been generally willing to acknowledge (Botsman 1993: 41–46).

Restructuring the economy for ecological sustainability

The need for ecologically sustainable development (ESD) has become an integral part of modern political rhetoric. Its implementation is another matter. Commonly, it is misrepresented as a threat to jobs. Of course, there are obvious cases, like logging of native forests, where existing employment structures could not be maintained. But the alternative employment opportunities which the application of ESD principles would open up are far greater. Indeed, the potential for simultaneous redress of environmental and unemployment problems is considerable. Most environmentally-sensitive technologies are more labour-intensive in their manufacture and their operation. The contrast between nuclear power and solar power as means of energy-provision is the classic illustration. More generally, the move towards ESD could open up employment opportunities in diverse areas of waste management, recycling, agriculture, transport, housing and recreational services. The implications for changing patterns of urban and regional development, so as to promote the development of more self-reliant communities which make less demands on non-renewable energy sources, are yet more far reaching.

Restructuring of this kind requires conscious planning. There is an obvious need for linkage to the issue of industry policy. There is also a need for the restructuring of taxes and user charges in order to promote more environmentally responsible production and consumption patterns. A 'carbon tax', providing disincentive to use fossil fuels, could replace payroll taxes which are a disincentive to employ labour. One estimate by the Australia Institute, a Canberra-based research group, suggests that these sort of measures could lead to the creation of approximately 250,000 jobs (Hamilton et al 1997).

Restoring the public sector

The public sector has been perhaps the greatest casualty of 'economic rationalism'. Public sector job losses have directly compounded the unemployment problem, as have the job 'rationalisations' typically associated with privatisation. In circumstances where the private sector is not willing to provide job opportunities to match the number of people seeking work, there remains a strong case for the public sector filling the vacuum. There are 'real jobs' to be done, involving improvements in the quantity and quality of the nation's infrastructure — transport systems, schools, hospitals, social services and so on.

The last decade has seen a dramatic run-down in investment in the public sector and this bodes ill for economic performance and living standards in the longer-term. The logic of public sector employment is that it mobilises the society's resources, including its otherwise unutilised labour resources, for socially-useful production.

It is in this context that 'work for the dole' could be re-cast as a more progressive policy rather than as a punitive measure. There is no fundamental economic reason why the unemployed cannot be provided with genuine public sector jobs at award pay-rates. It would be partly self-financing because of the reduction in social security payments, the extra tax revenue generated and the multiplier effects arising from the boost to the demand for goods and services. It makes better sense, as Keynesian economists have long emphasised, to mobilise our society's resources in this way rather than having people unemployed while important social needs — for better public infrastructure, social services and improved environmental quality — go unfulfilled.

Fostering the conditions for long-term economic development

Cooperative relationships are the key to success in economic life, as in other aspects of social life. A sense of shared purpose, a say in decision-making processes and perceived fair shares in the outcomes are the key ingredients. It goes without saying that the unemployed are excluded from any such participation. But so too are increasing numbers of the employed, fearful of their employment prospects as a result of top-down organisational 'rationalisations', facing increased economic insecurity, and with little confidence in the fruits of economic 'progress' being equitably shared. It is hard to imagine a context less conducive to the cooperation necessary for collective economic success.

Turning this situation around requires the widespread application of industrial democracy — the participation of the workforce in business decision-making processes. It requires a broad-based incomes policy to rein in the growth of income disparities and to ensure that the fruits of improved productivity are equitably shared. It requires controls on the escalation of executive and managerial salary packages. It requires a more equitable and progressive tax system. It requires that a higher proportion of tax revenues be used to finance social infrastructure in order to overcome the imbalance between private wealth and public squalor. Also, of course, it requires that a larger proportion of such funds goes to finance education, research and development, on which our long-run capacity for innovation depends.

These policy issues are indicative of how the economic and social context bears on the prospects for long-run economic development and growth of employment opportunities. The contrast with the current political emphasis on individualistic 'incentivation' could hardly be more striking. Among other things, the posited alternative emphasises that unemployment is not just an issue concerning 8–10% of the population which can be 'solved' by policies targeted at this economically-marginalised group. Rather, the unemployment issue raises questions about the whole relationship between society and economy.

Conclusion

There is no prospect of unemployment disappearing of its own accord. Measures that penalise the casualties provide no effective solution, whatever may be their political appeal. The unemployment problem is deeply embedded in the technological and economic characteristics of contemporary capitalism. Without radical reform, the unemployment problem will be with us indefinitely, with all the economic wastes and social tensions the implies.

It is a measure of the society's collective purpose to take on difficult problems. The policies suggested here, working together, would make a major contribution. The unemployment problem can be solved. Do our political leaders have the will to do so?

References

Australia Institute 1996, *Redistributing Work: Solutions to the Paradox of Overwork and Unemployment in Australia*. Discussion Paper No. 7, Canberra, June.

Botsman, P. 1993,*Creating Jobs in Europe: Strategies and Lessons for Australia*, Evatt Foundation, Sydney, December: 41–46.

Hamilton, C., Hundloe, T., and Quiggin, J. 1997, *Ecological Tax Reform in Australia*, Australia Institute, Discussion Paper No. 10, April.

Schofield, D. 1996, *The Impact of Employment and Hours of Work on Health Status and Health Service Use*, NATSEM discussion paper No. 11, University of Canberra, March.

Stilwell, F. 1995 'Reworking Australia', in *The Human Costs of Managerialism*, Eds. S. Rees & G Rodley, Pluto Press, Sydney.

A Policy Program for Growth, Jobs and the Current Account[1]

Roy Green and John Burgess

The purpose of this paper is to identify policies which will increase the rate of economic growth — and reduce unemployment — on the basis of a commitment to high quality jobs and an equitable distribution of work and pay. The paper argues that the growth rate must be higher than the unemployment stabilising rate, which is given by the combined growth in the labour force and labour productivity on a per person basis. The Okun coefficient suggests that for every 2.1 per cent GDP growth is above the unemployment stabilising threshold, the unemployment rate will decrease by 1 per cent.

The paper shows that in Australia the unemployment threshold is around 3.5 per cent, but it is falling as a result of the forecast decline in the labour force and productivity growth. Using the DEET Workforce 2005 projections, the paper estimates an unemployment stabilising growth rate of 2.8 per cent. This implies an annual reduction in the unemployment rate of around 0.4 per cent through to 2005 if GDP growth can be sustained at about 3.5 per cent, which is less ambitious than the targets set in the 1993 Green Paper but takes account of Australia's current account and foreign debt constraint.

The paper argues that the policies of the present Government are unlikely to maintain the required rate of growth to reduce unemployment. The deflationary effect of fiscal consolidation will not be offset by lower interest rates, which Keynes once likened to 'pushing on a string' since aggregate demand is the critical factor in generating investment and growth. The paper canvasses the economic models and proposes an alternative set of policies which include active demand management, labour market programs, an interventionist industry policy and a new industrial relations framework.

Unemployment is the central economic problem confronting Australia's policy-makers. While it is sometimes portrayed as the price to be paid for low rates of inflation, it is a price not just for the unemployed themselves but for the whole economy. Unemployment reflects foregone output to the extent that resources are not used to their full productive potential, and it places a direct cost on the budget through lower tax revenue and higher expenditure on unemployment benefits.

There is general acceptance of the view that unemployment stems from inadequate rates of economic growth over the last 25 years, accentuated by the boom-bust cycle, but there is less unanimity about the policy measures required to deal with it. The present Coalition Government has put its faith in the alleged self-regulating properties of the market and it has proceeded with a strategy of 'fiscal consolidation', including cuts of $1.8 billion to a range of labour market programs. While these cuts were partially offset with the introduction of the Green Corps and Work for the Dole programs, the main policy emphasis has shifted to the establishment of a private market in employment services, based on the purchaser-provider model. The result so far has been a slowdown in economic growth overall, and widening disparities between high growth and low growth sectors, which may have been even sharper without the series of reductions in interest rates corresponding with global trends.

However, interest rate reductions, as Keynes pointed out, are like 'pushing on a string'. They lower the cost of borrowing but will not in themselves persuade capitalists to invest in new capacity in the absence of more direct measures to increase the level of effective demand in the national economy — and to make firms more competitive internationally. Nor will such investment necessarily be encouraged by holding down wages, which simply increases the profit share of national income, or by accelerating the trend towards a two tier labour market. Currently, most investment and expansion in Australia is focused on property and capital-intensive resource projects with limited domestic value-adding or job-creation potential. As a result, employment growth has not been able to meet the modest target of 1.5 per cent a year, which was essential just to stabilise the rate of unemployment below 8.5 per cent, and, more worrying still, long-term unemployment (LTU) has resumed its upward trend. After falling by a fifth between 1993 and early 1996, LTU has since increased again to just under 250,000, with the major impact in regional Australia.

The purpose of this article is to propose an alternative set of policies for maximising employment growth — and reducing unemployment — with a commitment to the creation of high quality jobs and an equitable distribution of work and pay. Drawing upon classical (not neoclassical) value and distribution theory as well as Keynes' analysis of the determination of output, we argue for a new approach that integrates active demand management with a comprehensive supply side strategy encompassing industry policy, labour market programs and industrial relations reform. This approach addresses the traditional criticism of Keynesian demand management that it neglects the supply side of the economy and hence any potential impact on inflation and the balance of payments.

In other words, expansionary macro policy can create jobs and growth, but that growth will only be sustainable if it is supported by longer term supply side measures aimed at building a stronger, more competitive economy at the micro level, hence overcoming the contraint imposed by the current account and external debt. In specific terms, the measures must be designed to shift firms to a high skill, high productivity path — a path that will not be generated and diffused automatically by a market model based on deregulation and microeconomic reform. Instead, supply side measures must embody an interventionist approach to the development of competitive advantage for Australia's export and import replacement industries.

The article is structured as follows. First, we make the case for a faster rate of economic growth as a precondition for reducing unemployment and moving towards full employment. We then critically examine the three models most widely drawn upon to analyse the problem of unemployment globally and in Australia and to provide policy solutions. Finally, we propose an 'integrated approach' to the problem which emphasises the interdependence of demand and supply-side analysis. This approach forms the basis of a strategy for long-term growth and jobs.

The Case For Faster Growth

Although a faster rate of economic growth does not in itself provide the complete answer to unemployment, let alone long-term unemployment, it is a fundamental precondition for making progress towards any realistically defined full employment goal. Nor is this 'growth at any cost', for the quality and composition of growth should be such as to ensure ecological sustainability. For example, if growth is driven by natural resource extraction, it will be more likely to come into conflict with ecological sustainability than if it is based on knowledge-intensive, value-adding activities, including resource recovery and recycling, which are more likely for reasons spelt out below to lead to net additional employment.

The nature and extent of the relationship between trend changes in economic growth and unemployment is central to the argument. It has significant implications for theoretical analysis and policy debate in the area, and it may be influenced by a range of factors at work in the labour market. As a general rule of thumb, GDP growth must equal the combined growth in the labour force and labour productivity on a per person basis. If GDP growth exceeds this threshold — the 'unemployment stabilising growth rate' — then and only then will the unemployment rate decline. This relationship between GDP growth in excess of the unemployment stabilising threshold on the one hand and the unemployment rate on the other is captured by the 'Okun coefficient' (Okun, 1970).

In Australia, the Okun coefficient is around 2.1 (Indecs, 1995, ch 4); that is, for every 2.1 per cent GDP growth is above the unemployment stabilising threshold, the unemployment rate will decline by one per cent. Currently, the unemployment threshold is around 3.5 per cent, but it is not widely recognised that the threshold is now falling largely because of the trend decline in labour productivity growth. This is because sectors with the most rapid productivity growth account for a diminishing share of output and employment and because the composition of the workforce is shifting from full-time to part-time employment. The relationship between economic growth and the unemployment rate was a major issue discussed in the employment 'Green Paper' (Committee on Employment Opportunities, 1993, ch 2), which concluded that GDP growth of 4.75 per cent for eight years would be sufficient to bring down the unemployment rate from 11 per cent in 1993 to 5 per cent in 2000.

However, for the 1990s, annual economic growth is averaging less than 3 per cent and annual employment growth is around 1 per cent. In addition, current policy sits uncomfortably between the demands of financial markets, which favour microeconomic reform over macro activism, and the dynamics of 'reform fatigue' in an electorate which gives priority to secure employment. The consequence is policy paralysis and an unemployment rate anchored for the foreseeable future at nearly 9 per cent. On the other hand, it is important to note that the GDP growth requirement is declining because of a slowdown in the growth of the labour force. In the DEET (1995) *Workforce 2005* projections, the labour force is expected to grow by 1.6 per cent per year over the next decade. This represents a decline from the long-term trend and is a response to the decline in natural population growth, the fall in net immigration and an ageing population.

The DEET projections also forecast a trend increase in the female employment share and a continuation of the growing part-time employment share (to over 30 per cent in the next century). Hence, we estimate that the projections imply an unemployment stabilising growth rate of 2.8 per cent (Burgess and Green, 1997). Using an Okun coefficient of 2.15 suggests an annual reduction in the unemployment rate of around 0.4 per cent through to 2005 if GDP growth can be sustained at about 3.5 per cent. This is not spectacular, but it does give recognition to Australia's current account and external debt constraint, which we address below.[2]

As a result, despite the favourable structural developments, economic growth well above 3 per cent per year remains imperative over the next few years if the unemployment rate is to be reduced. Even if this is achieved, the Green Paper persuasively demonstrated that special labour market measures are required to address long-term unemployment and different forms of labour market disadvantage (Committee on Employment Opportunities, 1993, chs 4–6). In other words, it is not enough to secure sustainable rates of economic growth of 3.5 per cent per year. There is also a need for supplementary policies to address long-term unemployment, regional unemployment disparities and the uneven access to jobs and income across the community. In the next section, we discuss the competing models and approaches to job creation and economic performance.

Overcoming the Limits to Growth

What are the barriers limiting the growth of output and employment in Australia? Is economic growth above 3.5 per cent sustainable on a continuing basis over the medium to longer term? Is it feasible to aim for even higher growth to ensure a rapid and permanent reduction in unemployment, with additional measures to tackle LTU? On the face of it, finding the right answer to these questions should provide the basis for developing new policies that address the barriers more effectively and overcome the limits to growth. However, there are at least three different models or views on what direction analysis should take and how the barriers might be identified and tackled in practical policy terms.

The perfect competition model

The first view is based on the idea of 'perfect competition' in orthodox neoclassical economics. This view assumes a functional relationship between prices and quantities, which are determined simultaneously in all commodity markets, including those for factors of production such as labour. Equilibrium is achieved when markets 'clear' and the economy, treated as a self-regulating mechanism, produces optimal efficiency and welfare outcomes. Unemployment is explained here by 'imperfections' which prevent the labour market from clearing. These imperfections or impediments include, predictably, trade unions attempting to gain 'monopoly rents' from driving wages above market-clearing levels, and minimum wage regulation that distorts price signals by 'artificially' raising the floor price of labour. There is no role in this model for macroeconomic stabilisation policy, which cannot affect the long-run growth rate except by 'crowding out' private investment, and policy is therefore best directed to the elimination of budget deficits and market impediments.

The main policy implications of the perfect competition model, or 'economic rationalism' as it has become known in Australia, lie in the area of microeconomic reform. Since the barriers to full employment are unions and wage regulation, they must be eliminated to the extent that their operation and impact are inconsistent with desired market outcomes. This is the rationale in neoclassical economics for deregulation and wage flexibility throughout the world. It means, in the first place, pursuing a political and legislative strategy to restrict collective bargaining and union organisation and, secondly, marginalising or abolishing wage fixing tribunals, including their role in establishing industry-wide agreements and awards (Brown and Wadwhani, 1990). The model suggests that only when wages are set individually between employers and employees without external 'interference' will they be able to reflect both the marginal productivity of labour and the forces of demand and supply in the labour market.

The policies associated with the perfect competition model have been embraced by many governments and are currently championed by Australia's Treasury and Reserve Bank. While the model was moderated and adapted in various respects under the Labor Government, its more extreme version has an ideologically receptive audience in the Coalition. Labor was prepared to deregulate financial markets, through the floating of the dollar and removal of exchange controls, and to deregulate product markets to the extent that it introduced a program of tariff reductions and national competition reform. However, it baulked at the 'last frontier' of micro reform — deregulation of the labour market — given that this compromised the core principles of its Accord with the trade union movement, including the commitment to social justice objectives (Green, Mitchell and Watts, 1997). While Labor's caution in this area was supported by evidence on the existing scope for flexibility, the debate was no longer about evidence but ideology. Without the distraction of the GST, labour market 'reform' may have formed the basis for a Coalition victory at the 1993 election.

Labor was adept at retaining the overall support of business groups while it continued to shift the focus of wage bargaining to a more decentralised level, and correspondingly to restrict the role of the Australian Industrial Relations Commission (AIRC), but it lost support when the limits to further micro reform became apparent. The then Prime Minister's ambitious post-1993 election pledge to make enterprise agreements not 'add-ons' but full substitutes for awards, which raised employer expectations, was not delivered in subsequent legislation, though bargaining was opened up under AIRC scrutiny to the non-union sector. Significantly, the Coalition has now seized the opportunity to implement the *same* pledge through its Workplace Relations Act, despite amendments in the Senate, by stripping back awards to minimum standards and expanding the role of non-union bargaining and individual contracts. This strategy, like its counterpart in 1980s Britain, is thought to have a greater chance of success if it weakens organised labour through the promotion of high unemployment as part of the fiscal consolidation strategy.

The 'imperfectionist' model

The second view challenges not so much the conceptual basis of the perfect competition model but rather its practical efficacy. This view is influenced by the Institutionalist tradition of economics, which has treated the imperfections of neoclassical economics not as impediments to the working of the economy but as a necessary part of it. In the 'imperfectionist' approach, which characterised policy-making under the Accord, the legitimate role of institutions such as unions and tribunals is recognised, and the policy focus is shifted to achieving wage and price-setting behaviour that holds unemployment as close as possible to its 'natural rate' or non-accelerating inflation rate of unemployment (NAIRU) (Indecs, 1995, ch 4). In other words, union activity and minimum wage regulation are still seen as impediments to full employment in a theoretical sense, but it is not acceptable to try to eliminate them. Instead, a value judgement is made that a moderate level of unemployment, accompanied by policies to control inflation, is a price worth paying for greater equity in the labour market than would otherwise be justified. The debate here turns on whether higher unemployment should be tolerated, as in Europe, or more wage dispersion and 'low quality jobs', as in the US (Freeman, 1994; OECD, 1996).

There is also a further component to this view, which identifies a fundamental contradiction between the determination of wages by demand and supply in the external labour market (as assumed in the perfect competition model) and by factors such as skill, responsibility, performance, loyalty and commitment in the *internal* labour market of the firm or organisation. These factors were highlighted initially in industrial relations research on the 'open-endedness' of the employment contract, rehabilitating Marx's notion of 'labour power', which showed that employers purchase not labour as such with a given marginal productivity but only the *capacity* of workers to perform labour (Nolan and Brown, 1983). According to this research, the quality and productivity of labour will be contingent upon the way in which management structures its relationship with the workforce, including the nature of work organisation, the role of employees in decision-making and the design of the payment system.

In mainstream economics, the research has given rise to 'implicit contract' theory and the 'efficiency wage' hypothesis, which maintains that wages set within the firm to maximise employee commitment and performance in product markets are largely impervious to fluctuations in the labour market (Ackerloff and Yellen, 1986). Indeed, the recent experience of the UK has resulted in 'evidence that unemployment has, at most, a very small depressent effect on wage increases' (Gregory, Lobban and Thomson, 1987). However, the research also points to the emergence of a two tier labour market - with a high status, high skill core gaining access to efficiency wages in permanent, stable internal labour markets, while an insecure, low skill periphery of part-time and casual workers, comprising mainly women and disadvantaged groups, is subject to the vagaries of the external labour market. The jobless may be said to constitute a third tier, which is increasingly part of a growing 'underclass', for while it may enter the periphery, it has only limited opportunities to join the core workforce.

While unemployment in excess of the NAIRU is generally attributed to over-expansionary fiscal and monetary policy settings, a high level for the NAIRU itself, especially when it includes a significant proportion of long-term unemployed, is attributed by the imperfectionist view to 'market failure'. Moreover, a perverse 'hysteresis' effect may be at work as well; since the NAIRU is not independent of the actual unemployment rate, any growth deficiency can soon result in a build up in the numbers of long-term unemployed and a growing NAIRU (Indecs, 1995, ch 4). This is the essential justification for intervention by public agencies and the operation of active labour market programs throughout the OECD, such as the former Labor Government's *Working Nation* programs. In this context, the programs are designed for the most part not to create net additional employment, which is generated by economic growth, but to provide the long-term unemployed, young people and other disadvantaged groups with relevant skill attributes and entry points to the core workforce.

The Keynesian model

While the imperfectionist approach has much to commend it in practical policy terms, especially its commitment to labour market programs, it is flawed to the extent that it shares theoretical underpinnings with the neoclassical perfect competition model. In particular, it is implicit in the concept of the NAIRU and the associated operation of wage subsidies that unemployment can be reduced most effectively by lowering wage costs for business. Alternatively, the Keynesian or post-Keynesian view would suggest not only that wage subsidies are ineffective when unemployment results from deficient demand, since they merely promote the substitution of cheaper for more expensive workers, but that a policy of wage reductions in general is counter-productive. If such a policy were actually to succeed in reducing wages to any significant extent, it would further depress demand in the domestic economy as a whole and hence contribute to higher not lower unemployment. This was the key message of Keynes's *General Theory of Employment, Interest and Money* in 1936, which confronted the Treasury orthodoxy and its use of supply and demand assumptions in the determination of output.

However, with the more recent emergence of internal labour markets in firms and organisations, a wage reduction policy is unlikely to affect all groups equally, for its impact will be largely confined to workers in low skill, low paid and insecure jobs with little or no union organisation. The evidence suggests that the policy will not in itself expand job opportunities for these workers in the long-term, since labour demand throughout the OECD is moving upmarket to high skill jobs, but will only serve to accelerate the growth of wage dispersion and a two tier workforce (OECD, 1996, ch 3). In addition, the efficiency gains from a more flexible use of labour will be dwarfed by the huge costs to the economy in lost production, together with the cost to the budget in unemployment benefits and foregone tax revenue, that results from persistent mass unemployment (Junankar and Kapuscinski, 1992). Any short-term gains in international competitiveness will be more than offset by the inherent disadvantages of a low wage strategy in a world of even lower wage economies.

Keynes argued that there is no inherent tendency for a market economy to adjust to a position of full employment, and that even in savings-investment equilibrium, output can fall short of its full employment level for an indefinite period in the absence of additional sources of effective demand. Rather than devising measures to remove impediments from the labour market, and to pursue a self-defeating wage reduction strategy, Keynes made the case for stabilisation policy, primarily through deficit-financed government spending, to increase aggregate demand and generate a full employment level of output. While this marked a theoretical departure from the perfect competition model, it did not overcome the problem of the limits to growth of output and employment, which had their source in the structure of the market economy. Keynes himself conceded that interventionist policies might be required to raise the level of capital accumulation, and even to undertake the 'socialisation of investment'.

However, Keynes' analysis of supply side issues did not progress beyond the orthodoxy of the 'marginal efficiency of capital', and it is still the classical economists and their post-Keynesian interpreters who provide the most coherent alternative to neoclassical value and distribution theory (Eatwell and Milgate, 1984). These economists address the structural dynamic of capitalism in a global context, the drivers of growth and accumulation and the need for supply-side policies going beyond the Keynesian prescription. The dilemma for policy makers has been characterised as follows

For the patterns of interest rates and prices of financial assets, and the exchange rates which keep overseas holders in particular happy, may well not be the levels which are consistent with the rate of domestic investment spending — both public and private — that may be needed to bring about the desired restructuring and provide the proper level of activity and employment overall, and with which is associated a suitable supply of exports and demand for imports. (Harcourt, 1992, 8)

Without a strategy that takes account of the structure of Australia's economy and its position in world markets, the limits to growth are likely to be imposed by the balance of payments constraint and an associated deflationary bias to monetary policy. The current account deficit for 1996/97, for example, was over $20 billion, which at 4 per cent of GDP is at the upper end of the OECD range. This largely reflects the net income deficit, especially interest payments required to service Australia's foreign debt. Although lower world interest rates, the conversion of debt to equity and the recent strength of the Australian dollar have reduced these payments from around a third to just over 10 per cent of export revenue, the net income deficit continues to be 'lead in the saddle' for domestic fiscal policy. It is perpetuated by the deterioration of the trade balance in elaborately transformed manufactures (ETMs), offset only by Australia's traditional surplus in primary products (see Figure 1).

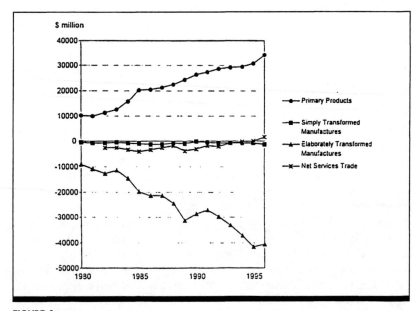

FIGURE 1

Australia's Balance of Trade

Source: ABS, DIST, Mortimer (1997)

As we have seen, Australia needs at least 3.5 per cent economic growth to bring down unemployment on a consistent basis. However, in present circumstances, if this objective is pursued through demand expansion, our propensity to import will result in a corresponding increase in the current account deficit.[2] Does this matter so long as the rest of the world is prepared to finance the deficit through capital inflows? There are at least two reasons why it must matter to an open trading nation like Australia. The first reason, as Thirlwall explains, is that 'interest rates will be higher than otherwise would be the case in order to finance the deficit, or to stop the currency from depreciating' (Thirlwall 1992). This is illustrated by the relationship between real interest rates and the current account in Australia's recent economic history (Figure 2), which has had a damaging effect on investment plans. It is also illustrated by the $A depreciation against a trade weighted average over the last decade. While this has increased competitiveness, it has also exacerbated the level of debt, which is denominated in overseas currencies.

The second reason why the current account matters is because 'no country in the long run can grow at a rate faster than that rate consistent with balance of payments equilibrium on current account unless it can finance an *ever growing* deficit — which in general it cannot' (Thirlwall 1992). In other words, the balance of payments becomes the ultimate constraint on growth, and, in the absence of supply side measures to address the current account deficit, it establishes the conditions for a damaging 'stop-go cycle' and increasing levels of unemployment, especially long-term unemployment, with each successive cycle. At the same time, reliance on currency depreci-

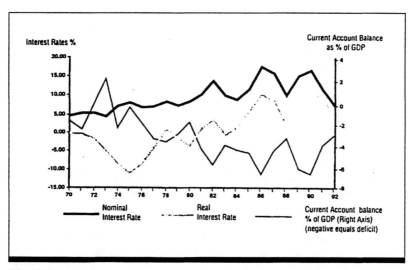

FIGURE 2

Interest Rates and the Current Account, March

Source: Reserve Bank Bulletin, various

ation will encourage the adoption of an export strategy based on low wage competition rather than a high skill, high productivity economy. Meeting this challenge calls for a more integrated approach to economic policy than has previously been contemplated in Australia, combining active demand management with an interventionist supply side strategy encompassing industry policy, labour market programs and industrial relations reform.

A Strategy for Jobs

The most effective strategy for overcoming the balance of payments constraint on growth and jobs is to tackle the merchandise trade component of the current account deficit, since the net income deficit problem is unlikely to be resolved on its own. This would address the major weakness in the Keynesian position without necessarily accepting the free market model underlying the perfect competition and imperfectionist approaches discussed above. It will strengthen the case for expansionary fiscal policy and associated public sector job creation by modifying it to include additional components, such as a more coherent framework for industry policy. The aim should be to create a trade surplus that offsets the net income deficit, and provides the scope and capacity for the nation to reduce external debt as a proportion of GDP to more sustainable levels. At the time of the last recession, for example, a number of scenarios were developed on adjustment paths for export growth subject to assumptions about import penetration (EPAC, 1992) and on the size of the surplus required for debt stabilisation (Green, Mitchell and Watts, 1992).

All these scenarios implied, however, that the key to success must be found in effective supply side measures to develop Australia's export and import replacement capabilities. This is not to suggest that all or even most of the net additional employment will be created *directly* by exports or the replacement of imports, for they simply generate the conditions for demand-led growth in the economy as a whole through their effect on the balance of payments. As we have seen, the additional employment is more likely to take place in other areas, including public sector industries and services, which now have greater scope for expansion without increasing the current account deficit. Such industries have a low import requirement, are labour-intensive and, in some cases (health, education, community services) generate considerable externalities and in others (transport, communications) also form part of the infrastructure for the private sector (Burgess, 1992).

Supply side linkages

The question now arises, what is the source of export growth and import replacement that can at least potentially underpin this broader impact on employment? According to the traditional doctrine of comparative advantage, Australia should concentrate on its primary commodity exports, which are still a large component of our total exports, but these have experienced a secular decline in their terms of trade over the post-war period. In other words, they may increase in volume, but export revenue has not increased correspondingly in value, and is unlikely to do so in the foreseeable future. While primary commodities experience declining terms of trade, the reverse is the case for manufacturing, particularly ETMs, which comprise the largest and fastest growing area of world trade. Globally, the most successful economies have relied not on comparative advantage, but on creating 'competitive advantage', based on investment in knowledge and skills rather than natural endowments and high value added production as opposed to high volume production (Reich 1991).

Although manufacturing has contracted in Australia as a *proportion* of GDP, and the role of the services sector has correspondingly increased, manufacturing output and productivity have risen markedly and the decline of total employment in manufacturing has stabilised in recent years.[4] In addition, ETM exports, which grew very slowly between 1979 and 1985, tripled between 1985 and 1993, with even more rapid growth in the ASIC categories targeted by the former Labor Government's industry plans (see Figure 3). While it is also true that the net trade deficit in ETMs also increased from around $21 billion in 1985 to $40 billion in 1995, this represented a significant slowdown in the *growth* of the deficit and a fall in the ETM deficit/GDP ratio over the period up to 1990 from 9 per cent to 7.9 per cent (Sheehan et al, 1994). Whether this slowdown continues under current economic policies, which have reduced support for ETM exports, remains to be seen. The evidence indicates that the services sector is also becoming a major source of export growth, but not yet to the extent or with the value-adding capacity of manufacturing.

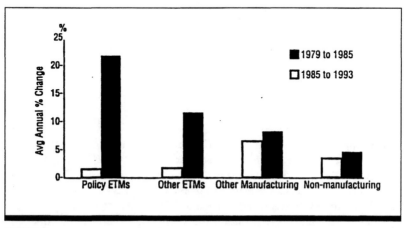

FIGURE 3

Components of Australia's Export Growth, 1979–1993

Source: Sheehan *et al* (1994)

The next question is, how does manufacturing create jobs? What are the linkages and mechanisms? First, while the manufacturing sector itself has limited scope for jobs growth, it is undergoing a fundamental shift in the nature and composition of employment as a result of the introduction of new technologies and skills. This is reflected in the fact that the industries experiencing the most rapid and sustained employment growth on a global scale are those making knowledge-intensive products and services, and that *within* most of these industries the main areas of employment growth are characterised by high complexity and high skill. On the other hand, low skill jobs are generally declining in the OECD, except in traditionally labour-intensive industries, or are being outsourced to low wage economies.[5] The relationship between technological change and the growth of high skill jobs has been depicted as follows:

> Technology both eliminates jobs and creates jobs. Generally, it destroys lower wage, lower productivity jobs, while it creates jobs that are more productive, high-skill and better paid. Historically, the income-generating effects of new technologies have proved more powerful than the labour-displacing effects: technological progress has been accompanied not only by higher output and productivity, but also by higher overall employment. (OECD 1994, 33; also Green 1995)

Moreover, the recent trend in the manufacturing sector has been to out-source not only low wage activities but also a range of high wage services, such as design, marketing, training and maintenance, which are then count-ed for statistical purposes as services rather than manufacturing employ-ment. It is in this sense that we live not in a 'post-industrial' society, but one in which the distinction between manufacturing and services is increasing-ly blurred (Jaikumar, 1986; Reich, 1991). This touches upon the second mechanism by which manufacturing creates jobs, which is through its rela-tionship to services that are directly or indirectly dependent upon it. An example of the former are business and financial services, and the latter includes retail outlets and personal and recreation services. Historically, manufacturing has given rise to a 'clustering' effect, with the establishment of formal and informal customer-supplier chains which include services as well as other manufacturers.

The third mechanism by which manufacturing creates jobs is less visible but, as already indicated in the earlier discussion, of even greater signifi-cance. Here, improvements in productivity and competitiveness enable manufacturers to export to world markets and to replace imports at home. It is this process, based on private and public sector investment[6] that allows the nation to reduce the current account deficit and hence to overcome the balance of payments 'speed limit' on economic growth. While it does not automatically generate faster growth, it provides policy-makers with the opportunity to do so through investment in public infrastructure and com-munity services, which not only creates new jobs directly but also via multiplier effects across the economy. Indeed, the public sector can and should be the major source of additional employment in the next century, because as manufacturing becomes more productive, government is in a better position to mobilise resources, including people, to tackle unemployment and meet clearly identified social needs (Langmore and Quiggin, 1994).

An integrated policy approach

An integrated approach to policy is required to maximise employment growth. In the first place, macro policy will stimulate demand within the limits set by the balance of payments and create jobs directly in the public sector and through multiplier effects in the private sector as well. However, this policy stance will not be sufficient on its own to achieve sustainable jobs growth, even if it is targeted at public sector activities with a low import propensity (European Commission, 1993). It must also be supported by an interventionist supply-side strategy, which promotes exports and import replacement as a means of overcoming the balance of payments constraint. The main component of such a strategy will be a sector-based industry policy, which, after the burst of industry plan activity in the early 1980s, became virtually a policy void by the 1990s. The adoption of generic cross-sector programs aimed at boosting 'competitiveness' and the export-orientation of companies may have satisfied the desire of market orthodoxy for a 'non-discriminatory' approach, but it was not the most cost-effective use of resources.[7] In Australia, industry policy will require new tripartite institutions outside the machinery of government to enable employers and unions to develop coherent strategies and visions for their sectors. In a world of smaller, more interdependent units of production, sectors and regions are the most efficient levels for determining investment, research and development and training plans, as well as for organising customer-supplier linkages and networking arrangements. While investment may not always lead at once to jobs growth, the long run relationship is a strong one (see Figure 4). The role of government in this context is to assist in the coordination of the plans and to provide assistance on the basis of transparent criteria related to the agreed goals of sector strategies and the mechanisms by which they may be translated into reality.[8] The strategies will also provide a clear framework for enterprise bargaining and ensure that a connection is made between decision-making at the workplace and the plans and priorities developed beyond the workplace at sector level. This is essential not just to industry policy but to 'articulated trade unionism' (Evatt Foundation, 1995)

There will also be a role for active labour market programs to channel the impact of economic growth, develop the skills base and replace passive income support for the unemployed. Such programs are now an integral part of economic and social policy in most advanced countries (OECD, 1995b), and their rationale may be conceptualised in the short and longer term. In the short term, the effectiveness of programs will depend largely on their 'strategic fit' with macro policy. In a recession, public sector job creation

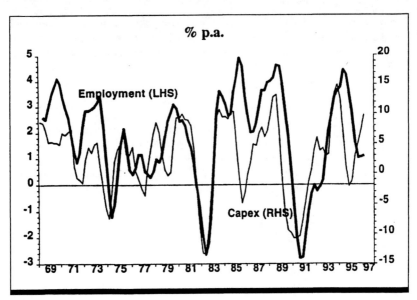

FIGURE 4

Growth in Employment and Real Fixed capital Expenditure

Source: Australian Economic Analysis (1995)

programs are inherently cost-effective because they generate employment directly and increase aggregate demand through their multiplier effects, whereas wage subsidies tend to lead to job substitution and displacement (Burgess, 1992). However, during a recovery, wage subsidies can play a part in distributing employment growth equitably and ensuring that the long-term unemployed and other disadvantaged job seekers have a better chance of entering the permanent workforce. This is a function which can also be performed by work-sharing and reductions in working time.

In the longer term, the key programs will be those that promote training and retraining for the whole range of client groups, including school leavers, new workforce entrants, current and displaced employees, women re-entering the labour market, as well as the unemployed and groups excluded from the labour market. These programs are not just the responsibility of government but of employers in the context of industry policy who recognise that training is an investment rather than simply a cost. Nor can the worth of training programs be judged by a 'cost per net impact' evaluation, since this confuses training with job creation, as well as encouraging discrimination against 'harder to place' client groups. While training can provide skill attributes that assist in job search, the creation of net additional employment is a separate process.[9]

Finally, industrial relations reform has a part to play not only in the job creation task itself but also in the type of jobs created. As Australia's wage fixing system becomes more decentralised, it is inevitable that workplace productivity gains will be pursued at the expense of comparability (Green 1996b). If this approach is pursued too far, however, it will actually undermine the drive to a high productivity, high skill economy for three reasons. First, achieving dynamic long-term efficiency gains at the workplace depends on a cooperative, motivated workforce, which will in turn be affected by perceptions of fairness. Second, an agreed industry-wide 'going rate' for the job ensures that employers compete on the basis of quality and innovation rather than wage undercutting. Third, the skill-based classification structures that are currently being established at an industry level could be rendered unworkable by excessive pay variations within and across workplaces. Industry agreements allowing scope for local flexibility, as in Germany, would provide the best fit with a sectoral approach to industry policy, competency-based training and skill formation.

Conclusion

In this article, we have analysed the rate of economic growth required to reduce unemployment, taking account of recent projections of labour force growth and productivity, as well as structural change in industry and the labour market. We argue that the projections of the 1993 Green Paper on restoring full employment should be modified to the extent that the trend to part-time employment and falling labour force growth has significantly lowered the unemployment stabilising growth rate. Our conclusion is that a 2.8 per cent growth rate is now required to stabilise unemployment and 3.5 per cent to reduce it by 0.4 per cent a year. The problem is that current and projected growth rates will not be sufficient to make a sustained impact on unemployment, and the present Government's fiscal consolidation strategy is likely to make it considerably worse. This strategy will (1) reduce public sector employment directly, (2) damage the job chances of the long-term unemployed and disadvantaged groups through cuts in labour market programs, (3) reduce private sector employment in those firms affected by cuts to export assistance programs and (4) bring about further job losses through multiplier effects in the rest of the economy.

Even in the absence of a deflationary strategy, however, there are limits to the speed at which the economy can grow. While market orthodoxy blames impediments to the operation of market forces, such as trade unions and minimum wage regulation, Keynesian approaches locate the limits to growth in the market itself. Even in saving-investment equilibrium, the market may not deliver a full employment level of output. This does not require wage reductions, which restrict effective demand, but an expansionary fiscal policy to increase demand, output and employment. Yet it must also recognised that macroeconomic policy on its own will not overcome the limits set by the balance of payments constraint. This in turn calls for a more integrated approach to policy, including industry policy, labour market programs and industrial relations reform. None of these policies on their own, or pursued as compartmentalised portfolio responsibilities, will be able to address the increasingly complex and challenging jobs task.

The key to overcoming Australia's balance of payments constraint is to create 'competitive advantage' through investment in the fast growing global markets for high valued added, knowledge intensive products and services. This will reduce our current account deficit by adding to exports and replacing imports, thus offsetting the net income deficit associated with servicing foreign debt. While the approach will not create many new jobs directly in manufacturing, it will increase the speed limit for expansionary fiscal policy, especially in public sector job creation. It also resolves the dilemma of having to choose between promoting low skill jobs, which help to reduce the unemployment stabilising growth rate, or a high skill, high productivity path which increases competitiveness at the cost of jobs growth. The latter option may not create direct jobs, but it can do so indirectly via the macroeconomic response to relaxation of the balance of payments constraint. If the response is to create a large number of low skill jobs in, say, community services, the unemployment stabilising growth rate may still be held down to manageable levels.

To sum up, achieving high productivity and high employment growth simultaneously will require a combination of (a) macroeconomic policy to increase demand and employment, (b) industry policy to raise the level and quality of capital accumulation, (c) labour market programs to address the needs of the long-term unemployed and disadvantaged groups, and (d) industrial relations reform to balance productivity with equity in wage determination. Consequently, in the strategy that we propose to reduce unemployment, the role of an independent tribunal like the AIRC will be crucial to maintaining an integrated labour market through an effective award framework and test cases, including fair award wage adjustments, equal pay and reduced working time. International experience demonstrates that the single-minded pursuit of productivity gains at the expense of socially derived notions of fairness and comparability in the wages system leads to a two tier labour market. It is unsustainable in the long-term as an employment strategy.

Endnotes

1. This paper forms part of a larger project on jobs, growth and structural change commissioned by the Brotherhood of St Laurence, Melbourne. The paper was presented to the Fourth National Conference on Unemployment, Adelaide, June 18–20, 1997.

2 The recent Mortimer report on industry policy sets a similar overall target, but offers no practical mechanism for its achievement (Mortimer 1997, ch 2). In this it is reminiscent of the 1965 National Plan in Britain, which was abandoned in all but name after the currency crisis of 1967. A further attempt in the 1970s was equally unsuccessful because it relied upon the state to substitute itself for the market, rather than tripartite mechanisms which involved employers and

unions. The lesson of this period was that government could *enable* but not prescribe the pattern of economic growth.

3   This does not imply acceptance of the 'twin deficits' theory, which rests on the pre-Keynesian assumption that savings are a pre-condition for investment, rather than the consequence of investment, and that public expenditure, or 'dissaving', necessarily crowds out private expenditure. This theory confuses an identity with causality.

4   ndeed, a recent study suggests that the declining employment share of manufacturing in leading industrialised economies has its source in rising labour labour productivity (Rowthorn and Ramaswamy, 1997).

5   Australia resisted the trend temporarily as a result of the wage restraint policies of the 1980s, which resulted in the substitution of labour for capital and a low rate of productivity growth (Green 1996a).

6   The 'crowding in' effect of public investment on private investment is now well established (Aschauer, 1988).

7   In a classic case study of industrialisation, Rodrik shows that in South Korea and Taiwan high levels of investment rather than exports were the 'main driver of growth' (Rodrik 1995). The same short-sighted preference for generic programs over sector-based programs is evident in the Mortimer report on industry policy (Mortimer 1997, p 164).

8   The problem of 'coordination failures' in investment markets, where returns from investment are so low or returns demanded by finance capital so high that investment remains stuck at low levels, is discussed by Cooper and John (1995) and Gill (1996).

9   Calmfors (1994) emphasises the need for a 'balanced portfolio' of labour market programs and the tendency to decreasing marginal returns, including substitution and deadweight effects, in the absence of a broader approach to employment creation.

References

Ackerloff, G. & Yellen, J. (1986), *Efficiency Wage Models of the Labour Market.* Cambridge University Press, Cambridge

Aschauer, D. (1988) Is Public Expenditure Productive? *Journal of Monetary Economics*, 23.

Australian Bureau of Statistics (1991), *Labour Force Projections 1992–2005.* Catalogue 6260.0, Canberra.

Australian Economic Analysis (1996), *A Fresh Look at Industry and Trade Policy: Some Preliminary Suggestions.* AEP, Sydney.

Brown, W. & Wadwhani, S. (1990), The Economic Effects of Industrial Relations Legislation since 1979', *National Institute Economic Review*, 131

Burgess, J. (1992), A Case for Public Sector Job Creation Schemes. *Economic and Labour Relations Review*, 3, 2.

Burgess, J. & Green, R. (1997), Economic Growth and Employment Reduction in Australia: The Changing Equation but Where are the Policies? *Journal of Economic & Social Policy*, 2(1) 96–110.

Calmfors, L. (1994), Active Labour Market Policy and Unemployment: A Framework for the Analysis of Crucial Design Features. OECD Labour Market and Social Policy Occasional Paper No 15, Paris.

Committee on Employment Opportunities (1993), *Restoring Full Employment: A Discussion Paper* (Green Paper). AGPS, Canberra.

Cooper, R. & John, A. (1995), Coordinating Coordination Failures in Keynesian Models. In G. Mankiw and D. Romer (eds), *New Keynesian Economics*. MIT Press, Cambridge Mass.

DEET (Department of Employment, Education and Training) (1995), *Australia's Workforce 2005: Jobs in the Future*. AGPS, Canberra.

Eatwell, J. & Milgate, M. (eds) (1984) *Keynes' Economics and the the Theory of Value and Distribution*, Duckworth, London.

EPAC (1992), *Current Account Adjustment: Options for the 1990s*. Council Paper No 50, AGPS, Canberra.

European Commission (1993), *Growth, Competitiveness and Employment*. EC, Brussels.

Evatt Foundation (1995), *Unions 2001: A Blueprint for Trade Union Activism*. Evatt Foundation, Sydney.

Freeman, R. (1994), Jobs in the USA. *New Economy*, 1, 3.

Gill, F. (1996), The Road to Full Employment: Coordination in a World of Interdependent Decisions. Department of Economics Working Paper No 229 (University of Sydney), February.

Green, R. (1995), How Manufacturing Can Help Young People to Get High Wage Jobs. ESC Working Paper No 20 (University of Newcastle), October.

Green, R. (1996a), Productivity: Current Trends and Prospects. In *Industrial Relations under the Microscope*, ACIRRT Working Paper No 40 (University of Sydney), April.

Green, R. (1996b), The 'Death' of Comparative Wage Justice. *Economic & Labour Relations Review*, 7, 2.

Green, R. Mitchell, W. & Watts, M. (1992), *Economic Policy in Crisis: A Proposal for Jobs and Growth*. Evatt Foundation, Sydney.

Green, R. Mitchell, W. & Watts, M. (1997), The Accord, Trade Unions and the Australian Labour Market, in P. Kriesler (ed), *The Australian Economy*. Allen & Unwin, Sydney.

Gregory, M. Lobban, P. & Thomson, A. (1987), Pay Settlements in Manufacturing Industry, 1979–84. *Oxford Bulletin of Economics and Statistics*. XLIX.

Harcourt, G. (1992), *Markets, Madness and a Middle Way*. The Second Donald Horne Address, National Centre for Australian Studies, Monash University.

Indecs (1995), *State of Play 8*. Allen & Unwin, Sydney.

Jaikumar, R. (1986), Post-Industrial Manufacturing. *Harvard Business Review*, November-December.

Junankar, P. & Kapuscinski, C. (1992), *The Costs of Unemployment in Australia*. EPAC Background Paper No 24, AGPS, Canberra.

Langmore, J. & Quiggin, J. (1994), *Work for All: Full Employment in the Nineties*. Melbourne University Press, Melbourne.

Mortimer, D. (1997), *Going for Growth: Business Programs for Investment, Innovation and Export*, Commonwealth of Australia

Nolan, P. & Brown, W. (1983), Competition and Workplace Wage Determination.

Oxford Bulletin of Economics and Statistics, XLV.

Norris, K. & Wooden, M. (1996), The Changing Australian Labour market An Overview. In K. Norris and M. Wooden (eds), *The Changing Australian Labour Market*. EPAC Commission Paper No 11, AGPS, Canberra.

OECD (1994), *The Jobs Study: Evidence and Explanations*. Pt I, OECD, Paris.

OECD (1995a), *Economic Outlook*. OECD, Paris.

OECD (1995b), *Employment Outlook*. OECD, Paris.

OECD (1996), *Employment Outlook*. OECD, Paris,

Okun, A. (1970), *The Political Economy of Prosperity*. Brookings Institute, Washington DC.

Quiggin, J. (1993), Growing Our Way to Full Employment. *Labour and Industry*, 5, 3.

Reich, R. (1991), *The Work of Nations*. Simon & Schuster, New York.

Rodrik, D. (1995), Getting Interventions Right: How South Korea and Taiwan Grew Rich. *Economic Policy*, April.

Rowthorn, R. & Ramaswamy, R. (1997), *Deindustrialization: Causes and Implications*. IMF Working Paper, April.

Sheehan, P. Pappas, N. & Cheng, E. (1994), *The Rebirth of Australian Industry*. Centre for Strategic Economic Studies, Victoria University, Melbourne.

Thirlwall, T. (1992), The Balance of Payments and Economic Performance. *Royal Bank of Scotland Quarterly Review*, May

The Scourge of Inflation? Unemployment and Orthodox Monetary Policy

Stephen Bell

Macroeconomic policy in Australia and elsewhere in the last decade has been dominated by 'sound finance' policies aimed at low inflation and monetary stability. Typically, these goals have been pursued through restrictionist monetary policies which, at best, have imposed economic speed limits on the economy and at worst helped plunge the economy into major recessions. This paper argues that the benefits of low inflation may have been overestimated and the costs if disinflationary policy underestimated. Hence the rationale for a policy fixation on price stability or very low inflation is questionable. In an era of high and persistent unemployment, it may be time for a more robust debate on the goals and efficacy of contemporary monetary policy.

The dominant strands of macroeconomic theory and policy in the advanced capitalist economies have been transformed in the last two decades (Gourevitch 1986; Armstrong et al. 1991; Bell 1997a). A key shift has been the abandonment of the post-war commitment to full employment in favour of a commitment to low inflation. Hence, in a turn back to pre-Keynesian doctrine, 'full employment' has disappeared from the fiscal policy lexicon, with that arm of policy now directed towards the passive medium-term goal of balanced budgets. For its part, monetary policy has taken over as the key 'swing instrument' of macroeconomic policy, one seen as having the 'comparative advantage' and flexibility to fight inflation. Although a few episodes of expansionary policy have been tried, compared to the post-war policy order, the broad stance of macroeconomic policy, particularly in the last decade has been deflationary (Eatwell 1995). The official view in Australia seems to be that growth much beyond 3.5 or perhaps 4 per cent per annum will trigger inflation and that this rate of growth should be the economic speed limit (Wood 1996). In a context of mass unemployment, Prime Minister Howard recently admitted that such growth rates will make little or no impact on unemployment.

Two major changes have driven all this. First, international financial deregulation has helped produce what can only be described as *the* major structural change in global political economy over the last quarter century: namely, the burgeoning growth of financial markets, greatly increased global financial interdependence, and the rise (or return) of financial interests as powerful players in the new order. In Australia, the full impact of these changes occurred after 1983 in the wake of domestic financial deregulation (Argy 1995, 1996). A second major factor driving policy realignment was the inflationary capitalism of the 1970s and 1980s, which, amongst other problems, wrecked monetary stability and often punished financiers and holders of monetary assets through negative real interest rates. In response, financial interests have formed the core of a wider and increasingly power-ful coalition that has fervently championed low inflation polices (Crotty and Epstein 1996; Eatwell 1995).

The new inflation priority, the new monetary policy activism, the firm grip that central banks now have over the instruments of monetary policy (Bell 1997b), as well as global financial integration, have restructured power relations within the state, placing central banks and monetary policy in the policy cockpit (Jayasuriya 1993: 131; Maley 1994; Dabkowski 1994). In this context, Maxfield (1991) sees the core of the low inflation coalition con-sisting of a 'bankers alliance' of powerful private and public financial inter-ests, organised at both domestic and global levels. The creed of this coali-tion can be summed as 'sound finance': aimed essentially at low inflation and monetary stability, moderate growth and the avoidance of sharp market gyrations and financial panics (Woolley 1991: 338–39).

So far, and somewhat surprisingly, the shift towards sound finance and has gone largely unchallenged. In Australia, industry complains about high interest rates, but so far, debate about the orthodox fixation on low inflation rates is still embryonic. In the meantime, the Reserve Bank (1993: 25) states that 'faster growth is a big part of the answer to unemployment',[1] and yet the fixation on very low inflation means that policy will deliberately limit growth. In an era of persistently high unemployment it is time to question the doctrinal supremacy of the low inflation fixation. In recent years a raft of economic literature has done just that. This paper reviews the relevant findings and argues that the orthodox policy fixation on very low inflation appears weak and is certainly open to debate.

Policy Orthodoxy

Central to the current view is that orthodox Keynesian manipulation of the macroeconomy is likely to be ineffective and damaging. On the inflation and monetary policy front, Don Brash (1997), Governor of the Reserve Bank of New Zealand, has recently spelt out the prevailing orthodoxy as follows:

> there is in fact no evidence that monetary policy can, by tolerat-ing a little more inflation, engineer a sustainably higher rate of growth, or a sustainably higher level of employment... To be sure, monetary policy can engineer faster growth and higher employ-ment in the short term — by tolerating a bit more inflation right now, there is not much doubt that growth and employment would be a little higher...than otherwise... Most of that faster growth and higher employment would be bought at the cost of

tricking working New Zealanders into accepting a reduction in their real wages, as prices rose ahead of wages. However, it would not last. Before too long, people would recognise the deception and would demand compensation in the form of higher wages and salaries. Within a very short time, inflation would be rising, growth would be back to its previous, lower level and we would be left contemplating the cost of reducing inflation again....Not only is there no evidence that tolerating more inflation can engineer sustainably faster read growth, there is now overwhelming evidence that high inflation positively damages the way in which the economy works...

Associated with this is the view is that there is an equilibrium rate of unemployment (symbolised by the NAIRU, or the Non-Accelerating Inflation Rate of Unemployment) at which the rate of inflation is stable. Artificial attempts to reduce unemployment below the NAIRU will only produce *accelerating* inflation, so the argument goes. The upshot of the orthodox analysis is a somewhat sceptical assessment of short-term 'activist' policy and the conclusion that the only sensible approach is a *medium-term* focus on achieving low inflation.

Low Inflation?

'Many economists', as Sarel (1996: 200) argues, are thus 'convinced that inflation is undesirable and should be avoided completely'. Recent research, however, has cast some doubt on this argument. According to one Canadian economist, there is an 'unbearable lightness' to the anti-inflation case (Fortin 1993). True, and particularly since the 1970s (Sarel 1996: 199–200), a number of studies have found that inflation has a negative impact on growth (see Smyth 1994; De Gregorio 1993; Fischer 1993; Bruno 1995; Barro 1996). Stanley Fischer (1993), for example, a leading monetary economist and now deputy President of the IMF, found in a study involving panel regressions for eighty countries for the period 1961–88, that a ten percentage point increase in inflation (from 5 percent to 15 per cent per annum) is correlated with a decline in output growth of 0.4 per cent per annum. Another study conducted at the Bank of England by Robert Barro (1996), a leading Harvard economist, examined over 100 countries covering the period 1960–90. Barro found that increasing inflation by 1 per cent reduces the rate of economic growth by between 0.02 and 0.03 per cent per annum.[2] What is striking about these studies, however, is that the supposed effects of inflation on growth are so small. Referring to Barro's study, when it was released in England, the *Economist* (1995: 90) was forced to admit that the results are not 'exactly earth-shattering'. As it notes, according Barro's estimates:

> a country that reduced its inflation rate from, say, 7 per cent to 2 per cent would see its growth rise by only a little more than one-tenth of a percentage point. Since reducing inflation is itself cost-

ly — it demands a (temporary) loss of output and jobs — governments that took Mr. Barro's numbers seriously would be forgiven for wondering whether that price was not often too high.

If the studies above find weak effects, a range of other studies have found no effects from inflation on growth (Kyriakopoulos 1991; Stanners 1993; Fortin 1993; Levine and Zervos 1993). Barro's (1996) research could not find a statistically significant relationship between inflation and growth for rates of inflation below 20 per cent. Moreover, For example, Levine and Zervos (1993: 428–29), after examining inflation and growth in 119 countries between 1969–89, conclude that their analysis:

> shows that inflation is not significantly negatively correlated with long-run growth....Given the uncharacteristically unified view among economists and policy analysts that countries with high inflation rates should adopt policies to lower inflation in order to promote prosperity, the inability to find simple cross-country regressions supporting this contention is both surprising and troubling.

Some researchers point to non-linearity and to the possibility of a structural break in the effects of inflation. Thus, low to moderate inflation may not be very harmful at all, but at some point, higher inflation will be damaging. Stanner's (1993) findings, for example, suggest that things may start going wrong when inflation starts to average around 14 or 15 percent. Sarel (1996), however, detects a structural break at about 8 per cent inflation.

Other studies have looked for a connection between growth and productivity (which analysts generally see as partly driving any links between inflation and growth). Fisher (1993) found that a 10 percent increase in inflation was associated with a decline in productivity growth of 0.18 per cent per annum. Again the presumed effects are small. In another study, on US data, Rudebusch and Wilcox (1994) found the relationship between inflation and productivity growth to be insignificant, if corrections are made for cyclical effects (see also Fortin 1993; Seccareccia and Lavoie 1996). On the question of the effects of inflation on investment, McClain and Nichols (1996) recently found not a negative link but a positive link between (moderate) inflation and investment. As these authors conclude, 'This surprising finding casts some doubt upon policy judgements that moderate inflation is more costly to an economy than increasing unemployment' (McClain and Nichols 1996: 218).

It is also important to note that the studies above explore correlations and not causation. Here, and at a somewhat more fundamental level, there is, as Fischer (1995) admits, *no* evidence of any causal relationships that would support the orthodox anti-inflation case, whatever the correlations. The problem is that growth and productivity etc. are driven by a wide range of factors making it difficult to untangle cause and effect. There are even claims that any causation at work might be 'reverse causation'; wherein, for example, growth and productivity are stymied not by inflation but by disinflationary policy (Fortin 1993: 5; Seccareccia and Lavoie 1996: 537). Even in the future, as Fischer (1995: 279) acknowledges, it 'will be impossible or extremely difficult to deal with the issue of causation'.

The conclusions from the above seem clear. The evidence for a strong case against inflation is, at best, mixed, and, at worst, weak. This suggests that hairy chested policy approaches aimed at 'price stability' or very low inflation could be misplaced.

This argument is strengthened if we consider the costs of a hairy chested disinflationary policy. Notwithstanding orthodox arguments about relationships in the medium to long-term, all analysts agree that in the short-term there *is* a trade-off between inflation, on the one hand, and growth and unemployment on the other. Thus, periods of disinflationary policy will help drive up unemployment and in Australia, it was the policy induced recessions of the early 1980s and early 1990s that played a central role in ratcheting up unemployment (RBA 1993: 4).

The orthodox view is that the costs of a restrictionist policy of slower growth and higher unemployment will be *short-term*. Moreover, such costs, so the argument goes, will be more than compensated for by a more sustainable pattern of growth once inflation is purged from the system. On this note Ian Macfarlane, Governor of the Reserve Bank, has recently predicted a new golden age of growth on the back of current low inflation (see Dwyer 1997). Yet a more negative assessment is possible. Indeed, for over twenty years the battle against inflation has raged and during this time the broad stance of disinflationary policy has helped produce rates of economic growth in Australia and the OECD that have averaged only half that achieved during the post-war era (Bell 1997: 88–89; Mathews 1996). The tough monetary policy response of the late 1980s, although a king hit against inflation, helped produce the worst recession since the 1930s.

In the post-recessionary era, Australia's shell shocked economy has produced a patchy and uneven recovery, whilst growth has averaged only 3.5 per cent per annum and unemployment has remained high. Still, Australia's rate of growth has been better than in many other OECD countries (see below). Nevertheless, in late 1994 the Reserve Bank moved decisively to damp down a minor recovery in the name of fighting an inflationary surge that was nowhere visible (Wright 1995). This action may have helped the Bank's 'credibility' with financial markets, but it continued a trend whereby growth rates are kept below that which will make any dent on unemployment. As the Australian Chamber of Commerce and Industry (ACCI, 1997: 8) puts it, 'the apparent willingness to accept 3.5 % as the maximum rate of growth achievable without serious inflationary consequence is itself one of the greatest obstacles preventing a major rise in employment'. This speed limit on growth (compared to a higher rate of say 4.5%) has cost the Australian economy $81 bn in lost output over the last five years according to the ACCI (see also Langmore and Quiggan 1994: 30).

In Europe the situation is worse. There, the kind of growth rates that might make an impact on unemployment are increasingly a distant memory of the post-war era. In Germany, traditionally Europe's Hawk on monetary policy, growth has averaged only 2.3 per cent per annum between 1981 and 1994, and in the five years to September 1996, German growth averaged a meagre 1.2 per cent. Over the same period, France's growth averaged 1.3 per cent, Italy averaged 1.1 percent and the UK 1.9 per cent. As Thurow (1996: 193) concludes 'rapid growth never resumes'. Hence, in Europe, as in Australia, monetary authorities have triumphed against inflation. But the European economies lie in a state of rigor mortis as unemployment climbs above 10 per cent and the number out of work in the European Union approaches twenty million. The orthodox analysis ascribes this to a high natural rate of unemployment rooted in labour market inflexibility and expensive welfare entitlements for workers and the unemployed (*Economist*, 5 April, 1997). One problem with such an explanation is that European labour market and welfare conditions have remained largely unchanged over the last twenty years and if anything have become more 'flexible'. Yet this is the same period in which unemployment has increased four fold (Ormerod 1995: 126). As Krugman (1994: 25) states: 'If the welfare state is so bad for employment, why were European countries able to achieve such low unemployment rates before 1970'?

Moreover, in the light of persistent mass unemployment, the notion of *short-term* adjustment costs looks shaky. The orthodox notion that disinflation will deliver only short-term unemployment shocks is seriously weakened if we admit the notion of hysteresis in labour markets (Fortin 1993; Junor 1995: 59; Phipps and Sheen 1995). The concept implies, as Langmore and Quiggan (1994: 81) put it, 'that episodes of high unemployment [through policy-induced recessions] engender greater likelihood of unemployment in the future. Once the level of unemployment has risen, the base level of unemployment appears to rise permanently'. As the Reserve Bank (1993; 6) has admitted, 'A number of European countries seem to have experienced this over the past decade. Some Australian research also suggests that there has been substantial persistence in unemployment'. Hence, hysteresis effects may be important. To the extent that they are, it means that the prospects for reconciling low inflation with full employment may be bleak. It also means that the 'sacrifice ratio', or the amount of growth or employment forgone to reduce inflation by a given quantum, may be higher than the authorities expect. Based on Canadian evidence, Fortin (1993: 15), for example, estimates that a one unit decrease in inflation could reduce one year's GDP by as much as 15 or 20 per cent, 'three or four times the previous standard estimate'.

One of the reasons for this dismal state of affairs is that current anti-inflation policy primarily amounts to a blunt form of labour market regulation that relies on the ongoing discipline of high unemployment and/or low wages and job insecurity (Arestis and Marshall (1995: 9). The high unemployment variant of this strategy is most clearly apparent in Europe, whilst the lower (official) unemployment, high job insecurity variant is most evident in the US. Australia seems stuck with both.[3] Either way, the strategy amounts to an historic victory over the kind of labour strength promoted by post-war full employment. From this perspective, as Glyn (1990: 117) and his co-authors argue, the leading capitalist states have little motive to move away from policies of relatively low growth and low inflation. 'If expansionary policies were followed and the world rate of economic growth rose on a sustained basis to anywhere near its golden age [post-war] level, it will again lead to an increase in the power of unions as well as a sharp rise in commodity prices, including oil'. In short, inflationary pressures would once again be rekindled. The prospect then 'is at best, continued slow growth' (Glyn et al. 1992: 118).

Reviewing the Australian evidence on growth-inflation trade-offs and the costs and benefits of disinflation, Junor (1995) cites McTaggart's (1992) estimate of a gain in output of 0.25 per cent per year as a result of a 1 per cent reduction in inflation. Set against this, studies by Ball (1993) and Stevens (1992) estimate a 1 per cent reduction in inflation will induce a cumulative loss of real output by between 1 and 2.7 percent (Ball) or 1.5 and 3 per cent of GDP (Stevens). As Junor (1995: 59) comments, on this evidence, 'it is likely that for output losses at the upper end of the range, the present value of these transitionary losses would exceed that of the permanent output gains. This suggests that anti-inflation policy is likely to impose net output losses, which is not consistent with the consensus view that a cost-benefit analysis would always favour lower inflation'. As Junor adds, 'this conclusion is given further support' if we take account of the findings in a study by Junankar and Kapuscinskiu (1992) which lifts the estimate of potential output losses to as much as 7.7 per cent of GDP. Junor further adds that if we accept there is significant hysteresis in the labour market, and that the output or employment losses from a restrictionist policy are thus unlikely to be temporary, then the case against such a policy is further strengthened (see also Fortin 1993).

Beyond this, other writers have argued that instead of being bad for the economy moderate rates of inflation (say in the range of 4–8 per cent) might actually be good for the economy. James Tobin (1972) argued some time ago that a little inflation helped oil the wheels of the economy, especially in terms of assisting labour market adjustment. This kind of adjustment is central to the process of structural change in the economy and requires wages to fall in some areas and to rise in others. Yet in a context of very low inflation, wage declines will usually involve actual reductions in *nominal* wages. Akerlof et al. (1996a), show, however, that wages display a marked downward rigidity and that 'employers almost never [directly] cut wages'. Akerlof and his co-authors then run a series of simulations of the effects of low inflation policy in a context of downward wage rigidity and detect permanent unemployment losses. As they explain:

> As expected, unemployment rises at low rates of inflation. This is
> a permanent cost to pursuing low inflation. The employment loss-
> es are permanent because the churning of the economy always pro-

duces some firms that need to cut relative wages to preserve employment. When inflation is very low, they cannot do this, because as we have seen, nominal wages are rigid downward. Unemployment rises instead. Not only are these losses permanent, we find that they are also much larger than any reasonable estimate of the gains of targeting low inflation (Akerlof et al. 1996a: 15).

The discussion above suggests that the orthodox approach to inflation is open to dispute and that positive assessments of the benefits of very low inflation may be misplaced. Beyond this, the costs of deflationary policy, costs that are quite possibly more than short-term, plus the hints above that moderate inflation might in some respects be good for the economy, suggest it is time for a wider debate on the efficacy of current policy. If there is a structural break beyond which the costs of inflation rapidly mount, then policy should aim to keep inflation below that level. As noted above, Sarel (1996) suggests this level may be around an inflation rate of 8 per cent.

Conclusion

Michl (1995: 54) writes that 'the danger of inflation is perhaps the most common excuse for policies which shrink from aggressively reducing unemployment'. Yet, as argued above, the evils of inflation may have been overstated and the costs of deflationary policies understated. It seems time to more openly question prevailing monetary orthodoxy and, if need be, rethink our approach to inflation and unemployment. Certainly, the Reserve Bank should be more accountable to the public on these issues.

Endnotes

1   There is no need here to examine the debate on links between growth and employment/unemployment. In the short term there are positive links between faster growth and employment growth. In the longer term, however, (say over several decades) the links are less clear (Ormerod 1995: 147–51). Boltho and Glyn (1995: 454–55) argue this applies mainly to the 1980s and see a stronger growth/employment link re-emerging in the 1990s (thus casting at least some doubt on 'jobless growth' claims).

2   It should be pointed out that much of this effect is achieved by including many third world countries with high to very high inflation rates.

3   In terms of growing job insecurity in Australia, most of the jobs created since 1990 have been part-time, whilst higher growth job areas have generally had below average wages.

References

Akerlof, G., Dickens, W. and Perry, G. 1996a, 'The Macroeconomics of Low Inflation', *Brookings Papers on Economic Activity*, No. 1: 1–76.

Arestis, P. and Marshall M. 1995, 'Introduction', in *The Political Economy of Full Employment*, eds. P. Arestis and M. Marshall, Edward Elgar, London.

Argy, F. 1995, *Financial Deregulation: Past Promise — Future Realities*, CEDA, Sydney.

Argy, F. 1996, 'The Integration of World Capital Markets: Some Economic and Social Implications', *Economic Record*, V 15: 1–19.

Armstrong, P., Glyn, A. and Harrison, J. 1991, *Capitalism Since 1945*, Blackwell, Oxford.

Australian Chamber of Commerce and Industry 1996, *Pre-Budget Submission*, Canberra, February.

Ball, L. 1993, 'How Costly is Disinflation?: The Historical Evidence', Federal Reserve Bank of Philadelphia, *Business Review*, Nov–Dec: 17–28.

Barro, R.J. 1996, 'Inflation and Growth', Federal Reserve Bank of St Louis, *Review*, V 78: 153–69.

Bell, S. 1993, *Australian Manufacturing and the State: The Politics of Industry Policy in the Post-War Era*, Cambridge University Press, Melbourne.

Bell, S. 1997a, *Ungoverning the Economy: The Political Economy of Australian Economic Policy*, Oxford University Press, Melbourne.

Bell, S. 1997b, 'Towards Orthodoxy: The Political Economy of Monetary Policy and Central Banking in Australia Since Financial Deregulation', Mimeo.

Brash, D. 1997, 'The New Inflation Target and New Zealanders' Expectations About Inflation and Growth', Address to Cantebury Employers' Chamber of Commerce, Christchurch, 23 January.

Brittan, S. 1995, 'Elusive Case for Stable Prices', *Financial Times*, 18 May: 9.

Bruno, M. 1995, 'Does Inflation Really Lower Growth', *Finance and Development*, V32: 35–38.

Crotty, J. and Epstein, G. 1996, 'In Defence of Capital Controls', *Socialist Register 1996*, Merlin Press, London.

Davidson, K. 1992, 'The Failures of Financial Deregulation in Australia,' in *Business—Government Relations in Australia* eds. S. Bell, and J. Wanna, Harcourt Brace Jovanovich, Sydney.

De Gregorio, J. 1993, 'Inflation, Taxation and Long-Run Growth', *Journal of Monetary Economics*, V31: 271–98.

Dwyer, M. 1997, 'Back to the Golden Age: RBA', *Australian Financial Review*, 21 March.

Eatwell, J. 1995, 'The International Origins of Unemployment', in *Managing the Global Economy* eds. J. Michie and J. Grieve Smith, Oxford University Press, Oxford.

Economist 1995, 'The Cost of Inflation', 13 May: 90.

Economist 1996, 'Who's Afraid of Inflation?', 6 July.

Economist, 1992, 'Zero Inflation', 7 November.

Economist, 1997, 'The Politics of Unemployment', 5 April: 17–19.

Economist, 1997a, 'Up the NAIRU Without a Paddle' 8 March: 98.

Fischer, S. 1995, 'Modern Central Banking', in *The Future of Central Banking* eds. F. Capie, C. Goodhart, and N. Schmidt, Cambridge University Press, Cambridge.

Fischer, S. and Huizinga, J. 1982, 'Inflation, Unemployment and Public Opinion Polls', *Journal of Money, Credit and Banking*, V14 (1).

Fisher, S. 1993, 'The Role of Macroeconomic Factors in Growth', *Journal of Monetary Economics*, V32: 485–512.

Fortin, F. 1993, 'The Unbearable Lightness of Zero-Inflation Optimism', *Canadian*

Business Economics, V1: 3–18.

Glyn, A., Hughes, A., Lipietz, A. and Singh, A. 1990, 'The Rise and Fall of the Golden Age', in The Golden Age of Capitalism: Reinterpreting the Post-War Experience eds. S.A. Marglin, and J.B. Schor, Clarendon Press, Oxford.

Gourevitch, P. 1986, Politics in Hard Times, Cornell University Press, Ithaca.

Henley, A. and Tsakalotos, E. 1995, 'Unemployment Experience and the Institutional Preconditions for Full Employment', in The Political Economy of Full Employment eds P. Arestis, and M. Marshall, Edward Elgar, London.

Hibbs, D.A. 1987, The American Political Economy: Macroeconomics and Electoral Politics, Harvard University Press, Cambridge, Mass.

Junankar, P.N. and Kapuscinskiu, C.A. 1992, The Costs of Unemployment in Australia, EPAC Background paper, No. 24, AGPS, Canberra.

Junor, B. 1995, 'Inflation', in The Australian Economy ed. Kriesler, P., Allen and Unwin, Sydney.

Krugman, P. 1994, 'Europe Jobless, America Penniless?', Foreign Policy, N95: 19–34

Kyriakopoulos, J. 1991, 'Does Moderate Inflation Affect Economic Growth?' in Contemporary Issues in Australian Economics ed. Johnson, M.R., Macmillan, Melbourne.

Langmore, J. and Quiggan, J. 1994, Work for All: Full Employment in the Nineties, Melbourne University Press, Melbourne.

Levine, R. and Zervos, S. 1993, 'What Have We Learned About Policy and Growth from Cross-Country Regressions?' American Economic Review, V83: 426–30.

Lucas, R.F. 1989, 'The Bank of Canada and Zero Inflation: A New Cross of Gold', Canadian Public Policy, V15: 84–93.

Luttwak, E. 1996 'Central Bankism', London Review of Books, 14 November.

Mathews. R.L. 1996, 'Financial Markets and Failed Economic Policies', in Dialogues on Australia's Future eds. P. Sheehan, et al., Centre for Strategic Economic Studies, Victoria University, Melbourne.

Maxfield, S. 1991, 'Bankers Alliances and Economic Policy Patterns: Evidence From Mexico and Brazil', Comparative Political Studies, V24: 419–58.

McClain, K.T and Nichols, L.M. 1993–94, 'On the Relation Between Investment and Unemployment', Journal of Post-Keynesian Economics, V16: 205–20.

McTaggart, D. 1992, 'The Cost of Inflation in Australia', in Inflation, Disinflation and Monetary Policy ed. A. Blundell-Wignall, Reserve Bank of Australia, Sydney.

Michl, T. 1995, 'Assessing the Costs of Inflation and Unemployment', in The Political Economy of Full Employment eds. P. Arestis, and M. Marshall, Edward Elgar, London.

Ormerod, P. 1994, The Death of Economics, Faber and Faber, London.

Phipps, A.J. and Sheen, J.R. 1995, 'Macroeconomic Policy and Employment Growth in Australia', Australian Economic Review, 1 st Quarter: 86–100.

Reserve Bank of Australia 1993, 'Towards Full Employment', Occasional Paper, No. 12, RBA, Sydney.

Reserve Bank of Australia 1996, Australian Economic Statistics 1949–50 to 1994–95, RBA, Sydney.

Rogerson, R. 1997, 'Theory Ahead of Language in the Economics of Unemployment', Journal of Economic Perspectives, V11: 73–92.

Sarel, M. 1996, 'NonLinear Effects of Inflation on Economic Growth', *IMF Staff Papers*, V43: 199–215.

Sayer, M. 1995, 'Obstacles to Full Employment in Capitalist Economies', in *The Political Economy of Full Employment* eds. P. Arestis, and M. Marshall, Edward Elgar, London.

Seccareccia, M. and Lavoie, M. 1996, 'Central Bank Austerity Policy, Zero-Inflation Targets and Productivity Growth in Canada' *Journal of Economic Issues*, VXXX: 533–543.

Smyth, D.J. 1994, 'Inflation and Growth', *Journal of Macroeconomics*, V16: 261–70.

Solow, R. 1986, 'Unemployment: Getting the Questions Right', *Economica*, V53 Supplement: 23–34.

Stanners, W. 1993, 'Is Low Inflation an Important Condition for High Growth?', *Cambridge Journal of Economics*, V17: 79–107.

Stevens, G. 1992, 'Inflation and Disinflation in Australia: 1950–91', in *Inflation, Disinflation and Monetary Policy* ed. A. Blundell-Wignall, Reserve Bank of Australia, Sydney.

Tobin, J. 1972, 'Inflation and Unemployment', *American Economic Review*, V62: 1–18.

Financial Deregulation, Unemployment and the Late 1980's Asset Price Inflation: A Post-Keynesian Perspective

James Juniper

The Wallis Committee's Inquiry into the Australian Financial System has foreshadowed increasing financial deregulation which moves further in blurring current regulatory distinctions between banks and other financial institutions, serves to further isolate prudential controls from other instruments of macroeconomic policy, and seeks to make control of price instability into the principle, if not sole, objective of monetary policy.

These proposals have been endorsed uncritically by the media and by most financial institutions, despite the late 80's experience of asset-price speculation and over-investment in property and housing. The fact that the worst episode of global speculative excess since the Great Depression has done little to check the momentum for further deregulation of the financial system owes much to dominance of conventional economic narratives.

Monetarists and New Classical theorists argue that loose monetary policies, adopted during the early 80's, were largely responsible for the on-set of asset-price inflation. They then proceed to examine how this speculative boom, once started, could have been unintentionally prolonged. Plausible reasons for such persistence which have been advanced in the literature include: the unexpected breakdown of functional relationships which had previously held between high powered money and broader monetary aggregates as a result of financial deregulation; a skills shortage and associated disruption to traditional practices of risk management due to the rapid growth of the financial sector following deregulation; the fading of corporate "memories" of the last "boom-bust" cycle; and, the adverse consequence of a global injection of liquidity prompted by the October, 1987 share-market crash.

Regulatory policies and practices such as those considered by the Wallis Report have been assessed in relation to this narrative as to their ability to prevent further laxity and irresponsibility on the part of governments, central banks and other financial institutions. Needless to say, a contrasting perspective on the late 80's speculative boom could lead to profound changes in this policy evaluation framework. In this paper, I vigorously oppose the conventional monetarist view of what occurred over the late 80's, on the basis that there was little evidence of slackness, either in wages policy or monetary policy, over the period leading up to the boom.

To provide an alternative perspective of the asset-price boom, I draw on and combine the insights of two post-Keynesian papers — the first of these, by Paul Dalziel, argues that asset-price inflation can arise solely as the outcome of rational, optimising behaviour on the part of firms; and the second, by Lynn Mainwaring, examines the phenomenon of rational "Tugan-bubbles" within a Marxian accumulation framework. I suggest that Mainwaring's model allows for the operation of Keynesian "paradox-of-thrift" effects which, I argue, may have played an important role in triggering-off the late 80's speculative cycle. I briefly consider evidence in support of this proposition. The final section of my paper examines the practical implications of these two theoretical models in a more detailed manner, drawing where necessary, on other policy-relevant material.

This paper reports on work-in-progress, which was initially stimulated by the release of the Wallis Committee's *Financial System Inquiry* Discussion Paper in 1996. The Wallis Inquiry's analysis is the embodiment of a conservative *New Monetarist*[1] perspective on the nature of the Australian financial system and the appropriate structure for its future regulation. Essentially, the recommendations favour a narrowing of the RBA's responsibilities for monetary management away from a concern with a broad range of macroeconomic objectives, including financial stability and full employment in the context of price stability and external viability towards a single-minded concern with anti-inflationary policy[2]. To this end, the recommendations favour, first, greater independence for the RBA so that it can resolutely, and therefore credibly, pursue anti-inflationary targets free from political hindrance or distraction[3], and second, the transfer of responsibility for prudential control of the banking system to a new authority which would have extended powers to similarly control the activities of the non-bank financial institutions.

The objective of the paper is to provide a critique of these recommendations on the basis of a post-Keynesian interpretation of inflation and unemployment. This critique will endeavour to demonstrate that (1) prudential controls should never be isolated from a coordinated approach to macroeconomic policy which should encompass manipulation of a spectrum of relevant interest rates, activist fiscal policy, redistribution of wealth and income, and, in this broader context, prices and incomes policies (2) incomes policies must be especially responsive to inflationary pressures within the capital goods and construction sectors, and (3) a combination of contractionary fiscal policy, regressive redistributive policies, and inadequate prudential controls are primarily to blame for the speculative asset boom of the late 1980's.

Post-Keynesian Perspectives on Unemployment

Orthodox macroeconomic theorists fall into two major camps. At the risk of some simplification, we can identify Real Business Cycle theorists as those who view unemployment as the outcome of rational choice on the part of workers, who withdraw labour in the expectation that interest rates will be lower, and wages will be higher in future periods (see Blanchard and Fischer, 1990; Chapter 7). On this view, adjustment lags in investment (the propagation mechanism) are seen to be responsible for transforming unanticipated shocks in either preferences, productivity or liquidity effects (the impulse mechanism) into cyclical movements in real output and employment. At all times, the resultant levels of output are determined as an optimal response under the presumption that goods, labour and financial markets clear. In these models, government intervention only compounds the severity of the business cycle by imposing additional impulses in the form of shocks associated with unpredictable policy responses.

New Keynesians, while accepting the foundational principle of rational expectations, view unemployment as the outcome of rigidities in goods, labour and credit markets. A diverse range of models, each founded on rigorous microeconomic principles, attempts to articulate the variety of processes, both real and nominal, underlying slow price adjustment, lags in the adjustment of wage contracts, lags in the adjustment of inventory, and the imposition of financial rationing (see Blanchard and Fischer, 1990, Chpts. 8 & 9). While markets attain optimal outcomes in the long-run, government intervention can speed the process in the short run, to the greater benefit of the community at large[4]

Neither of these schools of thought interrogates, let alone builds upon, the capital-theoretic style of analysis favoured by Keynes in *The General Theory*[5]. Keynes believed that unemployment primarily arose due to the volatility of investment in an environment of fundamental uncertainty. In contrast to the neoclassical synthesis, a series of recent Post-Keynesian interpretations of *The General Theory* (Minsky, 1975; Chick, 1983; Panico, 1988; and Rogers, 1989) has deliberately emphasised factors associated with the capital market, including liquidity preference, animal spirits — as reflected in psychological expectations about the prospective yield on capital equipment, and financial instability.

Minsky, in particular, argues that Keynes rejected simplistic marginal approaches to the analysis of investment because he believed that changes in the components of the value-marginal product of capital were overwhelmed in their effects by changes in the financial positions adopted by banks, firms and households. This latter cluster of variables would influence investment primarily through variations in liquidity premia, and subsequent changes to borrowers' and lenders' risk (Minsky, 1975).

Minsky suggests that fluctuations in liquidity preference not only influence speculative and precautionary demands for money balances, but also affect desired gearing ratios, and the differential capitalisation ratios which investors apply to prospective cash-flows which may be derived from alternately: holding liquid assets; purchasing bonds; engaging in lending activity; or, commissioning productive investment[6]. He stresses the importance of the fact that economic stability is undermined over time, because in a stable environment, agents — savers, lenders and borrowers — are encouraged to adopt increasingly speculative, and ultimately unsustainable, financial positions.

Carlo Panico, however, adopts a more fundamental position. He argues that, in rejecting Wicksellian notions of the natural rate of interest, Keynes was engaged in, but never fully accomplished, a far deeper critique of marginal theory, one which had its roots in Sraffa's 1932 debate with Hayek over the nature of monetary equilibrium. Panico advances a long-period interpretation of *The General Theory*, which integrates Keynesian notions of long-run asset-price equilibrium with a classical multi-sectoral pricing system. In his preferred model, industrial sectors are represented as earning a rate of profit sufficient to cover both advances for wages and circulating capital, and also net interest payments on bank borrowings over and above their interest earnings on deposits. The banking sector charges an interest rate on loans to industry sufficient to earn the going rate of profit on its own advances for capital and wages and cover the interest it must pay to depositors. Changing monetary conditions can raise both the long-period interest rate on bank deposits, and also, long-period illiquidity discounts on short-term bonds, long-term bonds and bank lending to industry. Over a certain adjustment period, rates of profit are equalised across each industry and the banking sector, and in consequence the initial changes in deposit rates and illiquidity premia would come to be fully reflected in increases in the economy-wide rate of profit (Panico, 1988).

The late 80's Asset Price Inflation

Shinasi's extensive empirical evidence (Shinasi, 1994) confirms that asset-price inflation amongst the industrialised nations over the late 1980's, was most pronounced in economies with the lowest levels of generalised inflation (i.e. as measured by the CPI or GDP deflator). Monetarists and other orthodox theorists argue that loose monetary policies applied during the early 80's, were largely responsible for the on-set of asset-price inflation. They then proceed to examine how this speculative boom, once started, could have been unintentionally prolonged.

Plausible reasons for such persistence which have been advanced in the literature include: the unexpected breakdown of functional relationships which had previously held between high powered money and broader monetary aggregates as a result of financial deregulation; a skills shortage and associated disruption to traditional practices of risk management due to the rapid growth of the financial sector following deregulation; the fading of corporate "memories" of the last "boom-bust" cycle; and, the adverse consequence of a global injection of liquidity prompted by the October, 1987 share-market crash (e.g. see Meltzer, 1996; Shinasi, 1994; and Lewis, 1994).

However, far from being too loose, monetary policy was tightened in most of the advanced economies, following on the heels of the second oil shock in the early 80's. At the same time, stringent anti-inflationary policies of wage-restraint were applied in most OECD nations, leading (notably in Australia, under the various prices and incomes accords), to a sizeable transfer of national income from workers to capital. Even in Japan's case, while the official discount rate was lowered from 5.0 percent in 1985 to 2.5 percent in 1987 in response to favourable declines in inflationary expectations, and was maintained at this low rate until 1989, this minor reduction in real interest rates, alone, could not account for the dramatic rise in asset-price inflation[7]. This evidence, in opposition to the conventional view of what caused the asset-price inflation phenomenon, begs the question of how post-Keynesian theory might account for what took place.

Post-Keynesian Perspectives on Asset-Price Inflation

Typically, Post-Keynesian writers have applied conflict theories of wage and price determination to the analysis of inflation (see Davidson: 1994, Chpt. 9; Palley: Chpt. 11, for a review). In this type of model, inflation is driven by incompatibility between the differential objectives of the workforce and of firms — the former in regard to the target real-wage, and the latter in regard to the target price mark-up. However, although this approach is useful in illuminating the nature of wage-price spirals (see Watts and Mitchell, 1990), unfortunately it is not particularly helpful in explaining asset-price inflation.

A coherent Post-Keynesian view of the late 80's speculative boom ought to account for the effects of the above-mentioned changes in the distribution of income between wage-earners and profit-takers. In other words, it would explicitly investigate the link between "paradox-of-thrift" effects and asset-price inflation, by recognising the effect that regressive income redistribution has, in the absence of compensating increases in public investment, on both the marginal propensity to consume and the marginal efficiency of investment.

Before proceeding further down this track, it would be useful to consider ways in which stable levels of asset price inflation could arise, in the absence of paradox-of-thrift effects, and without any distortionary intervention on the part of monetary authorities. In a simple process-model with three assets (money balances, equities, and debt), and endogenous money creation, Paul Dalziel has shown that asset-price inflation can be generated because firms are maximising the returns to existing shareholders by choosing a marginal debt-to-total-capital ratio which is greater than the ratio money stock desired by households, relative to their accumulating wealth (Dalziel, 1995)[8]. Notably, because the model contains has no government sector, asset-price inflation can only be generated as an outcome of the collective decisions of *private* firms and households.

Dalziel asserts that raising interest rates to lower asset-price inflation which has arisen under such circumstances, would puncture the speculative bubble at potentially great cost in terms of growth, income and employment. A better policy mix would aim to directly reduce the marginal debt-to-capital ratio, while keeping interest rates low. This could be achieved through certain types of institutional reform which cause the *effective* interest rate on firm borrowing to rise sharply once the marginal debt-to-capital ratio rises above the money stock-to-capital ratio of the economy (i.e. such reforms would be targeted at reducing the marginal benefits of inflation to shareholders). However, I would suggest that more flexible prudential controls may also play an important role in reducing credit-financed speculation (even when speculative activity is expressed through highly-leveraged management buy-outs or high levels of acquisition, merger and take-over activity).

In a recent contribution to the *Cambridge Journal of Economics*, which has an obvious kinship with Panico's classical interpretation of *The General Theory*, Lynn Mainwaring has analysed the phenomenon of "Tugan" or T-bubbles (Mainwaring, 1995). He first argues that both absolute and relative levels of wealth can operate as a source of utility and should therefore be explicitly incorporated into agents' utility functions (for example, accumulation of capital goods can yield utility even when their owners have no thought of converting them into future consumption). He then demonstrates, that as a consequence, paradox-of-thrift effects can give rise to rational, real bubbles in which wealth accumulation becomes an end in itself.

Departing from the neoclassical literature on bubbles in which accumulation is undertaken in the expectation of converting assets into future consumption, Mainwaring constructs a Marxian accumulation model. He shows that, in a steady state, the economy consists of a vertically-integrated subsystem (i.e. one in capital is reduced to dated-labour, workers are effectively represented as a mere cog in the production process, and their consumption is regarded as a necessary part of the means of production) containing two departments, one of which — department two — produces wage goods for both itself and the other department — department one — which is devoted to the production of machines.

In his model, asset values have a fundamental component reflecting their utility and usefulness — ultimately driven by capitalist consumption — and a bubble component reflecting the fact that certain assets may yield utility, but not usefulness *per se*. Real T-bubbles arise in the model, not through the revaluation of a fixed asset stock over time, but through the expansion of a physical stock at (possibly) fixed prices. Mainwaring distinguishes between the fundamental component of the economy — the T-fundamental — which is that part of the economy assigned to meet the consumption requirements of capitalists, and the bubble-component of the economy — T-bubble — which is "...dedicated to the production of machines and nothing else.". Lower wage costs, for example, which are necessarily reflected in a higher rate of profit, can trigger-off a T-bubble if capitalist consumption does not rise sufficiently to fully compensate for the ensuing reduction in worker consumption[9].

Mainwaring goes on to demonstrate that increasing risk associated with the (finite) probability that the T-bubble will burst at the end of a year, will be reflected in a risk premium or differential in the rates of return between the two departments. If capitalist confidence diminishes as the T-bubble expands in relative magnitude, raising the probability of a crash, "...recurrent, though not precisely periodic, booms and crashes are generated.".

Mainwaring's seminal model must now be related back to the model presented in Paul Dalziel's paper. In Dalziel's model, asset price inflation reflects a process in which firms impose an optimal "inflation tax" on holders of money balances which takes into account the offsetting effects on growth of the firm resulting from risk-related increases in the interest rate. In Mainwaring's model, as I understand it, as the economy expands along a given T-bubble path, asset price inflation reflects increasing risk (i.e. it is the expression of a necessary increase in the differential between the rate of return required by investors in the bubble-component, relative to that required by investors in the fundamental component).

Mainwaring's model explains how poverty-of-thrift effects can initiate a bubble in the absence of compensatory increases in capitalist consumption. It can also account for the short duration of the equity price bubble in comparison with the property boom, as observed in industrial economies over the late 80's. Ultimately, the return on equities is derived from production and sale of goods and services. In a multi-sectoral T-bubble model, the return to both the property sector and the sector responsible for the production of capital goods (ie. the machines that make machines) would rise relative to returns in the sector producing goods for capitalist (and worker) consumption. Under the circumstances of a generalised increase in equity prices, paradox-of-thrift effects would quickly lead to a widening disparity between equity prices and the underlying fundamentals in the consumption goods sector which could spill-over to burst the equity-price bubble for shares in the capital goods producing sector (primarily due to the fact that the consumption goods sector is a major purchaser of capital goods). In this context, an easing of liquidity conditions, as occurred in industrial economies in response to the October share-market crash, would be likely to encourage on-going asset-price inflation in the remaining "capital goods" producing sector — property.

Concluding Comments on Policy

Viewing macroeconomic policy from a global perspective, Post-Keynesian monetary theorists have pointed to the collapse in the international system of managed trade in the early seventies (eg. the failure of the Bretton-Woods international monetary system) as responsible for thwarting efforts to coordinate fiscal and monetary policies amongst nation states (e.g. see Wray, 1996; Davidson, 1994, Chpts. 13–16). In consequence, real interest rates have risen, prompting in turn a series of disasters such as a blowing out of budget deficits (via both declines in revenue and rising interest payments and transfer payments as components of government expenditure), a rise in debt-to-GDP ratios, current-account imbalances and the consequent imposition by the World Bank of severe programs of structural adjustment and fiscal conservatism on 'delinquent' nations. It is argued that these policies have been applied not only to the detriment of victim nations but also at significant cost to overall world growth, stability and employment. Similarly, "beggar-thy-neighbour" policies which have transferred national income from wages to profits, restricted imports and raised national savings rates, have also contributed to mutual immiseration (Sarantis, 1993). In other words, policies which might have allowed individual nations to selfishly export unemployment to other nations have, instead, promoted global stagnation.

This paper gives credence to the notion that these policies of fiscal and wage restraint have, as a somewhat paradoxical additional side-effect, encouraged periodic bouts of speculative excess and asset-price inflation. The exact nature of this process has been illuminated in a tentative fashion by drawing on two seemingly unrelated strands of Post-Keynesian thought. Much work remains to weld these embryonic models into a more substantial, and empirically testable, theoretical synthesis. Nevertheless, the policy implications are hopefully clear.

Achieving sustainable increases in employment will require the coordinated application of a wide range of policies including: prices and incomes policies — to control the wage-price spiral; financial and prudential policies which influence the balance-sheet positions of households, banks and firms — to nip speculative cycles of asset-price inflation in the bud; strong fiscal policies — to control effective demand; and, accommodating monetary policies — both to prevent high interest rates from choking-off growth, and to prevent the flow of excessive and unwarranted remuneration to profit-takers.

Endnotes

1 The New Monetarism is here defined to mean the revival of traditional monetarist views, but underpinned by the New Classical Macroeconomic theory.

2 See Lewis, 1994, for some discussion of these issues.

3 e.g. see Blake and Westaway, 1996 for a recent extension and Fuhrer, (1997) for an empirical critique.

4 Another strand, not discussed here for reasons of space, is that of the Coordination Failure School (e.g. see Durlauf, S. N., 1993).

5 Notable neoclassical exceptions include Blanchard's q-theoretic treatment of the IS-LM model (1981), Nagatani's temporary-equilibrium model (1981, Chpt. 7), Begg's rational expectations model (1982, Section 7.3), and more recent options theories of investment behaviour under risk.

6 In chapter 7 of his book on Keynes, Minsky also analyses capital goods price inflation, arguing in favour of price and income policies as a possible control mechanism (Minsky, 1975).

7 Ito and Iwaisako show that even if this 2.5 percentage point decrease in interest rates was expected to last for ten years before returning to its original level (a highly unlikely expectations scenario), this would have accounted for a modest 20 percent rather than the 200 percent increase in asset prices which would arise under the assumption of a *permanent* decline (cited in Ito, 1996; fn 9. p.216). Moreover, Ito presents evidence to show that, between 1987 and 1990 Japanese monetary policy passively responded to demand shocks. In addition, he cites

regression analysis which indicates that demand-driven growth in bank lending to the real estate sector, rather than low interest rates, was a significant predictor of changes in land prices (Ito, 1996).

8 In a longer version of this paper I examine the implications of modifying Dalziel's model to account for cyclical movements in his key parameters.

9 See Mainwaring (1995; p.307) for clarification of the similarities and differences between T-bubbles and conventional bubbles..

References

Blake, Andrew P. and Peter F. Westaway (1996) "Credibility and the Effectiveness of Inflation Targeting Regimes" *The Manchester School Supplement*, pp. 28–50.

Begg, David, K. H. (1982) *The Rational Expectations Revolution in Macroeconomics: Theories and Evidence*, Oxford, Phillip Allen.

Blanchard, Olivier J. and Stanley Fischer (1990) *Lectures on Macroeconomics*, London, The MIT Press

Blanchard, Olivier J. (1981) "Output, the stock market and interest rates", *American Economic Review*, 71, pp. 132–143.

Chick, V. (1983) *Macroeconomics After Keynes: A Reconsideration of the General Theory*, London: Phillip Allen.

Dalziel, Paul (1995) "Inflation and Endogenous Money: A Process Analysis" A Paper presented to the *24th Conference of Economists*, University of Adelaide, 24–27 September.

Davidson, Paul (1994) *Post-Keynesian Macroeconomic Theory: A Foundation for Successful Economic Policies for the Twenty-first Century*, Edward Elgar, Aldershot

Durlauf, S. N. (1993) "Nonergodic Economic Growth", *Review of Economic Studies*, 60 (2), pp. 349–366.

Fuhrer, Jeffrey C. (1997) "Central Bank Independence and Inflation Targeting: Monetary Policy Paradigms for the Next Millenium" *New England Economic Review*, January-February, pp. 19–36.

Ito, Takatoshi (1996) "Japan and the Asian Economies: A 'Miracle' in Transition" *Brookings Papers on Economic Activity*, No. 2, pp. 205–272.

Ito, Takatoshi and Tokuo Iwaisako (1996) "Explaining Asset Bubbles in Japan" *Bank of Japan Monetary and Economic Studies*, 14 (1), pp. 143–193.

Kelly, Paul (1997) "The Wallis Revolution", *The Weekend Australian*, April 12–13.

Lewis, Mervyn, K. (1994) "Monetary policy — do we need a new agenda?" *Discussion Papers in Economics*, No. 94/17, University of Nottingham, November.

Mainwaring, Lynn (1995) "Tugan's 'bubble': underconsumption crises in a Marxian model" *Cambridge Journal of Economics*, Vol. 19, pp. 305–321

Meltzer, Alan (1995) "Monetary, Credit and (Other) Transmission Processes: A Monetarist Perspective", *Journal of Economic Perspectives*, V. 9, No. 4, Fall, pp. 49–72

Minsky, H. P. (1985) "The Financial Instability Hypothesis: A Restatement" in Arestis, P. & Skouras, T. ed. *Post Keynesian Economic Theory: A Challenge to Neo-Classical Economics*, Wheatsheaf Books, Sussex.

Minsky, H. P. (1975) *John Maynard Keynes*, Columbia University Press, New York.

Nagatani, Keizo (1981) *Macroeconomic Dynamics*, Cambridge, Cambridge University Press.

Palley, T. (1995) *Post-Keynesian Macroeconomics*: Edward Elgar, Aldershot.

Panico, Carlo (1988) *Interest and Profit in the Theories of Value and Distribution*, Macmillan Press, London.

Rogers, Colin (1989) *Money, Interest and Capital: A Study in the Foundations of Monetary Theory*, Cambridge University Press, Cambridge.

Sarantis, N. (1993) "Distribution, aggregate demand and unemployment in OECD countries", *The Economic Journal*, 103, (March), pp. 459–467

Schinasi, Garry J (1994) "Asset Prices, Monetary Policy, and the Business Cycle", *Economic Papers*, Vol. 12, No. , –, pp. 108–131

Watts, M. and Mitchell, W. (1990) "Australian wage inflation: real wage resistance, hysteresis and incomes policy: 1968(3) – 1988(3), *The Manchester School*, 58, June, pp. 142–64.

Wray, L. Randall, (1996) "Deficits, inflation, and appropriate monetary policy" paper presented at the Fourth Post Keynesian Workshop at the University of Tennessee, Knoxville, June 27 – July 3.

Globalization, Political Capacity and Unemployment: A Comparative Analysis of 15 OECD Countries 1974–1992

Rachel Parker

Significant changes have occurred in the nature of international economic interaction in the postwar period. These changes have created new challenges for national governance and have resulted in some convergence in the advanced capitalist economies in terms of the widespread adoption of neo-liberal policy options. However, a growing body of literature has drawn attention to divergences between nations, particularly in relation to systems of innovation which are derived from national industry policy frameworks and prevailing production regimes. This literature suggests some continuing political capacities in the face of pressures from a volatile global economy. This paper builds on comparative approaches to industry policy and proposes a future research agenda which links industry policy with organizational characteristics to explain unemployment, manufacturing success and wage levels in advanced capitalist economies.

Globalization and Political Transformation

Scholars of any era are apt to conclude that the present is distinct from the past. In the 1980s and 1990s the uniqueness of current events is derived from changes in the global economy and their implications for national political capacities and policy regimes. The proliferation of business activity which crosses or transcends national boundaries has been interpreted by many social scientists as constituting a significant impediment to the development of distinctive policy regimes at the national level. This view suggests that unique national traditions and institutional arrangements will not be strong enough to resist the pressure to merge towards pro-market policy regimes which have characterized Anglo-Saxon countries (Berger 1996:12).

In particular, the internationalization of financial markets resulting from the break down of the Bretton Woods arrangements constitutes the clearest break with earlier forms of international economic interaction. The power of financial markets has increased dramatically as a result of deregulation and has enabled these markets to become dominant influences on the policy choices of national governments (Goodman and Pauly 1993). The transnationalisation of financial structures and instruments has created a pool of mobile financial capital that is thought to pose a significant obstacle for national governments seeking to depart from the austerity measures favoured by international financial players (Cerny 1996:85,89).

Linked to transformations in national policy regimes are changes in organizational structure and production processes in advanced capitalist economies. The regulation school has drawn connections between what has become widely viewed as Keynesian style political intervention in the immediate postwar period and closed national economies, mass consumption and mass production. According to this view, when national economies were relatively insulated because of high barriers to trade and exchange controls, Keynesian political intervention was utilised to prevent under-consumption, a necessary role for the state while fordism (which depended on mass consumption) continued as the principal mode of production. As 'Schumpeterian entrepreneurialism' and global production strategies continue to replace the old fordist production line and the insulated structure of many economies, the role of the state must correspondingly change to cope with the volatility, turbulence and competitiveness of the contemporary economic environment (Boyer and Drache 1996:12; Jessop 1994; Moses 1994).

For some, the competitive interaction of global corporations in international markets that are relatively unconstrained by regulatory barriers will eventually result in a process of natural selection whereby successful organizational structures and production regimes will survive while less effective or inefficient regimes will disintegrate. This process will ensure that 'best practice' is adopted throughout the world. Some commentators argue strongly for the transferability of proven organizational approaches to foreign environments (Womack et al 1991). However, this view does not necessarily privilege a particular system of corporate governance for universal adoption. Some have suggested that the best elements of a range of different approaches will merge to form the dominant organizational structure or production system (Kester 1996:136).

There is therefore a broad range of debates which discuss the nature of changes in the international economy and their implications for policy regimes and production strategies within nations.

The Capacities of Politics:
Domestic Institutions and Structures

There is another growing body of literature which, although it recognizes dramatic changes have occurred in the international economy, seeks to explore historical traditions and the domestic institutional and political characteristics of nations which are resilient in the face of global pressures and help to explain the different impact of globalization in domestic economic contexts. Although this literature accepts that the role of the state has changed in the post-Bretton Woods era, it argues that state capacities remain and are important in explaining continuing differences in social and economic outcomes within nations in the contemporary context. While there have been common trends of deregulation and privatization in advanced economies, there remain significant differences between nations (Milner and Keohane 1996:20).

From this approach, it is possible to develop an argument that the role of the state cannot be limited in the long term, as some versions of the globalization thesis suggest, to simply reinforcing market arrangements and outcomes (Boyer and Drache 1996:6,18). In particular, there is a role for the state in the promotion of manufacturing (particularly high value-added and technologically advanced manufacturing) because of its link with employment in other sectors of the economy (particularly high-technology services sector employment) and its association with high-skilled and high-quality employment (Cohen and Zysman 1987).

In an attempt to elaborate continuing political capacities in recent times, interest in the political philosophies of Friedrich List (1789–1846) has been reinvigorated. Friedrich List provides an important contribution to the understanding of the role of the state in the full development of national productive powers as a means of generating national wealth, employment and civic pride. Levi-Faur (1997) has identified four responsibilities for the state which were enunciated by List in the *National System of Political Economy* and which remain relevant in the contemporary context. These are the development of a cooperative environment between individual producers which promotes the consolidation of disparate interests towards common goals of economic development, the establishment of an institutional framework which overcomes political resistance to productive development, the introduction of policies which ensure that participants in the economy adopt a long term perspective in economic decision making, and the development of national political and cultural institutions within society which are conducive to manufacturing development (1997:162–169). The range of policies which remain critical to the promotion of innovation in national manufacturing (infrastructure spending, labour market policies, research and development policies, education systems) are the basis for the continuing importance of the state to national industrial development (Boyer and Drache 1996:4).

As the approach of nations to the pursuit of industrial success varies, continuing distinctiveness can be identified in the production regimes within nations. Wolfgang Streeck (1996) has argued that the lean-production model invented by Japanese firms cannot simply be transported to other nations because of political and institutional impediments (p.144). Differences in both the level and nature of skills in the workforce (whether high or low skills, whether broad occupational skills or organizationally specific skills), the nature of employment (whether long or short term, occupational or organization centred), modes of work organization and broader industrial relations characteristics are among the variables which inhibit the ready importation of alternative modes of production from other nations (Streeck 1996). Links between distinctive policy environments and production systems might be sustained even in the face of pressures and trends towards convergence in other areas (Boyer and Drache 1996:14).

Both these factors (state and production regimes and links between them) will be pertinent to the attainment of industrial success, a strong manufacturing base, low unemployment and high wages into the future. The following section raises questions about the changing role of industry policy in 15 OECD countries from 1974–1992 and the links between industry policy, manufacturing success and unemployment. The paper concludes with the suggestion that a future research agenda might be concerned with the identification of the links between the changing nature of industry policy and production regimes within advanced economies and their association with manufacturing performance, unemployment and wage levels.

Industry Policy and Unemployment in 15 OECD Countries 1974–1992

Table 1 reports the unemployment and manufacturing output scores for 15 OECD countries for the period from 1974 to 1992. The only countries to have sustained lower than average unemployment and higher than average manufacturing output are Austria, Germany and Japan. In all three countries, the state has played a significant role in national industrial development. In Austria, the state's role in the promotion of national manufacturing can be traced to the immediate postwar period when Austria faced significant problems of reconstruction and was threatened with high levels of foreign investment in national industries. In the 10 year period of postwar occupation, Austrians developed a strong sense of economic nationalism and were supportive of state building aimed at national industrial development (Luther and Mhller 1992:8–9). Germany also departs from the neo-liberal approach to industry policy prevalent in Anglo-Saxon nations both through its unique model of industrial banking which established close links and common goals between the manufacturing and financial sectors of the economy and the social market principles which have guided industrial policy and involved sectoral interventions to promote industries such as shipbuilding, information technology, steel, telecommunications and aerospace (Deeg 1993:169; OECD 1992:51). Finally, Japan is renown for its close government-business relationship, its unique organizational structures and practices and the significant role played by the state, principally through MITI, in national industrial development (Johnson 1995:51–68).

The economic measures contained in Table 1 also indicate that Norway, Sweden and Finland are relatively successful, although manufacturing output is below the average in Norway and Sweden and unemployment has increased recently in Finland. Norway's success is sometimes attributed to its system of 'credit socialism' which established the state as the central influence on the allocation of finance for industrial development and agricultural investment (Mjrset et. al. 1994). The fact that its manufacturing sector is small is thought to be a function of its high dependence on North Sea Oil (Landesmann 1992:276). In Finland, the state's role in industrial development, production and restructuring is well established and not subject to significant opposition by major economic interests (Pekkarinen 1992:302–303), although the close links between the Finnish and Russian economies has resulted in high unemployment in Finland in recent times. Finally, Sweden's success in achieving full employment until the 1990s is linked to the existence of active labour market policies, rather than industry policy. The failure of Sweden to address problems of investment and production is well documented (Pontusson 1992) and is a possible explanation of its lower than average manufacturing output.

Not all nations which have a history of state involvement in industry have performed well. Indicative planning and the promotion of national champions in France has not resulted in sustained economic success, although this historical approach to industry policy was significantly departed from in the late 1970s during Raymond Barre's Prime Ministership (Erbes-Seguin 1991:54).

Those countries which have taken a market-oriented approach to industry policy and are characterized by limited state involvement in industrial restructuring, an absence of sectoral policies, lack of infrastructure support, capital-market based finance systems, lack of coordinating administrative apparatus and poor support for research and development are not successes in terms of the level of manufacturing output and unemployment. Countries which fall in this category to varying degrees are the Anglo-Saxon countries such as Australia, Canada, UK and USA. In addition, Belgium, Denmark, Italy and the Netherlands have weaker states than many of there European counterparts and have followed a non-interventionist approach to industry policy with some limited exceptions (Kurzer 1993). They also cannot be characterized as successes on the measures in Table 1.

TABLE 1

Unemployment and Manufacturing Output 15 OECD Countries 1974–1992

Country	Unemployment			MOUT	Country	Unemployment			MOUT
	74–79	80–89	90–92	74–92		74–79	80–89	90–92	74–92
Australia	6.7*	7.2*	9.0*	18.1*	Italy	6.6*	9.5*	10.2*	25.0
Austria	1.5	3.1	3.4	27.2	Japan	1.9	2.5	2.1	29.6
Belgium	6.3*	10.8*	7.4*	23.9	Netherlands	4.9*	9.7*	6.7	19.4*
Canada	7.2*	9.3*	9.9*	17.4*	Norway	1.8	2.8	5.5	16.7*
Denmark	5.5*	8.9*	10.4*	16.8*	Sweden	1.9	2.4	3.0	21.7*
Finland	4.4	4.9	8.0*	22.8	UK	5.0*	10.0*	8.6*	22.9
France	4.5	9.0*	9.6*	23.1	USA	6.7*	7.2*	6.4	20.8*
Germany	3.2	5.9	4.5	32.2	Average	4.5	6.9	7.0	22.5

Source: OECD (1995) *Historical Statistics* p. 71; OECD National Accounts (various years)
*worse than average performance

Variations in national approaches to industry policy appear to have some relationship with manufacturing performance and the level of unemployment which prevails within nations. Although the evidence does not suggest that there is a single 'best approach' to industry policy, it implies that departure from the neo-liberal approach is necessary for sustained economic success.

Most countries have demonstrated a shift from sectoral interventions in recent times to a greater emphasis on research and development policy and policies to promote small and medium sized enterprises. These common trends in industry policy have not, however, resulted in complete convergence in approaches to industrial policy intervention. There remain differences between nations, especially in terms of their capacity to deal with structural and technological change through the use of research and development policies, training policies, educational policies, investment and infrastructure support (Boyer and Drache 1996:14). As noted above, distinctions remain in the production regimes which prevail within nations (Hollingsworth, Schmitter, Streeck 1994). Importantly, recent research has drawn links between innovation policies and organizational structures within nations. Studies of comparative economic performance (including explanations of manufacturing success, wage levels and unemployment) might usefully discern elements of the national industry policy framework which link with organizational distinctiveness within nations to explain continuing variations in economic performance.

References

Berger, S. 1996, 'Introduction', in National Diversity and Global Capitalism, eds. S. Berger and R. Dore, Cornell University Press, Ithaca, pp. 1–28.

Boyer, R. and D. Drache 1996, 'Introduction', in States Against Markets: The Limits of Globalization , eds. R. Boyer, and D. Drache, Routledge, London, pp. 1–27.

Cerny, P. G. 1996, 'International Finance and the Erosion of State Policy Capacity', in Globalization and Public Policy, ed. P. G. Cerny, Edward Elgar, Cheltenham, pp.83–104.

Cohen, S. and J. Zysman 1987, Manufacturing Matters: The Myth of the Post-Industrial Economy, Basic Books, New York.

Deeg, R. 1993, 'The State, Banks, and Economic Governance in Germany' German Politics V2(2):149–176.

Erbes-Seguin 1991, 'Industrial Policies in France' in Managing Modern Capitalism: Industrial Renewal and Workplace Democracy in the United States and Western Europe eds. M. D. Hancock, J. Logue, and G. Schiller, Praeger, New York, pp. 43–64.

Goodman, J. B. and L. W. Pauly 1993, 'The Obsolescence of Capital Controls? Economic Management in an Age of Global Markets', World Politics V46: 50–82.

Hollingsworth, J. Rogers, P. C. Schmitter, W. Streeck 1994, Governing Capitalist Economies: Performance and Control of Economic Sectors Oxford University Press, New York.

Jessop, B. 1994, 'Post-Fordism and the State' in Post-Fordism: A Reader, ed. A. Amin, Blackwell, Oxford, pp.251–279.

Johnson, C. 1995, *Japan: Who Governs? The Rise of the Developmental State*, W.W. Norton, New York.

Keohane, R. O. and H. V. Milner 1996, *Internationalization and Domestic Politics*, Cambridge University Press, Cambridge.

Kester, W. C. 1996, 'American and Japanese Corporate Governance: Convergence to Best Practice?', in *National Diversity and Global Capitalism*, eds. Suzanner Berger and Ronald Dore, Cornell University Press, Ithaca, pp. 107–137.

Kurzer, P. 1993, *Business and Banking: Political Change and Economic Integration in Western Europe*, Cornell University, Press Ithaca.

Landesmann, M. 1992, 'Industrial Policies and Social Corporatism' in *Social Corporatism: A Superior Economic System* , eds. J. Pekkarinen, M. Phjola and B. Rowthorn Clarendon Press, Oxford, pp. 242–279.

Levi-Faur, D. 1997, 'Friedrich List and the Political Economy of the Nation State', *Review of International Political Economy*, V4(1):154–178.

Luther, K. R. and W. Mhller 1992, 'Consociationalism and the Austrian Political System' in *Politics in Austria: Still a Case of Consociationalism?* eds. K. R. Luther & W. C. Mhller, Frank Cass, London, pp.1–15.

Mjrset, L., C Cappelen, J., Fagerberg, B., Sofus Tranry 1994, 'Norway: Changing the Model' in *Mapping the West European Left*, eds. P. Anderson and P. Camiller, Verso, London, pp. 55–76.

Moses, J. W. 1994, 'Abdication From National Policy Autonomy: What's Left to Leave?' *Politics and Society*, V22(2):125–148.

OECD 1992, *Industrial Policy in OECD Countries : Annual Review 1990*, OECD, Paris.

Pekkarinen, J. 1992, 'Corporatism and Economic Performance in Sweden, Norway and Finland' in *Social Corporatism: A Superior Economic System?*, eds. J. Pekkarinen, M. Pohjola and R. Rowthorn, Oxford University Press, Oxford, pp. 298–337.

Pontusson, J. 1992, *The Limits of Social Democracy: Investment Politics in Sweden*, Cornell University Press, Ithaca.

Womack, J. P., D. T. Jones and D. Roos 1991, *The Machine that Changed the World: The Story of Lean Production* , Harper, New York.

Maintaining Low Unemployment in Hong Kong: By State or Market?

Simon Chi Fai Li

In the postwar industrialization era, Hong Kong has maintained a remarkably low unemployment rate — so low that people in Hong Kong pay little attention to it. Even in academic circles, little effort has been put into studying it. It was not until early the 1990s that a debate emerged on the surge of unemployment. Even the highest unemployment rate of 3.6% in the third and fourth quarter of 1995 is still very low when compared with other countries, particularly developed countries. How can Hong Kong maintain such a low unemployment situation?

Unlike the neo-classical economists and others, I argue that it is not the market but the state, in Hong Kong's case, whose policy intervention makes possible the low unemployment rate. Policy interventions such as providing public housing as an effective subsidy to wages, enable the Hong Kong economy to keep growing. Adjustments are made to the definition of unemployed which may also indicate hidden unemployment.

In Hong Kong's case, we may conclude that the political will of a government is very important in dealing with the unemployment problem.

The oil crisis in early 1970s has been recognised as the watershed for the end of Golden Age of Capitalism and the commencement of massive unemployment in most of the industrialized countries. Unemployment issues, which include the cause, consequence and remedy, have been thoroughly discussed and debated from all levels in society and disciplines in the global village.

Various international organizations, for example the International Labour Office and OECD, have provided global labour force statistics, so that we can have a global picture of the unemployment situation. Different scholars have tried to classify countries with regard to their level of unemployment and analyse causes (Therborn 1986). These literatures focus on the industrialized countries. It is only in recent years that more attention has been paid to the Pacific Rim and performance on employment and unemployment in countries other than Japan.

The newly industralizing countries *ie.* Hong Kong, Singapore, South Korea and Taiwan have been noticed by scholars from various disciplines, especially development economists (Chowdhury and Islam 1993). In Hong Kong's case, concerns are more for the continuity of present levels of freedom, democracy and prosperity. Little attention is paid to the growing unemployment crisis resulting from industrial restructuring, and its subsequent social, political and economic consequences.

This paper argues that it is not the market but the state whose policy interventions have maintained the remarkably low unemployment rates in the postwar era of industrialization. These policy interventions included effective subsidy to wages, enabling Hong Kong economy to keep growing. It is also the government's refusal to review the definition of unemployed that hides some of the genuine unemployed from the unemployment figures. Unless the coming Hong Kong Special Administrative Region government is willing to exercise political will in this area, as in the past, the problem of unemployment will be hidden but not resolved.

Hong Kong in the Global Context

Unemployment has haunted most of the industrialized countries for almost two decades and there is no sign of it easing. Hong Kong has enjoyed a long period of low unemployment when compared with the industrialized countries. Figure 1 shows the comparison of the unemployment rate among OECD countries as a whole, Australia and Hong Kong.

A detailed analysis of the above unemployment rate found that European Union countries have a slightly higher unemployment rate than all European member countries of OECD since 1981. Moreover, the unemployment rate of all European member countries of OECD was increasing while North American member countries of OECD had a declining rate. Hong Kong's unemployment rate pattern more or less followed the OECD and Australia but at a much lower level.

Over the twenty year period from 1976 to 1996, the highest unemployment rate Hong Kong encountered was 5.1% in 1976, whereas it was 10.8% for Australia in 1993 and 8.3% for all OECD countries in 1983. The lowest unemployment rate for Hong Kong, Australia and OECD countries in the past two decades were 1.1% in 1989, 4.7% in 1976 and 5.1% in 1979 respectively. How has Hong Kong maintained such a low unemployment rate?

Maintaining Low Unemployment By Market?

Hong Kong has always been described by neo-classical economists (Friedman and Friedman 1980) as a laissez-faire economy in which market mechanisms govern the supply of and demand for resources at an optimal price. In the postwar industrialization processes of Hong Kong, industrialists demanded abundant low cost labour in order to carry out labour intensive production processes, and the influx of immigrants from mainland China provided such a supply. Thus, riding the wave of the golden age of capitalism and of the efficiency of market, Hong Kong could sustain growth without high unemployment.

Using a laissez-faire economy model to describe Hong Kong in the early years in the postwar era may be accurate, but this is not the case more recently. As the former Financial Secretary of Hong Kong, Sir Philip

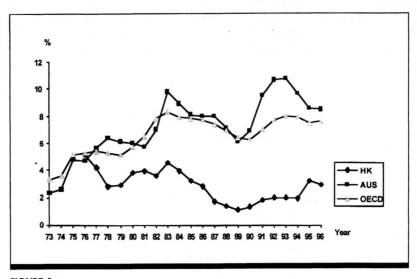

FIGURE 1

Unemployment Rate of Hong Kong, Australia and OECD Countries

Sources: Hong Kong Annual Digest of Statistics, Labour Force Survey and Quarterly Report of
General Household Survey, various years; OECD Quarterly Labour Force Statistics No. 1,
1997: p. 21–2 & 92 and OECD Labour Force Statistics 1973–1993: p. 32–3

Haddon-Cave pointed out, the description of the Hong Kong Government's attitude to the economy as based on laissez-faire is inadequate. He coined the term 'positive non-interventionism' which describes a government which will not normally intervene in the market unless there is a necessity.(Haddon-Cave 1985:xiv and 1982:84)

State Intervention to Maintain Low Unemployment

For Haddon-Cave the idea of positive non-interventionism — to intervene when there is a market failure and market imperfection explained Hong Kong's economic situation. Yet many scholars (Sit and Wong 1989; Chen and Li 1991; Castells et al 1990; Schiffer 1991) found that policy interventions other than those Haddon-Cave mentioned have been adopted by the government to sustain low unemployment in Hong Kong's industrialization period from 1960s to early 1980s. Among these policy interventions, the provision of social wages and a growth policy for the Hong Kong economy were two prominent measures.

One of the competitive edges Hong Kong had throughout its industrialization process was low wage labour. The government countered the low wages through the provision of decommodified housing, health services, education services and social welfare as social wages. Figure 2 shows the social expenditures as a percentage of the total government expenditures. We can notice that the social expenditures increased sharply from less than

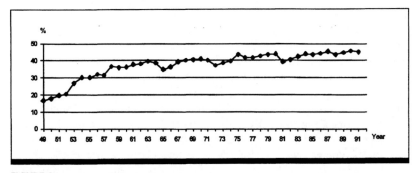

FIGURE 2

Social Service Expenditure as a Percentage of Total Government Expenditure

Source: Tang, Shu Hung (1992) Table 8-1

16% in the postwar era to over 40% since the end of 1960s. Compared with other newly industralizing countries, Hong Kong has the highest percentage of social wages. (Deyo 1992:290–293)

The other strategy used by the Hong Kong government to maintain low unemployment was to enable the growth of economy, and thus provide sufficient employment opportunities for the population. These interventions, as summarized by Sit & Wong (1989) and Chen & Li (1991) are infrastructural and developmental. On the one hand, the Hong Kong government ensured infrastructure such as industrial land, water, electricity, fuels and other raw materials, telecommunication, transport system, efficient public service and skilled labour force were available for industrialization. On the other hand, the government provided developmental services 'which contribute to industrial development via productivity growth, improvement of quality and product innovation' (Chen & Li 1991:42). Unlike other newly industrializing countries, the Hong Kong government did not select industries as a focus for development. Rather, the government ensured a favourable environment for industrial development.

The low unemployment in the 1960s and 1970s was achieved by government's policy to keep the Hong Kong economy growing, whereas the low unemployment in the 1980s and beyond is questioned by scholars as not reflecting the real situation of unemployment. Some even argue that the government is 'manufacturing' the low unemployment rate (Wong 1995). Whether the unemployment rate truly reflects the seriousness of unemployment or whether it hides some of the unemployed has been hotly debated in recent months.(Legislative Council 1997; Li 1997b; Hui 1997)

There is no doubt that Hong Kong is still undergoing industrial restructuring. Statistics reveal that there were almost 900 000 manufacturing workers in 1985, which constituted one-third of the working population. This figure declined to around 300 000 in 1996, or one-tenth of the working population. At the same time, the number of people engaged in the service sector rose sharply to 80% of the working population at the end of 1996 (Census and Statistics Department 1997). This industrial restructuring process was induced by the open door policy of China as well as the restructuring of the world economy from the Fordist to the information and communication techno-economic paradigm (Freeman 1994).

In facing economic restructuring, the government, unlike in previous decades, has taken a more reactive role. For example, the much urged Employee Retraining Board was set up in 1992 and the sample size of the General Household Survey enlarged in 1994 to get more detailed information on the unemployed e.g. unemployment in relation to the industrial sector. In society, many organizations found that the unemployment situation was much worse than the government figure revealed (Hong Kong Federation of Trade Union; Chan et al). The largest trade union in Hong Kong, the Hong Kong Federation of Trade Unions, have conducted their labour force survey quarterly since 1994 and revealed a more serious unemployment situation. Recent published research by academics of three universities in Hong Kong also found a much higher unemployment rate than the government claimed.(Chan et al 1997)

The current definition of unemployed adopted by the Hong Kong government is based on the resolution adopted by the Thirteenth International Conference of Labour Statisticians convened by the International Labour Organization in October 1982. The ILO guideline consists of three criteria: without work; currently available for work; and seeking work (ILO 1990:364–365). An examination of the definition of an unemployed person in Hong Kong revealed that it either mis-categorizes the unemployed as part of the economically inactive population or underemployed population. As pointed out by the author and other scholars (Chan et al; Wong), there are several types of hidden unemployment in Hong Kong.

The first type of hidden unemployment is found within the category of partial unemployment. According to the current definition, if the interviewee has only one hour of work for pay or profit, he or she will be excluded from the unemployed population. Consider a female worker who originally worked in the manufacturing sector but was laid off because of the relocation of the factory to mainland China. She finds a job as a cleaner in a fast food outlet during meal times. Her situation is partial unemployment more than underemployment.

The second type of hidden unemployed are those have the desire to work. Under the current definition, if the interviewee has the desire to work but did not actively seek a job during the thirty days before the survey, he or she will not be counted as unemployed. Rather, they are classified as part of the economically inactive population. There are various reasons for not seeking work, for instance the belief there is no work available to them. The industrial restructuring has discouraged workers to take action rather than it being a case of a worker's unwillingness to find a job.

The third type of hidden unemployed are those unemployed women who are forced to become full time housewives. In the industrial take-off period, a lot of women joined the workforce and this was reflected in the rise of the female labour force participation rate. But when the industrial restructuring occurred, they were the first to be dismissed as their skill lost its value in the labour market. They were forced to become full time housewives and classified as part of the economically inactive population.

Similar to the situation of unemployed women is that of middle aged and skill specific workers who were expelled from the labour force and forced into early retirement. The last type of hidden unemployment is found in those who cannot find a job and return to education institutions where they can survive upon loans and grants.

Conclusion

The case of Hong Kong shows that government policy interventions sustained employment in the industrialization period. However, government practices have served to hide the real situation of unemployment in the industrial restructuring period. The political will of the coming Hong Kong Special Administrative Region government will be crucial if a revised definition of unemployment is to be made in order to gain a clear picture of the problem. Only then can the government appropriately put forward a solution for the problem. In short, the Hong Kong case shows that the determination of a government has an impact on the level of employment in a country.

References

Castells, M, Goh L. and Kwok Y.W. 1990, *The Shek Kip Mei Syndrome: Economic Development and Public Housing in Hong Kong and Singapore*, Pion, London.

Census and Statistics Department 1997, 'Introduction to the Composite Employment Estimates.' *Hong Kong Monthly Digest of Statistics*. March.

Chan, K.W. et al. 1997, *Preliminary Report on the Unemployment Crisis of Hong Kong Labour*. mimeograph.(in Chinese).

Chen, Edward K.Y. and Kui-wai Li 1991, 'Industry Development and Industrial Policy in Hong Kong.' in *Industrial and Trade Development in Hong Kong*, eds. Edward K.Y. Chen, Mee-Kau Nyaw and Teresa Y.C. Wong., Centre of Asian Studies, University of Hong Kong, Hong Kong.

Chowdhury, Anis and Islam, Iyanatul.1993, *The Newly Industrializing Economies of East Asia*, Routledge, London.

Deyo, Frederic C.1992, 'The Political Economy of Social Policy Formation: East Asia's Newly Industrialized Countries.' in *States and Development in the Asian Pacific Rim*, eds. R.P. Appelbaum and J. Henderson, Sage Publications, U.S.A.

Freeman, Chris & Soete, Luc 1994, *Work for all or Mass Unemployment?* Pinter Publishers, Great Britain.

Friedman, Milton and Friedman R. 1980, *Free to Choose*, Penguin Books, Harmondsworth.

Haddon-Cave, Philip 1982,'Government Policy and Economic Success.' in *Hong Kong Economic Journal Monthly* V5 (12):82–5(in Chinese)

Haddon-Cave, Philip 1985, 'Introduction.' in *The Business Environment in Hong Kong* ed. D.G. Lethbridge, Oxford University Press, Hong Kong.

Hong Kong Federation of Trade Unions. *Report on the Members' Employment Situation*. various issues. mimeograph.

Hui, Sze Yan (Secretary for Finance)1997, 'Debate on the Definition Will Not Help to Resolve Unemployment Problem.' *Economic Times*, May 5,(in Chinese).

International Labour Office 1990, *Statistical Sources and Methods Vol 3 Economically Active Population, Employment, Unemployment and Hours of Work(Household Surveys)*, ILO, Geneva.

Legislative Council Sitting, April 23, 1997, Oral Question by the Hon. Chan Wing-chan on unemployment measurement.

Li, Simon Chi Fai 1997a, 'Statistical Profiles of Employment and Unemployment in Postwar Hong Kong.' paper presented at the East Asian Research Seminar organized by the School of Social Science, Bath University on Jan. 24.

Li, Simon Chi Fai 1997b, 'Extended the Unemployment Definition to Show the Real Situation of Unemployment.' *Economic Times*, May 24, (in Chinese).

Lui, Tai-lok and Samuel K. Chiu 1996, 'Interpreting Industrial Restructuring in Hong Kong: State, Market and Institutions.' in *Unravelling the Asian Miracle: Explorations in Development Strategies, Geopolitics and Regionalism*, eds. Jayant Lele and Ofori-Yeboah Kwasi,. Dartmouth, U.S.A.

Schiffer, J.R. 1991, 'State Policy and Economic Growth: A Note on the Hong Kong Model.' *International Journal of Urban and Regional Research*. V15(2): 180–196.

Sit, V.F.S. and Siu-lun Wong 1989, *Small and Medium Industries in an Export-Oriented Economy: The Case of Hong Kong*, Centre of Asian Studies, University of Hong Kong, Hong Kong.

Tang Shu Hung. 1992, *Hong Kong Public Finance in the Transition Period*, Joint Publishing(H.K.) Ltd, Hong Kong.(in Chinese).

Therborn, G. 1986, *Why Some People are More Unemployed than Others?* Verso, London.

Wong, Hung 1995, 'Government Suppress the Unemployment Rates Deliberately?' *Economic Times*, Nov. 9.

After Graduation, What? — Dilemmas of Vocational Integration in the New Global Economy

Peter J Dwyer

The purpose of this paper is to examine the emerging dilemmas confronting the post-1970 generation of young people concerning their career outcomes. It draws on a variety of research data from Canada, the US and Australia, and discusses the problems of 'vocational integration' related to the restructuring of labour markets in the new global economy.

The paper is divided into three parts: one looking at some Australian data on career aspirations of young Australians; a second discussing the concept of 'vocational integration' with reference to a variety of research data from Canada, the US and Australia; and the third reflecting on the emerging dilemmas confronting the post-1970 generation.

Career Aspirations of Young Australians

We have passed through a watershed in the world of work and old expectations and aspirations concerning the nature of the workplace and what a personal career might mean have been superseded. Beck (1993) in *The Risk Society*, Reich in *The Work of Nations* (1992), Rifkin(1995) in *The End of Work*, and Perkin (1996) in *The Third Revolution* refer to similar evidence and highlight the social implications of the workforce transformations taking place within the major industrialised nations.

To what extent that theme is commonly shared at a public level is another question. In fact, there is some evidence that the emergence of new highly-skilled and highly-paid jobs for a small professional elite has conveyed a misleading message to large numbers of young people that there will be plenty of these jobs for them to legitimately aspire to in the future. Thus, for example, a 1992 study of NSW Year 10–12 students' attitudes to post-compulsory education and training found that four times as many aspired to university (64 per cent) as TAFE (15 percent) and that over half aspired to professional occupations (DEET 1993: 6).

As Table 1 demonstrates, there is a considerable gap between the aspirations of these young Australians and the actual make-up of the workforce. Seven out of ten have set their sights on the highly-skilled professional and related sectors of the labour market that in 1992 accounted at most for only three out of ten of all employees. In other words, over half of these students — four out of the seven — are likely to miss out on their aspirations.

Similar career aspirations were evident in a 1996 Youth Research Centre survey of 1,908 Victorian students, the majority of whom had completed their schooling in 1991 and proceeded in the intervening years to participate in further study (Dwyer et al 1997). Details of social characteristics of the respondents in the sample are given in Table 2.

In the sample 81 per cent believed that there is a strong or very strong link between further study and better jobs, and as many as 72 per cent considered that this was definitely true in their own case. At a more detailed level the participants were asked what type of employment they would like

TABLE 1

NSW Year 10–12 Career Aspirations (%)

	Workforce 92	Males Aspire	Females Aspire	Total Aspire
Professionals	14	51	61	56
Managerial/Admin	11	9	9	9
Para-Professional	6	9	8	8
Sales/Services	15	4	11	7
Clerks	17	1	4	3
Trades	15	20	3	11
Labourers etc	22	11	12	12

(Source: DEET 1993: 7)

TABLE 2

Social Characteristics of Respondents

Respondents' Details	(%)
From Government Schools	60
Female	65
Australian-born	88
A-Born Female Parents	65
Male Parents with less than Yr 12	44
From Metropolitan areas	63
TAFE/VET post-secondary study	45
Completed studies	60

to have in the future, but also what they would 'realistically expect' to do. Again, not only did the majority (66 per cent) indicate that they have ambitions towards professional/managerial careers, but, as Table 3 indicates, almost all of these asserted that they also 'realistically expect' to achieve this (61 per cent).

These high aspirations were confirmed in other questions about their likes and dislikes concerning future employment situations. The picture of adult life they project is one of full-time secure employment in a two-income family (Table 4).

On the negative side, the majority indicated degrees of unhappiness if they could only find casual work, were dependent on welfare, were limited to 'home duties' or had a non-working partner (Table 5).

TABLE 3

Future Employment Expectations

Future Employment	Would like (%)	Expected (%)	1992 actuals
Professional/management/etc	66	61	31
Clerical/Office worker	4	9	17
Sales	2	3	15
Tradesperson	3	4	15
Factory worker or labourer	0	1	22
Not listed	25		

TABLE 4

Likes about Future Employment Situations

Job Features (% Response)	highly approve	approve
the job is a secure one	61	34
the job is full-time	55	29
had a partner with full-time job	39	43
work while children still at school	16	49

TABLE 5

Dislikes about Future Employment Situations

Job Features (% Response)	unhappy	very unhappy
had casual or irregular work	46	21
dependent on welfare	19	74
no work outside home duties	28	53
couldn't get a full-time job	31	59
had a non-working partner	32	19

They did not expect this to happen. In response to a final question about what they thought their situation in five years time was likely to be, the majority (Table 6) rejected the possibility that they might be unemployed (86 per cent rejection), dependent on welfare (90 per cent), only in casual or irregular work (67 per cent) or consigned to home duties (84 per cent).

Overall, the picture that emerges from this study is one of high-aspiring qualified young adults who fully expect to enter into full-time professional employment with little risk of irregular or intermittent work and in a living partnership with a similarly secure professional. Given the extensive restructuring that has taken place within the workforce, the down-sizing within professional occupations and the continuing high levels of prolonged unemployment, how realistic are these aspirations? The next section examines likely outcomes revealed by data from Canada, the United States and Australia.

Vocational Integration

Surveys in Australia and other English-speaking nations indicate that the transition of graduates into the labour market is not as immediate and direct as these young Australians might hope. If they are ever to fulfil their aspirations many of them must face an extended period of 'vocational integration' — with uncertain outcomes. This process has been the subject of considerable research by Canadian authors. Trottier, Cloutier and Laforce (1996) have recently developed a three-fold typology for the process which allows for some change of career-choice. According to their definition of 'vocational integration', the process is successfully realised by those graduates who within three years after graduation 'have a permanent full-time job and envisage making a career in the type of job which they hold' (p. 95) — 'even if the job is not the one he or she initially hoped for' (p. 94).

Chart 1 displays the varied degrees of success which Canadian graduates from different areas of specialisation have in finding a suitable career path for themselves within three years of graduation.

In the Youth Research Centre survey referred to earlier there is also evidence that 'vocational integration' is not an immediate or automatic outcome for young Australians either. When the respondents were asked about their own work situations in 1996, their answers suggested that the hopes of

TABLE 6

Prediction of Future Employment Situation

In 5 Years Time (% Response)	less likely	unlikely
unemployed	25	61
dependent on welfare	17	73
in casual or irregular work	36	31
no work outside home duties	21	63

many of them have not yet been realised. Only about half were in full-time employment and only 34 per cent described their job as being 'in my preferred career area' (Table 7).

Similar outcomes can be gleaned from other Australian data concerning graduate employment outcomes. In the Australia-wide Graduate Destination Survey, there has been a gradual decline in the proportion of those finding full-time jobs. Chart 2 compares figures for 1986 and 1995 for example, and we find that the proportion of first degree graduates who are only in part-time jobs, or who are not working but seeking work of some kind, has increased significantly. Some loosening of the link between university qualifications and direct entry into the full-time labour market has occurred, as is evident from Chart 2.

It is also interesting to observe how the graduates themselves view their

TABLE 7

Current Employment Situation

Current Job	(% Response)
a full-time job	49
a part-time job	26
job in my preferred career area	34
'stepping stone' job related to career	20
in a job not directly related to that	18
in a job, without career prospect	8
no job at present	19

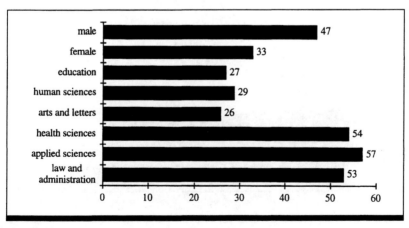

FIGURE 1

Vocational Integration of 3-year Canadian Graduates (%)
Source: Trottier, Cloutier & Laforce, 1996, p. 98.

employment outcomes. Thus, of the University of Melbourne Bachelor degree graduates who have been successful in finding employment in 1994 and 1996, only about one-third saw their job as 'a desired career position', with close to half in one defined only as 'a stepping stone' and almost a further fifth in 'an interim job not leading to a career position' (Chart 3).

When we turn to the United States, we also find parallels. Despite claims about rapid employment growth in the United States in recent years and the creation of new forms of 'highly-skilled' occupations, a process of delayed vocational integration is just as evident there for its College graduates. The Michigan State University College Employment Research Institute reported in 1993 that 'the job market for college graduates is now the poorest since World War II' (Rivkin 1995: 172). Thus, if we look at the College graduates of 1992–3, we find that while at least two-thirds of them have been able to find full-time jobs, once we look more closely at the types of jobs they have found the outcomes are not as promising. Only about half of those who graduated in 1992–3 are employed in jobs 'related to their field of study' or with 'career potential', and only four out of ten of them consider their jobs to merit the qualifications they themselves have brought to them (Table 8).

Dilemmas Facing the Post-1970 Generation

The identification of vocational integration problems affecting the current generation of graduates suggests that they are faced with a series of dilemmas regarding their future careers.

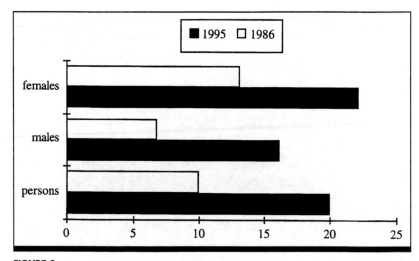

FIGURE 2

Australian First Degree Graduates in Part-Time Work or Seeking Work

Source: Graduate Careers Council, 1996, P. 64

First, a note of caution is necessary about perpetuating a definition of 'careers' in terms of a straightforward *linear* progression from study to work in a chosen field of specialisation. In developing their typology of vocational integration, Trottier et al take this into account by acknowledging that a settled career-choice may not necessarily bear a one-to-one relationship to actual qualifications or original intent.

This stable job may not correspond to the one that the graduate hoped to hold based on his or her initial plans for the future and on the training that he or she acquired because he or she had to reassess his or her situation and plans according to aspirations and competitive position in the job market (Trottier et al 1996: 94).

Other Canadian scholars (Anisef and Axelrod 1993) would argue that two or even three years is too short a time-span to allow for the process of

TABLE 8

US College Graduate Employment Outcomes

US 1992–3 College Graduates Per Cent	
graduated and in full-time jobs	67
grads. in F/T related to field of study	52
grads. in F/T with career potential	51
grads. in F/T 'college-degree-type' jobs	40

Source: US Digest of Education Statistics

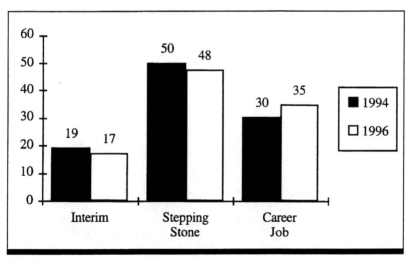

FIGURE 3

University of Melbourne Undergraduate Job Outcomes (%)
Source: Life After Graduation

vocational integration to take full effect. Even though, for example, some graduates initially experience periods of unemployment, 'care should be taken in drawing conclusions' about possible mismatches between qualifications and employment 'a short time after graduation' (Anisef and Axelrod 1993: 107). However, even if we allow for a longer time span it remains true that many still encounter 'obstacles in finding or sustaining employment consistent with their qualifications'. This may be particularly true for the post-1970 generation because they are entering into a radically restructured labour market in which greater flexibility and contingency are at play, and for whom a dilemma arises because the meaning of 'career' has changed.

Secondly, therefore, some doubts must be held about claims that the demand for increased skill levels is the likely explanation for the employment and career problems experienced by the current graduate generation. The study by Anisef et al referred to above was specifically devoted to the examination of this 'skills shortage' hypothesis and the authors came to the conclusion that 'it is reasonable to assume that the long-term mismatch rate among our highly qualified subjects was not the outcome of sharp increases in skill level requirements' (Anisef et al 1996: 171). Other data from Canada (Livingstone 1996), the United States (Rivkin 1995) and Australia (Gregory 1996) would support this conclusion. Data from Gregory suggest that the growing mismatch between educational levels and job market realities is much more likely to be a consequence of the narrowing of opportunities within the middle range of occupations, particularly for males. He concluded that 'the increased education levels of the young have not protected them from bearing the major adjustment from the lack of job growth' (Gregory 1995: 321). Given this evidence, it is clear that the professed employment benefits of increased participation in education and training have been exaggerated. The link between the two markets is not as direct or predictable as policy-makers claim.

Thirdly, as long as the global financial markets continue to dictate to labour market policy and high levels of prolonged unemployment are regarded as inevitable, it is likely that significant numbers of graduates will be denied a commensurate return on their (and their parents') investment in their post-secondary education and training. Côté and Allahar (1994) describe the current post-1970 generation as a *Generation on Hold*, and observe that

> Clearly, young people are the biggest losers as the conditions of advanced industrial society have become entrenched. The contradiction between credentialism and occupational disenfranchisement sends many of those attempting to come of age on an extended journey that does not lead them to the independence of adulthood, but rather to the uncertainties of prolonged youth (p 48).

It is worth commenting that already a decade has passed in Australia since the overwhelming majority of that generation entered upon the path of post-compulsory education and already the first cohorts of highly skilled tertiary graduates of the generation are ready to fulfil the promises that were made to them at the beginning. There is a question of accountability at stake here that demands a response in terms of *an economics of livelihood*. In one sense it could be argued that the prolongation of their youth was a price that had to be paid until they were properly trained for a restructured labour market and that market was ready for their entry. That time has come, and a final dilemma arises: what evidence can be found that those from preceding generations who in the meantime have benefited from that restructuring are willing to settle the account?

References

Anisef, P. and Axelrod, P. eds. 1993, 'Universities, Graduates and the Marketplace', in *Transitions: School to Work in Canada*, Thompson, Toronto.

Anisef, P., Ashbury, F., Bischoping, K. and Lin, Z. 1996, 'Post-secondary education and underemployment in a longitudinal study of Ontario baby boomers', *Higher Education Policy*, V9(2): 159–74.

Baker, M., Carne, S., and Ha, V. 1995, *Life After Graduation*, Institute of Applied Economic and Social Research, The University of Melbourne, Parkville.

Beck, U. 1993 *Risk Society: Towards a New Modernity*, Sage, London.

Byrne, S., Constant, A., and Moore, G. 1992, 'Making transitions from school to work', *Educational Leadership*, V49(6): 23–6.

Commonwealth of Australia 1994, *Working Nation: Policies and Programs* AGPS, Canberra.

Côté, J. and Allahar L. 1994, *Generation on Hold*, New York University Press, New York.

Davies, S., Mosher, C., and O'Grady, B. 1994, 'Trends in Labour Market Outcomes of Canadian Post-Secondary Graduates, 1978–1988', in *Sociology of Education in Canada*, eds. L. Erwin, and D. MacLennan, Copp Clark Longman, Toronto.

Dwyer, P. 1996, *Opting Out: Early School Leavers and the Degeneration of Youth Policy*, National Clearing House for Youth Studies, Hobart.

Freeman, R. & Katz, L 1994, *Working Under Different Rules*, Russell Sage, New York.

Gregory, R. 1995, 'Higher Education Expansion and Economic Change in Australia', *Australian Bulletin of Labour*, V21(4): 295–322.

Gregson, J. 1995 'The school-to-work movement and youth apprenticeship in the U.S.: Educational reform and democratic renewal.' *Journal of Industrial Teacher Education*, V32(3), pp. 7–29.

Levine, D. 1994, 'The School-to-Work Opportunities Act: A flawed prescription for education reform', *Educational Foundations*, V8(3): 33–51.

Livingstone, D. 1996, *The Education-Jobs Gap: Underemployment or Economic Democracy*, Westview Press, Boulder.

Looker, D. and Dwyer, P. 1997, *Pathways and Life's Patterns: Rethinking Research on Youth Transitions in Modern Societies* , forthcoming.

Nickell, S. and Bell, B. 1995, 'The Collapse in Demand for the Unskilled and Unemployment Across the OECD', *Oxford Review of Economic Policy*, V11(1): 40–62.

Perkin, H. 1996, *The Third Revolution*, Routledge, London.

Rifkin, J. 1995, *The End of Work*, Putnam, New York.

Smith, C. and Rojewski, J. 1993 'School-To-Work Transition, Alternatives for Educational Reform', *Youth & Society*, V25 (2): 222–50.

Teichler, U. 1989, 'Research on higher education and work in Europe', *European Journal of Education*, V24(3): 223–48.

Trottier, C., Cloutier, R., and Laforce, L. 1996, 'Vocational Integration of University Graduates: Typology and Multivariate Analysis', *International Sociology*, V11(1): 91–108.

Wyn, J. and White, R. 1997, *Rethinking Youth*, Allen & Unwin, Sydney.

Young Australian Women and Their Aspirations for Work, Education and Relationships[1]

Deidre Wicks and Gita Mishra

It is recognised that while women make up over half of tertiary enrolments, this outcome is not reflected in the gender composition of occupational structure, career patterns and pay distribution. There are a number of different explanations for this including a recent contribution from British sociologist Catherine Hakim who identified the main causal factor as women's own lack of career orientation and work commitment. Hakim's contribution has produced a lively debate with all sides acknowledging the lack of, and need for, longitudinal data on women's workforce participation.

The present paper investigates data from the first stage of the Australian Longitudinal Study on Women's Health which provides a valuable opportunity to inform this debate through an analysis of the aspirations of a large group of young Australian women aged 18–22 years. The investigation will be conducted in relation to young women's aspirations for work, relationships and further education. In this context, the implications for the 'Hakim debate' will be discussed.

Analysis of the initial data casts light on debates about women's workforce participation at the same time as establishing baseline data for future research on the work and family patterns of this group of young women. The information will have significance for policy debates in several areas, including those concerned with child care, access to higher education and workforce planning.

Over the last two decades, there has been a thoroughgoing reassessment of many of the taken for granted 'truths' concerning women, their supposed 'essential' natures and their biological destinies. Part of this reassessment has involved a re-evaluation of women and paid work, its history (Davidoff and Hall 1987; Scott 1988) as well as more recent trends and issues. Researchers and writers working from feminist perspectives have been concerned to examine such issues as the segmentation of the labour market by gender, women's level of participation in the paid workforce, patterns of women's employment, comparative pay rates of women and men, and the impact of domestic responsibilities on workforce participation (Walby 1986; 1988; Beechey 1987; Beechey and Perkins 1987; Game and Pringle 1983; Probert 1989). Research on these and related areas has contributed to a picture of workforce participation which is now recognised as being fundamentally marked by inequalities of gender. Research has shown that in Australia women predominate in jobs which are characterised by poor pay, high turnover, insecurity, a high incidence of part-time and casual work and little autonomy over the work itself (Baxter and Gibson 1990; Edwards and Magarey 1995).

While there is general agreement about the unequal roles and rewards for women and men in the labour market, there is much debate about the causes. Most agree that women's disadvantage in the workforce can be attributed to their child-care and domestic responsibilities. However, the explanatory differences lie in whether or not these responsibilities are imposed through the operation of power, or are willingly embraced. While conservative (or functionalist) writers have emphasised the latter, those writing from more radical traditions (Marxist and feminist) have, understandably, emphasised the former. Feminists have generally focussed on the concept of power for an explanation of the pervasiveness of gender inequalities, including those relating to work. Recently, Catherine Hakim (1991;1995) has launched an attack on the notion that a segmented labour market with unequal rewards is the result of gendered power relations rather than women's choice. She argues that 'feminist orthodoxy' has replaced objective assessment of the position of women in the labour market with the result that women are presented as victims who have little or no responsibility for their situation (Hakim 1995:448)

To support this view, Hakim explores the paradox of 'grateful slaves' that is, the fact that while women are concentrated in the lowest paid, least skilled jobs with the poorest benefits and prospects, they report disproportionately high levels of satisfaction with their jobs (1991:101). Hakim's explanation for this is that women have different life goals and priorities than men. She states:

> The majority of women aim for a homemaker career in which paid work is of secondary or peripheral importance, with strong support from their husbands for this strategy. A minority of women are committed to work as a central life goal, achieving jobs at higher levels of status and earnings. (Hakim 1991:101)

In her most recent (and most controversial) contribution, Hakim (1995) examines what she considers are 'Five feminist myths about employment'. The 'myth' which is of relevance here, is the 'myth' which holds that there is no sex differential in work commitment and work orientation between men and women. Hakim further develops her earlier argument concerning women's lower commitment and orientation to paid work and concludes by stating that working women comprise at least two qualitatively different groups. In her words:

> In effect, the adult female population divides into two fairly equal sectors. The first group of women are committed to careers in the labour market and therefore invest in training and qualifications, and generally achieve higher grade occupations and higher paid

jobs which they pursue full-time for the most part. The second group of women give priority to the marriage career, do not invest in what economists term 'human capital', transfer quickly and permanently to part-time work as soon as breadwinner husband permits it, choose undemanding jobs 'with no worries or responsibilities' when they do work, and are hence found concentrated in lower grade and lower paid jobs which offer convenient working hours with which they are perfectly happy. (Hakim 1995:434)

There is certainly other research which confirms that many women define outside work as secondary to their role as housewives and mothers (Yeandle 1984; Wearing 1984; Baxter and Gibson 1990). The key questions are firstly, are there really two distinct groups of women or is the situation not more fluid? In particular, what are the factors which influence the ease with which women move in and out of different employment categories? Secondly, to what extent is this supposed 'free choice' a real choice and to what extent is it the result of historically and culturally shaped limits, opportunities and expectations for women? Probert, for instance, when discussing the possible polarisation of work and earning experience of middle class and poorer women in Australia, makes the point that it is not very plausible to view these changes as simply the result of women's choices. She argues that it is far more likely that these changes are a response to changing educational and employment opportunities (1996:45). This point has also been made in relation to the high numbers of women in part-time work. Again, Probert suggests that there is a strong case for arguing that women's labour force participation is strongly determined by 'demand side' factors. It is these factors which determine whether there is a demand for female labour by employers in the small range of occupational groups within which women are concentrated (1994:319) .

It is within this context that the present study of young Australian women and their aspirations for work, education and relationships ought to be situated. This study is part of the baseline survey of the Australian Longitudinal Study on Women's Health (Women's Health Australia — WHA) which provides a unique opportunity to explore the relationship between women's aspirations, their success in achieving them and the consequences for their health. The WHA study is designed to track the health of three cohorts of women over a period of up to twenty years. The project, which was established as a result of an Australian government initiative to conduct a longitudinal cohort study on women's health (Brown et al 1996), aims to clarify cause-effect relationships between a range of biological, psychological, social and lifestyle factors and women's physical health, emotional well-being, and use of and satisfaction with health care services. To date, baseline data have been collected from three large cohorts of women, aged 18–22, 45–49 and 70–74 years. This component of the study examines baseline data from the young cohort in relation to their aspirations in the areas discussed above.

Methods And Analysis

Details of recruitment methods and baseline measures have been reported elsewhere (Brown et al 1996). To summarise, 39,000 women aged 18–22 years were randomly selected by the Health Insurance Commission (the agency which administers Medicare on behalf of the Federal Government of Australia), with deliberate over-representation of women from rural and remote areas. Women from these geographical areas were selected in twice the proportion which exists in the Australian rural and remote population in each age group (54% of the sample were from rural areas, and 3% were from remote areas). Women from capital cities and other metropolitan areas made up the balance of the samples. Surveys were sent to the selected women by mail during June and July 1996, using a modified Dilman proto-col (Dilman 1991). We now have 14,804 women in the young cohort. The baseline measures included 260 questions on a wide range of issues designed to explore the social and environmental aspects of women's lives as well as the psychological and biological determinants of health. The young cohort were asked specific questions concerning their aspirations for work, educa-tion and relationships at age 35. To correct for over-sampling of women from rural and remote areas, all responses were weighted (area adjusted) so that the study population was representative of the Australian population for women of this age group. Chi-square analyses were used when compar-ing proportions.

Results for Cohort as a Whole

Work and Further Education

When asked what type of work they would like to be doing at aged 35, 60% of the cohort responded that they wanted full time paid work. A further 31% wanted part time paid work. Together this constituted a majority of 91% who wanted either full or part time work with a significant majority declaring their desire for full time paid work. A further 4% wanted unpaid work in the home with the remaining 5% wanting another (unspecified) option.

Consistent with the results on work, 74.5% of respondents stated that at 35 they would like to have more educational qualifications than at present. Another 19% were not sure and 7% stated a definite 'no'.

Occupational Choice

From our survey, we ended up with approx. 14,000 individual responses to the question concerning which job each respondent would like to be doing at age 35. This made fascinating reading and included everything from accountant, animal trainer to truck driver and prime minister. In order to organise the responses into something more manageable, we classified their written responses on their ideal job into the Australian Standard Classification of Occupations (ASCO). The results are as follows in table 1.

At present, only 29.7% are working in jobs classified as professional, so another 14% aspire to professional jobs in the future. This also throws light on the high percentage who desire to improve their educational qualifications. It is also instructive to compare the aspirations of the young cohort with the occupational realities of our mid-life cohort (see table 2). For instance, while 23.8% of our mid-life cohort are working as clerks, only 3.5% of the young cohort want to be clerks.

It is apparent, however, that this group of young women is not solely focussed on work and qualifications. When asked about their aspirations for relationships, 85% responded that at 35 they wanted to be married. A further 11% wanted to be in a stable relationship (but not married), while 1% did not want to be either married or in a stable relationship (3% unspecified other).

Children

TABLE 1

Number and Percentage of Women Who Aspire the Following Types of Occupation

	N	%
Professional	5617	42.4
Para-Professional	1735	13.1
Manager/Administrator	1360	10.3
Sales/Personal	2362	17.8
Clerk	461	3.5
Tradesperson	404	3.1
Others (uncertain, unemployed, manual work, same as current job)	1292	9.7

TABLE 2

Number and Percentage of Mid-Life Cohort Who are in the Following Types of Occupation

	N	%
Professional	2154	16.0
Para-Professional	1220	9.0
Manager/Administrator	1573	11.7
Sales/Personal	1840	13.6
Clerk	3206	23.8
Tradesperson	413	3.1

Approximately 92% of this cohort want children by the time they are 35. The majority of the group (64.5%) want 1 or 2 children at age 35. More than one quarter (27%) want more than 2 children while 8% aspire to having no children at age 35. Of this large cohort of young women, 72% want either 2, 1 or no children at age 35.

Disaggregated Results

The data presented above constitute the baseline, aggregated data for the group as a whole. When the data is disaggregated a more complex and interesting picture emerges.

Social Class

As we lacked data on the respondents' parents' occupations and incomes, we followed several other studies which have used local government area or post code area as a marker for social advantage or disadvantage (Gregory and Hunter 1995; Birrell 1997). We chose two aggregated areas in Sydney, based on the numbers of high and low income households in Statistical Local Areas (ABS Census 1991). A low income household was defined as one where earnings were less than $25,000. The local areas which evidence a high number of low income households include, Blacktown, Bankstown, Canterbury, Fairfield and Parramatta while the areas containing few low income households were, Hunters Hill, Concord, Mosman, Strathfield, Lane Cove. We then compared the aspirations of the cohort from the low income and high income areas. Table 3 indicates the effect of social class on the aspirations of this group of young women.

Approximately 82% of the high income area group want to be in the professional, para professional or manager/administrator groups compared to approx 67% of the low income area group. This difference is statistically significant, ($\chi^2 = 26.2$, $df = 3$, $p < 0.0001$). In relation to the area of sales and personal services, traditionally an area of low pay, the trend is reversed.

Ethnicity

TABLE 3

Job Aspiration by Household Income Areas

| | Types of household income area | | | |
| | High | | Low | |
	N	%	N	%
Professional	67	49.3	148	40.6
Para-Professional	20	14.7	46	12.6
Manager/Administrator	25	18.4	52	14.3

Identified by country of birth, ethnicity was indicative of significant differences in aspirations for particular types of work at age 35. When we combine the three categories of professional, para-professional and manager/administrator, the results are interesting. While 75% of those born in Asia, 70% of those born in Europe (not of English speaking background — NESB), 71% born elsewhere (English speaking background — ESB — Canada, USA, Sth Africa, NZ) aspired to have jobs within these categories at age 35, a statistically significant lower number, of those born in Australia — 65% — held aspirations for these jobs ($\chi^2 = 42.7$, $df = 9$, $p < 0.0001$). The trend for sales and personal services are reversed though not statistically significant. This is illustrated by table 4:

Work and Children

While the majority of this cohort (92%) aspire to having children by age 35, the number of children is related to the type of work to which they aspire. Table 6 indicates this relationship.

TABLE 4

Job Aspirations by Country of Birth

	N	%	p-value*
Professional/para-professional/manager/administrator			
Australia	7620	65	—
Other ESB	399	71	0.006
Europe(NESB)	122	70	0.1
Asia	369	75	< 0.0001
Sales/personal			
Australia	2154	18	—
Other ESB	90	16	0.27
Europe(NESB)	30	17	0.43
Asia	55	11	0.04

TABLE 5

Number of Children Aspired by Job Aspirations

	Number of children aspired					
	One or two		More than two		No children	
	N	%	N	%	N	%
Professional	3217	65.8	1188	24.3	481	9.9
Para-professional	917	63.5	400	27.7	127	8.8
Manager/Administrator	808	69.0	259	22.1	104	8.8

It is worth noting that the majority of the cohort aspire to the top three occupational categories and want one or two children.

Discussion

These data, which at this stage represent a cross sectional cohort study, provide a useful contribution to several of the current debates concerning women and work. At the very least, they cast doubt on assertions made by Hakim concerning the supposed low level of work commitment evident among either a majority (1991) or a roughly equal (1995) segment of women workers. In this study, a majority of the cohort (60%) stated that at age 35 they would like to be in full-time work outside the home. Only a very small group (4%) stated that they wanted to be in full-time, unpaid work inside the home (home duties). This figure ought to be seen in the light of the even larger group (74.5%) who stated that at age 35 they wanted to have higher educational qualifications. In fact, a further 19% stated that they were 'not sure' with only 7% stating a definite 'no' to further educational qualifications at age 35. This appears to indicate a serious commitment to a future in which paid work plays a significant and ongoing role in their lives.

It is worthwhile to compare the aspirations of the cohort regarding full-time work with current workforce participation realities. While it is true that between 1986 and 1990 there has been a steady upward trend in the average labour force participation rate for women, most of this can be explained by an increase in women's part-time employment. During this period, women in the labour force were about three times more likely than men to be employed part-time. The full-time labour force participation rate increased by one percentage point for women and decreased by six points for men. In both 1986 and 1996, just over one quarter of the female population was in full-time employment (Australian Women's Year Book (AWYB) 1997:70). Clearly, if the aspirations of this large cohort of young women are representative of the aspirations of the national population of this age group, this constitutes a far reaching change in attitudes to and desire for full-time paid work. Whether or not these aspirations are realised will depend on many factors including the availability of full-time work and the provision of 'family friendly' social support services.

Occupational Choice

The other significant feature of these data concerns the type of work aspired to by the women in the study. While in 1996, 56% of all employed women worked in the two occupational groups of clerks and sales and personal service, it appears that young women today are aspiring to very different occupations (AWYB 1997:73). Within this cohort, a much lower proportion (21.5%) aspire to these two occupational groups. In fact, by far the biggest proportion, (42.4%), aspire to professional occupations. The picture becomes more complex, however, when we disaggregate the group. When we divide our respondents into areas marked by low and high income households, we find that there are significant differences in their occupational aspirations. Among the respondents in the households of the high income areas, 49% aspire to professional occupations while in low income areas, 41% hold these aspirations. The results are consistent when we look at the aspirations for the more traditional (and traditionally low paid) occupations. Within the areas of high income households, 7% of the young women surveyed aspire to the occupational groups of clerks, sales/personal services, compared with 23% of the low income households.

These results are consistent with the literature on social class which focuses on the connections between poverty and the distribution of life chances, including social mobility. Bourdieu (1977), for instance, has theorised the centrality of the education system in reproducing class inequalities. This approach is supported by the statistical analysis of social mobility data by writers such as Goldthorpe (1980) and Gallie (1988), who demonstrate that the chances for entering secure, well paid, 'middle class' jobs are much higher for the sons, and to a lesser extent the daughters, of middle class parents than for the children of working class parents. This also holds true for children from disadvantaged ethnic backgrounds, or the disabled, where we find higher barriers to social mobility within and between generations (Bilton et al., (1996). To these general findings on class obstacles to social mobility have been added the recent, detailed statistical analyses by Gregory and Hunter on inequalities among Australian neighbourhoods (1995, and Hunter 1995). Hunter, for instance, has found that the group of people who are most at risk of becoming permanently alienated from the economic system are those who live in neighbourhoods with low socio-economic status. Furthermore, living in a low status neighbourhood may have a detrimental effect on employment or level of participation in the labour market (Hunter 1995:14). In this context, it is possible to see the lower occupational aspiration levels of the young women from the low income areas as depressingly realistic in relation to their overall life chances. Yet, at the same time, the aspirations of the young women from the low income areas are still higher than the current female participation rates in professional occupations. While a lower 40.6% of the cohort from the low income areas aspire to professional occupations, this still represents a massive change from the current 29.7% of women who currently work in occupations classified as professional.

These data are particularly significant in the light of other longitudinal research on work orientations. In the National Longitudinal Surveys (NLS) initiated in the US in the mid 1960's, five cohorts of young and mature women and men were surveyed and followed up almost every year to 1983 on various aspects of their work orientations. Of special interest for this study is the cohort of young women aged 14–24 in 1968, who were asked what they would like to be doing when they were 35 (whether they planned to be working; marry; keep house; raise a family). Hakim, who refers to this study, makes the point, that despite the 'crudity of the question', it turned out to have 'astonishing analytical and predictive power' (Hakim 1991:111). Hakim goes on to point out that there are several independent analyses of the extent to which the early workplans were fulfilled by age 35. They all show that, for the most part, the 'career planning' women achieved their objectives in terms of occupational grade and earnings (Hakim 1991:111). The important point to make here is that in the NLS study, the proportion of young women who aspired to be career planners were only a small proportion of the total. Indeed, Hakim makes much of the fact that the career planners were a small minority of one quarter of the young women cohort. This contrasts dramatically with the WHA study where 60% of the young cohort aspire to full-time jobs at age 35. If the predictive power of these questions holds true for this study, there are enormous implications for several areas of policy, including social, employment, industrial and health policy.

Relationships and Children

The majority of the young cohort also state that they want to be married and have children by age 35. Combined with their work and education aspirations, this constellation of aspirations indicates a prospective desire and need for a cluster of education and family support services which would have to be greatly expanded from the current (shrinking) base. It also indicates the prospective need for continuing industrial relations reform such as parental leave and greater flexibility for both women and men to combine work and family responsibilities and pleasures. However, recent changes to Federal Government policies, including the new parenting allowances for women engaged in at-home child care and the cutbacks in subsidies for community based child care centres, appear to be moving in the opposite direction.

On the demand side, the possibility of these aspirations being realised assumes an employment market where the desired sorts of jobs, in the desired number, will be available to these young women. At present, the indications for jobs growth are not optimistic. In fact, recent research indicates that from the September quarter 1993 to the June quarter 1997, female employment growth has slowed dramatically. Much of this is due to the fact that the industries in which female jobs are mainly located are weaker than in the 1980's. The question remains as to whether the downturn in female unemployment is a temporary departure or marks the beginning of a significant structural change in the Australian labour market (Borland 1997). It would be disappointing to find that our longitudinal research is focussed on tracking the health effects of thwarted aspirations rather than on the rich interplay of individual hopes and plans in the context of a full range of life opportunities.

Conclusion

These data offer a beginning to a substantial, long term contribution to current debates concerning women and work. While it is acknowledged that the richest data will be longitudinal, the baseline data provide some interesting insights into young women's aspirations for work, career, relationships and education. In particular, they challenge recent arguments developed by Hakim concerning the supposed lower level of work orientation and commitment on the part of women. Clearly, the issues surrounding the multiple demands, orientations and opportunities in women's lives are complex and may have no simple explanations or clear cut analyses. It certainly seems simplistic in the extreme to claim that women neatly divide into two groups with different interests. It is apparent that women's interests, activities and priorities change over time, often as a consequence to changing life circumstances and employment opportunities. In the past these changes have occurred very much as a response to others needs and priorities. It is clear that given a free choice, the majority of this group of young women want both full-time paid work and family relationships as a significant, ongoing part of their lives. It remains to be seen how much power these young women have over the future direction of these key aspects of their lives.

Endnote

1. The research on which this paper is based was conducted as part of the Australian Longitudinal Study on Women's Health, coordinated by the University of Newcastle. We are grateful to the Australian Department of Health and Family Services for funding.

References

Australian Bureau of Statistics 1993, Sydney — a social atlas [map]: census of population and housing, 6 August 1991, Catalogue No. 2840.1, Canberra.

Australian Bureau of Statistics 1997, Australian Women's Year Book, Catalogue No. 4124.0, AGPS, Canberra.

Baxter, J. and Gibson, D. 1990, Double Take, AGPS, Canberra.

Beechey, V. 1987, Unequal Work, Verso, London.

Beechey, V. and Perkins, T. 1987, A Matter of Hours: women, part-time work and the labour market, Polity, Cambridge.

Bilton, T. et al. 1996, Introductory Sociology, Macmillan, London.

Borland, J. 1997, 'Women's work fast declining', Australian Financial Review, 22 July.

Bourdieu, P. 1977, Outline of a Theory of Practice, Cambridge University Press, Cambridge.

Brown, W. et al. 1996, 'Women's Health Australia: Establishment of the Australian Longitudinal Study on Women's Health', Journal of Women's Health, V5: 467–472.

Davidoff, L. and Hall, C. 1987, Family Fortunes. Men and Women of the English Middle Class, 1780–1850, Century Hutchinson, London.

Dilman, D. 1991, 'The Design and Administration of Mail Surveys', Annu. Rev. Sociol., V17: 225–49.

Edwards, A. and Magarey, S. eds. 1995, *Women in a restructuring Australia: Work and welfare*, Allen and Unwin, Sydney.

Gallie, D. ed 1988, *Employment in Britain*, Blackwell, Oxford.

Game, A. and Pringle, R. 1983, *Gender at Work*, Allen and Unwin, Sydney.

Goldthorpe, J. H. 1980, *Social Mobility and Class Structure in Modern Britain*, Clarendon Press, Oxford.

Hakim, C. 1991, 'Grateful slaves and self-made women: fact and fantasy in women's work orientations', *European Sociological Review* V7: 101–21.

Hakim, C. 1995, 'Five feminist myths about women's employment', *British Journal of Sociology*, V46(3): 429–455.

Hartmann, H. 1979, 'The unhappy marriage of Marxism and feminism: towards a more progressive union', *Capital and Class*, V8: 5–14.

Probert, Belinda 1994, 'Women's working lives' in *Contemporary Australian Feminism*, ed. Kate Pritchard Hughes, Longman, Melbourne.

Scott, Joan Wallach 1988, *Gender and the Politics of History*, Columbia University Press, New York.

Walby, S. 1986, 'Gender, class and stratification', in *Gender and Stratification*, eds. R. Crompton and M. Mann, Polity Press, Cambridge.

Wearing, Betsy 1996, *Gender. The Pain and Pleasure of Difference*, Longman, Melbourne.

Yeandle, S. 1984, *Women's Working Lives*, Tavistock, London.

Recruitment and Non-standard Employment

Ed Carson and Audrey VandenHeuvel

While there is considerable discussion in the literature on the supply of workers and their job search methods, the demand side of the labour market, including the recruitment and selection practices of employers, has received much less attention, especially in Australia.

This paper canvasses the published research to date in Australia and considers the impact on recruitment of factors such as occupational category, firm size, industry and the state of the labour market. Although there is conceptual uncertainty about the link between recruitment practices and workforce flexibility, the paper suggests that recent developments can be conceptualised in terms of the concept of the flexible firm.

The uncertainty about recruitment practices is compounded, however, by uncertainty about the implications of the impending reconfiguration of the employment services market on recruitment practices. Accordingly, the paper identifies the need for empirical research on changing recruitment practices of Australian employers.

There is little doubt that there has been a dramatic growth in non-standard employment in Australia in the last two decades — by some measures greater than that seen in most OECD countries. While there is considerable discussion in the literature on the supply of workers and their job search methods (Carson 1995, 1989; Devine & Kiefer 1993; Fevre 1992), the recruitment practices of employers have received much less attention, especially in Australia.

Evidence from the UK suggests that a move towards numerical flexibility might be leading to increased use of informal, word-of-mouth strategies (Boyer 1991). At the same time, research from the US suggests that a common recruitment strategy being used by firms is to move towards the use of employment agencies, for all skill levels, effectively sub-contracting to recruit workers (Standing 1996). By the mid-1990s the largest single employer in the USA was Manpower, a private temporary employment agency.

In the coming months in Australia, fundamental reforms to the nature and scope of labour market program assistance will, in part, involve the establishment of a contestable and competitive employment services market.

While the consequences of that change are still unclear, the nature of employment assistance agencies will be important for recruitment practices of employers because they are being developed at a time when many analysts predict that employers' search for numerical flexibility in their workforces will increase. In view of the uncertainty about the link between employment assistance agencies and recruitment practices, an empirical study is warranted to investigate the way recruitment practices have been integral to the growth of non-standard employment in Australia in the 1990s. This paper is part of the preliminary work in one such research project.

As a precursor to the empirical research it is necessary to theorise the changes in the nature of recruitment. An assessment of the impact on recruitment practices of factors such as occupational category, firm size, industry and the state of the labour market can be developed in a more integrated way with reference to the debate on the concept of 'the flexible firm' (Atkinson 1987) even though there is some debate about the relevance of that concept as either description, prescription or explanation of workforce restructuring in Australia (Burgess 1997).

Preliminary Distinctions: Informal/Formal and Degrees of Closure

Even where there is a body of research on recruitment issues in Australia and overseas, it is not clear whether there is a common understanding of the concept of recruitment among employers and researchers[1]

Recruitment methods used by the firm are often classified as being either formal or informal. While there is some disagreement in the literature as to what constitutes these two forms of recruiting (contrast Marsden & Campbell 1990 and Koch 1995 for example), in the main it can be said that formal strategies are aimed at disseminating information outside the organisation in systematic ways. In the case of informal recruitment, the aim is the transmission of information about vacancies via the employer's networks, such as current employees, business contacts, friends and relatives, in order to set in motion a process of information transmission out into the wider community.

At the same time, this latter point highlights the fact that rather than there being a clear dichotomy between internal and external labour markets, and in turn between internal and external recruitment methods, it is widely recognised that some labour markets do not fall neatly into either category (Doeringer & Piore 1971; Manwaring 1984). Rather, there are varying degrees of closure of labour markets. The most obvious example of this is firms which recruit through existing employees or their own contacts. Through this 'word-of-mouth' recruitment method, labour markets are closed to those who are outside of the social networks of the firm's employees or employer, but are open to those outside of the firm who are within these social networks (Manwaring 1984). In turn, the social networks (friends, relatives and acquaintances) of the existing workforce can be usefully conceptualised as the extended internal labour market (Jenkins et al. 1983; Manwaring 1984).

Recruitment Patterns: Is Australia Distinctive?

Research on recruitment methods used by Australian employers is considerably less developed than is the overseas research on this topic. The Australian studies tend to be based on data from a small number of employers who are based in select geographical areas and who represent a limited numbers of industries (Bankstown Technical College 1981; Dufty 1986; Nowak 1988; Roy Morgan Research Centre 1995; Savery & Soo 1984; Wright & Thong 1989). Nevertheless, there have been at least two more broadly based studies of relevance.

The first of these was undertaken by Charlton West Associates for DEET in 1991 and could reasonably claim to provide the most comprehensive and representative survey of employer recruitment practices ever undertaken in Australia. It involved a telephone-based survey of a stratified random quota sample of 1170 establishments drawn from Australian businesses in the eight largest industry divisions.

The second study (Callus et al. 1991) was based on the 1989 Australian Workplace Industrial Relations Survey, and looks only at those firms which had had a vacancy in the preceding year and had experienced difficulty in filling one or more of their vacancies. Thus general recruitment methods of firms are not considered.

A brief summary of Australian studies is provided in Table 1. Despite the variety of ways in which use of recruitment methods is defined and measured across studies, this body of research does give rise to a consistent conclusion — that in Australia formal recruitment methods, and especially advertisements in newspapers, are used more frequently than more informal methods of recruitment. The only exception to this general pattern is the Roy Morgan Research Centre (1995) study which reports evidence that direct applications and employee referrals are used just as frequently, if not more. This finding, however, may reflect the (deliberate) over-representation in their sample of employers with relatively high concentrations of foreign workers.

For the purposes of international comparison, Table 2 presents a summary of information from studies on recruitment methods undertaken overseas in the past 15 years. (As when comparing different Australian studies, caution must again be exercised when comparing results between countries.) The results suggest that firms overseas are more likely to make use of referrals from staff and contacts as a means to recruit staff. The use of unsolicited applications also seemed somewhat more popular overseas than in Australian firms. Thus overall, the data suggest a greater reliance on informal methods of recruiting and internal methods of filling job vacancies in international firms than in Australian firms.[2]

Does the same pattern of similarities and differences hold when we distinguish between the effects of occupation, firm size, industry and the state of the labour market? Consider what the existing literature has to say on each of these factors.

TABLE 1

Australian Studies on Recruitment Methods: 1980 Onwards

Study	Sample	Recruitment measure	Job levels considered	Results (%)					
				Newspaper advertising	CES	Private agency	Employee referral	Direct application	Internal
Bankstown Tech. College (1981)	140 Sydney	Primary method used	Unskilled	43	37	—	—	—	—
Savery & Soo (1984)	181 Perth firms, 1983	Methods used successfully	Managerial, professional	68	17	29	23	14	50
			Tradespeople	62	36	9	25	22	19
			Office workers	82	40	30	33	22	31
			Labourers	50	52	12	31	25	20
Duffy (1986)	20 large WA firms, 1986	(i) Relative use of all methods	Professional	40	0	15	10	13	—
			White collar	26	18	12	15	21	—
			Skilled	24	21	3	21	24	—
			Non-skilled	18	23	0	16	25	—
		(ii) Primary method used	Professional	89	0	—	—	0	—
			White collar	55	27	—	—	14	—
			Skilled	64	9	—	—	9	—
			Non-skilled	21	16	—	—	47	—
Nowak (1988)	156 Melbourne manuf. & service	(i) Relative use of all methods,	Executive, managerial	39	14	18	6	—	—
			Professional, technical	46	6	17	5	—	—

TABLE 1 (Continued)

Study	Sample	Recruitment measure	Job levels considered	Results (%)					
				Newspaper advertising	CES	Private agency	Employee referral	Direct application	Internal
		(ii) Methods successfully used, weighted	Clerical, sales	45	21	9	12	—	—
			Tradespeople	48	25	3	12	—	—
			Semi-skilled and unskilled	47	37	0	18	—	—
			Executive, managerial	41	12	20	5	5	—
			Professional, technical	46	8	22	33	—	—
			Clerical, sales	44	16	14	11	3	—
			Tradespeople	47	22	3	11	6	—
			Semi-skilled and unskilled	32	32	2	19	7	—
Wright & Thong (1989)	408 Victorian private sector firms, 1985	Methods used very often or always	Managerial	48	8	16	6	—	27
			Professional & administrative	49	6	12	7	—	20
			Supervisors	32	7	4	8	—	33
			Clerical	31	16	10	8	—	18
			Sales, service & technicians	38	10	4	7	—	14
			Industrial/manual	25	37	1	11	—	11

TABLE 1 (Continued)

Study	Sample	Recruitment measure	Job levels considered	Results (%)					
				Newspaper advertising	CES	Private agency	Employee referral	Direct application	Internal
Callus et al. (1991)	1341 firms who had difficulty filling a position, 1989	Method most successful	Management, professional, para-profess.	40	2	18	6	—	13
			All other occupations	42	13	5	13	—	6
Roy Morgan (1995)	100 employers in 4 regions, 1992; 240 employers in 4 regions, 1994	(i) Methods used in last 6 months by firms who had recruited	22	13	3	30	31	—	
		(ii) All methods used							
		1992	26	10	2	13	25	99	—
		1994	90	74	26	99	100		—
			88	81	23	97		8	—
Charlton West (1991)	1170 establishments, May 1991	Two most common methods used in last 2 yrs — relative use	Manager/prof	46	3	31	8	5	—
			Trades	49	16	10	13	8	—
			Clerks	40	19	16	8	11	—
			Sales	35	21	8	14	19	—
			Machine operators	36	27	3	17	14	—
			Labourers	25	33	2	19	19	—

Note: Indicates category not separately identified.

TABLE 2

International Studies on Recruitment Methods: 1980 Onwards

Study	Sample	Recruitment measure	Job levels considered	Results (%)					
				Newspaper advertising	CES	Private agency	Employee referral	Direct application	Internal
Wray (1984)	25 UK clothing manuf. firms, 1980	methods used successfully		46	3	5	42	2	—
Manwaring (1984)	66 UK large manuf. firms, 1980/81	methods which account for ≥ 30 % of recruitment	Non-manual	45	29	20	39	6	—
			Skilled manual	28	41	6	54	26	—
			Unskilled & Semi-skilled manual	13	54	0	69	48	—
Keil et al. (1984)*	41 UK manuf. & service sector firms, 1981	(i) all methods used	Managers	76	2	22	10	2	42
			Routine non-manual	83	73	24	42	32	59
			Craft workers	68	54	5	34	39	27
			Manual	61	78	0	59	66	44
		(ii) methods used ≥ 50 % of time to recruit	Managers	73	3	8	8	0	43
			Routine non-manual	68	44	7	32	17	51
			Craft workers	75	56	0	22	22	31
			Manual	49	72	0	39	34	39
		(iii) methods successfully used to recruit applicants	Managers	68	2	17	2	7	49
			Routine non-manual	83	59	32	29	29	44
			Craft workers	63	39	7	32	22	15
			Manual	61	76	2	59	54	24

TABLE 2 (Continued)

Study	Sample	Recruitment measure	Job levels considered	Results (%)					
				Newspaper advertising	CES	Private agency	Employee referral	Direct application	Internal
		(iv) methods used to hire applicants ≥ 50 % of time	Managers	54	3	0	0	3	25
			Routine non-manual	68	13	3	8	0	13
			Craft workers	49	10	0	7	0	3
			Manual	34	39	0	11	3	3
		(v) methods used for most recent vacancy	Non-manual	34	16	7	4	2	16
			Manual	20	22	3	14	6	11
		(vi) methods successfully used to recruit for most recent vacancy	Non-manual	39	17	7	2	2	12
			Manual	26	21	0	13	11	3
Wood (1985)	150 UK & West German large firms. 1980/81	methods used to fill ≥ 30 per cent of vacancies	Low-level white collar	—	49	—	35	18	80
			Skilled manual	—	36	—	57	36	62
			Unskilled manual	—	36	—	59	39	50
Ford et al. (1986)	306 UK firms, 1985	methods used for recent vacancy	Manual or shop assistant	37	61	11	40	17	25
			Clerical	47	50	10	25	7	31
Windolf (1986)	124 UK & West German firms, 1980/81	methods used to recruit ≥ 50 % of work force	Unskilled	30	33	—	36	—	48
			White collar	27	22	—	33	—	77

TABLE 2 (Continued)

Study	Sample	Recruitment measure	Job levels considered	Results (%) Newspaper advertising	CES	Private agency	Employee referral	Direct application	Internal
Holzer (1987)	3500 USA firms, 1982	(i) methods used in previous 10 days		37	20	—	53	—	—
		(ii) method for most recent hire		13	3	—	36	19	—
Bureau of	245 USA firms	all methods used	Managers, supervisors	85	7—30	60	64	46	95
			Professional, technical	94	11—37	58	78	64	88
			Salespersons	84	7—49	44	76	52	75
			Office, clerical	84	19—85	28	87	86	94
			Production, service	77	20—88	11	83	87	86
van Ours(1990)	1780 Dutch firms, 1988	methods used for existing vacancies		54	36	—	—	—	—

Notes:　— indicates data were not available.
* This data source is also discussed in Ford et al., 1984.

The Effect of Occupational Category

It is commonly accepted that employer recruitment methods differ according to the occupational level of the job vacancy, whereby occupational classification is considered to be a proxy for expected mean productivity (Nowak 1988). At higher occupational levels, it is assumed that there is greater variability in productivity among job applicants. In turn, the value of information on potential applicants and their expected productivity is greater at higher occupational levels. Therefore, it is expected that employer recruitment patterns differ systematically between occupational groups, whereby employers make use of more extensive and more formal recruitment methods more frequently for the recruitment of higher skilled workers.

As Table 1 indicates, with the exception of the Roy Morgan (1995) study, Australian studies show that advertising (usually in newspapers) is the most common form of recruiting among Australian firms for all types of vacancy except for the least skilled staff (Charlton West 1991; Dufty 1986; Nowak 1988; Savery & Soo 1984; Wright & Thong 1989).

For the least skilled staff, some studies show that firms have tended to rely more on the CES as the main recruitment channel (Bankstown Technical College 1981; Charlton West 1991; Savery & Soo 1984; Wright & Thong 1989). More commonly, though, the informal recruitment methods, namely referrals from employees or other contacts and direct applications, played the largest role in recruiting unskilled staff. Furthermore they were used for the recruiting of employees at all occupational statuses to some degree (Charlton West 1991; Dufty 1986; Nowak 1988; Savery & Soo 1984; Wright and Thong 1989).

By way of comparison with Australian findings, the results from the international research on recruitment again indicates the prevalence of advertising as a means of recruiting candidates (Keil et al. 1984; van Ours 1990; Wray 1984). However, the results are less consistent than the Australian research in suggesting the dominance of this form of recruiting for occupational levels other than lower-skilled jobs (Ford et al. 1986; Holzer 1987; Windolf 1986). For example, key overseas studies suggest that the use of public employment agencies is more likely than the use of advertising for clerical staff (Ford et al. 1986) and that employee referrals were more common than advertising (Holzer 1987).

In terms of recruiting methods for lower-skilled positions, the results from the international research are varied, with studies suggesting that the most commonly used recruitment method for such employees is employee referrals (Manwaring 1984), public employment agencies (Keil et al. 1984; Wood 1985) and internal recruitment (Windolf 1986).

As was observed for Australian firms, the use of private employment agencies is generally reserved for the hiring of managers and other highly-skilled staff, while the public employment agency was used much more commonly for the recruiting of lower-skilled workers.

The Effect of Firm Size

There are a number of reasons why the size of the firm is likely to be related to recruitment methods. First, large firms can afford to specialise internally in hiring activities. With bigger recruiting budgets and economies of scale in recruiting, they are thus are likely to make use of more intensive and extensive search procedures (Koch 1995; Marsden and Campbell 1990; Nowak 1986, 1988).

Second, it may be in the interests of larger firms to do so, if they have higher internal monitoring costs than smaller firms, and thus they may undertake more extensive and costly recruitment procedures (Barron et al 1987; Mellow 1982) such as the use of private employment agencies. It is assumed that such hiring practices can then assist in reducing staff monitoring costs.

Third, larger firms are more likely to receive unsolicited applications from job seekers given that job seekers are more likely to apply to organisations with a higher likelihood of requiring staff (Marsden & Campbell 1990).

Fourth, while all firms in Australia are subject to equal employment opportunity legislation, only larger firms are required to report annually on their affirmative action program. When there is direct legal oversight of hiring practices of firms, formal recruiting methods are encouraged (Marsden & Campbell 1990). This would suggest more formalised hiring practices by larger firms, at least in Australia.

Fifth, larger firms may be unable to fill all staff needs from local labour markets and thus may be more likely to resort to formal recruiting methods that cover a wide geographic area (Marsden and Campbell 1990). Smaller firms, on the other hand, may be able to fill all of their staff needs from local labour markets and can thus rely more heavily on informal methods and unsolicited applications.

Finally, those in charge of hiring in smaller firms are likely to hold a range of responsibilities, and will be unable to devote as much time and energy to hiring practices. The use of word-of-mouth recruiting is thus more likely to be relied upon. Further, the need to recruit will be relatively less frequent in small business. Nevertheless, errors in staff selection can be more costly for small firms, in terms of the impact on productivity and the relatively higher dismissal costs. Thus, it is suggested that small firms are more inclined to make use of methods that reduce uncertainty, yet cost little, such as relying on referrals from employees.

Relatively little empirical Australian research has dealt with how recruitment practices differ according to the size of the firm. Perhaps the best Australian evidence on this issue comes from the study of Charlton West Associates (1991) which confirms that direct contacts are relatively much more important for recruitment at small establishments (and by inference, small firms), while use of employment agencies is relatively less important. Differences in the use of both advertising or the CES, however, were not large (though the incidence of use of advertising did clearly rise with establishment size).

The other study that examined this issue in considerable detail was undertaken by the National Training Council (1987) but dealt only with the issue of the recruitment of apprentices. Their survey of 1273 firms in Victoria and South Australia concluded that advertising and the CES were more commonly used to recruit apprentices by large businesses, while small businesses were more likely to recruit through referrals from employees and other personal contacts. Another study, by Wright and Thong (1989), addresses the issue of firm size briefly and suggests that smaller firms tend to make less use of advertising, consultants and internal promotion.

Overseas research also tends to identify differences in recruiting methods according to the size of the firm. A number of findings match expectations of differences. First, the use of employment agencies (Deshpande & Golhar 1994; Holzer 1987), recruitment through educational institutions (Deshpande & Golhar 1994) and unsolicited applications (Holzer 1987) were found to be more widespread in larger firms, while the use of employee referrals (Holzer 1987) was more common among smaller firms. Second, results from three studies suggest that internal promotion is more likely as a means of filling vacancies in larger than smaller firms (Dalton & Kesner 1983; Deshpande & Golhar 1994; Lauterbach & Weisberg 1994). Third, total recruiting costs were found to be higher in larger firms than in smaller firms (Barron et al 1985).

The Effect of Industry

The information-gathering processes of firms are also expected to differ by industry for several reasons. First, the industry the firm operates in will determine the mix of labour required, and differences in the need for educational and skill requirements will relate to hiring methods used. For example, if an industry is characterised by a narrow spread of skills and qualifications between jobs, or requires on-the-job training, internal recruitment methods may be more likely (Nowak 1988). Second, it is believed that industries develop an approach to recruitment and selection over time, and the way these approaches evolve differ from one industry to another (Koch 1995).

Few studies have compared recruitment practices across industries and, with the exception of the Charlton West (1991) study, all those that did were overseas studies. The Australian study by Charlton West (1991) found important inter-industry differences, which can be summarised as follows:

- advertising, while the most dominant form of recruitment in all industries, was relatively most dominant in public administration and community services;

- personal contacts were extremely important in the agriculture sector, but of relatively little importance in public administration;

- the most intensive users of the CES were found in wholesale and retail trade and in public administration, while the least intensive users were in finance and business services;
- use of agencies was relatively common in construction and, to a lesser extent in finance and business services and manufacturing, and relatively uncommon in agriculture, public administration, community services and personal services.

Of course, it may be that these differences simply reflect differences in the occupational mix of the workforce across industries. The Charlton West study made no attempt to test for this.

Although no other Australian studies have looked at industry differences to any extent, two Australian studies did consider recruitment practices in specific industries. Norris et al. (1995) used a case study approach to examine recruitment in the tourism industry. They found that in this industry, virtually all external recruitment took place at base-level job classifications and for casual positions, while all other positions were filled by internal recruitment. The exception to this was the filling of a few specialist positions (such as accountant or chief chef) where external recruitment did occur. To find the unskilled casual workers they required, methods of recruitment commonly used were direct applications, the CES, employee referrals and newspaper advertisements.

The other example of an industry-specific study examined small- to medium-sized businesses in the finance sector in Brisbane (Boreham, Roan & Whitehouse 1994). As in the majority of Australian studies noted so far, newspaper advertising was found to be dominant, with the majority of employers (64 per cent) claiming they would use newspaper advertisements if they needed to hire clerical staff. Other commonly noted methods used to recruit clerical staff were private employment agencies (43 per cent) and the CES (36 per cent). In this study, employers were also asked for their attitudes toward private employment agencies and the CES. The main finding was that a greater percentage of employers said that the CES was less able than private employment agencies to meet employer needs. First, the association of the CES with the unemployed limited its ability to refer preferred types of job applicants, whereas private employment agencies were prized for being able to deliver a more personal service. Second, the commitment of the CES to adhere to legislative requirements and guidelines on discrimination and equal opportunity meant that it was less likely to accommodate requests for applicants with particular ascribed characteristics (sex, age, ethnicity, appearance).

Overseas studies tend to suggest some differences across industries. For example, a UK study suggests that when recruiting for a manual or a clerical worker, public sector organisations were much more likely than manufacturing or service sector firms to make use of advertising, and somewhat more likely to have made use of public employment agencies and direct applicants. Both public and service sector organisations were more likely than manufacturing industries to have made use of internal advertising. On the other hand, recruitment through referrals was much more common in the manufacturing industry than the two other industries considered. Another study, by Holzer (1987), included industry measures in multivariate analyses of the recruitment method that was used to hire the most recent employee. Industry differences were also noted in this study. For example, manufacturing firms were most likely to have used the public employment agency to fill their most recent vacancy, while service sector and agricultural firms were least likely to have hired a staff member recruited through a direct application. The use of newspaper advertisements were least likely among manufacturing, construction and trade organisations.

The Effect of the State of Labour Market

During times of recession, recruiting efforts on the part of firms are expected to decrease and internal promotion is likely to be relied upon more extensively (Jenkins et al. 1983; Wood 1985). At least four reasons for this change can be suggested. First, cutting recruitment budgets is one way for the firm to save money during recessionary periods (Jenkins et al. 1983). Second, voluntary staff turnover is likely to be less common during recessions, thus reducing the total need for recruitment. Third, internal recruitment is more likely during recessions since it can serve as a means to fill vacancies with redundant workers from other areas without requiring payouts (Jenkins et al. 1983). Finally, during periods of high unemployment, it is expected that there will be a greater number of employee referrals and unsolicited applicants of high-quality (Barron et al. 1985; Stone 1995), thereby reducing the need for more active (and expensive) recruitment methods on the part of the firm.

Thus less expensive methods, such as employee referrals, direct applications and internal promotions are more likely to be used, while methods which are more costly in terms of both time and fees (such as newspaper advertising or consultancy firms) are more likely to be avoided. On the other hand, however, it is possible that recruiting patterns of some firms remain constant regardless of the state of the labour market. They might respond to recessionary periods by becoming more selective about the person they hire or by lowering the wages offered rather than by altering recruitment methods. The ideal study of the relationship between the state of the labour market and recruitment methods would involve a longitudinal survey that examined recruitment patterns in specific firms at times of high and low unemployment. No such study was found.

Alternatively, one could attempt to study this issue by simply comparing results from studies conducted during times of recession with those conducted during times of full employment. It must be noted, however, that any observed differences over time may be due to many reasons other than changes in the state of the labour market, such as differences in the samples or different methods of measuring recruitment practices.

Nonetheless, results from Australian studies completed in the 1960s and 1970s are shown in Table 3 . Given the cautionary note, a review of these earlier research projects suggest four main differences compared with more recent surveys. First, in earlier decades, a greater number of recruitment methods may have been used (Godfrey 1973). Second, advertising was even more commonly used as a recruitment method for all occupational levels (Department of Productivity 1978; Godfrey 1973). Third, the data suggest that more frequent use was made of the CES to hire unskilled staff in the past (Godfrey 1973; Smith & McCalman 1965; Spencer and Singer 1970).

Two studies from the UK that claim to look at the effect of the recession on recruitment used a comparative method to investigate change over time in response to the state of the labour market — in both cases data from the early 1980s were examined and differences in the results in comparison to earlier years are suggested (Jenkins 1983; Wood 1985). Both suggest that internal recruiting and employee referral were much more common during times of recession.

There are nevertheless major gaps in the literature that need to be filled, about how recruitment methods have changed over time. In particular, no literature was found that considered how recruitment processes have changed in line with the trend to hire more casual and part-time workers, in line with the putative shift to a more 'flexible firm'.

Summary

It has been established that, first, in Australia there is a reliance on formal methods, particularly newspaper advertisements, rather than informal methods of recruiting. However, the research also indicates that employer recruitment practices differ by nature of the job vacancy.

It was found that more costly and extensive search methods which provide more information to the employer have tended to be used relatively more often for the hiring of more highly-skilled workers, while less costly methods were used relatively more often for hiring of unskilled workers. Furthermore, the use of private employment agencies was generally reserved for the hiring of managers and other highly-skilled staff, while the public employment agency and word-of-mouth was used much more commonly for the recruiting of lower-skilled workers.

Relatively little empirical Australian research has dealt with how recruitment practices differ according to the size of the firm, but such evidence as exists indicates that direct contacts were relatively much more important for recruitment in small firms, while use of employment agencies was relatively less important.

Consistent with this is the finding that in industries such as the tourism industry, virtually all external recruitment took place at base-level job clas-

TABLE 3

Australian Studies on Recruitment Methods: Pre-1980

Study	Sample	Recruitment measure	Job levels considered	Results (%)					
				Newspaper advertising	CES	Private agency	Employee referral	Direct application	Internal
Smith & McCalman (1965)	60 WA medium-sized, manuf. firms, 1964	all methods used		88	88	—	—	—	—
Spencer & Singer (1970)	317 medium-sized firms, 1969	primary method used	Managers	48	—	22	10	—	51
			Supervisors	35	—	3	4	—	90
			Other workers	82	62	19	—	—	—
Godfrey (1973)	136 firms, 1972	all methods used		96	74	70	45	45	—
Department of Productivity (1978)	128 medium-sized firms, year not stated	primary method used	Managers	55	1	32	6	—	—
			Professional	75	0	17	1	—	—
			Clerical70	13	9	3	—	—	—
			Skilled74	12	0	5	—	—	—
			Unskilled	43	35	0	4	—	—

Note: — indicates data were not available.

sifications and for casual positions, while all other positions were filled by internal recruitment. To find the unskilled casual workers they required, methods of recruitment commonly used were direct applications, the CES, employee referrals and newspaper advertisements.

In light of the fact that there has been a dramatic growth in non-standard employment in Australia in the last two decades — by some measures greater than that seen in most OECD countries — it is critical to identify the changes in the nature of recruitment and to theorise those changes, as suggested below. It is particularly critical to do so at the time when the newly declared competitive employment services market is likely to change the recruitment practices of employers, particularly for less skilled workers.

Flexible Firms and Non-standard Employment

An assessment of the impact on recruitment practices of factors such as occupational category, firm size, industry and the state of the labour market can be developed in a more integrated way with reference to the debate on the concept of 'the flexible firm' (Atkinson 1987) even though there is uncertainty about the relevance of that concept as either description, prescription or explanation of workforce restructuring in Australia (Burgess 1997).

In the coming months in Australia, fundamental reforms to the nature and scope of labour market program assistance will, in part, involve the establishment of a contestable and competitive employment services market. Non-profit and for-profit Employment Placement Enterprises (EPEs) and a Public Employment Placement Enterprises (PEPE) will tender to provide a range of employment services including labour exchange services, job search assistance and employment assistance.

Clearly the abolition of the CES will have implications for recruitment practices of employers but, even more critical is the way in which EPEs position themselves to provide services to job seekers and employers.

It is reasonable to expect that some EPEs will emphasise the labour exchange role of a placement agency while others will be likely to emphasise the networking and mentoring role that emulates information transmission and support informally available through the extended internal labour market. While the consequences of these developments are still unclear, the nature of employment assistance agencies will be important for recruitment practices of many employers. In either case, the nature of employment assistance agencies will be important for recruitment practices of employers at a time when the employers' search for numerical flexibility of the workforce is predicted to increase.

Because of the conceptual uncertainty about the link between workforce flexibility and recruitment practices , and the empirical uncertainty about the link between employment assistance agencies and recruitment practices, an empirical study is warranted to investigate the way recruitment practices have been integral to the growth of non-standard employment in Australia in the late 1990s. This paper is part of the preliminary work in one such research project.

Endnotes

1 This is most evident when we consider the results of a 1980 survey of 3100 American employers (Barron et al. 1985). All of the employers included in the study had indicated that they had hired an employee in the previous two years, but when asked for details about the recruiting method used to fill this position, 28 per cent responded that they had not recruited in order to fill this position. It can be presumed that certain internal or informal methods of filling job vacancies are considered to be recruitment procedures by researchers and some employers but may not be considered as such by other employers.

2 This same conclusion was reached by Nowak (1988).

References

Atkinson, J. 1987, 'Flexibility or fragmentation? The United Kingdom labour market in the eighties', *Labour and Society*, vol. 12, no. 1, pp. 87–105.

Bankstown Technical College, 1981. *Selecting the Unskilled*, Management Research Group, Bankstown Technical College.

Barron, J. M., Black, D. A. and Loewenstein, M. A. 1987, 'Employer size: The implications for search, training, capital investment, starting wages and wage growth', *Journal of Labor Economics*, vol. 5, no. 1, pp. 76–89.

Boreham, P., Roan, A. and Whitehouse, G. 1994, 'The regulation of employment services: Private employment agencies and labour market policy', *Australian Journal of Political Science*, vol. 29, pp. 541–555.

Boyer, R. 1991, 'The eighties: search for the alternatives to Fordism', in B. Jessop et al. (eds), *The Politics of Flexibility*, Edward Elgar, Aldershot.

Burgess, J. 1997, 'The flexible firm and the growth of non-standard employment', *Industry and Labour*, vol. 7, no 3, pp. 85–102.

Callus, R., Morehead, A., Cully, M. and Buchanan, J. 1991, *Industrial Relations at Work: The Australian Workplace Industrial Relations Survey*, AGPS, Canberra.

Carson, E. 1989, 'Social networks in the labour market: The sociology of job search', *Australian Bulletin of Labour*, vol. 15, no. 4, pp. 287–313.

Carson, E. 1995, *Social Networks and Job Acquisition in Ethnic Communities in South Australia*, AGPS, Canberra.

Charlton West Associates, 1991, The Pattern of Job Filling in Australia, unpublished report to DEET, Canberra.

Clark, R. 1989, *Australian Human Resources Management: Framework and Practice*, McGraw-Hill Company, Sydney.

Department of Productivity, 1978, 'Recruitment, selection and induction — A survey', *Work & People*, vol. 4, no. 3/4, pp. 53–60.

Deshpande, S. P. and Golhar, D. Y. 1994, 'HRM practices in large and small manufacturing firms: A comparative study', *Journal of Small Business Management*, vol. 32, no. 2, pp. 49–56.

Devine, T. J. and Kiefer, N. M. 1993, 'The empirical status of job search theory', *Labor Economics*, vol. 1, pp. 3–24.

Doeringer, P. and Piore, M. 1971, *Internal Labour Markets and Manpower Analysis*, Heath Lexington, Massachusetts.

Dufty, N. F. 1986, *The Hiring Experience of Large Employers in Western Australia*, The Western Australian Labour Market Research Centre Discussion Paper No. 18, Murdoch University, Perth.

Fevre, R. 1992, *The Sociology of Labour Markets*, Harvester Wheatsheaf, Hemel, Hempstead.

Ford, J. R., Bryman, A., Beardsworth. A. D., Bresnen, M. and Keil, T. 1986, 'Changing patterns of labour recruitment', *Personnel Review*, vol. 15, no. 4, pp. 14–18.

Godfrey. J. 1973. 'Aspects of recruitment and selection.' *Personnel Practice Bulletin*, vol. 29, no. 2, pp. 148–152.

Hodes, B. S. 1995. 'Recruiting on the Internet — On your marks, get set ...', *Human Resources Professional*, vol. 8, no. 6, pp. 7–9.

Holzer, H. J. 1987, 'Hiring procedures in the firm: Their economic determinants and outcomes', pp. 243 to 274 in M. Kleiner, R. Block, M. Roomkin and S. Salsbury (eds.), *Human Resources and the Performance of the Firm*, Industrial Relations Research Association, University of Wisconsin, Madison, WI.

Jenkins, R., Bryman, A., Ford, J., Keil, T. and Beardsworth, A. 1983, 'Information in the labour market: The impact of the recession', *Sociology*, vol. 17, no. 2, pp. 260–267.

Keil, T., Ford, J., Bryman, A. and Beardsworth, A. 1984, 'Does occupational status matter? The case of recruitment', *International Journal of Social Economics*, vol. 11, no. 7, pp. 32–48.

Koch, M. J. 1995, *Hiring Practices and Productivity*, Garland Publishing, Inc., New York.

Manwaring, T. 1984, 'The extended internal labour market', *Cambridge Journal of Economics*, vol. 8, no. 2, pp. 161–187.

Marsden, P. V. and Campbell, K. E. 1990, 'Recruitment and selection processes: The organizational side of job searches,' pp. 59–79 in Ronald L. Brieger (ed.), *Social Mobility and Social Structure*, Cambridge University Press, Cambridge.

Mellow, W. 1982, 'Employer size and wages', *Review of Economics and Statistics* (August), pp. 495–501.

National Training Council. 1987, *Apprentice Selection by Small Business*, AGPS, Canberra

Norris, K., Stromback, T. and Dockery, A. M. 1995, *How Tourism Labour Markets Work*, Commonwealth Department of Tourism Research Paper No. 1, AGPS, Canberra.

Nowak, Margaret J. 1986, 'The search for staff — some employer practices', *Bulletin of Labour Market Research* No. 18: 10–13.

Nowak, Margaret J. 1988, 'Information theory and employer recruitment practices', *Journal of Industrial Relations*, vol. 30, no. 2, pp. 277–294.

Roy Morgan Research Centre 1995, *Employer Recruitment Practices Survey — 1994 Update*, Bureau of Immigration, Multicultural and Population Research, AGPS, Canberra.

Rynes, S. L. 1993, 'When recruitment fails to attract: Individual expectations meet organizational realities in recruitment', pp. 27 to 40 in H. Schuler, J. Farr and M. Smith (eds), *Personnel Selection and Assessment: Individual and Organizational Perspectives*, Lawrence Erlbaum Assoc., Hillsdale, New Jersey.

Savery. L. K. and Soo, R. Y.C. 1984, 'Recruitment and selection procedures in Western Australia', *Economic Activity*, vol. 27, no. 2, pp. 29–33.

Sayles, L. R. and Strauss, G. 1977, *Managing Human Resources*, Prentice-Hall, Englewood Cliffs, NJ.

Schuler, R. S., Dowling, P. J. and Smart, J. P. 1988, *Personnel/Human Resource Management in Australia*, Harper & Row Publishers, Sydney.

Schuler, R. S., Dowling, P. J., Smart, J. P. and Huber, V. L. 1991, 'Staffing the organisation: Recruitment, selection and placement', pp. 156–199 in *Human Resource Management in Australia*, 2nd edition, Harper Educational.

Smith, R. S. and McCalman, D. H. 1965, 'Employment practices in medium-small firms — A survey in Western Australia', *Personnel Practice Bulletin*, vol. 21, no. 4, pp. 34–41.

Spencer, C. and Singer, C. 1970, 'The personnel function in medium and small firms', *Personnel Practice Bulletin*, vol. 26, no. 1, pp. 42–47.

Standing, G. 1997, 'Globalization, labour flexilibity and insecurity: the era of market regulation', *European Journal of Industrial Relations*, vol. 3, no. 1, pp. 7–37.

Stone, R. J. 1995, *Human Resource Management*, second edition, John Wiley & Sons, Brisbane.

van Ours, Jan C. 1990, 'An empirical analysis of employers' search', pp. 191–213 in J. Hartog, G. Ridder and J. Theeuwes (eds.), *Panel Data and Labor Market Studies*, Elsevier Science Publishers, North-Holland.

Windolf, P. 1986, 'Recruitment, selection, and internal labour markets in Britain and Germany', *Organization Studies*, vol. 7, pp. 235–254.

Wood, S. 1985, 'Recruitment systems and the recession', *British Journal of Industrial Relations*, vol. 23, no. 3, pp. 103–120.

Wray, K. 1984, 'Labour market operation, recruitment strategies and workforce structures', *International Journal of Social Economics*, vol. 11, no. 7, pp. 6–31.

Wright, K. and Thong, M. 1989. *Recruitment Channels and Selection Methods of Victorian Private Sector Organisations*, Phillip Institute of Technology Occasional Paper No. 6, Coburg, Victoria.

The Role of Job Sharing in Regional Economies

Helen Nohilly, Margaret Drever and Bruce Armstrong[1]

> we can now produce our 1948 standard of living (measured in terms of market goods and services) in less than half the time it took in that year, yet Americans are now working longer hours. (Juliet Schor cited in Rifkin, 1996, p. 223).

The issue of job sharing as a labour market development policy has been elevated recently through the release of findings from a study entitled 'Reforming Work Time' by John Buchanan and Sue Bearfield (1997). A number of recommendations and findings were made in the report relevant to the Australian work environment. One of the issues raised was job sharing strategies.

This paper examines the current status of the Australian labour market. The material discussed includes data for Australia as a whole, and the employment patterns found from a study which examined employee and business profiles on the Mid North Coast region of New South Wales (NSW). This particular regional study shows very high levels of part time and casual employment in the region, with women more likely to be employed on a part time or casual basis in nearly all industry categories. The data for the entire Australian labour market also reveals the current extent of overtime work within Australia.

The paper then explores the practicalities and difficulties of implementing a job sharing strategy in a regional context. However, there are limits to its ability to help share the existing work hours. These limits are related to the decreasing number of full time jobs available to share, the lack of payment for overtime hours presently being worked, and the government and unions inertia in deciding to actively support job sharing. Furthermore, the greatest barricade is the current ideology and emotional expectation that full employment will solve the problem of social inclusion and participation which unemployment is said to cause The authors concluded that the recognition and acceptance of this type of policy approach, that is, sharing the work, is capable of challenging the current work paradigm in a more inclusive way than other employment and job creation strategies. Sharing the work gives a more equitable distribution of social time and earnings is discussed.

The analysis of findings illustrated in Table 1 show that 6.1 million people are currently working full time in Australia. This is 68% of the total labour force including the unemployed, or 75% of the currently employed workforce. This shows that the majority of those who are working are still working full time.

Currently, 2.6 million people are working overtime of whom only 0.9 million are working paid overtime. Table 1 also shows that 24% of the labour force is working part time, which means that 25% of the total employed labour force is employed on a part time basis (Buchanan & Bearfield, 1997).

Table 1 shows that despite Australia being 'one of the largest employers of part time labour among OECD countries (only Norway, Netherlands, Denmark and Sweden are more intensive in part time workers) that an overwhelming majority of those who are working do so full time' (National Institute of Labour Studies, 1994, p. 13). Table 1 also shows that 35% of those working are doing extra paid overtime while 0.7 million people remain unemployed. This seems to infer that there may be quite a few opportunities for job sharing through a redistribution of overtime.

The dichotomy of overtime is made evident in a survey conducted of 1000 companies based in Sydney, Melbourne and Brisbane by Recruitment Solutions. The study shows that the industry with the highest rate of unpaid overtime in the over $80,000 income bracket is the hospitality and travel industry, with 83% working more than 50 hours, up from 46 hours the previous year (Crothers, 1997). The industry with the highest unpaid overtime in the $40,000 to $80,0000 income bracket is the advertising, media and

TABLE 1

Labour Market Profile

Total Labour Force:	8.9 million	Unemployed: 0.7 million
Full-Time:	6.1 million (68% of total labour force) (75% of employed labour force)	
Work Overtime	2.6 million	42% (labour force)
Work Paid Overtime	0.9 million	15% (labour force) 35% (employed labour force)
Work Unpaid Overtime	1.7 million	27% (labour force) 65% (employed labour force)
No Overtime	3.5 million	58% (labour force)
Have 2nd Job	0.25 million	4% (labour force)
Work Standard Hours	3.2 million	52.5% (labour force)
Part-Time:	2 million (24% of total labour force) (25% of employed labour force)	
Happy with Working Hours	1.5 million	75% (total part-time employed)
	0.5 million	25% (total part-time employed)

Source: Buchanan and Bearfield, 1997, Reforming Working Time, p. 9.

marketing sector. This industry has 77% of employees working in excess of 45 hours per week. The industry with the highest unpaid overtime in the less than $40,000 income bracket, is the telecommunications sector, with an alarming increase from 16% working more than 40 hours last year, to 76% this year (Crothers, 1997).

If society is to be truly committed to the creation of employment opportunities, then these industries must discourage staff from working unpaid overtime. The sharp rise in unpaid overtime in the telecommunications industry over the past year, begs the question as to whether the supposed increases in efficiency are coming from privatisation or merely making those who are left with jobs, work more hours without being paid for it. Not only does this challenge the notion of privatisation, but also whether Australians are indeed working smarter or are simply working harder.

When a person is in a position that is paid for overtime worked, this can account for in excess of 20% of their total waged income. 'Using ABS figures, if overtime was shared, up to 500,000 jobs could be created. However, only one third of employees working overtime are paid ...unpaid hours account for about 300,000 of these possible 500,000 full time jobs.' (Buchanan & Bearfield, 1997, p. 4). This implies that if these jobs were shared, either those working paid overtime could not bear the decrease in wages, or the employer would have to find the money to pay those currently working unpaid overtime.

The report by Buchanan and Bearfield (1997) does not take into account that the estimated 500,00 created jobs will increase on-costs to business. It is likely that employers could only increase their number of employees by a percentage of the reported 500,000 jobs, while ensuring the viability and survival of their business.

Government policies which try to shift responsibilities such as superannuation and health care to employers, will reduce job and employment opportunities by raising the costs of employing staff. Policies such as this directly raise on-costs, as opposed to government provisions which spreads these costs across the community. These types of policies act as a barrier to the implemention of job sharing strategies on a large scale, particularly in areas such as the Mid North Coast region of NSW. Figure 1 shows the Mid North Coast has a much greater incidence of those working part time, compared to the national average. Figure 1 also shows that there are less full time jobs to share in this particular region.

The data illustrated in Figure 2 shows that 43% of men, as opposed to 23% of women, work full time on the Mid North Coast region of NSW. The majority of women who are working in the region are employed on a part time or casual basis. This could be related to the increase in the female participation rate in the work and labour force (see Figure 3). Whether or not this increase in women's participation has led to a greater demand for part time casual jobs is inconclusive. However it may be related to the findings

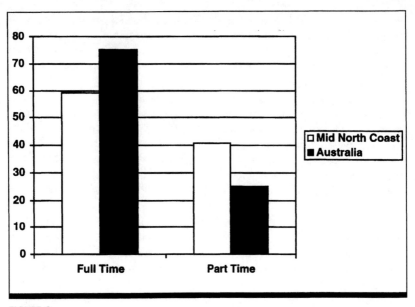

FIGURE 1

Comparison of Position Types using Data from the Business Enterprise Register and ABS Labour Force Survey

Source: Australia Catalogue 6203.0, Feb & Nov 1995.

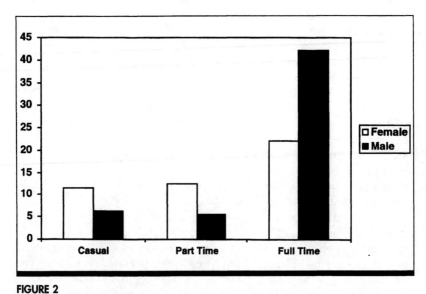

FIGURE 2

Comparison of Male/Female Employment on the Mid North Coast of NSW

Source: Armstrong and Drever, 1997, Mid North Coast Business Census Report.

in Figure 1, that show 75% of those working part time Australia-wide were happy with their hours of work (Buchanan & Bearfield, 1997, p. 9). There may also be a causal association with the fact that the majority of jobs created during the period are part time or casual, thereby providing only part-time or casual employment opportunities.

Figure 4 shows a comparison of female/male full time employment by industry. It shows that the industries where women have a greater share of the full time work, are:

- health and community services,
- education, and
- personal and financial services.

These three industries have also shown a large increase in job numbers. However, it should also be noted from Figure 5, that more women work on a part time or casual basis than men, in every industry, except construction and wholesale. Relative to full-time work, part-time and casual work results in lower pay, cumulative benefits, responsibility, job security, and promotion opportunities. Thus, the majority of women are in a disadvantaged position in the workforce.

Various studies related to overtime work (Buchanan & Bearfield, 1997) justify McCarthy's statement that:

> The preferred method of distributing leisure in recent decades has been to increase the number of people who do no remunerative work at all, but in some cases, nevertheless receive financial support. Unemployment itself could be considered such a form of leisure' 'When leisure is put on an all or none basis, it raises questions of social equity compared to those cited earlier in regard to

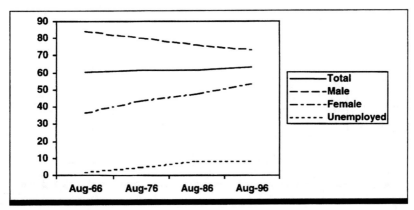

FIGURE 3

Labour Force Participation Rates

Adapted from Buchanan and Bearfield, 1997, Reforming Working Time.

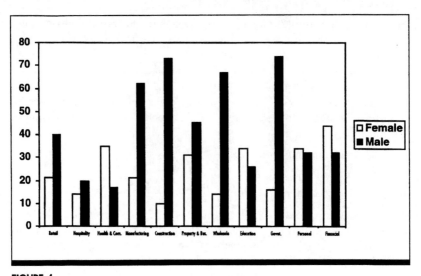

FIGURE 4

Comparison of Male/Female Full Time Employment by Industry on the Mid North Coast of NSW

Source: Armstrong and Drever, 1997, Mid North Coast Business Census Report.

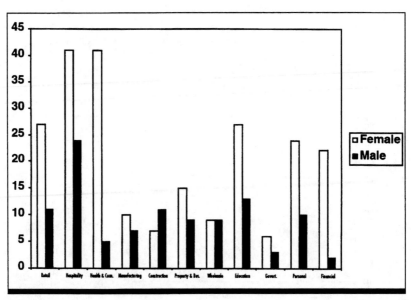

FIGURE 5

Comparison of Female/Male Part Time & Casual Employment by Industry on the Mid North Coast of NSW

Source: Armstrong and Drever, 1997, Mid North Coast Business Census Report.

the distribution of income... Like financial poverty, an inadequate provision of leisure time can become a source of misery and a type of social injustice (McCarthy & McgGaughey, 1989, p. 47–49).

The figures overall, have shown that those who are fortunate to have a full time job are also 'losing out' in that they are increasingly having to work more hours, usually without financial compensation.

Nevertheless, some argue that the trend towards part time and casual work is a form of job sharing. The authors of this paper argue that this presumption is incorrect as part-time and casual work does not lead to job security and other benefits. Most of these benefits, such as pension, sick leave, maternity leave, holiday pay and social recognition, are only paid or received in relation to either a minimum number of hours worked or earning a certain amount of income over a specific period. This is not normally a component of part-time and casual employment frameworks.

One of the major issues associated with part-time and casual employment is job security. This is especially relevant in the current industrial relations climate where many government bodies and employers are advocating (and sometimes sermonising) on the need for a flexible, just-in-time labour force.

The increasing use of part time and casual workers discussed previously, seems to reflect the ideas behind John Atkinson's model of the flexible firm (cited in Burgess, 1997). The idea behind this model being the emergence of a three tier labour. The three tiers are divided into a 'core group' of employees , and a periphery group of part-time and casual workers who are said to be 'numerically flexible'(Atkinson cited in Burgess1997, p. 87).

Burgess (1997) argues that Atkinson's model is 'descriptive..., perscriptive..., and not causal'. The debate about this model is diverse. However whether the model is 'a feature or signal of a new phase of capitalism;...a theory of new firm strategies;...a neo-classical perscriptive device;... or merely an explanation for workforce restructuring' the data validates the workplace structures espoused in the model. This has important implications for production efficiency, job security and consumer demand. Mares (1993) refers to the costs associated with having an insecurely employed work force in terms of output quality, employee loyalty, etc. In referring to the implementation of policy requiring jobs to be readvertised at certain periods, he concluded that:

> ...one would baulk at the idea of having one's position of husband or wife re-advertised every two or three years, with the incumbent just being allowed to re-apply for it in the open market. No doubt such an arrangement could somewhat enhance matrimonial flexibility. One must doubt, though that it necessarily would improve its productivity.(Mares, 1993)

Consequently, the conditions associated with part-time and casual jobs including remuneration, intensity, job satisfaction, security and cumulative benefits, must also be addressed. Another issue is to determine whether part-time and casual employment conditions improve economic demand for goods and services. It may well take a number of workforce generations to reform work and job expectations.

Connery (1937) stated:

> What does the country ultimately gain if we encourage business-men to enlarge the capacity of American industry to produce unless we see that the income of our working population actual-ly expands to create markets to absorb that increased production (Black Connery, 1937 Congressional Record, 75th Congress, 2nd Session, vol182, part 1, p6. cited in Rifkin, 1996, p. 29).

This implies that individuals must have sufficient income and income secu-rity before they will increase or change their consumption. In a survey con-ducted by the Business Council of Australiain 1992, half of the 146 large enterprises in Australia stated that 'they used subcontractors and part timers, although the use of part-timers and subcontracting was primarily linked to poor product conditions rather than a 'new' workforce strategy' (BCA, 1992, p. 18, cited in Burgess, 1997). Other research shows that prominent causes of this shift to part time/casual work include 'the bargaining regime', 'prod-uct market conditions', and the 'dramatic impact of the early 1990's reces-sion' (Green & Macdonald, 1991, Brosnan & Thornwaite, 1994, Campbell & Burgess, 1993). All of these authors suggest that lack of demand is having a strong impact on how management are structuring their workforce.

Job sharing spreads the existing income being returned to the labour force more evenly across the community. However, achieving this would require maintaining some form of guaranteed income level to counter the existing poverty traps created by the present social security system. Individuals must have an adequate , secure income level to maintain some sort of consistent spending power. Consequently, job sharing or extending the conditions of full time employment would achieve this aim in a way that the existing rise of insecure part time and casual employment does not. Unfortunately the trend is for new jobs to be created at the lowest end of the income stratum. In the USA '... since 1979 ... nearly 97% of net employment gains among white men have been in the low wage stratum. In 1984 there were 8 million new employees, but 58% earned no more than $7,012' (McCarthy & McGaughey, 1989, p. 30).

The benefits that can be obtained through implementation of effective job sharing include greater disposable income per hour worked due to the tax advantages, increased self esteem, greater output, shared parenting, increased labour force participation, more job satisfaction, less sick days, etc. Figure 6 shows the comparative tax advantages of job sharing in terms of dis-posable income versus single income families. The increase in disposable income occurs because the taxable gross income for each partner is halved rather than one partner bearing the brunt of the taxation burden in the household.

The greatest difference between shared and single disposable income occurs at a gross income of $70, 000. The shared disposable income at this salary level is 10.94% higher than if the equivalent salary was earned by one person. The disposable income for a single worker earning $70,000 is $45,448 compared against a disposable income by sharing the position of $53,106, a net difference of $7,658. Consequently, each individual receives $26,500. Allowing workers to job share on the lowest illustrated gross salary of $30,000 results in an additional $2,382 disposable income per annum per family (each individual receives $12,855).

From a regional perspective the adoption of such a strategy for 1,000 positions at the lowest illustrated salary level of $30,000 per annum, means that there would be an additional $1,191,000 (500 x $2,382) income injection. Given the tendency for low income earners to spend their disposable income, the bulk of this could be expected to be injected to the local economy.

However, such a strategy must be seen as redistributing working time and income, not merely an easy way to gain additional income to the region. Placing the desire to share the work first is most important in a region that has a large proportion of its population recieving and/or dependent on some form of government benefit(s).

Federal government support for job sharing is essential to ensure the existing tax incentives remain. The monetary gain to those who do job share dictates a loss to Federal government tax revenue. The Commonwealth government could choose merely to increase tax levels at the lower end of the income earning scale, and thus remove the financial incentives for individuals to job share. A conducive response to job sharing, is to investigate

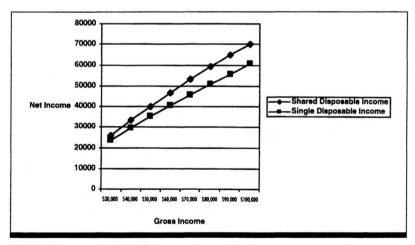

FIGURE 6

Shared and Single Income Comparisons

whether sharing the work is a more efficient form of income distribution as opposed to the current transfer payments system.

In addition, job sharing offers many benefits to employers such as:

- greater work satisfaction amongst employees,
- less sick leave,
- less stress,
- more jobs to cope with extra consumption,
- better quality work, and
- higher volume of output.

Another social and economic implication likely from such a strategy is that females will be more likely to consume and buy items for themselves if earning their 'own income' or an income separate from their partner. Research by Edith Edwards on the distribution of income within households revealed that only 20% of women said that they did not feel uncomfortable in asking their spouse for money (cited in Broom, 1984). Changing the structure of work allows more women to more fully participate in the workforce, move into higher positions, and has the added affect of increasing women's independence and self esteem. Broom's research also suggests that this change in work structure would create different consumption patterns.

Nevertheless, there are great challenges associated with re-organising and reforming work structures and worker expectations commensurate with the community-wide benefits of job sharing. Stocker and Hegeman (1996) allude to these ideas and relate them to the present dominance of economic rationalism over social participativeness. This infers that the value of work in itself has risen above family, leisure, community and other pursuits.

The implicit acceptance of the goal of work can be seen in the current community, and political and policy cries to re-establish full employment, subject of course to the current dominance of the non accelerating inflation rate of unemployment(NAIRU). This approach to work and unemployment mirrors what Huxley (1994) claimed would be a 'really efficient totalitarian state ... in that the political bosses and their army of managers control a population of slaves who do not have to be coerced, because they love their servitude'.

This demand for full time work can also be related to the need for a livable income level. However, as the government has been elected to pursue a policy which places the level of employment and wages second to that of inflation, some people's right to work and their right of passage to social participation, has been taken away. This raises the question of what the real problem is: the lack of work or the lack of an entitlement to an income and social recognition? This implies that the 'underlying cultural value of paid work involves elements neither revealed in public opinion polls nor addressed by post industrialists' (Pixley, 1993, p. 248). This is an issue which needs to be explored, not just by policy makers and business, but the community as a whole.

All of this raises the question as to whether there is a will to job share, not just amongst policy makers and politicians, but the community as a whole. A recent survey by Morgans and Banks which questioned 3,200 employers nationally found that:

> 69.4% of employers supported job sharing, 41.1% gave unconditional support, and 28.3% 'would approve if the government were to introduce a clearly defined national policy' (Tanner 1997, p. 35).

Therefore, some employers believe in job sharing but would be even more encouraged towards implementation if the government issued supporting policies and developed supporting structures. However it must be noted that some employers see this as a 'way of cutting down their permanent payroll' (Tanner, 1997, p. 35). Obviously, if the goal of such a policy is to include those previously excluded, and stimulate the economy through a more equal distribution of income and leisure, it must be designed so that it is not just used as a cost cutting measure by employers.

Conclusion

Government participation is essential if job sharing strategies are to achieve a redistribution of existing work. Policy initiatives must include equalising full time, part time, and casual employee conditions and entitlements. This means employers would not be biased in hiring one category of worker over the other, as employee entitlements would be equal regardless of employment category. Research by Bertola (1992) shows that lowering hiring costs while increasing firing costs, leads to employers employing more employees for less hours. However, these types of policy initiatives must be backed up with some type of guaranteed minimum income level, to allow for the varying weekly hours and income that such work involves. This type of policy also implicitly recognises that part time and casual work constitutes a legitimate guarantee to full citizenship and social acceptance (See Pixley and related debates, 1993).

In addition, Unions also have a role in allowing the community to redefine work. The goal of sharing the work must include unions demanding adequate wages so that workers are not forced to work overtime just to make ends meet.. However, unions also need to extend their membership to those who do socially useful work outside the paid labour force. To some extent this has been done in both Sweden and Denmark with the result that unions are no longer labelled as representatives of workers' trying to protect their jobs to the exclusion of non workers (Bertola, 1992). Such a union system would have obvious benefits in making demands for wages and conditions, as their claims would be in the interests of both groups, and thus circumvent the present rationalists' claims that unions keep the unemployed as outsiders. This could also lift the present falling union memberships. Moreover, the unions, through surveys and appealing to both groups may be able to achieve a more democratic redefinition of work than any government effort ever could (Pixley, 1993).

Furthermore, job sharing allows a more equitable distribution of both income and leisure. However, there are limits to its ability to help put social pursuits and leisure on an equal footing with work. These limits are related to the ever decreasing amount of full time jobs to share, and the payment of excessive work presently being done without any reward. Nevertheless, the greatest barrier or challenge to redistributing working time is the current attachment the community, politicians, and unionists have to the present definition of full time work, its mandatory requirement for social inclusion, and their perception of what full employment will solve.

The final point is that, Keynes (1936, p. 37) stated 'the power of vested interests is vastly exaggerated compared with the gradual encroachment of ideas ... sooner or later, it is ideas, not vested interests, which are dangerous for good, evil, tyranny, or democracy'. *Whether one believes that the power of vested interests is vastly exaggerated or not, it is through these ideas that they wield their power.*

References

Armstrong, D.B., & Drever, M.A. (1997). *Mid North Coast Business Census Report*, Southern Cross University & Mid North Coast Regional Development Board.

Bertola, G. (1992). 'Job Security, Employment and Wages' *The Dynamic Labour Demand and Adjustment Costs*, Edward Elgar Publishing, UK.

Broom, D. (1984). *Unfinished Business*, Allen and Unwin, Australia.

Buchanan, J., & Bearfield, S. (1997). *Reforming Working Time*, Brotherhood of Saint Lawrence, Melbourne.

Burgess, J. (1997). 'The Flexible Firm and the Growth of Non-Standard Employment'; *Labour and Industry*, 7(3) 287–313.

Crothers, F. (1997). 'Less Pay, More work', Sydney Morning Herald, 24/4/97

Huxley, A. (1994 edition). *Brave New World*, Harper Collins Publishers.

Mares, S.C. (1993). *Economic Papers*, 12(2) 6/93.

McCarthy, E., & McGaughey, W. (1989). *Non Financial Economics*, Praeger Publishers.

National Institute of Labour Studies (1994). *Working Paper Series no 129*, Flinders University, South Australia.

Pixley, J. (1993). *Citizenship and Employment*, University of Cambridge Press.

Rifkin, J (1996). *The End of Work*, Putnam and Son's.

Stocker, M., & Hegeman, E. (1996). *Valuing Emotions*, University of Cambridge Press.

Tanner, D. (1997). 'Labor Wins Support for Work Share Call', Morgans and Bank Survey, *The Australian*, 17–18/5.

Immigrant Unemployment and Ethnic Small Business in Australia

Jock Collins

NESB immigrants continue to bear the greatest burden of economic recession and economic restructuring in Australia in the 1990s. Some groups of NESB immigrants, like the Vietnamese and Lebanese, continue to have rates of unemployment four to five times the national average. There is the danger of the emergence of an underclass of economically disadvantaged and socially isolated immigrants. Given continued downsizing by the corporate and public sector, the best hope of jobs for these NESB immigrants is the ethnic small business sector. In the Australian immigration debate, the economic contribution of immigrant small businesses — and the potential they have in creating jobs and wealth in coming years — seems to have been underestimated. This paper draws on original research generated by surveys of more than 1,600 ethnic small businesses in Australia. It explores in detail the relationship between ethnic small businesses and employment growth and argues that innovative strategies designed to increase both the rate of ethnic small business formation and the success of existing ethnic small businesses will strengthen the Australian economy in general and employment creation in particular. It also shows that Asian immigrants in small business in Australia predict the greatest employment growth potential and the most significant trading growth of all Australian small businesses

Although the Australian economy has experienced more than six years of relatively high economic growth since the 1990–91 recession, unemployment has remained above 8 per cent. The contractionary fiscal policy of the first two Howard/Costello budgets and structural factors related to globalisation are leading to increasing retrenchment in the public sector and the corporate sectors of the Australian economy. This paper focuses on immigrant unemployment in Australia in the 1990s. Average unemployment rates for all first-generation immigrants are about 2 per cent higher than the national average. But these averages mask very different unemployment experiences among immigrant men and women. Some NESB immigrant birthplace groups have very high unemployment rates. For example, the Vietnamese-born and Lebanese-born have demonstrated unemployment rates that have been more than three times higher than the average for more than a decade. Issues related to the emergence of a social underclass emerge when some groups are consistently far worse off in terms of unemployment. How can these entrenched pockets of immigrant unemployment be redressed? A related issue is the problem of an overall reduction to immigrant unemployment rates.

Immigrant unemployment is a complex phenomenon. It is shaped by factors such as language and literacy; recognition of overseas qualifications; perceptions of immigrants' ability to communicate; direct and indirect racial discrimination; globalisation and the restructuring of Australian industry; business cycle fluctuations and macroeconomic and microeconomic policy response; and regional dimensions within cities and regions. This paper explores but one aspect of immigrant unemployment, namely, the relationship between ethnic small business in Australia and employment creation for ethnic minorities. Small business employs nearly one half of all the private sector workers in Australia, with more than half of all small businesses owned and operated by first or second-generation immigrants (Collins et al., 1996). Small business has always been an alternative to unemployment or inferior employment for NESB immigrants in Australia (Collins et al., 1995: 39–50). In addition, many ethnic entrepreneurs employ family or members of their ethnic communities (*co-ethnics*). NESB immigrants are locked out of new jobs in the corporate or public sector, both of which continue to downsize. It is therefore the small business sector in general, and the ethnic small business sector in particular, that hold out the greatest hope for jobs for a large part of Australia's NESB ethnic minorities in the late 1990s.

This paper explores the existing relationship between ethnic unemployment and ethnic small business in Australia before exploring possible policy initiatives in the area. Section two looks at the labour market realities for NESB immigrants in Australia in the 1990s to sketch the contemporary dimensions of immigrant unemployment in Australia to day. Section three looks at dimensions of the over-representation of many ethnic groups in small business related activities in Australia. Section four presents the results from three surveys of ethnic entrepreneurs in Australia that are relevant to the consideration of the link between NESB unemployment and NESB small businesses. Section five looks at the possibilities of establishing a small business as an alternative strategy for unemployed immigrants, while section six identifies the major conclusions of the paper.

Labour Market Realities for Australia's NESB Immigrants in the 1990s

Access to employment is perhaps the most critical factor in determining socio-economic outcomes of Australia's immigrants from non-English speaking backgrounds. The fortunes of wage-earning immigrants have been largely constrained by the patterns of labour market segmentation that have accompanied post-war immigration (Collins, 1991: 78–92). For the period up until the late 1980s, immigrants from non-English speaking backgrounds were concentrated in the unskilled and semi-skilled manual jobs in the male and female labour markets, sometimes called the secondary labour market (Piore, 1980). Low wages, poor conditions, unstable employment and vulnerability to retrenchment are features of this segment of the Australian labour market. One consequence of this is that unemployment during the three post-war recessions — 1974–5, 1982–3 and 1990–91 — has been much higher for immigrants from non-English speaking backgrounds than for immigrants from English-speaking backgrounds or the Australian-born (Collins 1991: 114–9; Ackland and Williams 1992).

As the Australian and international economies restructure, the Australian labour market is transforming. This has differential impacts on NESB immigrants. For some, particularly recently arrived Vietnamese, Lebanese and Turkish immigrants, unemployment rates are four to five times higher than average. Hence in May 1983, when the unemployment rate for the Australian-born was 10.2%, the rate of unemployment among Lebanese-born was 33.6% and Vietnamese-born 30.5%. Much of the burden of Australian unemployment falls on younger people. A decade later, little has changed. The May 1993 unemployment rates for Vietnamese aged 15–34 years were 52% and Lebanese 43% (Moss 1993: 258).

At the same time, recent immigration flows demonstrate an increasing reliance on immigrants from Asia, mirroring the trends in the other major immigration countries of Canada, New Zealand and the United States (Abella and Lim 1993: 31; Low 1993). In 1990–91, for example, eight out of the top ten source countries of Australia's migrants were Asian (Inglis 1992: 25), and Asians have been the fastest growing overseas-born population group in Australia in the past decade (Khoo et al., 1993:1). Many of these recent Asian-born immigrants possess professional educational and/or managerial expertise, often moving into primary labour market jobs. Hence patterns of labour market segmentation in Australia are changing because of economic restructuring and changing immigration patterns that are themselves products of the international processes of globalisation (Collins, 1996).

Unemployment

Just as NESB immigrants appeared to bear the greatest burden of the 1974–5 and 1982–3 recessions in terms of disproportionately high unemployment rates (Collins 1991: 115–119), recent studies have confirmed that this is also the case in the 1990s recession. Ackland and Williams (1992:28) conclude that "[i]n the last three recessions, immigrants from NESBs have fared worse in the labour market than either those from ESBs or those born in Australia". Jones and McAllister (1991) reviewed the unemployment experience of immigrants up to 1989 to find that Lebanese and Vietnamese unemployment rates were about four times greater than that of the Australian-born. They also found that immigrants of non-English speaking background who were recently-arrived suffered an unemployment rate two to three times higher than immigrants of English-speaking background who arrived during the same period.

Recent unemployment data for November 1996 allows a picture of immigrant unemployment five years after the economic recession that began the decade. It shows very high rates of unemployment among male and female immigrants born in

While these official unemployment rates indicate unambiguously that non-English speaking background immigrants experience unequal labour market outcomes, they actually underestimate the severity of the extent of

TABLE 1

Unemployment rates by birthplace and gender, November 1996*

Birthplace	Male Nos.'000	Male %	Female Nos.'000	Female %
Middle East & N. Africa	7.2	19.7	3.7	23.8
Lebanon	2.8	31.7	2.9	50.0
Africa	1.2	4.8	3.1	15.0
South Africa	0	0	1.6	11.8
North America	1.7	9.5	0.3	2.0
USA	1.1	10.2	0	0
Sth, Central America	1.9	12.7	1.5	10.0
Chile	0.9	12.8	1.5	18.0
Northeast Asia	3.3	7.3	3.7	13.5
China	2.7	11.1	3.4	25.0
Southeast Asia	9.6	10.6	9.8	11.3
Philippines	1.3	5.0	0.8	2.4
Vietnam	5.9	18.0	4.7	21.5
Southern Asia	6.6	17.5	3.6	14.9
India	0.6	4.4	0.6	5.2
Europe (include USSR)	15.0	6.9	13.4	9.1
Former Yugoslavia	2.0	9.6	3.2	19.1
Germany	0.5	5.9	0.6	16.1
Greece	0	0	1.6	47.9
Italy	0.2	11.1	0	0
Netherlands	2.8	57.6	0	0
Poland	0.3	3.3	0.3	3.7
UK & Ireland	7.4	5.7	6.3	7.3
New Zealand	4.9	6.4	1.6	3.8
Total	52.6	9.1	42.9	10.5

Source: Australian Bureau of Statistics, *Labour Force Status and Other Characteristics of Migrants*, November 1996 (Catalogue No. 6250.0), p. 14.
* Migrants who arrived after 1970 and were aged 18 years and over on arrival
NB: unemployment rates of those who arrived before 1970 not included so that southern and eastern European unemployment rates underestimated.
Lebanon, Vietnam, Chile and South Asian. It also shows disproportionately high unemployment rates among women born in Africa and the former Yugoslavia.

unemployment. Official unemployment rates do not include the "hidden unemployed", that is, those without jobs but who are not counted in official statistics. Wooden (1993: 41) concluded in a more recent report, "if discouraged job seekers were included as part of the unemployed...1.8 percentage points would be added to the official unemployment rate for the Australian-born, while the rate for immigrants would be increased by 2.9 percentage points". If the immigrant rate is disaggregated, the real unemployment rate for immigrant men and women from a non-English speaking background would be even higher than 2.9 percentage points above the official rates.

Australian Immigration, Ethnic Diversity and Small Business

Australia has the greatest proportion of immigrants of all contemporary western societies. In 1995, 22.7 per cent of Australia's population were first generation immigrants (that is, were born overseas). This exceeds the immigrant presence in Switzerland and Canada and greatly exceeds the immigrant presence in Germany, USA, France and the United Kingdom. (see Table 2).

Post-war immigration has also increased the ethnic diversity of the Australian people. The immigration net has been cast across Europe, North and Latin America, Asia, Eastern Europe and Africa, with some 150 nationalities joining in the great immigrant pilgrimage to Australia (Collins, 1991: 19–38). Many of these immigrants have moved into small business in Australia (Collins et al., 1995). The census data shows that in 1991, 88,363 first generation immigrant men – and 38,662 first generation immigrant women — were employers, comprising 25.3% of male and female employers in Australia. Most of these would be in small business, since 97% of enterprises are small. In addition, 141,257 first generation immigrant males and 65,673 immigrant females were self employed in 1991. They comprise

TABLE 2

First generation immigrant presence in major countries today

Country	%
Australia	22.7
Canada	15.6
USA	7.9
Switzerland	18.1
United Kingdom	3.5
France	6.3
Germany	8.5

Source: System of Observation of Permanent Migration (SOPEMI) 1995:27

27.8% of self-employed males in Australia and 26.5% of self-employed females. In 1995, an estimated 239,700 (29%) first generation immigrant males were business operators. (ABS, 1996:12).

Clearly the ethnic diversity of Australian society is matched with an ethnic diversity of Australian small business. Many ethnic groups are, in relative terms, more likely to be in small business than the Australian-born. At the 1991 census, 14.2 per cent of the Australian-born were in small business, if we define the latter as the sum of those who are employers and self-employed. While this slightly over exaggerates the number of small business owners, a few of the employers will be in big business, while a few self employed will be 'relabelled' workers, it is a useful proxy. According to this definition, in 1991 14.2% of the Australian-born male were in small business.

In comparison, as Table 3 shows, nearly one in three Korean males were in small business, as were around quarter of Greek, Cypriot, Dutch and Italian males and one fifth of Lebanese males. These same ethnic groups are over-represented among female small businesses. 11.6 % of Australian-born women were in small business, less than half the rate of small business formation for women born in Korea, Greece, Cyprus, Netherlands and Italy. Women from other birthplace groups, such as Lebanon and Israel also have a significantly higher rate of small business formation than the Australian-born.

If we break down the national aggregates, the significance of immigrants to Australia's small business sector becomes more evident. Hence in 1991 as Table 4 shows, over one in three businesses were owned by first generation immigrants in WA (38.6%) Northern Territory (35.7%), ACT (33.75), while they comprised more than one quarter of all small businesses in

TABLE 3

Proportion of workforce who are entrepreneurs by gender and birthplace 1991

Birthplace	Male %	Female %
Korea	30.5	27.7
Italy	25.3	21.7
Greece	25.0	22.1
Cyprus	24.2	21.3
Netherlands	23.2	20.2
Hungary	23.3	19.5
Lebanon	20.2	18.5
Israel	16.9	16.9
Average of above	23.6	20.1
Australia	14.2	11.6

Source: 1991 census

Victoria (28.9%), NSW (27.7%) and South Australia (27.5%). In some states, if we add in the small businesses owned by second generation immigrants, ethnic business would comprise the majority of small businesses in WA, NT and ACT and around half of those in VIC, NSW and SA.

The significance of ethnic small business can be seen when we disaggregate the data to look at fish and chip shops and fruit and vegetable shops in Australia. Here we can see that first generation Italian immigrants, who comprise around 2% of the total population, make up one in three of the fruit and vegetable shops in Australia. Similarly, Greek immigrants own one in three fish and chip shops, but are one in fifty of the Australian population. Ethnic entrepreneurs dominate some sectors of small businesses, but are a minority in others (Collins et al, 1995).

There are, however, some birthplace groups of migrants who have a similar or lower presence as employers or self employed than the Australian-born. NESB birthplace groups in the Australian labour market with a lower proportion of self-employed and employers include Japan, India, Sri Lanka, Vietnam, Indonesia and Turkey. Other birthplace groups have a similar proportion of employers and/or self-employed compared to the Australian-born: China, Singapore, Malaysia, Egypt, Lebanon, Poland, Ukraine and Yugoslavia. ESB migrant groups, such as those born in the United Kingdom, New Zealand, Canada and the USA have a very similar spread to the Australian-born. This pattern varies only slightly between males and females in the Australian labour market.

Clearly ethnic small businesses are of considerable importance, comprising around one half of the small businesses in many states. They are clearly an important part of the story of small business growth in the past decade. Over the period 1983–4 and 1994–5, the number of small businesses in Australia increased by 43%, at a rate of 3.35% per annum. Over the same period, small business employment increased by just under one third (31.8%), or 2.5% per annum. Today the Australian small business sector provides just under half of all private sector employment in Australia. Small business is therefore an important dynamic for economic growth in the Australian economy in general, and to employment growth in particular. The Australian small business sector is a vital cog of the current economy,

TABLE 4

Ethnic small business as a percentage of all small business, by state, 1991

State	%	State	%
New South Wales	27.7	Western Australia	38.6
Victoria	28.9	Tasmania	17.9
Queensland	21.2	Northern Territory	35.7
South Australia	27.5	ACT	33.7

Source: ABS, Characteristics of Small Business, Australia, 1995, p.13

and will also play a role in the internationalisation of the Australian economy through trade, investment and cultural links.

Ethnic Small Business and NESB Immigrant Unemployment

This section reports on the findings of two major studies on Australian ethinc enterprises. The first is a study of 280 ethnic small businesses in Sydney conducted in two stages (1988 and 1991) called the *Sydney Survey* (Collins et al., 1995). The second is a 1996 survey of over 300 small business owners in Sydney, Melbourne and Perth, 85 per cent of whom were from a NESB, called the *National Survey* (Collins et al., 1996). The third is a survey of over 1000 small business men and women who were enrolled in TAFE courses in 1996, called the *TAFE Survey* (Collins et al., 1996). These surveys enable us to better understand how ethnicity and gender influence dynamics in Australian small business. They provide information on employment size, ethnicity of employees, recruitment strategies, training activities, and international trading activities of ethnic enterprises. This research highlights the employment growth potential of the ethnic small business sector and has important implications for strategies relating to reducing NESB unemployment rates.

One emerging feature from the *Sydney Survey* was the importance of "family" in small business activities and relates to the employment of family members in the business. Family members were a significant proportion of the employees in Sydney small businesses regardless of the ethnicity of the business owners. Hence just over one third of the businesses run by NESB immigrant men — and one half of the businesses run by NESB women — reported that between 75%–100% of their staff were family members. Family is most important as a source of labour in businesses run by South American women — over 80% of which rely on family members to fill between 75% and 100% of all jobs — and South American men, where half of all businesses surveyed relied on the family to provide over three quarters of all workers. It is also very important in businesses owned by Asian women: in 60% of such businesses, more than three-quarters of employees were family.

Overall, over one half of the labour employed in businesses owned by NESB women were family members. This is more than double the non-immigrant rate. Similarly, over one third (35.4%) of staff in businesses owned by NESB men were family members. That is, businesses run by NESB males rely on family labour by at least 50% more than non-immigrant males. In this way, the *Sydney Survey* supports the findings from the study of ethnic businesses in other countries (Waldinger et al, 1990).

However non-immigrant businesses were also very reliant on family labour: in one third of the businesses run by non-immigrant women — and in between one-fifth and one quarter of the businesses run by non-immigrant men — more than three-quarters of the employees were also family members. The importance of family labour does not appear to be solely part of a distinctive "ethnic" strategy for small business in Australia. Rather, family labour is very important in all Australian small businesses.

Clearly, one of the characteristics of ethnic small business in Australian is the high rate of employment of co-ethnics. This finding has important implications for employment creation strategies for NESB immigrant minorities. Specifically, the greater the number and success of ethnic small business in Australia, the greater will be the number of jobs created and the greater the chance of reducing the very high rates of unemployment among some ethnic groups.

One important aspect of the relationship between employment creation and ethnic small business relates to the dynamics of employment recruitment. Current recruitment networks indicate the profile of those who are most likely to be able to gain employment from small business sector growth. Those small businesses that were surveyed in the 1996 *National Survey* were asked: "How do you recruit your employees?" The responses — presented in Table 5 — show that family, community and business networks are by far the most important sources of employment recruitment of ethnic small business. Nearly half of the small business owners born in the Middle East recruit from their family as do about one in three of Asian and Latin American entrepreneurs. European-born female entrepreneurs are the least likely to use family networks to create workers. Family and community networks account for half of the employment recruitment among Middle East, Asian and Latin American-born entrepreneurs. The implication from this is that on average one in every two small businesses is likely to directly recruit co-ethnics via family and community networks. Moreover, given the community nature of ethnic business networks, most of those recruited from this source will also be co-ethnics, while newspapers referred to will often be ethnic newspapers. In other words, existing sources of recruitment of employment by ethnic small business suggest strongly that ethnic businesses do and will employ co-ethnics if their employment base is expanded.

TABLE 5

NESB small businesses sources of employment recruitment, (%) by birthplace and gender, (1996 National Survey).

| | Europe | | Asia | | L.A.* | | M.E.** | |
	m	f	m	f	m	f	m	f
family	22.4	12.5	28.2	29.7	30.0		47.1	42.9
community networks	18.4	20.8	26.9	32.4	20.0		17.6	28.6
business networks	20.4	20.8	9.0	13.5	30.0		17.6	0
newspapers	22.4	29.2	16.7	10.8	10.0		11.8	14.3
CES	14.3	12.5	12.8	5.4	0	20.0	5.9	14.3

*Latin America; ** Middle East

The employment profile of first and second-generation immigrant entrepreneurs in the 1996 TAFE *Survey* is shown below in Table 6. The results
confirm other observations that most ethnic small businesses employ fewer
than five workers. Two in three NESB female small business operators and
three in four NESB male small business operators employed fewer than five
workers, including the self-employed who comprised more than one quarter
of the NESB male sample and less than one fifth of the NESB female sample.

As Table 7 shows, there were strong indications of employment growth
by ethnic entrepreneurs in the Australian small business sector in 1996. The
survey revealed that employment growth was predicted to be strongest in
the small businesses ran by third or later generation Australian-born respondents, although the numbers of these businesses contained in the sample, as
a "control" was small. Two in three Australian-born male small business
respondents — and nearly one in two Australian-born male respondents —
predicted an increase in employment in their firms in the coming year. But
NESB ethnic small businesses also predicted employment. One in five
NESB female and one in three NESB male respondents said that they would
increase employment in the next year. Very few entrepreneurs surveyed predicted that their employment would fall in the coming year, with most predicting the same or increased employment size. It is also important to note
that the growth in employment was predicted to be greater in those businesses ran by males in each category surveyed.

TABLE 6

Current employment size of Australian ethnic small business, 1996 TAFE survey
(% of small businesses surveyed)

	Self only male	1 to five male	6 to 10 male	11 plus male	Self only female	1 to five female	6 to 10 female	11 plus female
NESB G1	25.0	41.5	4.9	3.5	16.4	45.9	9.6	2.8
NESB G2	31.1	40.0	8.9	7.7	17.0	53.2	6.4	4.3
ESB*	38.7	37.2	3.6	5.1	17.6	33.0	9.9	6.6

G1 = first generation; G2 = second generation; ESB = English-speaking-background

TABLE 7

Predictions for small business employment growth in coming year (%) by ethnicity and gender, (1996 National Survey)

	NESB males	NESB females	AUST males	AUST females	ESB males	ESB females
Increase	32.7	21.2	71.4	44.4	20.0	0
Decrease	2.8	0	0	0	0	0
Remain same	41.1	23.1	14.3	55.6	66.7	66.7

It is possible to break down the NESB data to look at the responses to the question of whether employment in their small business will increase in the coming year by continental grouping. As Table 8 shows, Asian immigrant small business operators predicted the greatest rate of employment creation, with on average one in three predicting that they would take on more employees in the next 12 months. About one in four small business operators born in Europe and Latin America also predicted that they would take on more workers in the next year.

The survey of 774 small business people engaged in vocational education and training revealed an expectation of even greater employment growth than the 1996 survey of ethnic small business. Just over a half of all first and second-generation immigrants in the TAFE Survey expected to take on more workers in the following year. The greatest expectation of employment growth was among the second generation of NESB businesses. Moreover, it appeared that male-owned businesses were generally more likely to report that they will increase employment in the next year than were female-owned businesses. It is interesting to note that those ethnic small business operators who were currently engaged in vocational education and training were generally twice as likely to report that they would hire workers in the next 12 months. Here is evidence of the economic benefits of vocational education and training.

One important issue that relates to small business and employment creation is whether entrepreneurs set up the business themselves or merely take over an existing one. The former process is clearly more innovative with potential for net employment creation. The latter is merely a change in ownership of existing arrangement which could lead to employment growth if the business expands. Two in three male NESB entrepreneurs in the TAFE Survey had set up the business, as had one in two female NESB entrepreneurs. This shows the potential for new small business formation is very strong, across all industries, but particularly in construction, health community and personal services and property, business services and finance.

Ethnic Small Business and the Unemployed

A piece of research relevant to the discussion about the relationship between NESB unemployment and small business comes from a project designed to investigate the potential of small business as an alternative to

TABLE 8

Proportion of NESB small businesses that predict that their employment will increase in coming year (%) by ethnicity and gender (1996 National Survey)

	European	Asian	Latin American	Middle East
males	37.5	39.6	14.3	6.7
females	17.6	28.0	33.3	6.7

unemployment for NESB immigrant women. The key question of the research was: "Is it possible to get unemployed NESB immigrant women together to combine their — often unrecognised — skills to form small businesses as a pilot study of what may be possible on a larger, national, scale? If the answer to this question was affirmative, a number of other important questions emerged: What areas would the small businesses be in? How should the organisation of the small business be arranged? And what about financial and legal matters? What assistance would these NESB immigrant women need in establishing their small business? Could these women also tap into TAFE courses on different aspects of small business? What about marketing? What about using ethnic connections to promote the pilot study and publicise the pilot small businesses established? How could funding to support his pilot program be arranged? Could low-cost start-up loans be arranged? Is a co-operative the best legal/social/economic form of organisation for the small business?

The research found (Collins, mimeo, 1993) that one feasible alternative strategy for unemployed NESB immigrant women was to assist them to set up co-operative small businesses. Co-operatives allow unemployed NESB immigrants to come together in a critical mass to form a business enterprise which would be not possible through the traditional private ownership model because of the lack of start-up capital and access to finance and training that they face as unemployed. A public meeting of unemployed NESB women, held in 1992, revealed their enthusiasm for the chance to attempt to take the small business option to their unemployment situation. Women from across ethnic backgrounds expressed willingness to form small business collectives across four areas: cleaning, clothing, cooking and childcare. The main conclusion was that the small business sector offered an excellent chance for NESB women to escape unemployment.

The main recommendation from this research project was for a pilot program based on setting up four pilot small business co-operatives in the areas of clothing, childcare, cleaning and cooking. The small businesses would be registered as co-operatives to ensure legal and other matters are properly arranged. A low interest loan was found to be the preferred way to raise capital for the business. For such a pilot program to get off the ground, funding for one full-time community worker would be required to assist in the administration and organisation of this pilot program. Duties would be to liaise with funding and loaning bodies, provide advice about registering as a co-operative, arrange TAFE or other training programs, provide advice on other matters of business.

Unfortunately, government departments approached about this study did not agree to provide the funds required to establish this pilot program. Nevertheless, the research indicates that there is a demand for such innovative programs and that the co-operative model may have much more relevance given the very high rates of unemployment that prevent the traditional path to private small business ownership to be pursued.

Policy initiatives to encourage small business growth and success require further investigation. The Carr Government in New South Wales is at present developing a strategy for supporting ethnic small business, and is exploring the ways in which through co-operatives or other arrangements whereby ethnic small business growth might be linked to strategies to reduce high unemployment rates in particularly disadvantaged NESB communities.

Conclusions

This paper has reported on the importance of the Australian small business sector for employment growth in the late 1990s. Australia's ethnic communities have a strong small business tradition. Many ethnic groups are — in relative terms — over-represented among the small business sector, while others have a significant, though lower, small business presence. At the same time, many of the newer NESB immigrant communities face rates of unemployment much higher than the national average.

The research has shown how reliant ethnic small businesses are on employees from their family or community: there is a strong trend to employ co-ethnics in their small businesses. The corollary of this is that one strategy to reduce Vietnamese and Lebanese unemployment in particular — and NESB and other unemployment in general — is to focus on increasing the rate of small business formation of NESB immigrants from Vietnam of Lebanon and/or to introduce strategies to enable existing ethnic small businesses in Australia to grow and expand their employment base. This research indicates that about one in three NESB small businesses intend to increase their employment in the coming 12 months. This is hard evidence of the wealth and employment generation of contemporary ethnic small business in Australia.

At the same time, the very forces that have generated apparently permanent higher unemployment rates in Australia in the 1990s also generate barriers to new ethnic small business formation. Long periods of unemployment increase the desire for — but substantially reduce the opportunity of — NESB immigrants to establish new businesses. There is much more work to be done to encourage unemployed NESB men and women to make the transition from unemployed to entrepreneur. This paper suggests that co-operative small businesses might be ideal in enabling people — otherwise incapable of establishing a small business in their own right because of their unemployment — to establish a new small business enterprise.

At the same time, programs and policies to help ethnic small business formation among the employed and to help existing ethnic small businesses to expand will have the pay off — if successful — of increasing employment opportunities particularly for those in the same ethnic group as the small business owner. Hence one strategy to reduce Vietnamese and Lebanese unemployment to fall substantially would be to establish a package of policies ranging from:

- Improving unemployed NESB immigrant access to — and success in — New Enterprise Incentive Schemes;
- Establishing help for unemployed NESB immigrants to form small business co-operatives;
- Developing policies to encourage a greater number of employed NESB men and women to establish their own business, including improving matters relating to access to bank finance and access to relevant education and training ;
- Developing policies to enhance the performance of ethnic small business, including those who are engaged in export/import activities.
- Developing ethnic-specific strategies for small business creation and expansion, with a high priority targeted at those with the highest and most intransigent unemployment rates.

For whatever reason, immigrants of all types and backgrounds have been attracted to small business ever since immigration has been a feature of Australian life. This chapter in the story of Australian immigration has often been overlooked in the eagerness of many to link immigration with economic costs rather than benefits. Despite these voices, it is important to establish the rightful place of ethnic enterprises in the Australian immigration history, to acknowledge the economic contribution that they have made to date and to utilise ethnic small businesses more effectively in the fight against the development of an immigrant underclass in Australia.

Clearly ethnic small businesses in Australia make a very significant economic contribution. Jobs, wealth and exports are the products of this contribution, with ethnic small business men and women leading the charge in the renaissance of the Australian small business sector over the last two decades. This point is often overlooked in the debate about Australian immigration in much the same way as the Australian small business sector is often overlooked in debates about the Australian economy.

References

Abella, M. and L.L. Lim, (1993), "The Movement of People in Asia: Internal, Intra-regional and International Migration", paper to the *Conference on Asia-Pacific Migration Affecting Australia*, Darwin, 14–17 September.

Ackland, R. and Williams, L. (1992) *Immigrants and the Australian Labour Market: The Experience of Three Recessions*, Bureau of Immigration Research, Canberra, AGPS.

Australian Bureau of Statistics (1996). *Small Business in Australia*, AGPS, Canberra.

Collins, Jock (1991) *Migrant Hands in a Distant Land: Australia's Postwar Immigration*, Pluto Press, Sydney and London, second edition,

Collins, Jock (1993) "NESB immigrant women and small business co-operatives", unpublished mimeo.

Collins, Jock (1996a) "The Changing Political Economy of Australian Racism" in

Stephen Castles and Ellie Vasta (eds.) *The Teeth are Smiling: the persistence of racism in multicultural Australia*, Sydney: Allen & Unwin, pp. 73–96.

Collins, J., Morrissey, M. and Grogan, L. (1995) "Employment" *1995 State of the Nation: A Report on People of non-English Speaking Background*, Federal Race Discrimination Commissioner, Canberra: AGPS.

Collins, Jock, Gibson, K., Alcorso, C., Tait, D. and Castles, S. (1995) *A Shop Full of Dreams: Ethnic Small Business in Australia*, Sydney and London: Pluto Press.

Collins, J., Sim, C.-L., Dhungel, B., Zabbal, N. and Noel, G. (1997) *Training for Ethnic Small Business*, Sydney: University of Technology Sydney (UTS).

Department of Employment, Education and Training (1995). 'Self Employment Programs for the Unemployed, Australia', a paper presented at the *Conference on Self-Employment Programs for the Unemployed*, Washington DC, 13 June, 1995.

Inglis, C. (1992) "An Overview of Australian Migration Policy and Flows" paper to the *Conference on Immigration and Refugee Policy: The Australian and Canadian Experiences*, York University, Toronto, Canada, 2–5th May.

Khoo, Siew-Ean et al. (1993) Asian Immigrant Settlement and Adjustment in Australia", paper to the *Conference on Asia-Pacific Migration Affecting Australia*, Darwin, 14–17 September.

Low, L. (1993), "People Movement in the Asia Pacific: Issues and Prospects", paper to the *Conference on Asia-Pacific Migration Affecting Australia*, Darwin, 14–17 September.

Moss, Irene (1993) *State of the Nation: A report on people of non-English speaking backgrounds*, Canberra: AGPS.

Piore, M.J. (1990) "The United States of America" in Sengenberger et al. (1990), pp. 261–308.

Stricker, P. and Sheehan, P. (1981) *Hidden Unemployment: The Australian Experience*, Melbourne: University of Melbourne Press

SOPEMI (1995) *Trends in International Migration: Annual Report 1995*, Paris: OECD.

Waldinger, R., Aldrich. Ward, R. and Associates (1990) *Ethnic Entrepreneurs — Immigrant Business in Industrial Societies*, Newbury Park, London, New Delhi: Sage.

Wooden, M. (1993) *Underemployment, Hidden Unemployment, and Immigrants*, Canberra: AGPS.

Quasi-markets and Insecure Employment in the Health and Welfare Bureaucracy: The Impact on Professional Occupations

Lou Wilson

Austrian and State Governments have transformed public sector services into quasi-markets, or 'market bureaucracies' as part of a wider restructuring of the economy. Market bureaucracy may create an insecure work environment which presents a challenge to the working conditions of some professional occupational groups that are employed predominantly in the public sector. Members of these occupations may experience greater insecurity in employment, lessened control over how their work is done and competition from lower skilled workers for their jobs.

In recent years, Australian and State Governments have transformed their health and welfare services into quasi-markets as part of a wide ranging restructuring of the economy (Scott 1996: 97, Kelly 1995: 26).

I will argue that public sector reform of this nature generates insecure workplaces that present challenges to the interests of particular professional occupational groups.

The occupational groups referred to in this paper are those which fall into the 'Professionals' major group classification of the Australian Standard Classification of Occupations (ABS 1993a). In Australia, occupations such as medical doctors, lawyers, physiotherapists, social workers and nurses all fall under this definition.

I will begin to examine these issues with a brief discussion of public choice theory and the introduction of quasi-markets into the bureaucracy. Subsequently, debates about the future of the professions will be discussed in the context of an emerging "market bureaucracy", followed by a description of some of the implications of a commercialised public sector for particular occupations, and for subsets of those occupations.

Public Choice Theory

A raft of Australian studies, including those of Salvaris (1995), Stretton and Orchard (1994), Self (1993) and Pusey (1991) have suggested that public policy at a Commonwealth and State level in this country is now driven largely by an economic rationalism inspired by public choice theory.

Public choice theory holds that society is no more than the sum total of atomistic individuals pursuing their own interests in a market place (Salvaris 1995: 37). The theory emphasises the importance to the public interest of the ideal consumer who is assertive, knowledgeable and prepared to shop for the best deal. A study by Stretton and Orchard (1994: 123) suggested public choice theory rested on four assumptions:

> 'individual material self-interest sufficiently motivates most economic behaviour, which is sufficiently understood by the use of neo-classical economic theory; and since the same individual self interest sufficiently motivates most political behaviour, that also may be sufficiently understood by the use of the same neo-classical economic theory'.

For government policy planners who accept these assumptions, it is in the public interest to extend the principles of the market place, as understood in neo-classical economic theory, to as many aspects of human life as possible, including the provision of public services (Salvaris 1995: 37).

In practice, the extension of this perspective to the public services has been associated in Australia since the 1980s with attempts to commercialise the public sector.

Quasi-markets and the Market Bureaucracy

South Australia and Victoria pioneered commercialisation of the State public sector in the early 1990s with the establishment of competitive unit cost funding (case-mix) for health services and the introduction of the funder/purchaser/ provider split into the welfare and health bureaucracies of those States (Kelly 1995: 27, FACS 1994/1995).

The central idea behind the introduction of these quasi-markets was to make service providers compete for government funds by increasing the volume of service provided at the least possible cost to the State (Kelly 1995: 26).

This new organisational concept has been termed "market bureaucracy" (Considine 1996: 1). It is characterised by internal business units competing for capital, rewards, staff and attention. Other characteristics include internal incentives related to productivity measures, competition between public organisations and user fee systems. The new position of competition at the centre of organisational practices differentiates the new market bureaucracies from previous legal-rational and corporate models that considered bureaucratic action to be essentially rule bound rather than price driven. For example, consider Hegel's concept of State organisations endowed with a general interest distinct from that of private corporations, or Weber's position that public officials should be prevented from owning any part of the means of administration (Hegel and Weber cited in Considine 1996: 1).

Market bureaucracy can be illustrated by considering the introduction of the funder/purchaser/provider split to the funding and provision of community services. The South Australian Department of Family and Community

Services annual report for 1994/95 (FACS 1994/95: 1–5) described the restructuring of that department along lines of funder/purchaser/provider (FPP) as 'introducing contestability' into the distribution of Government funds by 'utilising an output based tendering' system for the provision and delivery of community services. Essentially, a Policy and Development Division (the funder) determined where Government human service funding would be allocated and to whom. A separate Community Services Division (the purchaser) purchased services in line with the determinations of the funder and then managed the resulting contracts. The contracted service providers (the provider) who sold their services to the department included both those sections of the department which previously provided direct services to the public, and/or new external private contractors.

There is a potential for quasi-markets such as the FPP to greatly increase the job insecurity of employees in the public health and welfare sector as permanent employment is replaced by work arrangements based on contracts and tenders. In this context, Rubery (1996: 25) argued that job permanency was to be transformed into 'a job for as long as you are not undercut at the next tender'.

Indeed, the tendering process employed in quasi-markets may create an element of formal insecurity for employees. Job security is limited to the length of the employment contract which may in turn be altered by the loss of a tender by the employing organisation. Individual workers may be subject to the will of the tendering organisation which may be entirely separate from their direct employers. Moreover, the terms of an employment contract may involve re-negotiating previously held entitlements, for example sick pay or overtime arrangements, and/or include a wage cut (Allen and Henry 1996: 69).

Furthermore, the potential of quasi-market arrangements such as the funder/purchaser/provider split to restrict professional autonomy has particular implications for professionals employed in restructured organisations. In professionalised service agencies such as hospitals, schools and social agencies, the central tasks around which all others work may be performed or controlled by professional workers with as diverse occupational identities as doctors, physiotherapists, and social workers. This central role allows professional workers to resist or escape administrative authority over their work and hence enjoy a high degree of autonomy in their work practices (Freidson 1994: 116).

Moreover, the occupational location of service professionals in public sector organisations has allowed, in the past, the creation of 'labor market shelters' in the Weberian sense. Professional workers have been able to protect their employment conditions by excluding non-professional workers from jobs they have had designated for themselves (Freidson 1994: 81). However, the creation of labor market shelters in the public sector by professional workers is seen by policy planners inspired by public choice theory as 'market closure'. These closed markets are incongruent with the consumer led, free market economic rationalist policy planners seek to create (Salvaris 1995: 37).

This suggests a conflictual tension between the occupational principle of professions and the creation of quasi-markets in the public health and welfare sector. What then is the prognosis for professional workers in an insecure market bureaucracy? A discussion of some of the sociological critiques of the position of professionals in Western capitalist societies from 1960s, 1970s and 1980s suggests some answers.

Debates on the Future of the Professions

The radical political climate in the USA, Britain and Australia of the late 1960s and early 1970s was characterised by the rise of the women's movement, and mass movements for civil rights and against the Vietnam war. This climate generated critiques of the power of professional occupations which had previously been viewed more benignly by functionalist theorists such as Durkheim and Parsons as important contributors to social order (Crompton 1990: 151). Two critiques that emerged in this period have particular salience for this discussion. These were the deprofessionalisation and proletarianisation theses. Marie Haug (1973, 1975, 1977, 1978) argued that the professions were in danger of losing their monopoly over sets of knowledge and power, a process of deprofessionalisation. Haug's pessimistic prognosis for the professions focused on the threat to professional monopoly over sets of knowledge from new, consumer friendly technology and the increasing education levels of the lay population. These factors made the lay population more independent of professional knowledge, and more challenging in their dealings with professionals.

The notion of the new sovereignty of the consumer was central to this thesis:

> "with the client in a position to seek alternatives, we will begin
> to see a consumer model, rather than a patient or client model,
> of the entire transaction and the concept of profession as now
> formulated will indeed be obsolete" (Haug 1977: 226).

While the concept of de-professionalisation focused on cultural factors and other elements external to the professional work-place, the related notion of proletarianisation emphasised the circumstances of professional work in large bureaucratic organisations (Oppenheimer 1973: 213).

A seminal study by Braverman (1974: 4) suggested monopolisation and deskilling were inherent trends in capitalist society which must lead to the reduction of control by all workers, including professionals, over their work and the removal of their monopoly over particular skills and knowledge. Likewise Oppenheimer (1973: 213) argued that professionals in bureaucratised work places increasingly faced conditions similar to those of production line workers in factories.

More recently, McKinley and Stoeckle (1988: 191) argued that commercialisation of the U.S. health system had reduced the price doctors could sell their labour to the hospitals for and placed increased controls over the pace and direction of their work. Similarly Arches (1991: 202) argued that the commercialisation of U.S. social services under government policies influenced by public choice theories had lessened the control of professional social workers over determining what work they did, how it was done and what its aims were. For these authors, the likely product of the processes described above was an insecure, deskilled, demoralised, stressed and alienated professional work force which was likely to serve its customers less well than in the past (Arches 1991, McKinley and Stoeckle 1988).

But the deprofessionalisation and proletarianisation theses have come under criticism from a range of scholars. For example, Freidson (1994: 134) argued that the quantity and quality of specialised knowledge and technical competence had continued to increase in recent years because of the location of professional training within Universities. Therefore, a knowledge gap existed which was difficult for lay people to bridge. Moreover, with reference to the proletarianisation thesis, Brewer (1996: 36) argued that continuing strong collegial loyalty between professionals reinforced by recruitment practices, and the egalitarian formation of partnerships between professionals and their employers, continued to protect the control professionals had over their work. To support this argument, Brewer (1996: 33, 35) cited, among others, recent studies by Mullis (1995) and Derber et al. (1990).

However, Mullis (1995) reviewed the collegial habits of medical doctors and Derber et al. (1990) based their study on interviews with 1000 salaried doctors, lawyers, scientists and engineers in the United States. Furthermore, much of the work of Freidson focused on the experiences of medical doctors, a popular group for researchers given their dominant position in the health system. It can be argued these are high status, male dominated professions which produce goods or services which the members of the public are willing to pay for privately and also provide services seen as essential by the State (Gardner and McCoppin 1995: 372).

Hence, the new market bureaucracy may present a threat to the interests of public sector professionals who are not members of high status groups such as lawyers or doctors, or of occupations that do not produce products that are in demand by consumer groups, or whose products are seen as expendable by the State.

In this context, Gardner and McCoppin (1995: 372) noted the division of Australian professionals into older, predominantly male professions, such as law and medicine, and newer, predominantly female professions, for example, physiotherapy, nursing and social work, with distinct power differentials between these categories of professionals in terms of their ability to affect market closure and raise the status and working conditions of their members.

Newer, predominantly female professions such as social work and nursing do not produce commodities for which there is a large private market but rather mainly service consumer groups which are subsidised by the State or non-Government welfare agencies, in contrast with higher status professions such as medicine and law.

The prognosis for these professions may be grim in the new market bureaucracy in the likelihood that they experience greater insecurity in employment, lessened control over how their work is done and competition from lower skilled workers for their jobs. It is pertinent here to consider the growth of these new professions in Australia.

The Growth of the New Professions in Australia

In recent years, much of the growth of the Australian public sector has occurred in the community services/health and welfare sector. Employment in this sector increased 147.7% between 1966 and 1986. Congruent with this increase, and over the same period, the numbers of persons whose occupations were classed as professional/technical rose by 129.8%. Two thirds of those employed in the health and welfare services sector were women (ABS 1986).

Furthermore, statistics from the 1991 census showed the employment ratio of women to men was higher in community service oriented professions. For example, in Australia in 1991, 80% of physiotherapists, 97% of speech therapists, 92% of nurses, 91% of occupational therapists and 78% of social workers were female (ABS 1993b).

These statistics suggest that the marketisation of the health and welfare bureaucracy has implications for social equity. In particular, marketisation may alter the gender balance of the predominantly female professions as the bureaucracy increasingly privatises its operations. For example, consider the changing gender balance in the Australian physiotherapy profession. The number of male physiotherapists increased from the beginning of the 1980s from an insignificant number to 20% of the total number by the 1991 census (census data cited in Gardner and McCoppin 1995: 373). The growth in the number of male physiotherapists coincided with the establishment in Australia during the 1980s of private "sports clinics" financed by lucrative contracts with public and private health organisations that attracted more men into the profession by offering higher salaries (Gardner and McCoppin 1995: 374).

In contrast, a study by Martin (1996: 30) suggested that the number of social workers employed by government organisations increased by greater numbers than those employed by non-government organisations between the 1986 and 1991 census. While not explicitly stated by Martin (1996), the increase in Government employment appeared to coincide with the number of women in the profession becoming greater.

The above suggests a relationship between public employment and gender which requires further exploration.

Public Employment and Gender

Statistics from the 1991 census showed that women in the 'caring' professions were more likely to be working in the public sector than men. For example, among persons employed in health occupations, 32.6% of males were employed in the Government sector and 63.6% in the private sector. Among females, 50.9% were employed by the public sector and 47.6% by the private sector (ABS 1993b).

The attraction of public sector employment for women may be related to the progressive employment policies of Australian public organisations compared with private counterparts. For example, employment targets, paid parental leave and the existence of working time arrangements advantageous to women were much more likely to occur in the public sector (Boreham et al. 1996: 60). In the private sector, equity considerations were likely to conflict with the need to be profitable (Boreham et al. 1996: 65)

Hence, the emergence of market bureaucracy may create a potential conflict between equity and profitability in the public sector. This may translate into the erosion of gender equity by the need to cut costs in the public sector so as to provide maximum service at a minimum price to the consumer.

Changing industrial conditions may also have a greater impact on women professionals because access to time is qualitatively different for men and women. In this context, a study by Seron and Ferris (1995: 27) argued that theories of occupations and professions have assumed a male experience. Professional workplaces, especially among service professionals, required an open ended series of implicit demands and processes. For example, networking to ensure client satisfaction, or deadlines to complete a report for a court of law. Time at the office seeped into private time as networking, socialising and informal politicking took place. Men were freer to pursue professional networking in flexible time frames than women, who were far more likely to require time for private roles related to home and child care (Seron and Ferris 1995: 23).

If, as has been suggested above, professional networking and politicking become more difficult and time consuming as the bureaucracy is atomised into competing segments and working conditions, including child care, are pared back in the interests of economic efficiency, women professionals and professions dominated by women are likely to be most affected.

However, an examination of the impact of a competitive market bureaucracy on 'women' professionals that treats this as an homogenous category and without also considering the impact on 'men' is one which is in danger of presenting male professionals as the 'norm' (Franzway in Pocock 1997: 5). In this respect, Seron and Ferris (1995: 36) found the pressures of professional networking affected married male professionals with care commitments to a greater extent than single females or males, albeit to a lesser extent than married females with care commitments.

Just as there is a need to disaggregate professional occupations by status and relative location in the private or public sector, in acknowledging the gender factor there is a need to unravel the gender categories themselves so as to fully understand their impact in a changing workplace. In doing so it is possible to suggest the outlook for diverse occupations in the increasingly insecure Australian workplace.

Summary

I have argued that Commonwealth and State policies inspired by public choice theory have driven the emergence of market bureaucracies in the public sector. Market bureaucracies may threaten the interests of newer, lower status, professional occupational groups that have traditionally been employed in significant numbers within the public sector. Many newer professional occupations are predominantly filled by women and the imposition of market disciplines in the public sector has the potential to undermine gender equity. Potentially, members of these occupations may experience greater insecurity in employment, lessened control over how their work is done and competition from lower skilled workers for their jobs. But the experience may differ for individual professional workers, depending on gender and care responsibilities.

In overall terms, I have suggested that the outlook for particular occupations in the new market bureaucracies can be forecast by addressing the relative location of occupational groups within the public or private sector, and by accounting for the impact of power differentials between and within gendered categories of analysis on the ability of occupational groups to compete in an insecure work place.

References

ABS (1993a) 'Australian Standard Classification of Occupations' 1st ed., *Catalogue No. 1223.0*: Australian Bureau of Statistics.

ABS (1993b) "Characteristics of persons employed in health occupations, Australia", *Census of population and housing*, 6 August 1991, Catalogue No. 4346.0: Australian Bureau of Statistics.

ABS (1986) '*The labour force Australia*' Catalogue No. 6203.0: Australian Bureau of Statistics.

Allen, J. and Henry, N. (1996) "Fragments of industry and employment" in *Changing forms of employment*, eds. Crompton R., Gallie D. and Purcell K., London: Routledge.

Arches, J. (1991) "Social structure, burnout and job satisfaction" *Social Work* 36 (3): 202–206.

Boreham, P., Hall, R., Harley, B. and Whitehouse, G. (1996) "What does enterprise bargaining mean for gender equity? Some empirical evidence" *Labour and Industry*, 7 (1): 51–67.

Braverman, H. (1974) *Labour and Monopoly Capital New York*: Monthly Review Press.

Brewer, L. (1996) "Bureaucratic organisation of professional labour" *Australian and New Zealand Journal of Sociology* 32 (3): 21–38.

Considine, M. (1996), "Market Bureaucracy? Explore the contending rationalities of contemporary administrative regimes" *Labour and Industry* 7, (1): 1–27.

Crompton, R. (1990) "Professions in the current context" *Work, employment and society* May Special Issue: 147–166.

Derber, C., Schwartz, W. and Magrass, Y. (1990) *Power in the highest degree, professionals and the rise of a new mandarin order* New York: Oxford Press.

FACS (1994/95), *The South Australian Department of Family and Community Services annual report for 1994/95.*

Freidson, E. (1994) *Professionalism reborn* Chicago: University of Chicago Press.

Gardner, H. and McCoppin, B. (1995) " Struggle for survival by health therapists, nurses and medical scientists" *Politics of health: the Australian experience* ed. Gardner H., 2nd ed. Melbourne: Livingstone.

Haug, M. (1973) "Deprofessionalization: an alternative hypothesis for the future" *Sociological Review Monograph* 20: 195–211.

Haug, M. (1975) "The deprofessionalization of everyone" *Sociological focus*, 8: 187–213.

Haug, M. (1977) "Computer technology and the obsolescence of the concept of profession" *Work and technology*, eds. M. Haug and J. Dofny, Beverley Hills: Sage.

Haug, M. (1988) "A re-examination of the hypothesis of physician deprofessionalisation" *The Millbank Quarterly* 66 (2): 48–56.

Kelly, R. (1995) "Privatising public health: private profit at public expense" *Just Policy* June 3.

Martin, E. (1996) "An update on census data: good news for social work?" *Australian Social Work* 49 (2): 29–36.

McKinlay, J. and Stoeckle, J. (1988) "Corporatisation and the social transformation of doctoring" *International journal of health services* 18 (2): 191–205.

Mullis, J. (1995) "Medical malpractice, social structure and social reform" *Sociological forum* 10: 135–163.

Oppenheimer, M. (1973) "The proletarianisation of the professional", in Halmos P. (ed) *Professionalisation and social change* Keele: University of Keele Press.

Pocock, B. (1997) 'Gender and Australian industrial relations theory and research practice' *Labour and Industry* 8 (1): 1–19.

Pusey, M. (1991) *Economic rationalism in Canberra: a nation building state changes its mind* Melbourne: Cambridge University Press.

Rubery, J. (1996) "The labour market outlook and the outlook for labour market analysis" *Changing forms of employment* eds. Crompton R., Gallie D. and Purcell K., London: Routledge.

Salvaris, M. (1995) 'Privatisation, citizenship and the public interest' *Just Policy* September 4: 37–43.

Scott, G. (1996) "The use of contracting in the public sector" *Australian Journal of Public Administration* 55 (3): 97–104.

Self, P. (1993) *Government by the market?* London: Macmillan.

Seron, C. and Ferris, K. (1995) "Negotiating professionalism — the gendered social capital of flexible time" *Work and Occupations* 22 (1): 22–47.

Stretton, H. and Orchard, L. (1994) *Public goods, public enterprise, public choice* London: St. Martins Press.

At What Price a Job?
Suicide Ideation as a Psychological Cost for Dissatisfied Workers and the Unemployed

Angelique Foran and Juanita Muller

The aim of this research was to examine the relationship between employment status and suicide ideation. One hundred and nine subjects were approached at a street shopping mall and asked to complete a questionnaire on the health of employed and unemployed people. All subjects completed the GHQ-28 and a survey that asked questions on employment status, job satisfaction and general demographics. Subjects were then divided into four groups: satisfied employed, dissatisfied employed, unemployed and students and compared with each other. Results indicate that those who were dissatisfied with their job had a significantly higher level of suicide ideation and psychological distress than the unemployed, followed by satisfied employed and students. This study had given impetus to changing the way we conceptualise work and its psychological effects.

Durkheim's research on suicide put forward the initial argument that suicide rates are related to unemployment levels (cited in Standish-Barry, Clayden & Sims, 1989). Recent research findings support this view (Platt & Kreitman, 1985; Standish-Barry et al, 1989 & Platt, 1984). Platt and Kreitman (1985) investigated the relationship between unemployment and attempted suicide in Edinburgh during the years 1968–82. They identified a general trend showing a strong positive association between unemployment and parasuicide. Parasuicide is defined as all forms of intentional self harming behaviour and the term is preferable to suicide attempt (Fremouw, de Perczel, & Ellis, 1990). In Platt's (1984) review of the literature on suicide and unemployment he reported that most research points to a relationship, with the exception of a few studies.

Goldney and Spence (1987) attempted to see if they could predict suicide using the information from 46 psychiatric patients in an Australian hospital who had committed suicide. One of the identified risk factors was being unemployed. Other risk factors included previous hospital admissions and schizophrenia. Current literature, however, suggests that the association is somewhat more problematic and no longer supports the assumption that suicide rates are determined by unemployment rates (Hawton & Rose, 1986, Furness, Khan & Pickens, 1985; Jones, Forster & Hassenyeh 1991).

Hawton and Rose (1986) studied trends in male suicide attempts in

Oxford between 1976 and 1982 when rates of unemployment were increasing. Results of the study reveal that attempted suicide is a greater risk for the long term unemployed. As there is no direct causal link between unemployment and parasuicide they believed a third indirect causal factor was operating, such as social or interpersonal difficulties which are exacerbated by unemployment. The explanation given was that those who are "vulnerable to having psychological problems may also be both more vulnerable to becoming unemployed and of remaining unemployed" (Hawton & Rose, 1986, p. 31).

Jones et al (1991) in a study on self-poisoning also suggest a third independent factor which may increase the risk of self harm. They found that personality differences independently increase the risk of both unemployment and self poisoning. Besides psychological problems and personality differences, age, sex, time and geographical differences have also been cited in some research as contributing to parasuicides. Platt and Kreitman (1985) found that geographical location played a role in the suicide attempts of the unemployed. They argue that the unemployed individual would have less social stigma in an area where unemployment was high and their findings supported this view. Furness et al (1985) did not find an association between unemployment and parasuicide but suggested that this was because the level of unemployment in Hartlepool was so high that there was no social stigma.

Trends in youth suicide in Victoria, Australia were studied by Krupinski, Tiller, Burrows & Hallenstein (1994) using Australian Bureau of Statistics (ABS) data to examine their relationship to youth unemployment. They found no apparent association between suicide and unemployment. They used available data from 1907 to 1990 to show steady increases in the youth suicide rate. The suicide rates showed differences in age, sex and area of living but there was no relationship between suicide and an increase in youth unemployment. These findings however may not reflect the problematic nature of studying suicide.

One of the major problems is that while suicide is a dramatic event it occurs only very infrequently in the community (Winefield, Tiggemann, Winefield & Goldney 1993). To address this problem researchers have used suicide ideation as a measure of suicidal behaviour. Pearce and Martin (1994) identified suicide ideation as a significant risk factor for attempted suicides. Winefield et al (1993) acknowledged that those who have thoughts of suicide are different from those who actually attempt suicide but there are also some similarities between these two groups. Goldney, Smith, Winefield, Tiggemann and Winefield (1991) conducted an Australian longitudinal study over 8 years and found suicidal ideation correlated with depression, hopelessness, self esteem and locus of control. They believe that this supports the view that suicidal ideation is not a transient phenomenon but a pervasive personality problem.

Goldney et al (1995) undertook a longitudinal study of school leavers between the years 1980 and 1988. Originally 3130 subjects were included in the sample but at every one year follow up 20% of subjects dropped out of the survey leaving 483 subjects in total after 8 years. Goldney et al aimed to look at the relationship between suicide ideation and unemployment. In the final year of the survey a job satisfaction questionnaire was introduced due to research by Winefield, Tiggemann and Goldney (1988). As a result they found that young people who thought their jobs were unsatisfactory were just as "badly off psychologically" as an unemployed person. The results which have been widely reported (Winefield, Tiggemann, Winefield & Goldney, 1991b; Goldney et al, 1995; Winefield, Tiggemann & Winefield, 1991a) did not support an association between unemployment and suicide ideation. There was a strong link, however, between unsatisfactory employment and suicide ideation. The 28 item General Health Questionnaire (GHQ) was used in this study and the dissatisfied employed scored higher than the unemployed overall. Satisfied employed scored lower than both groups (Goldney et al, 1995). Consequently, Goldney et al believe that suicide ideation is "independent of employment status and associated with more enduring personality or health related traits, at least within the young adult population" (p. 182). As such their findings directly contradict Jahoda's (1982) belief that any work is better than none at all no matter how bad the employment conditions. This research with young adults challenges the way that we conceptualise the benefits of work versus unemployment.

The findings of Goldney et al (1995) indicate that young people who are dissatisfied with employment have a higher suicidal ideation in comparison with those who are either satisfied with employment, unemployed or students. The aim of the present study is to examine this issue in the general population. The questions addressed in this study are:

1   Suicide ideation in this sample is expected to be similar to other population studies.

2   The dissatisfied employed are expected to have the highest suicide ideation and GHQ scores, followed by the unemployed group and then students and satisfied employed groups.

3   When unemployed groups and dissatisfied groups are compared together it isexpected they will have a higher suicide ideation than satisfied employedand student groups.

4   Older age groups will have a higher suicide ideation than younger age groups.

5   Males will exhibit a higher suicide ideation than females in all groups.

Method

Subjects
Participants in the survey were approached on the footpath at Stones

Corner Shopping Mall in which a Commonwealth Employment Service (CES) office was located. The original sample of 117 subjects were allocated into one of four groups: satisfied employed, dissatisfied employed, unemployed and students. The employment status and job satisfaction of a subject was decided by a self report measure. All subjects that said they worked part time or full time were included in the employed category. Subjects were classified as unemployed if they indicated they were on a disability support or sickness benefit pension or they were unemployed. Subjects were considered unemployed even if they were currently not collecting unemployment benefits. The eight remaining subjects were excluded as they listed themselves as retired, home duties person or were unsure if they were satisfied or dissatisfied with their jobs.

Data collected included 46 (42.2%) men and 63 (57.8%) women with ages ranging from 16 to 57 years of age. Of the 109 subjects, 63 were satisfied employed, 7 dissatisfied employed, 30 unemployed and 9 were students. The mean age of respondents was 28.68 years. The length of time unemployed ranged from 1 month to 48 months with the mean being 9.19 months.

Materials

The questionnaire had two sections and subjects were also required to complete a consent form. The first part of the questionnaire asked for background information such as age, sex, employment status, length of unemployment and for the employed group a job satisfaction question (Warr, Cook & Wall, 1979). The second part of the questionnaire was the 28 item General Health Questionnaire (GHQ-28) which is a self report inventory that is designed to assess psychological disturbance (Goldberg, 1972). The GHQ-28 has four subscales: somatic symptoms, anxiety and insomnia, social dysfunction and severe depression. Each scale has seven items and the sum of these scores gives an indication of the type of psychological disturbance as does the total score (LoBello, 1995). The Likert method of scoring for the GHQ was used as it is said to be better than the binary system as it increases the range of variability in scores and more closely approximates a normal distribution (Winefield et al, 1989). The Likert system consists of assigning values of 0, 1, 2 or 3 to each item with the maximum score possible being 84. In general, the higher the score the greater the level of distress the individual is experiencing. A meta-analysis of 43 studies of the GHQ-28 by Goldberg and Williams (1988) obtained a sensitivity of 84% and a specificity of 82%.

Suicide ideation scores were determined using four questions from Section D of the GHQ-28 (see Table 1 below). These four questions were chosen as they directly assess a subjects suicide ideation and have been used in other research as a measure of suicide ideation (Goldney, Winefield, Tiggemann, Winefield & Smith, 1989).

Procedure

When subjects were approached on the street they were asked if they would like to complete a questionnaire on the health of employed and unemployed people. Before completing the questionnaire subjects were instructed to read and sign the informed consent sheet. Subjects could then proceed to fill out the questionnaire. Subjects who indicated they were employed were classified as satisfied or dissatisfied on the basis of their answer to the job satisfaction question (Warr et al, 1979). This was scored on a seven point scale with one to three being satisfied employed and scores from five to seven being dissatisfied employed. Those who chose four or unsure were excluded from the sample.

Statistical Analysis

Descriptive statistics were computed for total GHQ-28 scores and suicide ideation scores. Mean differences in scores on the GHQ-28 and suicide ideation scores were subject to two way analysis of variance (ANOVA). Chi-Square was used to assess differences if those who reported some suicide ideation compared with those who did not report any suicide ideation. Regression analysis was used to examine the relationship between age and suicide ideation scores. All data was analysed using SPSS version 6.1 for windows.

Results

In this sample of subjects 22.9% had at least thought that life was not worth living while 12.8% reported that they frequently had the idea of taking their own life. On each of the measures of psychological distress and suicide ideation the dissatisfied employed group were significantly different from the other three groups. Alpha probability levels were set at 0.01 due to the large number of comparisons.

As Table 2 shows the dissatisfied employed group had the highest percentage of suicidal thoughts with 57.1% followed by the unemployed with 43.3% and then the satisfied employed and students both had 11.1%. When the four groups were compared for presence or absence of suicidal thoughts there was a significant difference (Chi-Square 17.39, $df = 3$, $p < .01$).

TABLE 1

Suicide Ideation Questions in the GHQ-28.

Section D: Suicide Ideation Questions (Goldberg, 1972)
Felt that life isn't worth living?
Thought of the possibility that you might make away with yourself?
Found that you were wishing you were dead and away from it all?
Found that the idea of taking your own life kept coming into your mind?

As can be seen from Figure 1 the dissatisfied employed have the highest mean suicide ideation score and the difference between the four employment status groups is significant $[F(3,105) = 104.18, p < .01]$. The unemployed group scored higher than both satisfied employed and the students but lower than the dissatisfied employed.

The dissatisfied employed have also scored the highest GHQ followed by the unemployed group, then students and the satisfied unemployed had the lowest mean score. A significant difference was evident between the occupational group and their GHQ scores $[F(3,105) = 2897.53, p < .01]$.

TABLE 2

Employment Group by Suicidal Thoughts

Employment Status	Suicidal Thoughts	No Suicidal Thoughts
Satisfied Employed	11.1%	88.9%
Dissatisfied Employed	57.1%	42.9%
Unemployed	43.3%	56.7%
Student	11.1%	88.9%

TABLE 3

GHQ score by Employment Group

Employment Group	Mean GHQ Score	Standard Deviation
Satisfied Employed	16.68	10.86
Dissatisfied Employed	31.29	21.16
Unemployed	26.57	20.48
Student	17.89	16.01

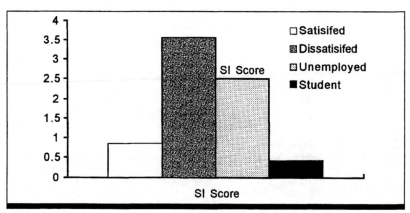

FIGURE 1

Employment Group by Suicide Ideation Score

When the unemployed and dissatisfied were grouped together and compared to satisfied employed and students, suicide ideation scores between the two groups were significantly different [$F(3,105) = 4.49, p < .01$].

No age differences in suicide ideation scores were evident in this sample of subjects [$F(2,104) = 1.48, p = .24$]. There was a significant difference when suicide ideation scores where compared with sex and occupational status with females showing significantly higher suicide ideation [$F(7,101) = 119.98, p < .01$]. Further analysis of these results reveal a significant difference in the female groups with the dissatisfied employed female group have a higher level of suicide ideation than all other groups[$F(3,59) = 209.35, p < .01$]. When male occupational status groups were compared with each other there was no significant difference between the groups [$F(3,42) = 9.05, p = .79$].

Discussion

The percentage of subjects (12.8%) who reported they frequently thought of killing themselves was in line with general population studies done by Sorenson and Golding (1988) and Schwab, Wharheit and Holzer (1972) who reported 13% and 15.9% of subjects had thoughts about suicide. Suicide ideation was higher in the dissatisfied employed and unemployed groups as predicted and this result supports the findings of Goldney et al (1995). Overall scores on the GHQ were also higher for dissatisfied employed and unemployed groups suggesting that psychological disturbance was evident in these groups.

In contrast to the findings of Goldney et al (1995), females had higher suicide ideation scores across all groups in comparison to males. Females suicide ideation was also significantly different across the four groups. Some of the reasons for the females having a higher suicide ideation than expected could be due the worse conditions, with regards to pay and status of jobs, in which women are generally employed (Winefield et al, 1991b).

While the results are significant, applying these findings to the whole population should be cautioned due to the sample size. The small number of subjects in the dissatisfied employed group is of particular concern. These issues are limitations of the current study and should be addressed in future research. The study differed from the Winefield et al (1991b) research in that they only measured suicide ideation in the last two weeks of a longitudinal study. If lifetime suicide ideation was assessed it is possible there may have been smaller differences between the groups if any. As the research was interested however in how they felt about their present employment status, this time difference in suicide ideation should not be problematic.

Using the 4/5 binary criterion for the GHQ-28 the percentage of positive 'cases' was 34.9% in this sample. This figure is comparable but slightly higher than the Winefield et al (1989) research with Australian youth. Measurement of suicide ideation using the GHQ is also a concern as the

GHQ is said to 'misclassify' cases (Winefield et al, 1989). The GHQ was developed using an English population and some of the questions use phrases that may possibly have confused some subjects such as 'make away with yourself'. As this was one of the questions used to assess suicide ideation it is possible that subjects scores may have differed if they did not understand the question properly.

As outlined earlier, Jahoda (1982) believes that any employment is better than no employment. The findings of this research do not support this view. The dissatisfied subjects had higher levels of suicide ideation and psychological distress than all of the other three groups. This suggests that job satisfaction plays a very important role in psychological well being and consequently, the employed, like the unemployed, should not be treated as a homogenous group. Future studies on suicide ideation will need to look further at what constitutes job satisfaction in the employed.

Given the findings of this study and previous findings of other researchers, it appears that being dissatisfied with employment is more of a psychological cost than being unemployed. We must then ask the question — "At what price a job?" Do we push the unemployed into jobs that they will find dissatisfying and therefore increase they risk of psychological distress? Or, do we start to act on the much talked about 'reconceptualization of work' and make it a more satisfying existence for all.

References

Fremouw, W.J., de Perczel, M., & Ellis, T.E. (1990) *Suicide risk: Assessment and response guidelines*. New York: Pergamon Press.

Furness, J. A., Khan, M. C., & Pickens, P. T. (1985) Unemployment and parasuicide in Hartlepool 1974–83. *Health Trends (London)*, 17, 21–24.

Goldberg, D. (1972) *Detection of Psychiatric Illness by Questionnaire*. London: Oxford University Press.

Goldberg, D., & Williams, P. (1988) *A Users Guide to the General Health Questionnaire*. Berkshire, UK: NFER-Nelson.

Goldney, R. D., Winefield, A. H., Tiggeman, M., & Winefield, H. R., & Smith, S. (1989) Suicidal ideation in a young adult population. *Acta Psychiatrica Scandinavica*, 79, 481–489.

Goldney, R. D., Smith, S., Winefield, A. H., Tiggeman, M., & Winefield, H. R. (1991) Suicidal ideation: its enduring nature and associated morbidity. *Acta Psychiatrica Scandinavica*, 83, 115–120.

Goldney, R. D., & Spence, N. D. (1987) Is suicide predictable? *Australian and New Zealand Journal of Psychiatry*, 21, 3–4.

Goldney, R. D., Winefield, A. H., Tiggeman, M., & Winefield, H. R. (1995) Suicidal ideation and unemployment: A prospective longitudinal study. *Archives of Suicide Research*, 1, 175–184.

Hawton, K., & Rose, N. (1986) Unemployment and attempted suicide among men in Oxford. *Health Trends*, 18, 29–32.

Jahoda, M. (1992) Reflections on Marienthal and after. *Journal of Occupational and*

Organisational Psychology, 65, 355–358.

Jones, S. C., Forster, D. P., & Hassenyeh, F. (1991) The role of unemployment in parasuicide. *Psychological Medicine*, 21, 169–176.

Krupinski, J., Tiller, J. W. G., Burrows, G. D., & Hallenstein, H. (1994) Youth suicide in Victoria: A retrospective study. *The Medical Journal of Australia*, 160, 113–116.

LoBello, S. G. (1995) General Health Questionnaire. In Conoley & Impara (Eds.) *The Twelfth Mental Measurements Yearbook*. Nebraska, U.S.A.: Buros Institute of Mental Measurements.

Pearce, C. M., & Martin, G. (1994) Predicting suicide attempts among adolescents. *Acta Psychiatrica Scandinavica*, 90, 268–291.

Platt, S. (1984) Unemployment and suicidal behaviour: A review of the literature. *Social Science and Medicine*, 19(2), 93–115.

Platt, S., & Kreitman, N. (1985) Parasuicide and unemployment among men in Edinburgh, 1968–82. *Psychological Medicine*, 15, 113–123.

Platt, S., & Kreitman, N. (1990) Long term trends in parasuicide and unemployment in Edinburgh, 1968–87. *Social Psychiatry and Psychiatric Epidemiology*, 25, 56–61.

Schwab, J. J., Warheit, G. J., & Holzer, C. E. (1972) Suicide ideation and behaviour in a general population. *Diseases of the Nervous System*, 33, 745–749.

Sorenson, S. B., & Golding, J. M. (1988) Suicide ideation and attempts in Hispanics and non-Hispanic whites: Demographic and Psychiatric disorder issues. *Suicide and Life-Threatening Behaviour*, 18, 205–218.

Standish-Barry, H. M. S., Clayden, A., & Sims, C. P. (1989) Age, unemployment and parasuicide in Leeds. *The International Journal of Social Psychiatry*, 35(4), 303–312.

Warr, P. B., Cook, J., & Wall, T. (1979) Scales for the measurement of some work attitudes and aspects of psychological well-being. *Journal of Occupational Psychology*, 52, 129–148.

Winefield, A. H., Tiggemann, M., Winefield, H. R., & Goldney, R. D. (1993) *Growing up with Unemployment: A Longitudinal Study of Psychological Impact*. London: Routledge.

Winefield, A. H., Tiggemann, M., & Goldney, R. D. (1988) Psychological concomitants of satisfactory employment and unemployment in young people. *Social Psychiatry and Psychiatric Epidemiology*, 23, 149–157.

Winefield, H. R., Goldney, R. D., Winefield, A. H., & Tiggemann, M. (1989) The General Health Questionnaire: Reliability and validity for Australian youth. *Australian and New Zealand Journal of Psychiatry*, 23, 53–58.

Winefield, A. H., Tiggeman, M., Winefield, H. R. (1991a) The psychological impact of unemployment and unsatisfactory employment in young men and women: Longitudinal and cross-sectional data. *British Journal of Psychology*, 82, 473–483.

Winefield, A. H., Tiggeman, M., Winefield, H. R., & Goldney, R. D. (1991b) A longitudinal study of the psychological effects of unemployment and unsatisfactory employment on young adults. *Journal of Applied Psychology*, 76(3), 424–431.

'In the Silence of the Heart': Rethinking the Youth Suicide and Youth Unemployment Link[1]

Rob Watts

Contemporary political and popular concern has been expressed about the rising youth suicide rate. It has become an increasingly accepted fact of our time that rising rates of youth suicide have sociological significance and are causally linked to social facts like the rising rate of youth unemployment. In this paper I challenge the belief that: (i) official youth suicide rates represent accurately a tangible 'social fact' which in turn (ii) can be structurally and/or 'causally' linked to other social-structural factors most notably youth unemployment. I begin by outlining the two closely related propositions that inform the 'classical sociological' inflection in suicidology, before subjecting them to four intersecting criticisms.

> Suicide like a great work of art, is prepared in the silence of the heart
> Camus, *The Myth of Sisyphus*, 1942

A recent *Age* editorial registers the contemporary concern in our community about youth suicide:

> ... is impossible to discount the influence of fears generated by high unemployment and the erosion of traditional communities, particularly in rural Australia, on youth suicide rates (*Age* 2 December 1996: A12).

The editorial is symptomatic of a broader 'sociological' approach given prominence by Eckersley who affirms that youth suicide rates:

> ... point unequivocally to an alarming escalation in the social and psychological problems facing young Australians today. Behind these problems are increases in family conflict and breakdown, increasing poverty, high youth unemployment, soaring youth homelessness and growing educational pressures (Eckersley 1988:1).

In a time of mounting unemployment and the near-complete destruction of the full-time youth labour market we can ill-afford to be blase about the scale of this problem. The social and ethical significance of youth unemployment however does not excuse sloppy thinking. My interest in this paper is in the way youth suicide is constituted as part of a 'classical sociological' paradigm which argues that social structure constrains or shapes individual identity and behaviour. This paradigm which has established a presence in a tradition of 'suicidology' (Anderberg 1989) privileges a methodology stressing the empirical and statistical analysis of variance. (Rather than repeat this lengthy formulation endlessly I will for ease refer to this as the 'classical sociological tradition').[2] This sociological tradition, which stresses in conscious memory of Durkheim's foundational study (1897;1970) the *anomic* forms of suicide, is represented in pop suicidology by Eckersley (1988) and by scientific suicidology (Baume in House of Representatives 1997: FCA 56–7).

Suicidology claims:

- There has been a significant increase in youth suicide rate.
- Rising rates of youth suicide have sociological significance and are causally linked to social facts like the rising rate of youth unemployment.

In this paper I challenge the belief that (i) official youth suicide rates represent accurately a tangible 'social fact' which in turn (ii) can be structurally and/or 'causally' linked to other social-structural factors most notably youth unemployment. I begin by outlining the two closely related propositions that inform the 'classical sociological' inflection in suicidology.

A Significant Increase in The Youth Suicide Rate?

The claim that the youth suicide rate has increased dramatically since the 1980s has become common knowledge and an accepted truth routinely announced, analysed and discussed by numerous writers. Although he was not the first to make the point, Eckersley drew attention to the rising rate of youth suicide in the late 1980s in ways which have not always been helpful. In 1988 Eckersley claimed that:

> Young Australians are now committing suicide at a rate of about one a day. This year more than 350 young Australians under the age of 25 will take their own lives. Suicide will be the second biggest killer of young people after traffic accidents (and many of these may also essentially be suicides). Thousands more teenagers and young men and women will attempt to kill themselves with varying degrees of seriousness (Eckersley 1988 : 5).

Five years later Eckersley was writing in even more alarmist terms:

> A striking feature of Western civilisation is that, for all our success in reducing the toll of lives taken by disease, we have failed to diminish that exacted by despair ... suicide has steadily increased for both males and females since the early 1950s. What makes the trend particularly tragic is that the increase in suicide is occurring mainly among teenagers and young adults especially males ... The suicide rate among young males has more than tripled since 1950 (1993: 8).

Eckersley drew on a body of expert research to support his claim that 'attempted suicide' (eg. Kosky 1987) and 'achieved suicide' (eg. Hassan 1987) was a major social and public health problem.

Since then a considerable body of expert and official research has confirmed that the youth suicide rate is on the rise. A growing body of 'empirical' (that is, statistical) research has been carried out, much of it by the medical profession deploying a 'sociological', epidemiological approach (Hassan & Carr 1989).[3] Official reports and the Australian Bureau of Statistics (ABS) support the claim that there has been a significant increase in the youth suicide rate (ABS 1993; ABS 1994). The ABS Report *Causes of Death* shows a 48% increase in young women killing themselves, with a growth in suicide for women aged between 15 to 24 years from 57 in 1994 to 84 in 1995. The most recent Australian youth suicide statistics for 1995–6 indicate an increase in the rate of youth suicide of 7% for Victoria — even though the national rate has remained static or is perhaps tailing off (*Age*, 9 November 1996: A9). There was a slight drop in the numbers of young men suiciding, although the total number for males continues to be much higher than those for young women. Suicides for young males have declined from 374 in 1994 to 350 in 1995 (*Age*, 9 November 1996: A9). Contrary to received opinion, Australia is not the country with the highest youth suicide rate, something Lithuania and the Russian Federation contest (UNICEF 1996). In 1996–7 youth suicide became an object of national concern, inquiry and policy development (Taylor 1994; Commonwealth Department of Human Services and Health 1995). Governments have begun to develop targeted interventions to address the problem (Health and Community Services 1995).

A certain kind of 'sociological imagination' has also informed the evolution of socially pessimistic, even apocalyptic social commentary that has linked social change, social dislocation, globalisation and moral disorder to increased rates of youth suicide in Australia (Eckersley 1988; 1992; 1993; McDonald 1995; 1996a; 1996b). These effects, singly or in combination, are then interpreted either as causes or as symptoms of a dramatic increase in the rate of youth suicide in Australia.

Rising Rates of Youth Suicide Can Be Explained 'Sociologically' in Terms of Factors Like Unemployment

With such apparently unimpeachable data to reflect on, some social commentators make links between youth suicide and a context of social change. The Commonwealth Department of Human Services and Health (1995) report allows that:

> ... broad movements in the general male rates for death by suicide correspond with periods of economic downturn with high male rates occurring in 1912, 1930, 1962–67 and again in 1987(1995: 29).

The report cites with approval the claim that:

> The reality is that many young people do have trouble making the psycho-social adjustments of adolescence. Understandably, the very high rates of youth unemployment, the fear of joblessness, and the prevailing materialistic, worldly values that equate individual success with wealth, good looks, and power make many young people feel quite worthless and cast out by society. Fatalistic attitudes are found more and more among young people (Commonwealth Department of Human Services and Health 1995: 32–3).

(It is noteworthy that ultimately this report does not support a sociological framework for understanding youth suicide).

Apart from drawing attention to recent increases in the youth suicide rate, Eckersley has also developed a 'Durkheimian sociological' interpretation of the problem of youth suicide and its aetiology. Eckersley has linked youth suicide causally to the dramatic social economic, cultural and technological changes — aggregated as 'globalisation' — which he claims is inducing despair, moral disarray and the disintegration of key institutions such as 'the family'.

Like Durkheim, Eckersley rejects individualist and psychological explanations of suicide:

> The broader [sociological] perspective ... emphasises the fundamental social, economic, and technological changes that underlie the strains and tensions occurring in families, education and employment, and also contribute directly to people's unease about life today (Eckersley 1988: 40).

Acknowledging that there might be some problems with the official statistics on suicide — and crime and drug use, Eckersley's other indicators of social breakdown — Eckersley nevertheless claims that:

> ... the figures point unequivocally to an alarming escalation in the social and psychological problems facing young Australians today. Behind these problems are increases in family conflict and breakdown, increasing poverty, high youth unemployment, soaring youth homelessness and growing educational pressures. Underlying these developments are social, economic and technological changes that may, in themselves be imposing a growing psychological stress on children and young adults — a stress that finds bleak expression in the fear and pessimism with which many of them regard the future (Eckersley 1988: 1).

'Australians' he wrote, 'are not facing the seriousness of the predicament facing youth today. It is because of "our failures" that more young people each year become "casualties of the changes" sweeping our society' (Eckersley 1988: 1).

Suicidology: A Critique

It is neither a surprise nor perhaps any comfort to read that 'It is probable that suicide is the most unremittingly studied human behaviour' (Baechler 1979: 3). Giddens notes that as early as the 1930s there were already some 3000 bibliographic references to suicide, a figure which had undoubtably doubled by the 1970s (Giddens 1977). Nor does it necessarily help to agree with Douglas, who after surveying much of that literature decided that:

> The *ad hoc* nature of the selection of the criteria [to define suicide] — has been largely unrecognised by the students of suicide ... the result has been endless, confusing, unresolvable arguments over defining suicide (Douglas 1969 : 382).

Despite the discouraging nature of such observations, they suggest there is more to be said about the crucial assumptions that sustain a 'classical' sociological approach to youth suicide, exemplified in Durkheim's generic approach to suicide and in the contemporary approach to interpreting youth suicide as an objective 'social fact' and as evidence of social structural constraints like youth unemployment acting on the lives of individuals.

Four assumptions underpin the 'sociological approach' to youth suicide:

- Suicide as a behaviour or event is deemed to be sufficiently unequivocal or unmistakable as to be both definable and objectively measurable by official statistics.

- The youth suicide rate is not a social artefact that merely reflects administrative classification processes, coronial or community attitudes subject to change over time, but is an objective measure of youth suicides.

- The youth suicide rate is a social fact and a stable index so that any alteration and/or increase in the youth suicide rate can be used to discover or point to some significant additional or novel features which have 'explanatory' value and can be causally linked to other independent variables.

- Establishing causal links between 'independent variables' (such as a youth unemployment, hopelessness, the speed of social change, anomie, etc) and the 'dependent variable' (the youth suicide rate) is possible and desirable. Such exercises may point to significant predictive measures of young people being at risk, and such exercises may be helpful in specifying useful preventive programs.

These assumptions provide an initial analytic framework for assessing the validity of the sociological approach to suicide.

Problem 1: Defining and Measuring Suicide Rates

The problems of 'measuring' suicide rates, as with many other official statistics like crime rates are notorious (Miles and Irvine 1979: 113–29). The idea that official suicide statistics reliably indicate the actual incidence of suicide is questionable because the identification of death as suicide in official statistics depends on the use of social meanings that are shared by officials involved (Giddens 1977: 298). As Giddens explains:

> Though it may be generally agreed that an 'intention to die' is in some way a necessary characteristic of what distinguishes 'suicide' from other causes of death, there is likely to be considerable vagueness and difference between those in different regions or different countries about what constitutes adequate grounds for inferring a person's intentions, and about what other defining features are presupposed in 'suicide'. (Giddens 1977: 299).

As Harrison indicates there is often ambiguity about what kinds of activities fit the criteria for an event to regarded as a suicide (House of Representatives 1997: FCA 9). As Cicourel (1968) and Tait (1994: 60–73) suggested, there are complex social processes involved in turning interactions between officials and citizens they encounter into official statistics. Atkinson (1978) in particular stressed that it becomes clear that far from being a 'social fact, a) suicide rates are very much the product of meaningful categorisation by officials investigating certain activities, and, b) it cannot be assumed that these officials share the same meanings on which they base their interpretations. c) Therefore what eventually appears as a 'suicide' in the official statistics is in fact the result of a long process of inference and the application of whole range of commonsense notions on the part of all the people involved in the investigation of a death.

Douglas (1967:185) cited examples of coroners who refused to label a death as suicide unless a note was found with the body. It is clear Douglas says:

> ... that coroners do in fact use different operational definitions of suicide. Moreover, different coroners' offices use very different search procedures in trying in get evidence for their decisions about categorisations of causes of death. These two facts must lead us to expect that suicide statistics are incomparable even within each local area (cited in Giddens 1977: 299)

There are also problems in distinguishing between accident, foolhardiness, and homicidal and/or suicidal intention when police and/or coroners courts attempt to determine the cause of death. Atkinson (1971) reported on coroners who disregarded road accidents as possible suicides while hangings were more likely to be recorded as a suicide. Coroners also use different search procedures and take into account widely divergent physical evidence to draw their conclusions.

While there is no clear research analysis on these matters it is possible to note that between 1982–92 the number of 'undetermined deaths' in Australia rose from 47 to 190, with a major jump in 1985 when the numbers increased from 56 to 100 (ABS, *Suicides Australia 1982–92*, Cat no. 3309.0). While it is reasonable to suggest that this might mean that the suicide rate may understate the number of suicides, it is also possible that the suicide rate conceals accidents, unserious attempts at suicide which succeeded and undetected suicides.

It is important to establish whether the data is recording a consistent, changing predilection by 'victims' to commit suicide, or whether it is simply recording changes in legal, policing and community attitudes and state policies to suicide. These considerations make it very difficult to assume safely that longitudinal data sets will actually be recording data that has been classified, counted and recorded in a consistent way (re: crime rates see Mukherjee and Dagger 1990: xiii; re: suicide rates see Douglas 1967; Atkinson 1978; Anderberg 1989).

Acknowledging these difficulties, there is need for caution in inferring (as the Durkheimian tradition has encouraged us to do) that official statistics give unequivocal objective evidence of states of mind or provide examples of suicidal behaviour. Douglas (1967) appears to hold out the hope that if we apply a lot of rigour to the task we could, in principle, arrive at an accurate set of suicide data, but Giddens seems to doubt this (1977: 300).[4]

However these considerations are by themselves not reasons to deny that youth suicide has been on the rise since the 1980s. There are more serious considerations which lead us to address these questions in a particular way .

Problem 2: Suicide Rates are Social Facts and Therefore Function as Bearers of Sociologically Significant Information

The incidence of youth suicide is not the kind of social phenomena best defined as a 'social problem'. The youth suicide rate is not amenable to, nor is it appropriate to subject suicide to, social statistical treatment. *Notwithstanding press claims about 'a suicide every day', the youth suicide rate is too rare a phenomenon to be regarded as a social phenomenon amenable to sociological investigation.* Indeed given its relative rarity there is little point in pursuing the idea that it is somehow to be read as a social indicator of other social facts.

As Delmas (1932) argued some time ago, suicide is simply too rare a phenomenon to be appropriately regarded in the same light as, for example, the unemployment rate, the birth rate, the rate at which people now either contract cancer or die from such a cancer, or any other social fact however defined.

The youth suicide rate is not a socially significant fact. Delmas (1932: 49) made this point when he argued that if we highlight some increase in the rate of suicide from 10 per 100,000 in year X (or country X) to 20 per 100,000 in Year Y (or country Y) we are not pointing to anything that has *social* significance. The youth suicide rate does not have *social* significance because when we point to the suicide rate, we need to note (using the example above) that in year/country X 99,990 people did not kill themselves while in year/country Y 99,980 did not kill themselves.

It needs to be stressed that when I argue youth suicide is not a social problem, it is not being argued that youth suicide is something we all need not be concerned with. The point being made relates to the distinction between what is a 'social problem' and what is a 'personal problem' and how we can best understand such problems. C. Wright Mills' intervention makes this point clear. Mills made his point in the context of outlining what he meant by 'the sociological imagination', which he argued, entails the capacity to range from the most impersonal and remote to the most intimate features of the human self and to see the relationship between the two:

> Perhaps the most fruitful distinction with which the sociological imagination works is between 'the personal troubles of milieu' and 'the public issues of social structure' ... [Consider the issues of unemployment] [W]hen in a city of 100,000, only one man is unemployed, that is his personal trouble, and for its relief we *properly look to the character of the man, his skills and his immediate opportunities*. But when, in a nation of 50 million employees, 15 million men are unemployed, that is ... [a social] issue, and *we cannot hope to find the solution within the range of opportunities open to any one individual* (Wright Mills, in Giddens 1992: 6) (My stress).

Youth suicide is simply too rare a phenomenon to be regarded in the same light as, for example, the youth unemployment rate, to which it is frequently and erroneously linked.

Problem 3: A Naturalistic and Structuralist Sociology

Suicidology relies on the presumption that it is possible to discover causal or probabilistic links between structural factors like unemployment and outcomes like suicide. Cressey outlines succinctly the methodological assumption about good, ie 'naturalistic', research when he writes:

> A theory explaining social behaviour in general, or any specific kind of social behaviour should have two distinct but consistent aspects. First there must be a statement that explains the statistical distribution of the behaviour in time and space (epidemiology) and from which predictive statements about unknown statistical distributions can be derived. Second there must be a statement that identifies, at least by implication, the process by which individuals come to exhibit the behaviour in question, and from which can be derived predictive statements about individuals (Cited in Braithwaite 1989: 98).

In the light of Cressy's ideal it is paradoxical that the largest of suicidology's general failures has been preoccupation with generating nomothetic/predictive causal or significant correlation statements about something called the suicide rate. The most significant failure committed by those employing suicide using a macro-perspectives approach has been the obsessive search for law-like regularities, causal or significant correlations linking the suicide rate to things like the youth unemployment rate.

Suicidologists since Durkheim claim that the behaviour of persons must be analysed as elements in an over-riding set of determinate relations in which both are construed as 'products of society'. On this reading, personal action and rationality may have apparently independent effects but are actually sub-sets of society-as-the-social.

A lay-person for example, might think that if we were to 'explain' suicide we would find out why it is that people kill themselves or attempt to do so. But in so much of the sociological approach to youth suicide, there is all too often simply no account of why it is some 'do it' and others 'don't'. Potter poses the question we need to ask in a general way:

> All things being equal ... how do we explain differences in behaviour? (1992: 229).

But those sociologically-inclined suicidologists, working largely under the impress of Durkheim's doctrine of 'social facts' have persisted in trying to do two things:

1 they have tried to measure the 'suicide rate' and then tried to explain the suicide rate by testing for significant causal or correlational 'independent variables' (ie. factors that might 'explain' the suicide rate like age, gender, employment status, religious affiliation, family status or social commitment).

2 they have insisted, however ambiguously, that suicide is a 'determined activity' in which some social structural feature/s causes suicide; this ontological prejudice allows no space for the possibility that suicidal action is rationalised action, 'that is to say ... conduct carried out for reasons reflexively applied by the agents involved' (Giddens 1977: 303). (Note: this determinism is also at work in much of the bio-medical approach to suicide).

A critical sociology of the sort advocated by Giddens (1977; 1984) should require us to enquire into the efficacy of durable intellectual and methodological assumptions about such matters as the primacy of 'structure', 'society', and 'social order' in relation to 'agency'. Too many sociological researchers in suicidology assume that the positivist project (that identifies 'explanation' with 'prediction'), and a reliance on statistical generalisations is a valid epistemic approach.

The suicide rate is a statistical artefact — a set of numbers. And the pursuit of an explanation for why a set of numbers changes over time or is different between one society and another, will usually be undertaken at least by those interested in constructing other statistical artefacts. This may be like Hesse's *Glass Bead Game* which fills many hours of the day and confers great prestige on the players, but ...

These observations are the prelude to certain other observations:

- We are not entitled to draw a link between a single independent variable like unemployment and the dependent variable (suicide). As Delmas again pointed out: 'Does one have to agree, from the sociological point of view, that there is an entity that in England protects 999,460 people from suicide, but that the same entity in Saxony only protects 999,665 people?' (Delmas, 1932: 50).

- We are also not entitled to attempt to draw a link using the statistical technique of replication, between a statistically significant variable and a statistically insignificant variable. This is precisely what, for example, the Department of Health and Human Services (1995: 29) does when it draws a graph showing a general parallel increase between the unemployment rate and the youth suicide rate between 1966–1990, with the clear implication that the rising rate of youth unemployment somehow has something to do with the rising rate of suicide. Goodman (1953) and Selvin (1965) argued that the kind of ecological regression that Durkheim used to claim a link between a major social phenomenon like the incidence of Protestantism and the suicide rate attempts to link a very common factor (Protestantism) with a rare phenomenon (suicide):

No amount of replication will lead to bounds for the individual association between suicide and Protestantism or between suicide and any of Durkheim's independent variables: suicide is too rare an event, compared with the rates of the other variables (Selvin 1965: 129).

A further corollary of this is that we are not entitled to assume that associations computed from group means or group proportions are also valid estimates of the associations that would be obtained from individual data. Making this assumption is to fall into the 'ecological fallacy' (Robinson 1950). (The 'ecological fallacy is the inverted form of the attempt to claim that what is true of an individual in a group must be true of the whole group: the ecological fallacy asks us to accept that what is true of a group *as group* is true of each of its members).

To put it another way, and in more general terms, social research broadly based on, or loosely inspired by Durkheim's conception of 'social facts' and by his 'rules for sociological method' has not worked especially well.

- Firstly we are *not* entitled to move from the use of structures (to explain large scale social transformation) to particular collective action/s by 'individual' persons without falling into the fallacy of composition. Durkheim and many who follow in his footsteps infer directly from certain real or alleged macro-structural conditions of a society (eg. anomie, mass unemployment or general despair) to individual behaviour without showing us how this occurs.

- Further if we set out to understand or explain large scale social processes we must assume a degree of repetition (or what in the jargon can be called 'qualitative structural stability') in patterns of action/structure and constraint. This is needed to either generate the predictive explanations or to make the explanations work as the scientistic and 'theoretically' minded say they must.

- Further, if the 'social' is said to supply the 'grounding of reason, action and affect' why is it that the search for effective causal-predictive explanations of particular social actions has been so elusive?

The reason for the failure of the positivistically grounded search for *causality in invariant relations* that constrain people to behave in predicted ways — and even when 'causality' is redefined in a less strict version to probability statements — has been clearly identified by Stanley Cohen and by Katz (1988). The following amendment of Katz's critique of empiricist criminology makes the point clearly:

1 Many of those in the identified causal categories (eg. young unemployed people, people from broken families) do not commit suicide.

2 Many people who do commit suicide do not fit the causal categories.

3 Many who do fit the background categories and later committed suicide, go for long periods without committing or attempting to commit the self destruction to which the theory directs them.

Such sociological accounts of suicide fail to offer a 'theory' which says why some individuals actually commit suicide. Equally importantly they also fail to identify why other people do *not* commit suicide. The fact that large numbers of young people do *not* kill themselves is a reminder that *the genuinely widespread experience* of 'family breakdowns', social transformations, unemployment and poverty is being mediated by other important, individual level variables when it comes to the decisions taken by some young people to kill themselves.

Conclusion

Youth suicide is a painful and difficult issue, but this should neither prevent nor dissuade us from thinking about it intelligently. Nor should that difficulty discourage seeking more insight into an issue that is generating so much community concern, a concern we are legitimately entitled to feel when numbers of young people are killing themselves. Death by suicide by any young person, apart from the obvious pain and misery the young person concerned experiences, is distressing and devastating for those closely connected to that young person. Anderberg's point, unpalatable as it is to those who believe everything is in principle determinable and knowable, nonetheless holds that:

> The *individual* suicide is a mystery and so will suicide as *a category* remain ... it is not likely that there is one component gluing together all of the diverse phenomenena brought together under the title 'suicide' (1989:165).

Endnotes

1   This paper is part of an ongoing project in collaboration with Dr Judith Bessant, Sociology and Youth studies, ACU, Oakleigh. We gratefully acknowledge a very illuminating paper sent to us by Dr Peter Whiteford and very useful discussions with Prof. Robert Kosky, University of Adelaide.

2   I certainly do not assume (a) that all sociologists would acknowledge that this paradigm encompasses everything that 'sociology' was, or is, or that the only researchers working on suicide are sociologists. But given the pervasive appeal of these arguments they seem to be worthy of detailed critical examination.

3   This is not to deny the role played within medicine and psychiatry of a strong preference for a bio-medical model of suicide grounded in claims about the chemical-genetic basis of depressive illnesses linked to suicide.

4   Even approaches like those of Douglas seem to produce a deterministic theory of suicide , which provides little if any room for human agency and the possibility that suicide can be understood as a rational action. The prospect that suicide could be attempted or completed, as Giddens explained, for 'reasons reflexively applied by the agents involved' is not provided for even in Douglas' interactionist approach (Giddens, 1977: 303).

Bibliography And References

ABS 1993, *Suicides Australia 1982–1992*, Cat. no. 3309.0, ABS. Canberra.

ABS 1994, *Trends in Mortality by Cause of Death in Australia*, cat no 3313. 0, ABS. Canberra.

Anderberg, T. 1989 *Suicide: Definitions, Causes, and Values*, Lund University Press, Lund.

Atkinson, J. 1971, 'Societal reactions to suicide: the role of coroners definitions', in *Images of Deviance*, ed. Cohen, S. Penguin, Harmondsworth.

Atkinson, J. 1978, *Discovering Suicide*, Macmillan, London.

Baechler, J. 1979, *Suicides*, (trans.) Basic Books, New York.

Braithwaite, J. 1988 *Crime, Shame and Reintegration*, Cambridge University Press, Cambridge.

Delmas, A. 1932, *Psychologie, Pathologie du Suicide*, Clement, Paris.

Department of Health and Human Services 1995, *Youth Suicide In Australia: A Background monograph*, AGPS, Canberra.

Douglas, J. 1967, *The Social Meaning of Suicide*, Princeton University Press, Princeton.

Durkheim, E. 1964, *The Rules of Sociological Method*, Free Press, New York.

Durkheim, E. 1970, *Suicide*, Routledge & Kegan Paul, London (first ed. 1897) ed. G. Simpson.

Eckersley, R. 1988, *Casualties of Change: The Predicament of Youth in Australia*, Australia's Commission for the Future, AGPS, Melbourne.

Eckersley, R. 1992, *Apocalypse No! Youth and the Challenge to Change*, Australia's Commission for the Future, Essay series No.1. ACF. Melbourne.

Eckersley, R. 1993, 'The West's Deepening Cultural Crisis', *The Futurist*, November December, pp. 8–12.

Eckersley, R. 1995, 'Value and Visions: Youth and the failure of modern Western Culture', *Youth Studies Australia*, V14(1): 13–17.

Eckersley, R. 1996, in Australasian Science and Technology Council, *Having Our Say about the Future: Young People's Dreams and Expectations for Australia in 2010 and the role of Science and Technology*, Commonwealth of Australia, Canberra, pp. 60–65.

Giddens, A. 1977, 'A Theory of Suicide', in *Studies in Social and Political Theory*, Hutchinson, London.

Giddens, A. 1977, *Studies in Social and Political Theory*, Hutchinson, London.

Giddens, A. 1979, *Central Problems of Social Theory: Action, Structure and Contradiction in Social Analyisis*, Macmillan, London.

Giddens, A. 1984, *The Constitution of Society*, Polity Press, Cambridge.

Giddens, A. 1991, 'Structuration Theory: Past Present and Future', in Bryant, C. and Jary, C. eds, 1991, *Giddens' Theory of Structuration: a critical appreciation*, Routledge, London.

Giddens, A. 1993, *The Consequences of Modernity*, Polity press, Cambridge,.

Goodman, L. 1953, 'Ecological regression and the behaviour of Individuals', *American Sociological Review*, V. XVIII: 663–64.

Hassan, R. & Carr, J. 1989, 'Changing Patterns of Suicide in Australia', *Australian and New Zealand Journal of Psychiatry*, V23: 226–234.

Hassan, R. 1987, 'Lives Unlived: Youth Suicide in Australia', Paper to *The Youth Suicide: The Australian Experience Conference*, Prince Henry's Hospital; Sydney November.

Health and Community Services, 1995, *Mental Health Services: Current Youth Suicide Prevention Activities in Victoria*, Psychiatric Services Division, HACS, Melbourne.

House of Representatives 1997, Standing Committee on Family and Community Affairs: Aspects of Youth Suicide, 28 February

Katz, J. 1988, *Seductions of Crime*, Basic Books, New York.

Kosky, R. 1987, 'Is Suicidal behaviour increasing among Australian youth?' *the Medical Journal of Australia*, V147, August.

McDonald, K. 1995, 'Morals is all you've got', *Arena Magazine*, December, pp. 18–23.

McDonald, K. 1996a, 'The Uncertain family', *Arena Magazine*, July pp. 38–41.

McDonald, K. 1996b 'The Other Side of Identity Politics', *Arena Magazine*, December pp. 5–7.

Mental Health Branch, Commonwealth Department of Human Services and Health, 1995, *Here For Life: A National Plan for Youth in Distress*, Commonwealth of Australia, Canberra.

Miles, I. & Irvine, J. 1979, 'The Critique of Official Statistics', in *Demystifying Official Statistics* Irvine, eds. J., Miles, I. & Evans, J., Pluto, London.

Potter, R.H. 1992, 'Crime Shame and Reintegration: Review, Questions and Comments', *ANZ Journal of Sociology* V28 (2): 13–19

Robinson, W. 1950, 'Ecological Correlation and the Behaviour of individuals', *American Sociological Review*, Vol. XV: 351–57.

Selvin, H. 1965, 'Durkheim's' *Suicide*,', in *Emile Durkheim*, ed. R. Nisbet, Prentice Hall, Englewood Cliffs.

Special Health Services Section, Commonwealth Department of Human Services and Health 1995, *Youth Suicide in Australia: a Background monograph*. AGPS, Canberra.

Taylor, B. 1994, *The Prevention of youth Suicide and Self harm: Promoting Intersectoral Action*, Victorian Health Promotion Foundation, Melbourne.

Wright Mills, C. 1992, 'The Sociological Imagination and the promise of sociology', in *Human Societies: An Introductory Reader in Sociology*, ed. Anthony Giddens, Polity Press, Cambridge, pp. 5–7.

Labour Market Programmes: Improvements in the Employment Prospects of Those Assisted

Derek Pigram and Michael Cameron

This paper summarises the findings of a study into the impact of labour market programmes on the job prospects of those assisted. The study, conducted by the Department of Employment, Education, Training and Youth Affairs (DEETYA), compared the unsubsidised employment levels of former programme participants with those of similar people who had not been assisted (controlling for key criteria such as duration of unemployment, age and gender). The study extended upon earlier programme evaluation research and for the first time examined the effect of programmes in reducing income support dependency.

The forms of assistance included in the study were JobStart wage subsidies, job search training in Job Clubs, work skills training delivered through JobTrain and SkillShare, and work experience under the JobSkills and New Work Opportunities (NWO) brokered employment programmes. The findings of the study were consistent with those of earlier departmental research in that all programmes were shown to improve the employment levels of participants. JobStart wage subsidies were found to have the greatest impact. Other programmes, which generally catered for people who were more disadvantaged, were shown to result in more modest gains.

All forms of assistance were found to bring about reductions in income support dependency. JobStart wage subsidies were again shown to have the greatest impact, with Job Clubs and JobSkills producing more moderate results. Small reductions in Department of Social Security (DSS) income support register numbers were attributable to JobTrain, SkillShare and NWO, with substantial proportions of employed former SkillShare and JobTrain participants remaining registered for benefits while in part-time, temporary or casual work.

Scope of the study

The scope of the study was determined primarily on the basis of programme expenditure and participant numbers. The programmes selected accounted for close to 70 percent of the clients assisted in 1995–96 and around $1.4 billion in expenditure. Placement numbers in the year ranged from approximately 46,000 for Job Clubs to 165,000 for SkillShare. Expenditure ranged from $30 million for Job Clubs to $498 million for NWO[1].

Programmes can of course have a range of benefits (as examples, brokered employment projects often drew on community needs and initiatives, while JobStart wage subsidies have the potential to result in the creation of additional jobs), some of which have been addressed in other departmental research. The study reported here was confined to examining the impact of programmes on the participants' chances of securing unsubsidised employment and consequently reducing their reliance on income support.

Methodology

Information on the employment and DSS registration status of the people included in the study was gathered by survey and compiled from departmental information systems between May and June 1996. The outcomes of programme participants were measured 3 months after the end of their participation. Programme participants were registered for income support at the time of commencing their placements. Non-participants were registered for income support at the end of February 1996. Some of the people who were registered with DSS while in part-time, temporary or casual work at the time of outcomes measurement would have been receiving reduced benefit payments. The available data did not extend to details of these reductions.

Programme participants and non-participants were matched on the basis of gender, age (in 5 year groupings) and duration of unemployment (in 2 month groupings). Departmental research has consistently shown that duration of unemployment, age and gender are major predictors of employment outcomes. As a consequence, accounting for age and gender, and in particular closely matching on duration of unemployment, would greatly diminish the potential influence of other factors on the measurement of employment outcomes levels. Notwithstanding this, sensitivity analysis was conducted to test for the possible impact of additional variables. Weighting for factors such as equity group membership (eg. the proportions of migrants with English language difficulties within the programme and non-participant groups), educational attainment and geographical location did not alter the study's findings.

JobStart — Wage Subsidies

The JobStart wage subsidy programme provided access to employment for job seekers who, because of long periods of unemployment or other difficulties, were unable to compete on an equal footing in the labour market. Job seekers finding work or placed into jobs by the Commonwealth Employment Service (CES) received support in the form of subsidies paid to their employers. Differing rates and duration of subsidy applied in accordance with job seeker age, educational attainment and length of unemployment. There were just over 100,000 placements in 1995–96, around 63 percent of which went to the long term unemployed. The net unit cost per JobStart placement, taking into account the estimated savings to government that could accrue through a person's participation, was $1,263[2].

As would be expected on the basis of previous departmental research (Byrne 1993), JobStart was found to significantly improve the employment prospects of participants. Three months after the end of subsidy payments, 50 percent of participants were in work, compared to 22 percent of similar unemployed people who were not assisted.

JobStart wage subsidies were also shown to be highly effective in reducing dependence on income support. Forty-three percent of former JobStart participants were in unsubsidised work and had left the DSS register. An additional 7 percent were in part-time temporary or casual work while remaining registered for allowance payments (some of these people would have received reduced income support payments as a result of their earnings from part time or casual employment[3]).

Of comparable unemployed people who were not assisted, 13 percent were in unsubsidised jobs and no longer registered with DSS. An additional 9 percent were in work, but remained registered for income support.

It is important to note that while participant and non-participant groups were matched on a range of criteria, the unobserved characteristics of motivation and skill levels could explain some part of the net impact found for JobStart. At the time of commencing JobStart placements, clients were assessed by employers as being potentially 'job ready', reflecting judgements as to appropriate levels of motivation and work related skills. In comparison, other unemployed people could have been less well prepared for work.

Job Clubs — Job Search Training

The Job Clubs programme provided individuals with intensive instruction in job search techniques. Job Club members were supported in their work search efforts through guidance and encouragement from a leader and other members. Participation was designed to improve the clients' chances of finding employment by re-building their self esteem and self confidence, developing their job search skills and increasing their job search efforts. Job Clubs participants were generally assessed as being potentially 'job ready' before commencing in the programme. Around 46,000 people were assisted through Job Clubs in 1995–96 with 62 percent being long term unemployed. The estimated net unit cost or cost per placement of Job Clubs was $625.

As is consistent with both earlier departmental research and the broader international experience with job search training (Redway and Patston 1994; Fay 1996; Bewick 1997), Job Clubs was shown to have a beneficial impact on participant outcomes.

Compared to 24 percent of those who were not assisted, 3 months after leaving the programme, 36 percent of former Job Clubs participants were in unsubsidised work. Job Clubs was also shown to have a positive effect in reducing reliance on income support.

Twenty percent of former Job Clubs participants were in unsubsidised work and had left the DSS register, compared to 14 percent of non-participants. An additional 16 percent of Job Clubs participants and 10 percent of non-participants were in work while remaining registered.

JobTrain and SkillShare — Work Skills Training

JobTrain was designed to provide the long term unemployed and other disadvantaged job seekers with formal training opportunities. The CES let contracts for the provision of courses and bought places on existing courses to meet the needs of local job seekers and the skill needs of the local labour market. Training providers included TAFE and community based organisations, private training agencies and industry bodies. Average course length was eight to ten weeks. There were around 93,000 JobTrain commencements in 1995–96 with 63 percent of places taken up by the long term unemployed. The estimated net unit cost of JobTrain was $1,173.

SkillShares provided assistance to close to 165,000 clients in 1995–96, with 57 percent of these people being long term unemployed. SkillShares were administered by community organisations and partially funded through the support of local communities. SkillShares assisted the long term unemployed and other job seekers with significant barriers to employment in finding work or gaining entry to further education and training. This was achieved through skills training, employment related assistance (including personal support and referral) and enterprise activities. Around 60 percent of SkillShare assisted people participated in formal training courses, with the remainder receiving support through access to self-help facilities and informal assistance. The estimated net unit cost of SkillShare was $970.

As would be expected on the basis of earlier research on SkillShare (DEET 1993) and JobTrain (DEET 1994), the improvements in employment levels resulting from participation in these programmes were found to be modest.

Three months after leaving programme assistance, 30 percent of SkillShare participants were in unsubsidised work. In comparison, 23 percent of non-participants were in jobs. For JobTrain, the employment outcomes levels of participants and non-participants were 31 percent and 24 percent respectively.

The extent to which employment related training or assistance provided through SkillShare and JobTrain resulted in reduced dependence on income support was found to be far less than was the case for either JobStart or Job Clubs. Over two thirds of the increase in employment levels resulting from SkillShare and JobTrain was associated with participants who were in temporary, casual or part time jobs while remaining registered with DSS.

Fifteen percent of JobTrain participants were in unsubsidised jobs and had left the DSS register, compared to 14 percent of non-participants. An additional 16 percent of JobTrain participants and 10 percent of non-participants were in jobs while remaining registered for income support.

Sixteen percent of SkillShare participants were in unsubsidised jobs and had left the DSS register, compared to 14 percent of non-participants. An additional 14 percent of SkillShare participants and 9 percent of non-participants were in jobs while remaining registered for income support.

JobSkills and New Work Opportunities — Brokered Employment

Brokered employment programmes involved community groups, local councils and commercial organisations being contracted to establish and manage projects with the objective of providing training and work experience to improve the job prospects of the long term unemployed.

JobSkills brokers provided assistance to people of 21 years of age and over who had been unemployed for 12 months or more. JobSkills placements were of 26 weeks duration with participants receiving a mix of supervised work experience and structured on the job or off the job training. Around 40 percent of the participant's time was allocated to training. There were over 27,000 JobSkills placements in 1995–96 with 96 percent being for the long term unemployed. The estimated net unit cost of JobSkills was $7,105.

The New Work Opportunities (NWO) programme funded projects that provided 26 weeks of work experience and training for the long term unemployed. Work and training placements were approved on the basis that they were additional to normal staffing levels, with NWO funded projects drawing on the initiatives and needs of the local community. There were over 49,000 NWO placements in 1995–96 with 93 percent being taken up by the long term unemployed. The estimated net unit cost of NWO was $10,009.

The findings on JobSkills were consistent with those of earlier research (Madigan and Murphy 1996) in that, when compared to those not assisted, former participants were more likely to be in unsubsidised work (30 percent compared to 19 percent). NWO was shown to have a small impact on employment prospects with 21 percent of participants in work, compared to 17 percent of non-participants.

The JobSkills brokered employment programme was shown to have a moderate impact on DSS allowee numbers. The impact of NWO in terms of reducing dependence on income support was small. Twenty-two percent of JobSkills participants were in unsubsidised jobs and had left the DSS register, compared to 11 percent of non-participants. There was no difference in proportions of participants and non-participants who were working while remaining registered for income support (8 percent for both groups).

Fourteen percent of NWO participants were in unsubsidised jobs and had left the DSS register, compared to 10 percent of non-participants. There was no difference in proportions of participants and non-participants who were working while remaining registered for income support (7 percent for both groups).

Conclusions

JobStart wage subsidies, job search training in Job Clubs, work skills training in SkillShare and JobTrain, and work experience gained through JobSkills and NWO were all shown to improve the participant's chances of finding unsubsidised work. Each programme was found to result in reduced dependence on income support with the extent of the reduction varying in accordance with the programme's impact on participant job prospects.

While the conclusions of international research are not entirely consistent (Fay 1996; Bewick 1997), the findings on Australian labour market programmes correspond with overseas evidence showing that wage subsidies and job search training are effective ways of assisting the unemployed to find work. JobStart wage subsidies were found to have a pronounced impact on participant job prospects. Job search training in Job Clubs produced a smaller gain, but at a lower cost per participant.

It was notable that most of the gains in employment levels following work skills training in SkillShare and JobTrain involved part-time, temporary or casual work that did not disqualify participants from income support registration. Nonetheless, the people who undertook placements in JobTrain and SkillShare would generally have been more disadvantaged than those assisted through JobStart and Job Clubs, and work skills training was found to achieve positive results at a moderate cost per participant.

The JobSkills and NWO programmes were directed towards people who faced serious and multiple barriers to employment. These people would of course need significant preparatory assistance before being in a position to compete for available jobs in the open employment market. However, the work experience provided through brokered employment programmes was not shown to be a particularly cost effective form of assistance. While JobSkills was found to result in a worthwhile improvement in participant job prospects, this was achieved at a cost per participant around 6 times higher than that of the work skills training delivered by JobTrain and SkillShare. NWO, by far the most expensive of all programmes with a cost per participant that exceeded $10,000, produced an improvement in participant employment levels of just 4 percentage points.

Endnotes

1 Readers should note that a full summary of DEETYA studies into the impact of programmes on participant job prospects has been published by the department (Pigram et al. 1997). This summary includes additional income support registration data and detailed estimates of the costs associated with achieving employment outcomes.

2 The method for calculating net unit costs was developed in consultation with the Department of Social Security (DSS), the Department of Finance and the Treasury. Net unit costs are derived from the average gross unit cost of assistance and estimated savings in Jobsearch and Newstart Allowance (JSA/NSA) payments accruing to DSS as a result of job seekers participating in programmes (both during and after their participation). The formula for calculation includes a range of parameters amongst which are the duration of programme assistance, the proportion of participants on JSA/NSA and average JSA/NSA rates. Net unit costs calculations do not take into account the secondary impacts of programmes resulting from improved labour market efficiency, for example, through either reduced pressure on wages growth or any impact on interest rates.

3 The income support data available on the people included in this study did not extend to details of reductions in allowance payments due to earnings. DSS statistics relating to payment fortnights in mid 1996, show that in the order of 4 percent of people registered for Job Search and Newstart allowances did not receive a payment. Of those who did receive a payment, around 17 percent also had earned income.

References

Bewick T. 1997, Active labour market policies: aA solution to unemployment?, *Working Brief*, Issue 83, April 1997, pp 17–21.

Byrne A. 1993, *An Evaluation of JobStart*, Department of Employment, Education and Training, EMB Report 2/93.

Department of Employment, Education and Training DEET 1993, *Evaluation of SkillShare*, EMB Report 5/93.

Department of Employment, Education and Training DEET 1994, *Summary Evaluation of JobTrain*, EMB Report 4/93.

Fay, R.G. 1996, *Enhancing the Effect of Labour Market Policies: Evidence from Programme Evaluations in OECD Countries*, Labour Market and Social Policy Occasional Paper no. 18, OECD, Paris.

Madigan S. and Murphy K. 1996, *Evaluation of the JobSkills Program*, Department of Employment, Education, Training and Youth Affairs, EMB Report 7/96.

Pigram, D., Cameron M., Lipp R., George A. and Szabo D. 1997, *The Net Impact of Labour Market Programmes: Improvements in the Employment Prospects of Those Assisted*, Department of Employment, Education, Training and Youth Affairs, EMB Report 2/97.

Redway D. and Patston K. 1994, *Net Impact Study of Job Clubs*, Department of Employment, Education and Training, EMB Report 5/94.

Case Managing Unemployment: A Comparative Perspective

Tony Eardley

The persistence of long-term unemployment in industrialised countries has led to a shift towards 'active' labour market policies. Increasingly, techniques of case management, borrowed from social work and other human services, are being applied to the delivery of labour market programs.

This paper draws on an international comparative review of the operation and impact of tailored job search assistance programs. Although there is evidence that individually-tailored assistance can have some impact, it is often at the expense of other unemployed people. Much of the effect is also achieved through deterrence and enforcement of activity testing. As yet, however, evaluations have been unable fully to open the 'black box' of service and delivery processes in case management, which act as a gateway to other programs and services. While it may make sense for other reasons to adopt individually-tailored assistance, the question is still open as to whether case management by itself has any major impact on long-term unemployment.

Over the last 20 years case management has become a dominant paradigm for service delivery in a wide range of fields. Its application to employment services is more recent, starting in the United States in welfare-to-work programs and gradually gaining a foothold in many of the industrialised countries as part of the shift from 'passive' to 'active' labour market policies. Australia, however, was the first OECD country to adopt an explicit national program of case management in its employment services.

The basic principle underlying case management is that of working outwards from the needs of individuals to pull together resources from different agencies — thus aiming to make provision 'client-shaped' rather than 'service-shaped'. This idea has much to recommend it. Yet there is relatively little solid evidence internationally about what the individualised assistance model in employment services actually achieves and how it works.

This paper attempts to provide some answers to these questions, drawing on a review of the international experience of case management-type interventions within labour market programs, commissioned by the New Zealand Department of Labour (Eardley and Thompson 1997). The first part of the paper briefly discusses the concept of case management and its application to services for unemployed people. I then turn to the question 'what do we know about what works?'.

What is Case Management?

The term 'case management' is generally recognised as deriving from the United States, as a response to the difficulties faced by people moving out of residential care in the de-institutionalisation process during the 1960s. The shortcomings of the fragmented and uncoordinated network of human services which grew out of this process led, in the 1970s, to a series of demonstration projects aimed at service integration and coordinated community support (Turner and Schiffren 1979).

Since then, the case management approach has become a model for client-driven service delivery wherever the demand for coordination, rationalisation and accountability has arisen. In the United Kingdom, for example, in the 1980s, it emerged in projects concerned with the delivery of care services for older people outside institutional settings and has since become a key feature of social work practice under the new 'care in the community' framework. In Australia the term 'case management' is now in use not only in community services and employment assistance, but also areas such as the Court system.

However, this expansion in the use of case management has brought some conceptual difficulties. While it has become accepted as a key tool for engaging with a set of societal problems, the character of case management has become 'indistinct and amorphous' (Rothman 1992:1). Rose (1992), for example, has argued that it must involve advocacy within a 'system reform strategy' aimed at tackling the lack of client-centred resources in organisational patterns of service delivery. Yet case management is also frequently regarded by governments as primarily a means to improve efficiency and contain costs in service delivery — central aims of the UK community care reforms, for example.

This paradox is of some importance in the context of case management for job seekers and underlies some of the differences in approach evident in the Australian experience. Gursansky and Kennedy (1997) have argued that the concept of case management is fraught with theoretical and practical ambiguities, and has taken on different meanings within the new public service managerialism.

Thus, although there may be broad agreement on the basic principle of case management, the literature shows that there are many important dimensions within which practices vary. These include:

- whether case management for an individual client is carried out by a single worker or can be delegated to other workers or agencies;
- the size of caseloads;
- the degree of client contact;
- the level of control over external resources exercised by case managers;
- enforcement of client participation.

The last point is in fact rarely addressed in the human services literature on case management, although the question of coercion clearly exists in areas such as child protection, probation and parole, and is one of the more controversial aspects of the use of case management in employment services.

What Do We Know About What Works?

As was stated earlier, Australia was the first country to adopt a national program of case management for job seekers and is one of the only countries to contract out substantial parts of its delivery to non-government providers. Other countries have tried elements of the approach in special schemes or experiments, or have introduced degrees of individualised assistance into their general schemes. The evidence here thus draws on a wide range of different types of program which have some features of the individualised assistance model.

Detailed information on how programs operate on the ground is hard to come by, except in a few countries. Also, the case management elements of programs are often inseparable from broader packages of policy. Nevertheless, it does appear that assistance aimed at improving the effectiveness of job search is, compared to other forms of labour market program, relatively effective for most groups of unemployed people (though less so for the young unemployed), and produces modest reductions in unemployment rolls. This is supported by evaluations of the Belgian 'Work Again' scheme (Geer 1992), France's Project 900,000 (OECD 1993), the Job Opportunities Program, Reorientation Interviews and another experimental counselling scheme in the Netherlands (van den Berg and van der Veer 1992; Bouman, cited in OECD 1993; Gorter and Kalb 1996), Restart and a number of other programs in the UK (White and Lakey 1992; Birtwhistle 1994; Dolton and O'Neil 1996), and Job Action in New Zealand (New Zealand Department of Labour 1995). The only substantive evidence to the contrary is that from a number of Canadian projects for the re-employment of recently retrenched workers, where job search assistance programs appeared to have had little impact, or even to have had a negative effect by delaying clients' actual job seeking (Human Resources Canada 1992; Ekos Research Associates 1993). This points to the need to keep the job search continuing even while people are participating in programs.

Nevertheless, what seems inescapable from all the international evidence is that in the absence of substantial job growth much of the impact of these interventions is to redistribute opportunities among the unemployed, especially between the short-term and long-term unemployed. This is not necessarily a negative effect *per se*. Given the corrosive effect of long-term unemployment, helping people to avoid extended periods without work can be a legitimate aim of public policy. But if the move off unemployment benefits becomes a carousel or revolving door, not only is this a dispiriting and infuriating experience for participants but it may also damage their future prospects through what Judith Sloan (1993) has called 'scarring' — the identification by employers of people whose employment program experience suggests that they may be poor employment risks.

So how do these individually-tailored interventions achieve their impacts? There seem to be three main elements. First, assessment or profiling of job seekers allows decisions to be made about whether and when to provide a particular type or level of assistance. These initial assessments are important in that they can identify those who might be at risk of falling into long-term unemployment. They also help to minimise deadweight effects by screening out people likely to find work unaided. There seems to be a strong argument for testing different kinds of assessment instruments for this purpose.

A second stage of assessment, used in some countries, aims to categorise the level of disadvantage faced by job seekers. The Australian experience suggests that this can be a useful way of allocating funding, in order to minimise creaming of easier-to-assist clients, but more work is needed on the measures involved. Client assessment tools developed in the USA may be of help (see, for example, Means et al. 1993), but profiling of clients in this way does not in itself give any clear indication of what sort of interventions would be the most effective for particular groups of job seekers. There is also a danger that problems or disadvantages faced by some long-term unemployed people may be reinterpreted as a psychiatric or psychological dysfunction. As Gosden (1997) argues, such labelling may become a convenient explanation for the 'inadequacies' of people who lose out in the competition for scarce jobs.

It is not clear at what point intervention is most effective in the duration of unemployment. Initial assessment to identify those at risk seems important. After that, the UK evidence seems to suggest that more intensive help at six months may be necessary. It was hoped that the evaluation of the *Working Nation* programs might also shed some light on this question, but administrative problems which led to delays in clients accessing assistance made it virtually impossible to determine the impact of interventions at different stages of unemployment.

The second way in which individually-tailored schemes operate is through the use of individual action plans or contracts with clients to specify what steps the client should follow to improve their prospects and what assistance will be provided in return. The literature suggests that the key to effective action plans is in working closely with clients according to their individual needs, rather than prescribing 'off the peg' solutions or routine plans of activity. This allows for appropriate referrals to other services, training schemes or job placements, and for clients to 'own' their plans. One point emphasised by Nicaise et al. (1995), in a review of European labour market programs, is that action plans or counselling for the unemployed should aim at all times to keep clients routed towards the goal of unsubsidised employment, even if only in the longer term. Otherwise long-term unemployed people especially run the risk of continually being recycled around dead-end or segmented special schemes.

However, the implication of any contract is that it is in some way enforceable. This leads to the third and perhaps the most controversial element of case management, which is the link with benefit control and surveillance of clients' compliance with activity testing. Evidence from many of the US schemes, and from the programs cited above suggests that they achieve a substantial part of their effect, in terms of public expenditure savings, by deterring claims or by enforcing activity through threat of sanctions.

Some may regard this as a positive effect, but little is known about what happens to people who are deterred and there is some evidence that excessive activity testing can actually divert effort from effective job seeking. In the UK context, Bryson and Jacobs (1992) have argued that increasing enforcement can have perverse effects, penalising those foolish or honest enough not to provide the 'right' answers to forms or interviews while leaving untouched the hard-core 'workshy'. Tough enforcement of sanctions may also end up being applied unevenly, and thus unfairly, if some staff are less comfortable with this approach. There can be particular difficulties in reconciling the watchdog and counsellor role where case management is contracted out to non-government providers, as in Australia (Thompson 1995).

One aspect of the coercive nature of individualised assistance is the practice of directing clients into any job available, on the principle that 'any job is better than none'. The GAIN program in Riverside County, California has attracted considerable interest for apparently demonstrating that such an approach can produce substantial welfare savings and improvements in client earnings. However, even its official evaluators urge some caution about the results (Riccio and Orenstein 1996), and analysis by Peck (1996) suggests that the Riverside model has been oversold, appearing successful only in comparison with the poor results of most US welfare-to work programs. The Employment Policy Institute has also pointed to the insecure work and poverty-level wages achieved by clients (who are mainly sole parents), and has argued that applying the Riverside approach more generally could have a highly detrimental effect on local labour markets by driving down already low wages (Mishel and Schmitt 1995).

On the other hand, some evidence from the UK Restart scheme suggests that getting into even a poor job may still be helpful as a way into a better one (White and Lakey 1992). The problem comes where jobs turn out to be highly temporary or inappropriate. Community sector case managers in Australia have argued that any funding system for employment services has to take a longer view about clients' incremental achievements rather than being driven by narrow, short-term outcome measures. The new structure of employment assistance which is to be introduced in 1998 places more emphasis on longer-term outcomes, but also on unsubsidised jobs as the preferable form of outcome. It remains to be seen how the new incentive structure will affect the kinds of help offered to job seekers.

In the US, a few studies have begun to trace the links between different ways of organising case management and overall program effectiveness (Doolittle and Riccio 1992; Riccio and Orentstein 1996). There seem to be a series of trade-offs: first, between relatively low-cost provision for a large, general caseload and intensive assistance for more tightly targeted groups; and secondly between the size of caseloads for individual case managers and the level of assistance possible. Evidence from one study where the effects of having different size caseloads have been assessed, seems to suggest that smaller loads were not necessarily more effective. It appeared that levels of 100–150 clients per case manager may provide an optimum balance between service and cost-effectiveness, though this will depend on the nature of the clientele. However, caseloads above this level in the Australian public case management service have tended to reinforce problems of poor training and skills which lead to ineffective outcomes (Thompson 1995; DEETYA 1996).

There is little hard evidence as yet on the impact of contracting out case management to the non-governmental and private sectors. The Australian experience was the first major national test of this policy. Although initial results were encouraging in the sense that contracted case managers were achieving comparable results to those of the public employment service, a number of problems with the competitive framework remained to be addressed.

In general the evidence as to what specific contribution case management has made to the wider outcomes of labour market programs is scarce. The policy shift following the 1996 Budget means that the original structure was only in place for a short period, which makes it difficult to reach a mature assessment of its effectiveness. It is also not clear that the methods of evaluation available would provide a definitive answer, since there has been no attempt to test the counterfactual through any kind of randomised trials. However, the Employment Services Regulatory Authority and Deakin University are currently undertaking research on the day-to-day activities involved in case management, which may help in opening up what is still largely a 'black box'.

The new structure for employment services outlined in the 1996 Budget represents a further shift in competition policy, from an idea of partnership between complementary but different sectors (as proposed in Labor's Green Paper), through managed competition by tender between sectors treated as similar (under *Working Nation*), to a fully contestable market. There are still many unanswered questions about how this will work in practice and whether, in the context of a much reduced budget for employment services, it will have any beneficial effects for job seekers.

Conclusion

Evidence from the US, the UK, Australia and to lesser extent from other European countries does suggest that individually-tailored approaches to employment assistance can have some impact, but information is still lacking about the most effective ways of organising such services. No evaluations as yet have been able fully to unravel the particular effect on unemployment which stems from interventions like case management, which act as a gateway to a host of other programs and services. Thus, while it may make sense for other reasons to adopt individually-tailored assistance, the question is still open as to whether case management by itself has any major impact on long-term unemployment.

References

Birtwhistle, A. 1994, *Jobplan Evaluation: Summary of Findings*, Research and Evaluation Branch Paper No.100, Employment Service, Sheffield.

Bryson, A. and J. Jacobs 1992 *Policing the Workshy*, Avebury, Aldershot.

Department of Employment, Education and Training and Youth Affairs 1996, *Working Nation: Evaluation of the Employment, Education and Training Elements*, EMB Report, AGPS, Canberra.

Dolton, P. and D. O'Neill 1996, Unemployment duration and the Restart effect: Some experimental evidence, *The Economic Journal*, V106, March, pp 387–400.

Doolittle, F. and J. Riccio 1992, Case management in welfare employment programs, in *Evaluating Welfare and Training Programs*, eds. C. Manski and I. Garfinkel, Harvard University Press, Cambridge, pp310–344.

Ekos Research Associates 1993, *Industrial Adjustment Services Program Evaluation*, Ottawa.

Geers, F. 1992, New strategies to combat long-term unemployment in Belgium, *International Journal of Manpower*, V13(2): 55–65.

Gorter, C. and G. Kalb 1996, Estimating the effect of counselling and monitoring the unemployed using a job search model, *Journal of Human Resources*, V31 (3): 590–610.

Gosden, R 1997, Shrinking the dole queue, *Arena*, V29: 39–41.

Gursansky, D. and R. Kennedy 1997, *Discourses of case management: A labour market program case study*, paper given to the 4th Conference on Unemployment, University of South Australia, 20 June.

Human Resources Development Canada 1992, *Evaluation of the Claimant Re-employment Service*, Job Creation and Employment Services Division, Program Evaluation Branch.

Means, B., N. Bross, E. Schaeffer, D. Kogan, F. Kelley and S. Golan 1993, *Improving Assessment for JTPA: A Technical Assistance Guide*, unpublished report for the US Department of Labor by SRI International, April.

Mishel, L. and J. Schmitt 1995, *Cutting Welfare: The Impact of Reform on the Low-wage Labour Market*, Briefing Paper 58, Economic Policy Institute, Washington D.C.

New Zealand Department of Labour 1995, *Evaluation of Job Action*, Wellington.

Nicaise, I., J. Bollens, L. Dawes, S. Laghaei, I. Thaulow, M. Verdie and A. Wagner 1995, Pitfalls and dilemmas in labour market policies for disadvantaged groups

— and how to avoid them, *Journal of European Social Policy*, V5(3): 199–217.

OECD 1993a, *Employment Outlook*, OECD, Paris, July.

Peck, J. 1996, Workfare California style: What lessons for Britain?, *Working Brief*, No. 77, Aug–Sept, 26–29.

Riccio, J. and A. Orenstein 1996, Understanding best practices for operating welfare-to-work programs, *Evaluation Review*, V20(1), Feb: 3–28.

Rose, S. 1992, *Case Management and Social Work Practice*, Longman, New York.

Rothman, J. 1992, *Guidelines for Case Management: Putting Research to Professional Use*, F.E. Peacock, Itasca.

Sloan, J. 1993, Some policy responses to long-term unemployment, *The Australian Economic Review*, 2nd Quarter: 35–40.

Thompson, D. 1995, Working Nation — The SkillShare Experience, paper presented at the 2nd National Conference on Unemployment, Queensland University of Technology, Brisbane, 15–16 June.

Turner, J. and I. Schiffren 1979, Community support system: How comprehensive?, in L.Stein ed. *Community Support Sytems for the Long-term Patient*, Jossey-Bass, San Francisco, pp 1–13.

van den Berg, H. and C. van der Veer 1992, The myth of "unemployable" people: an evaluation of a new employment service for the "hard core" unemployed, *Journal of Social Policy*, V21(2): 177–210.

White, M. and J. Lakey 1992, *The Restart Effect: Does Active Labour Market Policy Reduce Unemployment?*, Policy Studies Institute, London.

Assisting Young Unemployed People: Directions for Employment Services

Helen MacDonald

This paper draws on the service delivery, evaluation and policy development experience of the Brotherhood of St Laurence over the past decade in order to identify the aspects of employment and training assistance which seem most beneficial for disadvantaged young people.

In the light of recent evidence from overseas which suggests that young people 'are the most difficult group to help' in terms of active labour market assistance, and Federal Government initiatives, including the restructuring of employment services and targeted programs, the paper will address the question: Can the positive aspects of employment assistance be included within the new employment services market for young people?

Changes in employment outcomes for young people over the past 25 years have transformed their opportunities for participation in structured training. The current Federal Government has also proposed far-reaching restructuring of the delivery of employment and training assistance which has important implications for job seekers including younger unemployed people.

Work by the Brotherhood of St Laurence over the last decade has provided some insights into the positive features of employment and training assistance for disadvantaged job seekers. This paper draws on those lessons to examine if they can be integrated into the new arrangements for job seekers in order to enhance their employment prospects and self-esteem.

Structure of the Paper

The first section of this paper outlines changes in the youth labour market and identifies the impact on opportunities for structured training. Drawing on the Brotherhood's research and policy work, section two identifies the positive principles and elements of employment and training services for disadvantaged job seekers, in particular younger unemployed people. Section three provides an overview of changes to the delivery of employment services introduced by the Coalition Government in its first budget. The concluding section identifies the opportunities and limitations for integrating these positive service features into employment and training assistance for young people.

Overview of the Youth Labour Market

The major trends occurring in the youth labour market over the past 25 years can be summarised as:

- a marked increase in participation by young people in education;
- the collapse of full-time labour force participation by young people; and
- a partial compensation of this collapse in full-time employment with growth in part-time employment opportunities (Wooden 1996).

Through a comparative analysis of younger and older workers, Wooden (1996) further found that young people experience lower labour market participation rates, higher unemployment rates, more mobility, and have a higher incidence of both part-time and casual employment.

In April 1997, 153,800 15 to 19 year olds were unemployed — an unemployment rate of 20.4 per cent (ABS 6203.0). At that time, 78,100 young unemployed people were attending neither school nor a tertiary institution (ABS 6203.0).

Young People on the Margins of the Labour Market

Young people who are unemployed and who are not engaged in education or training are at particular risk in the labour market. These 'non-students' (who are not in secondary school, full-time or part-time tertiary education, nor in apprenticeships or traineeships) are likely to experience persistent unemployment (Flatau & Simpson 1996).

Flatau's & Simpon's (1996) analysis of the Australian Youth Survey indicates that 60 to 75 per cent of all part-time jobs for non-students were casual and were therefore less secure and carried fewer benefits. Over 60 per cent of those who were employed part-time did not obtain full-time work over a three year time period despite wanting to work longer hours. Furthermore these part-time non-student workers had the lowest incidence of formal training; and any training they did receive was likely to be on-the-job and more firm specific (Flatau & Simpson 1996).

The implications are that the labour market disadvantages experienced by the most marginalised young people are likely to be persistent and entrenched.

Trends for Young People in Training

The changing fortunes for young people in apprenticeships and traineeships have been driven by the broader changes in the youth labour market. Sweet (1996) found that 'at best one in four young Australians take part in recognised vocational preparation programs in the immediate post-compulsory years, compared to an average of one in two in OECD countries'. His analysis of this poor record includes identifying a decline in full-time employment opportunities which are likely to include apprenticeship training arrangements, and the growth of part-time and casual employment in the service sector which militates against expansion of structured training (Sweet 1996).

Increased upper secondary school industry programs in the last 2 years provide a more positive picture. Sweet (1996) suggests that school-industry programs which lead to accreditation within apprenticeships and traineeships, and part-time apprenticeships and traineeships combined with Years 11 and 12, will be attractive to young people. An additional need is for the development, recognition and reward of competence in the context of the broader youth labour market which is characterised by part-time, temporary and casual work for those who are not full-time students (Sweet 1996).

Positive Features of Employment and Training Assistance

From 1994 to 1996 the persistence of unemployment among younger age groups was somewhat ameliorated by the growth in specialised employment assistance provided in the previous Government's *Working Nation* initiatives. Such assistance sought to increase levels of self-confidence and motivation in participants and to provide them with relevant employment skills in order to enhance their job prospects (BSL 1995a).

The need for a mix of programs offering different types and combinations of assistance to meet the above aims and to fulfil the needs of disadvantaged job seekers was accepted by those involved in *Working Nation*.

Lessons from the OECD (1996) also show that the effectiveness of programs for young people are enhanced when combined to provide a range of assistance. That is, stand alone formal classroom training, or on-the-job training, or subsidies to employment appear not to help young people unless offered in combination with programs targeted to their specific labour market needs. 'A flexible mix of programs which can be adjusted to suit local and regional circumstances, particular client groups and the various stages of the economic cycle' is also required according to Finn (1997).

The Brotherhood has provided employment services and conducted evaluations to assess the benefits to program participants. This experience has enabled us to identify some features of assistance to disadvantaged job seekers which may enhance their self-esteem and job prospects. On this basis, the following service elements and principles have been developed.

Choice — 'responses to unemployment must be flexible enough to allow unemployed people to choose from a range of options and select those best suited to their needs and career choices' (BSL 1994). This principle is grounded in our obligations under the International Covenant on Economic, Social and Cultural Rights which safeguards 'the right to work, which includes the right of everyone to gain their living by work which they freely choose or accept'.

Supervision — appropriate supervision is required in workplaces to ensure participant requirements for personal and vocational support are met. Difficulties have been identified in work experience and training programs when participants perceived supervision to be ill-defined and inconsistent

(MacDonald 1995). The importance of training for supervisors working with disadvantaged job seekers has been further documented (MacDonald 1992, 1993).

Links to ongoing job prospects — the content of training must be relevant to employment needs and provide an opportunity to develop marketable skills. A quality training program should be provided in areas of employment growth so as to link it to real improvements in job prospects (BSL 1995b, 1996).

Building upon existing skills and aspirations — participants get value from training when it is suited to their skills and career aspirations. An appropriate assessment of individuals' needs, prior to a training placement, ensures that training is then tailored to build on existing skills (BSL 1995b, 1996).

Accredited and recognised training — formal acknowledgment of skills of participants at the end of the placement is important to ensure that their competencies are recognised by future employers (BSL 1995b, 1996).

Being attuned to the needs of individuals — training programs must accommodate the particular needs of individuals. Participants who have been out of the labour market for longer durations may require a longer period of time to successfully complete their training. Some participants' emotional, personal and housing needs require support during training, and after program completion, to ensure positive training and subsequent employment outcomes (BSL 1995b, 1996).

Income — employment programs should alleviate the considerable financial hardship experienced by unemployed people who may have relied on very low incomes for long periods of time (MacNeill 1995). Positive income incentives for participation should be provided. Participants require adequate remuneration and access to Health Care Card and other Department of Social Security benefits during the training placement to ensure they are not financially disadvantaged by their participation and to meet the additional costs of training (BSL 1995b, 1996).

Post placement assistance — assistance after completing the training, work experience or a labour market program placement should seek to capitalise on improved self-esteem by participants in order to enhance their subsequent employment prospects (MacNeill 1995).

Not all past programs offered all of these features of assistance to disadvantaged job seekers, but the most beneficial had many aspects of them. The question is whether these positive program features can be included in the new arrangements for job seekers.

Employment Services for Disadvantaged Job Seekers

The significant restructuring of employment and training services announced by the Government in 1996 provide both opportunities and restrictions on the provision of assistance for job seekers, particularly younger unemployed people.

Labour market program spending was severely reduced in the 1996/97 budget. With 802,300 people unemployed in April 1997, and about 30 per cent (239,800) of these job seekers unemployed for 12 months or more (ABS 6203.0) these reductions are not only premature but are going in the wrong direction. According to ACOSS (1997) 'only about one in four long-term unemployed people will receive substantial employment assistance in any given year, and that employment assistance will have to be strictly rationed'.

These cuts have been accompanied by extensive restructuring of employment and training assistance delivery arrangements and dismantling of the previous Government's *Working Nation* strategy. In addition to abandoning the Job Compact commitment of a work experience and training place for all those who are long-term unemployed, the Government proposes moving towards a competitive employment placement market based on 'price-based tendering'. The main features of these changes are listed below.

- Establishment of the tentatively named Commonwealth Service Delivery Agency (CSDA), from a merger of the existing network of Department of Social Security and Commonwealth Employment Service offices to provide, among other services, registration of job seekers, assessment for employment assistance, self-help facilities for job search, and referrals of eligible job seekers to providers (DEETYA 1997).

- Abolition of most labour market programs and 'cashing out' funds to provide a single main pool of resources available for buying employment assistance services for eligible job seekers.

- Employment Placement Enterprises (private and community-based agencies) and the Public Employment Placement Enterprise (the corporatised public provider) will tender to deliver assistance to eligible job seekers. For an initial period of about 18 months from March 1997, these contracts will be at fixed prices per outcome similar to the case management contracts.

- In addition to the New Enterprise Incentive Scheme, four types of services will be bought by the Department (DEETYA 1997):

  labour exchange services — to obtain job vacancies and place job seekers. Eligible young people include those registered with the CSDA who are aged 15 to 20 years and not in full-time education or training, irrespective of income support, and individuals placed in an apprentice or traineeship vacancy.

  job search assistance — to provide, over 15 days, training in job search techniques, access to facilities, and supported job search activity. Regardless of income support, eligibility for young people includes those registered with the CSDA who are not in full-time education or training.

employment assistance — to assist 'a diverse range of eligible job seekers to gain sustainable employment using flexible and innovative approaches targeted to the specific needs of the individual' over a period of 12 to 18 months. Eligible young people aged 15 to 20 years will not be in full-time education or training and have been registered with the CSDA as unemployed for at least 12 months or will be classified as at risk of long-term unemployment.

entry level training support — to provide an integrated support service for employers, apprentices and trainees. Apprentices, trainees and their employers may be eligible.

Additional assistance currently available to young job seekers are the Job Placement, Employment and Training (JPET) scheme for homeless and 'at risk' young people; the Jobs Pathway Program to improve student's transition from school to work; the proposed 'work-for-the-dole' scheme; an expansion of apprenticeship and traineeship opportunities; and an expansion of vocational education opportunities for students in senior secondary schools.

Integrating the Positive Features of Assistance into the New Arrangements

There are some positive opportunities emerging from the Government's remodelling of the apprenticeship and traineeship systems (BSL 1996). These include:

- Introduction of part-time apprenticeships and part-time traineeships which can enhance the flexibility of training arrangements to meet the needs of both job seekers and employers. However, adequate income support must be assured.

- Introduction of pre-apprenticeship and pre-traineeship accredited training which can improve the chances of some young people actually gaining and maintaining a training place.

- Modernisation of apprenticeships and traineeships to incorporate competency-based rather than time-based training can better meet the needs of young people and their employers.

Schools, too, are in a good position to assist young people to make informed decisions about their employment directions. Careers education, work experience programs and greater links with industry and employers are all positive trends in assistance for young people at the school level. However, the ability of schools to assist young people who are assessing their employment directions will be influenced by the resources available (Byrne 1996).

There are also risks in the new direction of employment, education and training assistance for young people, especially those who are unemployed and marginalised in the labour market. These include:

- Greater control of training arrangements being given to employers and group training companies may mean that young people who are very disadvantaged in the labour market will be overlooked. It also risks less consistency in the quality of training across employers. Training and accreditation which is provided to young people must be nationally recognised and portable; and uniform standards for good practice and quality training will be essential.

- Traineeships were initially introduced for young people who were early school leavers in order to enhance their pathways to employment. But broadening eligibility for traineeships to a wider range of young people will reduce access by those who are very disadvantaged in the labour market. This group must not become more marginalised in the context of the wide ranging reforms which are underway in employment, education and training systems.

- Clearer strategies and gender equity principles are needed to encourage and support young women who want to undertake apprenticeships which have typically been located in male dominated industries.

- Apart from JPET and the new Community Support Program, absent from reforms to structured training and employment assistance are opportunities to provide integrated assistance recognising that some young people will experience compounding vocational and personal barriers to employment. There needs to be a 'holistic' approach to the provision of employment and personal assistance to unemployed people, especially young people who experience multiple barriers to employment.

- Levels of remuneration for young people participating in different combinations of employment, education and training, either on a full-time or part-time basis, must be sufficient to meet their needs.

The new employment services market is slightly more problematic than aspects of the remodelling of structured training arrangements. While the new arrangements are creating significant problems and dilemmas for community sector providers, this does not mean that they will have to sacrifice quality services for quick outcomes.

In practice, however, job seeker outcomes will be determined by the extent of resourcing and whether providers are able to respond to the diversity of need or are driven to lower quality responses, ignoring the lessons of the past.

The availability of assistance to many job seekers has been severely reduced by recent expenditure cuts mentioned above. There is a danger that access to assistance will be denied to some and restricted for others who may require longer periods of assistance to overcome personal and vocational barriers to employment.

It will be essential that job seekers are able to make informed choices in the new employment service arrangements. Choice is at the heart of a competitive market. How much choice job seekers will have in the services they use will depend on, first, their assessment of eligibility by the CSDA, second, information job seekers have and the types and numbers of providers available, and third, the range of assistance which can be purchased for them.

Conclusion

Changes in youth employment outcomes and opportunities for structured training have created a challenging scenario for assisting young unemployed people in the labour market. It is both possible and necessary to now integrate into the new employment services market for job seekers the lessons from the past about the beneficial aspects of assistance, and lessons from overseas about effective assistance for young people.

References

Australian Council of Social Service 1997, *Submission to Senate Community Affairs Legislation Committee on the Reform of Employment Services Bill 1996 and the Reform of Employment service (Consequential Provisions) Bill 1996*, ACOSS, NSW.

Brotherhood of St Laurence 1994, *Making the future work: Submission to White Paper on employment opportunities*, Brotherhood of St Laurence, Fitzroy.

Brotherhood of St Laurence 1995a, *Submission to Senate Employment, Education and Training References Committee Inquiry into Long Term Unemployment*, Brotherhood of St Laurence, Fitzroy.

Brotherhood of St Laurence 1995b, *Quality training through employment programs: Submission to the Employment and Skills Formation Council*, Brotherhood of St Laurence, Fitzroy.

Brotherhood of St Laurence 1996, *Submission The House of Representatives Standing Committee on Employment, Education and Training: factors influencing the employment of young people*, Brotherhood of St Laurence, Fitzroy.

Byrne A. 1996, 'Young people's future employment decisions: the role of schools', in *Jobs for Young Australians: Proceedings of an international conference*, eds. J. Spierings, I. Voorendt, and J. Spoehr, Adelaide, 27–31 August 1995, pp. 119–124.

Department of Employment, Education, Training and Youth Affairs 1997, *Exposure draft: Service requirements for the Employment Services request for tender*, DEETYA, Canberra.

Finn, D. 1997, *Working Nation: welfare reform and the Australian job compact for the long term unemployed*, ACOSS, Sydney.

Flatau, P. and Simpson, M. 1996, *Part-time youth employment and training: evidence from the Australian youth survey*, Working paper series No. 137, National Institute of Labour Studies Inc, Flinders University of South Australia, SA.

MacDonald, H. 1992, *The Body Shop Linked Access Project, Stage 1 evaluation: Issues for consideration by the Project Steering Committee*, Brotherhood of St Laurence,

Fitzroy.

MacDonald, H. 1993, *The Body Shop Linked Access Project, Stage 2 evaluation*, Brotherhood of St Laurence, Fitzroy.

MacDonald, H. 1995, *Implementation of the Jobskills Program by the Brotherhood of St Laurence*, SPR Paper No. 9507, Brotherhood of St Laurence, Fitzroy.

MacNeill, K. 1995, *Labour market programs and policy beyond Working Nation*, Brotherhood of St Laurence, Fitzroy.

OECD 1996, *The OECD jobs strategy: enhancing the effectiveness of active labour market policies*, OECD, Paris.

Sweet, R. 1996, 'How well do our entry level training models fit the labour market of the 1990s?' paper presented to the Tasmanian Education consortium National Conference on *Rethinking Work — Re-inventing Education*, October 10–12, Hobart.

Wooden, M. 1996, 'The youth labour market: characteristics and trends', *Australian Bulletin of Labour*, V22, (2): 137–160, June.

Learning (not) to Labour

How (some) working class kids get (some) working class jobs (some of the time)
— with apologies to Paul Willis (1977)

Pat Thomson

Schools located in areas traditionally known as working class face an increasingly difficult task. Among the pressures they face are these:

- Apparent retention rates are plummeting: the nexus between high school graduation and the prospect of full time permanent employment is weak
- Poor communities are getting poorer and increasingly bereft of basic public services
- There is increasing youth alienation accompanied by media fuelled moral panic and pressure for schools to provide answers to the "youth problem"
- There is an imperative to "crash through" the low levels of information and communication technology use in schools
- Teachers are demoralised and their work intensifying
- The federal government has abolished the Disadvantaged Schools Program, funded vocational education and literacy instead and intensified the marketisation and privatisation agendas

The paper will raise questions about options that might enable working class schools to meet the needs of their students while avoiding the scenario of simply educating the casual workforce required by "fast capitalism."

What is to be understood by the disciplining of societies in Europe since the eighteenth century is not, of course, that the individuals who are part of them become more and more obedient, nor that they set about assembling in barracks, schools or prisons: rather, that an increasingly better invigilated process of adjustment has been sought after – more and more rational and economic — between productive activities, resources of communication, and the play of power relations. (Foucault 1982)

Questions about the relation of the school to the labour market are not new. The history of public schooling in Australia is inextricably linked to concerns about turning the unruly children of the working class into obedient persons of good moral character, productive male breadwinners and thrifty wives (Miller 1986). There is, therefore, a familiar debate about the degree to which compulsory education is utilitarian and how much it fosters personal and social development. This continuum has been discussed and enacted in policy settlements since the Education Acts of the 1870s made schooling mandatory until the age of thirteen. The role of the working class school has been, and is still, strongly directed towards the processes of schooling both citizens and workers by sorting and selecting, differentiating between children and young people so that each proceeds on to a vocation and civil life appropriately skilled and shaped. Working class schools do not simply reproduce existing inequity, they are implicated as active agents in the process.

In the immediate post war period (WWII), there was some agreement about the broad purposes of schooling. Education was an integral part of nation building: it shaped and passed on collective social, cultural and economic stories from one generation to the next. The rigid processes of sorting, through a divided system of technical and high schools that selected out the brightest working class students through streaming and testing, were challenged during the post Vietnam war period, and efforts were made to examine ways in which working class schools could become more equitable, less involved in producing social difference. The shift marked by 'Australia Reconstructed'(1985) and the subsequent translation of its implications for schooling (Dawkins 1988), was a move to an education that was no longer primarily to do with nation building, but was instead an integral part of the armory of the State used to fight the economic war — to stave off economic ruin through the production of multi skilled human capital.

The election of the new/old Howard government has seen educational economics developed further. The Commonwealth has, in policies if not in rhetoric, abandoned the orthodox liberal view of education, in which individuals can attain social mobility if they have merit, demonstrated by success through the school system. It has abolished the Disadvantaged Schools Program intended to ensure a more 'equitable basis for the distribution of social goods '(Codd 1988). Questions of income, of social division, of poverty are now off the agenda in a discursive sweep that obscures and obfuscates debate about the school as an agent for the creation of social cohesion and/or social difference.

There are two key mechanisms for selection and sorting that are being enacted in the new environment. They are changes in the nature of the curriculum, and the introduction of market forces through choice policy.

Key Mechanisms for Sorting and Selecting

1. Changes in the Curriculum: Education and Training

It is usual to conduct arguments about general and vocational education as if they are subjects — English is general, and Woodwork is vocational. This creates an unhelpful binary based on the historical practices used to divide teachers and students into Vocational and General streams. The general — vocational can better be understood as alternative views of schooling and knowledge, as generalist and vocationalist paradigms whose borders are overlapping and porous.

Generalist education does not equate to the curriculum of the old elite high school, nor to those subject divisions that now constitute the prerequisites for university entrance. Rather it represents the knowledges that are supportive of fully participating citizens in a democratic society. Sometimes it is suggested that to adopt a generalist education paradigm is to argue that schools should not get involved in vocational education. This is misleading. To employ the discourse relevant to the paradigm of generalist education is not only to assert that subjects such as the humanities, literature and liberal arts should be directed towards the development of mind that participation in social life requires (Apple and Beane 1995) but is also to argue that vocational subjects should always incorporate some opportunities for reflective understanding and critical examination of the genesis, context, norms and values of the world of work. Conversely, to use the vocationalist paradigm is to stress the market values of all school subjects and to restrict vocational subjects to providing the knowledge and skill required for successful market participation (Carr and Hartnett 1996).

The following table outlines, somewhat too simply, as such schemas always do, the dimensions of the two paradigms.

At present, the Australian vocational curriculum is controlled by industry and training providers and operates within the vocationalist paradigm. School teachers often find it difficult to come to terms with a vocational competencies based curriculum, not because they are hostile to work education, but because they operate within the parameters of a generalist education philosophy. Teachers want students to know more than the competencies required to work in automobile manufacturing: they want their students to understand something of the nature of the industry, the debates about the car, and the changing nature of work itself. Defenders of the vocationalist paradigm suggest that such learning can occur in the general education subjects that are left to the discretion of the school and the teacher, but this is a simplistic response to a more complex dilemma of credentialling, patterns of subjects, and the organisation of knowledge in the senior secondary years, also controlled outside of schools through state credentialling authorities. What may seem to be teachers' rejection or subversion of the vocational agenda is more aptly described as resistance to courses over which they have little control, and which they would wish to see considerably changed.

The debate therefore is not about whether education should prepare students for either public life or work, but whether education should respond to the current political demands to reproduce the *particular* world of work on which recent educational changes have been erected and legitimised (Arnold 1996), that is move from the generalist paradigm to the vocationalist, and from a long term holistic to a short term 'supply' perspective of work

TABLE 1

	Vocationalist Education	Generalist Education
Political orientation	Technocratic	Democratic
Main reproductive function of education	Economic regeneration	Public participation
Political and social values	Meritocratic (old form) Individualistic (new form)	Egalitarian
Guiding educational metaphors	Relevance, enterprise	Participation, collaboration
Policy exemplars	Australian National Training Agenda	National Goals for Schooling World of Work Curriculum Project
Type of school	Technical/vocational schools and colleges	Comprehensive community schools and programs
School organisation	Managerial Self managing	Democratic Part of mutually supporting and participatory community networks
Curriculum organisation	Differentiation of subjects Grouping on the basis of vocational needs. Weak division between classroom and world of work	Differentiation of subject matter around common activities and student negotiated needs. Weak division between classroom and community
Curriculum knowledge	Technical knowledge and practical skills Vocational applications Utilitarian value. Competency based. Arbitrary standards External syllabus management.	Critical knowledge, cultural awareness and social understanding always under review. Negotiated standards Broad negotiated frameworks.
Teacher's role	Managerial, maximising and testing learning outcomesl	Coordinator, organising learning around common tasks
Teaching Methods	Practical instruction Self paced.	Rich assessment processes Projects, group work, collaborative enquiry Authentic tasks.

(Adaptation from Carr and Hartnett 1996)

2. The Educational Quasi- Market and Choice Policy

The coming together at the national level of policy and accountability requirements, increased support for non government schools and the imposition of a national market philosophy, has led some commentators to speculate on the likely future. One emerging analysis suggests that there is increasingly little difference between public and private providers (Angus 1996; Pascoe 1996) since they are both funded from the public purse and will soon have to meet the same goals, deliver the same core of curriculum, meet the same accountability requirements, and be subject(ed) to competitive national benchmarking and reporting. It is argued that they have more in common than is different. This analysis conveniently omits the different remits for different providers - state systems have to provide for all children, no matter where they live or who they are, regardless of how uneconomic this might be.

It is not difficult, however, to see the emerging trend. In the not too distant future we could have a nation where policy treats all education providers as equal, and the consumer chooses between. In this landscape of 'equal provision', the traditional differences between public and private do not matter as much as the amount of money that parents can pay or the school can raise to add to the sum allocated by the government. The notion that all children have an equal claim on the educational resources of the community is increasingly replaced by the idea that some children *can* have a better education because their parents can afford to pay for it.

In the new marketised world, all providers are equal but some providers are more equal than others, that is, the difference is not between public and private, but between schools that serve the poor and schools that serve everyone else. There will not be a distinct line like an educational dingo fence with rich (private and public) schools on one side and poor (public and Catholic parish) schools on the other, but the differential funding base of schools, created through parent contribution and linked to general levels of income and related resources in local communities, will act as a major structuring force in school decision making and in students' learning. This is a trend already well underway elsewhere. In America, the choice, charter schools and voucher systems operate to create a schooling market in which parent capacity to pay and choose is paramount (e.g. Kozol 1991; Molnar 1996). There is a similar scenario in Britain (e.g. Ball 1990; Walford 1994; Gerwitz, Ball et al. 1995). And in Australia, most obviously in Victoria, the unequal providers are already overtly in competition with one another for students, image, networks, funds, and powerful sponsors.

There is enormous pressure on working class schools to move to avoid the prospect of becoming a marginalised fragment of the former public system, clinging to the goals of comprehensive education while catering only for those who are unable to exercise any other choice. This is already an emerging picture in parts of Australia and is well documented in England

and New Zealand (e.g. Marginson 1993; Smyth 1993; Lingard and Porter 1996). Many working class schools actively look for ways they can avoid this situation.

The Impact of the Two Trends Combined: Vocationalism and Choice

When there is "market" choice between schools, one of the chief factors in parent (consumer) choice decisions will be the curriculum that is offered. Commentators (e.g.Bowe, Ball et al. 1992; Ball, Bowe et al. 1996) suggest that choice policy leads to a conservative influence in the curriculum, as schools fight to offer what the market perceives to be the 'best'. In the first instance this is likely to be the most prestigious — that required for university entrance — and the most instrumental — higher education oriented and vocational.

As schools decide how to position themselves in the market, more wealthy communities and parents will ensure that the schools that they prefer offer either the common curriculum but specialise in 'gifted programs' or a narrow curriculum congruent with higher education entry. At the same time, a combination of factors is likely to push working class schools into increasing vocational curriculum offerings:

- Schools in working class communities are under public, political pressure to redress their plummeting apparent retention rates: one immediate response is to provide more vocational courses in an effort to retain those who are leaving..

- In South Australia the new Commonwealth vocational education funding tops up substantial state funding that is being directed in the first instance to regions where there is both high youth unemployment and poor school retention. Significant sums are available for the development of vocational curriculum. At a time when there is decreasing funding this is a strong incentive.

- Parents of working class students and teachers in the disadvantaged schools are acutely concerned to find ways to assist students to have a future, and that means to get employment.

- Students argue for schooling that will help them get a job as an alternative to a narrow competitive academic curriculum that appears removed from their everyday lives in the media saturated youth cultures.

Given these pressures and trends, we might expect to see in future more working class students engaged in vocational education in their own neighbourhoods with the 'cream' transported to the more academically prestigious state schools in wealthier communities or to university oriented schools run by newly funded private providers in working class neighbourhoods. Depending on the degree to which schools take up work related programs and projects, some could find themselves becoming highly specialised, that is becoming a 'common core plus niche market curriculum' school — where the niche curriculum is vocational. They would then become specialist vocational schools that:

- *Teach different knowledge and skills.* The vocational curriculum that is offered in schools is now, and will continue to be, grounded in the vocationalist paradigm, as will many of the other general courses on offer. They will accentuate utilitarian and applied learning rather than critical and analytic. This technicist knowledge commodity might be 'marketed' as a viable and attractive alternative to the academic vocational curriculum in a revitalised mind/manual, theory/practice binary.

- *Institute more intense student management.* There is considerable pressure in a market and image conscious environment to avoid anything that might cause public approbrium. Schools answer market pressure with tighter selection criteria (you can only come to this school if...) and with more rigid discipline and promotion procedures (you can only stay at this school if....) and with less open information and participation strategies. Schools initiate less flexible counselling and promotion processes in the face of public league tables (you can only do this course if you are likely to succeed ...).

- *Become less willing to address needs.* Annual public reporting demands create reasons to hide any issues that need addressing: school plans to address racism, harassment, and curriculum reform can all be interpreted by a mean minded media as deficiencies, rather than signs of courage in facing inevitable imperfections

- *Avoid dealing with the most vulnerable.* Many parents do not want their children to mix with those they might describe as 'a bad influence'. If schools choose to work hard at keeping homeless young people, young offenders, and aggressively alienated young people then their student population will be less attractive to some. In both Victoria and South Australia schools that have catered for the most vulnerable young people have been closed on the grounds that they no longer attract 'mainstream' parents (Sykes 1993). Such schools are also very costly, because these young people require specialised, often intensive support and their teachers require additional training.

- *Reinforce existing cultural and gender patterns.* Proposals such as measuring school effectiveness through the collection and publication of statistics on school leaver job placement, training or higher education outcomes are likely to encourage conservative counselling and restricted programs that take easy options - those that get numbers - rather than continue to work against entrenched gendered and cultured institutional and personal behaviours through pilot/trial/action research programs.

Through the educational policy market and the operation of social, economic and political forces, we could well face a return to our own conservative past - the technical vocationalist school for the majority of the working class, with academically specialised vocationalist schools for everyone else. This is a prospect that is actively supported by some. Salient issues such as the abundance of permanent full time unskilled work for all those post war students who left their technical school at the end of Year 10 seem to escape the reactionary romantics. They presume a link between credentials and labour market success that no longer exists (Marginson 1995), disallow the very considerable organised opposition that met and arguably sabotaged proposals to reform the senior secondary curriculum, and would cheerfully abandon the goal of a general education for all rather than reconsider how we might be more successful.

The New Vocationalist Curriculum

Baudrillard (1988) suggests that contemporary society has become a culture of simulacra, of constructs that have no referent, no reality. The archtypal theme park Disneyland is not like any real country or place, but operates instead in America to disguise the broader fact that all of the United States has become a theme park, unreal, surreal, hyperreal (p.172) In the theme park, the state, which has little role to play in the culture, creates crises to confirm that it has a reality, and a purpose (p173). Using the idea of the simulacrum, it is possible to argue that the Victorian casino operates to disguise the fact that living in Kennett's Victoria has become a social gamble (Webber and Crooks 1996) and to create the illusion that the government is in charge of a jackpot economy. The idea of the simulacrum helps explain the existence of a vocationalist curriculum that creates the illusion that there are jobs, while the concentration of technical — vocational courses in working class areas confirms that there will be jobs for working class young people. And indeed, those who work in such areas have little option but to operate as if this is both true and untrue, exactly as Baudrillard suggests.

But what kind of jobs? It is predicted that the future workforce will consist of 'core' knowledge workers, and 'peripheral' casual workers, with many engaged in service industries (e.g.Reich 1991; Beare and Slaughter 1993; Rifkin 1996) — a highly stratified and differentiated workforce. While there is debate about the number of highly skilled knowledge workers that the economy will require, there is more agreement about the likely demand for large numbers of casual workers in a range of human and physical services. Current thinking (e.g. Beasley 1991; Speirings and Spoehr 1996; AAP 1997) about work and employment in Australia indicates that while casual part time work is a future prospect for nearly all young people, for a substantial number it may be their entire work career.

The peripheral or contract labour force may be employed seasonally, part time, in peak periods, or other times of increased demand or to do specific specialised tasks (Handy 1994). They may be recruited and supplied to employers through specialised employment brokers or agencies, or through personal networks. The needs of the specific business or service will be determined by market forces: the organisation will be geared to maximising efficiency and effectiveness, meeting best practice at the lowest possible cost.

The casual worker available to such an enterprise will need to be:

- *Literate and numerate.* The literacy and numeracy requirements in the new manufacturing and human services workplace increasingly require both core and casual workers to operate with quality assurance processes involving considerable documentation — manuals of instructions, computer print outs of data, graphs of production targets, calculation of error rates, Pareto charts(Aguayo 1990). In McJobs this is not necessary.

- *Familiar with a range of digitised technologies.* Casual workers will require the skills to use advanced technologies for communication, to handle transactions, for information management and in production processes.

- *Able to fit in with the rest of the workforce.* Communication skills, the capacity to work in a team that you have only just met, preparedness to put personal feelings aside and focus on the job will be key inter-personal attributes. This must be coupled with intra-personal capacities, such as the ability to follow instructions, absorb the local work culture and live within its boundaries.

- *Motivated to work.* Contract and casual staff must be committed to high productivity and quality, to work as if their job was permanent even though it isn't (Gee, Hull et al. 1996). The prospect of being able to be easily replaced acts as to reinforce compliance and foster enthusiasm.

- *Already skilled for the job.* Because some jobs are changing so rapidly, it is necessary for training to be constantly changing to keep up. Casual workers must be training focussed, should understand that it is their responsibility to be job ready and must know how to learn varieties of new skills 'just in time.' They are responsible for managing their own learning and therefore their capacity to get a job is dependent on their motivation to come to work ready. They will have to pay for their own training, available from a phalanx of training providers, since it is they who will benefit from having income generating skills.

There are three notable things about this imaginary casual worker. Firstly, the requirements look remarkably like the Mayer Key Competencies (1993). The key competencies were probably never intended to be read in this way, but literacy and numeracy, technology, communication skills, operate as 'open signs'. They mean different things to different people in different contexts. The spin that I have put on them is not precisely the version that drove their inception but it may well be similar to the version that is implemented, since it is this 'imaginary' that is driving aspects of the vocationalist paradigm.

Secondly, life long learning has a sinister turn. Life long learning does not have to be read in this way but it can be. Life long vocational learning, when learning is seen as a personal benefit and a commodity, renders casual workers victim to continuous expenditure on training. If they are to 'get work', then it is their responsibility to buy the training. To refuse to engage in continuous training is to refuse to be job ready, is to cease to be a virtuous worker, is to join the ranks of the undeserving poor (welfare recipient, dole bludger). The responsibility for employment is shifted to the worker via the obligation to be trained appropriately.

Thirdly, there is a degree of disciplining of the self that is required of the casual that is not required of the full time, permanent core worker, who operates within the social setting of the workplace, and who has to meet externally sanctioned behavioural rules and norms on a daily basis. The casual must be obedient, adaptable, flexible, reliable, and friendly, able to fit in anywhere with a minimum of fuss.

An increasing emphasis on personal behaviours, character, and moral development are required to create the flexible, friendly but obedient casual worker, manifested in increased surveillance of the working class student, managed through the development of ongoing records that give evidence of the consistent performance of self discipline. And indeed, the extension of formal credentialled assessment into dimensions of the self is currently underway in all Australian schools through the key competencies and student portfolios.

Student Resistances

However, working class students have minds of their own. The dramatic decline in retention rates in working class schools indicates that all is not going smoothly. There is little other than anecdotal evidence at this time about the reasons for so many working class students leaving school early. Speculation about causes includes the following:

- The statistics are highly suspect because they do not take part time and repeat Year 12 students into account (South Australia has the highest number of part time students in Australia)
- Postcompulsory curriculum and schools are alienating and students are voting with their feet
- There has been an upturn in the number of part time casual jobs available and young people have left school to take them because they understand that the casual job is here to stay and believe that they will not be advantaged in the casual job market by completing twelve years of schooling.
- Schools have failed to adjust their structures to enable young people to continue on with both part time work and part time school
- Market pressures are operating to narrow the curriculum options for working class students and they will not stay if they cannot do the exact

combination of subjects they want

- Schools are policing the behaviour of working class students with increased rigour and are excluding many
- Young people are extremely pessimistic about the future and can't see the point of staying at school
- Young people have seen through the exhortations to stay at school — and out of the job market and unemployment statistics — and have walked out as an act of resistance towards duplicitous government policy.

There is unlikely to be a single or simple explanation for the phenomenon of falling school retention nor any magic bullet to fix it. Recent studies in Australia indicate that young people act in ways that assist their own marginalisation, and that acts of resistance vary, with gender, location and cultural factors creating observable specificities (Wyn and White 1997). The degree to which young people exercise agency through the act of leaving school or through acting in ways that ensure that they are required to go, is situational and contingent, dependent on the young person's 'time, space, activity, resources and identity…and upon their own biography and psychological makeup' [p143]. This is an area about which we need considerably more research and discussion, always mindful of the dangers of making young people into either victims or demons.

The early school leaver is an ongoing task: where the working class school failed, others must pick up. (The project of schooling the casual workforce continues.) A further series of programs must ensure that young people are managed, and become responsible, self disciplined labour market resources. We might call one of these strategies Work for the Dole.

Conclusion

Calls for more vocational programs and tighter adjustment between schools and the labour market work against the ongoing democratic schooling project — they work to deny some young people socially useful and important knowledge and fail to support continued progressive educational reform that includes a more balanced vocational education component. In the current market driven policy context such demands, which often come from the left as well as from the conservative right, may well exacerbate trends towards even more highly differentiated schooling and curriculum and a widening socio-cultural and economic gap between rich and poor.

One of the foundations of the post war public school system was that it was charged with the responsibility of working for the elimination of unfair differences: one of its basic roles was the redistribution of resources to ensure equity of access, provision and participation. It was specifically charged with educating all_students. The decision whether or not to abandon generalist /democratic schooling is always in train and requires particular determination and courage in the present circumstances. The diminution of a school education that enables young people to develop the knowledge and skills that support critical inquiry speak to us about the degree to which all young people will be equipped to deal adequately with the demands of the next century as citizens and workers, but this is most at issue for those young people who are likely to be sent to the societal margins. The future of Australia as a peaceful and democratic country surely relies on all citizens being socially, culturally, economically and politically productive, and it is to that end that we need to continue to pursue a just and democratic public education system.

Bibliography and References

AAP (1997). Schools Bear Brunt Of Jobs Market Collapse. *The Advertiser*. Adelaide: Nov 12 : 26.

ACTU/TD (1985). Australia Reconstructed: Report of the Joint ACTU — Trade Department Mission to Europe. Melbourne, Australian Council of Trade Unions.

Aguayo, R. (1990). *Dr Deming. The American Who Taught the Japanese About Quality*. New York, Simon and Schuster.

Angus, M. (1996). The integration of the public and private schooling sectors in Australia. A *National Approach to Schooling in Australia? Essays on the development of national policies in schools education*. B. Lingard and P. Porter. Canberra, Australia, Australian College of Education.

Apple, M. and J. Beane (1995). *Democratic Schools*. Alexandria, Virginia, Association for Supervision and Curriculum Development.

Arnold, M. (1996). "The High Tech, Post Fordist School." *Interchange* 27(3-4): 225–250.

Ball, S. (1990). *Politics and Policy Making in Education: Explorations In Policy Sociology*. London, Routledge.

Ball, S., R. Bowe, et al. (1996). "School choice, social class and distinction: the realisation of social advantage in education." *Journal of Education Policy* 11(1): 89–112.

Baudrillard, J. (1988). Simulacra and Simulations. *Jean Baudrillard. Selected Writings*. M. Poster. Stanford. California, Stanford University Press.: 166–184.

Beare, H. and R. Slaughter (1993). *Education for the Twenty First Century*. London, Routledge.

Beasley, B. (1991). Transitions to nowhere: the effects of government policies on young working class people's access to employment/training. *For Your Own Good, Young People and State Intervention in Australia*. R. White and B. Wilson. Bundoora, Latrobe University Press.

Bowe, R., S. Ball, et al. (1992). *Reforming Education and Changing Schools: Case Studies in Policy Sociology*. London, Routledge.

Carr, W. and A. Hartnett (1996). *Education and the Struggle for Democracy. The politics of educational ideas*. Bristol and Buckingham, England, Open University Press.

Codd, J. (1988). "The construction and deconstruction of educational policy texts."

Journal of Educational Policy 3(3): 235–247.

Dawkins, J. (1988). *Strengthening Australia's Schools*. Canberra, Australia, AGPS.

Foucault, M. (1982). The Subject and Power. *Michel Foucault: Beyond Structuralism and Hermeneutics*. H. L. Dreyfus and P. Rabinow. Chicago, University of Chicago Press: 208–226.

Gee, J., G. Hull, et al. (1996). *The New Work Order: behind the language of the new capitalism*. Australia, Allen and Unwin.

Gerwitz, S., S. Ball, et al. (1995). *Markets, Choice and Equity in Education*. Buckingham, Open University Press.

Handy, C. (1994). *The Empty Raincoat: Making Sense of the Future*. London, Great Britain, Hutchison.

Kozol, J. (1991). *Savage Inequalities. Children in America's Schools*. New York, Harper Perennial.

Lingard, B. and P. Porter (1996). *A National Approach to Schooling in Australia?* Canberra, Australian College of Education.

Marginson, S. (1993). *Education and Public Policy in Australia*. Australia, Cambridge University Press.

Marginson, S. (1995). "The decline in the standing of educational credentials in Australia." *Australian Journal of Education* 39(1).

Mayer, E. (1993). Key Competencies. Canberra, Australia, Australian Education Council - Ministers of Vocational Education, Employment and Training.

Miller, P. (1986). *Long Division State Schooling in South Australia*. Adelaide, Wakefield Press.

Molnar, A. (1996). *Giving Kids the Business. The Commercialisation of America's Schools*. Boulder, Colorado, Westview Press.

Pascoe, S. (1996). *Broadening Our Horizons*. Melbourne, Australian Council for Educational Administration.

Reich, R. (1991). The Work of Nations. A Blueprint for the Future. New York, Simon and Schuster.

Rifkin, J. (1996). *The End of Work. The decline of the global labour force and the dawn of the post market era*. New York, Putnam.

Smyth, J., Ed. (1993). *A Socially Critical View of the Self Managing School*. London, Falmer Press.

Speirings, J. and J. Spoehr, Eds. (1996). *Jobs for Young Australians. Vol 1*. Adelaide, Social Justice Research Foundation.

Sykes, H., Ed. (1993). *Youth Homelessness. Courage and Hope*. Melbourne, Melbourne University Press.

Walford, G. (1994). *Choice and Equity in Education*. London, Cassell.

Webber, M. and M. Crooks, Eds. (1996). *Putting the People Last. Government, Services and Rights in Victoria*. Melbourne, Hyland House.

Willis, P. (1977). *Learning to Labour*. London, Saxon House.

Wyn, J. and R. White (1997). *Rethinking Youth*. Australia, Allen and Unwin.

Volunteering for the Dole:
Toward a New Social Contract?

Lorraine Kerr & Harry Savelsberg

The Department of Social Security is implementing new policy on the amount and nature of volunteer work which may be undertaken by people receiving unemployment benefits. These people will be allowed to choose between participating in labour market programmes and job search strategies or to work in the community — on a voluntary basis — for longer hours per week than was previously permissible without jeopardising their unemployment cash benefit. This paper will argue that such a shift in government policy reflects free-market ideology which includes public sector withdrawal from provision of programmes and resources for unemployed people and emphasises a new social contractual relationship between the DSS recipient, the state and the 'community'. Ostensibly the policy arises to 'help the community' and improve recipients' employability, however it will be argued that the volunteering option represents the state's tacit recognition of the intractibility of wide-spread unemployment and a diminishing commitment and obligation to employment programmes. Such an approach accommodates non-interventionist strategies by government and reduced social expenditure, which are necessary principles for economic liberalism. Coupled with this is the expectation that welfare 'entitlements' are conditional upon reciprocal obligations and responsibilities between the individual, the state and the 'community'. Here, the volunteering option becomes a powerful ideological affirmation of civic responsibility owed by DSS recipients to the 'community', under the guardianship of the state. Introduction of this policy may be regarded as the next step in dismantling the welfare state and the legitimation of the new social contract.

In a society which, it has been argued, is traditionally based on a labourist model of welfare (Castles 1985: Jones 1990: Beilharz, Considine and Watts 1992), the relationship between recipients of social welfare — cash transfer — benefits and the state has been based on a bargain. The terms of this bargain have been couched within a framework of reciprocity and have been historically strongly linked to work and also to the needs of laissez faire capitalism. For example the old-age pension, referred to in s.xxiii of the Constitution, was seen as a 'gift by the state to citizens, who, during the prime of life, have helped to bear the public burdens of the State by the payment of taxes, and by opening up its resources by their labour and skill' (New South Wales Year Book 1908: 120, cited Jones 1990: 21). According to Jones (1990), Emy & Hughes (1991) and Beilharz et al (1992) the basis of such a bargain is underpinned not only by an ideology which distinguishes between the 'deserving' and 'undeserving' poor, but also by the principles of economic liberalism which rely on minimalist state intervention. The terms of the bargain can be seen to have dominated attitudes toward welfare benefits, and consequently social and economic policy formation.

The expectation that individuals, with specific exceptions for those considered not able-bodied through no fault of their own, such as the aged, orphans, and lunatics (Jones 1990 : 20), should generally be responsible for their own welfare persisted largely unchanged until the mid-1940s when benefits such as family allowance, widow's pension and — in 1945, unemployment benefits — were introduced. The introduction of unemployment benefits occurred in the same year as the 1945 White Paper Full Employment in Australia — a paper which, as Langmore and Quiggin (1994: 79) assert, represented a fundamental break with economic thinking of the past and an acceptance by governments of the state's responsibility to ensure that work be available for all. The relationship between the state and unemployed people changed at this time. There was now an ideological commitment by the state to not only provide cash benefits to people without work while they sought jobs but also to make certain the jobs were there to be found. What had effectively happened in 1945 was that the state had introduced another term into the welfare bargain. Not only was there a reciprocal imperative that individuals would receive a 'reward'(in the form of an old-age pension) from the state for having worked or financial support during periods of unemployment while the individual sought work but now the state undertook the responsibility for ensuring that there was work to be had. This represented a significant shift away from traditional non-interventionist strategies by the state and reflected the adoption of Keynesian economics. This commitment to full employment dominated economic policy until the mid 1970s and as Jones (1990), Bell & Head (1994) and Langmore & Quiggin (1994) maintain was not problematical during the 'long boom' period from the late 1940s through to the early 1970s, when economic conditions were favourable and near full-employment was possible, but was to herald significant problems from the mid-1970s onwards as the state was increasingly called upon to honour that commitment. In response to increasing globalisation and trends toward deregulation and dismantling protection the next twenty years saw a bi-partisan shift away from Keynesian principles toward economic-rationalist policies and free-market ideology, which may be regarded as satisfying the social and economic prerequisites of capital, but which was diametrically opposed to the state's asserted commitment to facilitate full employment. — and society's continuing expectation that it should do so.

Government Responses to Changing Labour Markets

During the period of economic restructuring since the early 1980s one of the most vexing problems for the state has been the changing nature of employment. There is a consensus that not only are many jobs — especially in manufacturing — disappearing, but the very character of the labour market has been transformed from a regulated, predominantly full-time structure to an increasingly casualised and fragmented one (Jones 1990:Rees, Rodley & Stilwell 1993; Healey 1994; ACOSS 1996; Gregory & Hunter 1996). The changing character of the labour market is seen to have been largely responsible for the consistently high levels of unemployment over the past two decades and indicators are that these trends will continue. For example Healey (1994) claims that between 1970 and 1993, the number of jobs in Australia increased by over 40%, but part-time jobs increased by over 200%. Healey cites some of the reasons for this trend as being the combined effects of the recession and economic restructuring, efforts by employers to reduce wage and non-wage costs and achieve greater flexibility in the workplace, award restructuring and the extension of workplace bargaining. There is no indication that this general over-all pattern will change and consequently there will be little — if any — change to the unacceptably high levels of unemployment in the foreseeable future. The form of economic restructuring undertaken during the 1980s and '90s involved two major strands. The first was labour market reform and deregulation, which was facilitated by the Accord (Ewer et al 1991) and the second was an emphasis on privatisation and reduction of protectionist practices. Whilst these measures were partially effective in increasing competitiveness, enhancing competition and promoting global integration, their effects on reducing unemployment were less than satisfactory, attesting to the intractability of unemployment (Watts 1990: Langmore & Quiggin 1994:Grewal 1996).

The government's response to continuingly unacceptably high rates of unemployment (though not necessarily the solution) was seen to be a series of job creation strategies and labour market programmes (LMPs). As unemployment rates worsened, labour market strategies proliferated as the state struggled to meet the competing social requirements of the welfare bargain and the economic demands of the market. The 1993 Committee on Employment Opportunities details the experiments with special employment and training programmes which were undertaken by the state from the 1970s onwards in an attempt to improve employment opportunities. Until 1985 the focus was on job creation schemes, but following the Kirby Report on the 1985 Committee of Inquiry into Labour Market Programs there was a shift in focus toward training programmes, rather than job creation strategies. The rationale given for this shift was the promotion of an 'active society' — a strategy very much in favour at the time in most OECD countries (Pixley 1994). The 'active society' approach included several programmes, with NEWSTART, which combined an income support system and an activity test, being the one most commonly adopted. In order to fulfill their part of the historically-determined terms of the welfare bargain and to satisfy perceived societal expectations concerning recipients of welfare benefits (as outlined above) — and hence continue to receive those benefits —

unemployed people had to be seen (by the state and by the 'community' in general) to be looking for work. The unemployed had a commitment to engage in LMPs, demonstrate that they were actively seeking work, move from an unemployed to an employed status and hence fulfil their part of the bargain by 'earning' their welfare benefit. As Bryson (cited Bell & Head 1994: 291–311) states, throughout the 1980s there was an increasing focus on removing any potential or perceived disincentives to the search for work.

Of particular interest to this paper was that volunteering, unless it was specifically linked to vocational training, was regarded as a disincentive to work, was severely restricted and, as Senator Newman (Minister for Social Security) said in September 1996 could occur only '...within very strict guidelines. These guidelines required that the [voluntary] work be vocationally useful'. Adherence to the guidelines was monitored by the state, via the Commonwealth Employment Service, with the overall imperative being that the priority for unemployed people was to undertake anything that would — and nothing that would not — facilitate the goal of becoming employed. However, unemployment rates overall did not fall, for as Watts (1990: 106) maintains, '... even if labour market programs are being developed and funded adequately, the central issue of jobs remains. Training programs only work finally when jobs are available for people who have come out of these programs.' So what was happening to the bargain? Unemployed people were engaging in LMPs, were actively seeking work, were receiving welfare benefits — but the state's economic reforms could not provide them with jobs. The bargain, the social contract, was not working and a serious dilemma faced the state. Training and employment programmes are costly, were not necessarily leading to jobs and the overall fiscal climate was increasingly hostile to public spending, yet there remained an ideological imperative that unemployed people 'earn' their welfare dollar. How could the dilemma be resolved?

A New Social Contract

In 1996 the newly-elected Coalition government faced the same dilemma as its predecessor and, this paper argues, has sought its resolution in ways which will have profound effects on the relationships between the individual, the 'community' and the state. Effects which indeed redefine not only reciprocal rights and responsibilities but also the nature of social citizenship itself because the government has proposed changes which will alter the terms of the bargain, will introduce a new social contract. The new bargain drawn up between the state and unemployed people can be detected in the Coalition government's Department of Education, Employment, Training and Youth Affairs (DEETYA) and Department of Social Services (DSS) proposed policies and include major reforms to labour market assistance, service delivery, unemployment classification, and volunteering and the unemployed. These policies, which are a major focus of this paper, are comprehensively detailed by the Minister for Employment, Education and Youth Affairs (Senator Amanda Vanstone) in the August 1996 DEETYA paper 'Reforming Employment Assistance' (hitherto referred to as REA) and in a series of News Releases ('A New Era in Customer Service', August 1996: 'Unemployment Payments', August 1996 & 'Voluntary Work Made Easier', September 1996) from the Minister for Social Security (Senator Jocelyn Newman).

The proposed restructuring of government employment services outlined above will be briefly detailed below:

- Services previously provided by the DSS and CES will be integrated into the Service Delivery Agency (SDA). This agency will focus on individual circumstances and will be, according to Senator Vanstone,'client-focused not programme-driven' (REA: 15). Furthermore, 'The government has decided that the current arrangements for the delivery of labour market assistance should be replaced with a contestable...fully competitive market in which private, community and public sector agencies would be contracted to place unemployed people into jobs' (REA : 17).Labour exchange services (previously performed by CES) will be delegated, primarily to EPE's.

- The Employment Placement Enterprises (EPE's) 'which operate in the new employment placement market could include business and industry associations, private employment agencies, community and voluntary organisations, education and training institutions...'(REA: 18). The EPE's will be outcome focused and 'There will no longer be a guaranteed level of dedicated funding for particular labour market programs...EPE's will make their own judgement about their client's needs for specialist assistance, entering into their own contractual arrangements with training providers only when they judge that the training on offer will significantly boost their client's chances of securing a real job outcome' (REA: 22). Performance payment arrangements and incentives will be an integral part of the restructuring. EPE's will be funded on outcomes with some up-front fee by government and the rest of the payment when a primary or secondary outcome (eg. a full-or part-time job) has been achieved. 'This means EPE's will get most of their payment after a job-seeker has got a job and kept it' (REA: 45). The EPE's will provide three main services, the most important being Intensive Employment Assistance (IEA).

- Intensive Employment Assistance: 'The government has decided that intensive employment assistance should be concentrated on those persons who are already long-term unemployed or at risk of becoming so' (REA: 39). 'Many short term unemployed people obtain work relatively quickly...[and] there is a minority of highly disadvantaged jobseekers for whom no realistically affordable level of employment-related assistance will be able to secure a real and lasting job'(REA: 39). 'Accordingly, the government intends to apply a 'capacity to benefit' test to ensure that assistance is targeted not only on the needy but also on those who stand to benefit significantly...'(REA: 39). Hence those assessed as 'job ready', or those who are highly disadvantaged would not meet the 'capacity to benefit' criteria. The Jobseeker Classification Instrument (JCI), a screening instrument, will be revamped to assist in the determination of IEA eligibility. Factors to be included in the JCI include: 'educational attainments, access to viable labour market, country of birth, reading and writing ability, ATSI status, duration of unemployment, recent work experience and stability of residence' (REA: 41). SDA staff will make an assessment regarding 'capacity to benefit', in addition to the JCI.

- Compliance. The EPE's will be responsible for 'monitoring compliance with the activity test requirement'. 'Activity tests for long-term unemployed jobseekers not selected for intensive assistance will be more flexible, with some being given the option of either meeting standard job search requirements... or participating in alternative activities which contribute to improving job-readiness, help to overcome barriers to employment or contribute to the community. Activities could include participation in voluntary work, community development activities, community education or other activities suggested by the jobseeker subject to approval by the agency'(REA: 55).

The proposed greater flexibility regarding compliance with activity test requirements then connects with the DSS new guidelines on volunteering. The volunteering option is an alternative to actively seeking work and/or participation in LMPs. Prior to September 1996, recipients of DSS unemployment benefits were largely discouraged from undertaking voluntary work on the grounds that such work hindered their compliance with the activity test, that is if they were volunteering they were regarded as not seeking work. It was possible to undertake voluntary work and still receive benefits, but only if individuals could also demonstrate satisfactory job search/LMP activity. After September 1996, unemployed people over the age of 50 years were able to meet the activity test requirement by volunteering for an approved, 'not for profit' organisation, provided the total time spent in volunteering exceeded 32 hours per fortnight. Of great significance is that, although DSS guidelines state that these people are required to be available and willing to undertake suitable paid work, they are not required to actively seek work. From September 1997, the new guidelines will be extended to include people under 50 years of age who have been in receipt of income support for 12 months and who have not been selected for IEA, plus those under 50 years of age who have received income support for at least three months and will now be able to satisfy the activity test through participation in voluntary work. According to DSS guidelines on the implementation of the new voluntary work strategies, unemployed people who fit the above criteria will, as is now the case with those aged over 50 years, be required to be available and willing to undertake suitable paid work, but will not be required to seek work in order to comply with the activity test. Voluntary work is quite clearly being offered as an option to paid work, with unemployed people fulfilling their part of the bargain — earning their welfare dollar — not by seeking work, but by volunteering in their 'communities'.

The rationale given for the changed policy on volunteering is, according to Senator Newman, because 'Voluntary work develops skills, social contacts and enhances self esteem. It also enables people to gain valuable work experience, maintain their skills, make employer contacts, obtain a reference and help them to return to paid employment' (September, 1996). This raises questions given that volunteering was previously regarded by DSS as a disincentive to seeking employment and is now apparently seen as the pathway to paid work. The rationale is also called into question when studies (eg. Rogers 1992) indicate that few people who volunteer as a means of gaining paid employment actually achieve that goal. Also of interest is that the voluntary work must be undertaken in 'not for profit' organisations which according to Senator Newman could include charitable organisations, community organisations, community centres or even schools. This paper questions the likelihood of volunteers gaining paid employment in the 'not for profit', community services sector given that this sector experienced severe funding cuts in the last two Coalition Budgets and is consequently shedding paid staff, rather than employing them.

Conclusions

This paper argues that the volunteering option satisfies two key aspects of the welfare bargain, that is the ideological imperative that those in receipt of welfare benefits must be 'deserving' of that benefit, and the notion that there be some form of reciprocity on the part of the beneficiary. As Senator Newman said,' The community has indicated very clearly that it is concerned people meet all their obligations when receiving taxpayer funded income support because they are unemployed' (August 1996). Unemployment benefits are not to be given unconditionally, but must be earned in order to avoid the 'dole bludger' tag.

So the welfare bargain has been renegotiated. The state will continue to provide a cash benefit to unemployed people but, as evidenced in the strategies outlined in 'Reforming Employment Assistance', has withdrawn its commitment to LMPs, placing its faith instead in the ability of market forces to provide 'real jobs'. Unemployed people will be assessed and will be directed into two broad streams, one 'suitable' for Intensive Employment Assistance and the other not. Members of the former group will fulfil their part of the bargain by engaging in LMPs and endeavouring to become employed, whilst those in the latter group will be given the option of volunteering in community services as an alternative to actively seeking paid work — and thereby 'earn' their benefit. The policing of both groups regarding compliance in fulfilling their part of the bargain will be undertaken by EPE's and approved 'not for profit' community organisations. Effectively that policing will be privatised, with the state acting only as guardian of the contract. Therefore, not only have the terms of the bargain been renegotiated, but the relationship between some individuals, the 'community' and the state has been radically changed. The state and the unemployed will no longer be partners in a direct bargain and will no longer be directly linked by the bonds of reciprocal obligations and responsibilities. For unemployed people who receive welfare benefits, that bargain will be brokered by private agencies and the 'community' — who may also be in a position to determine obligations and responsibilities. The policies which expedite this new bargain or social contract could be considered as either the state's further withdrawal from the 'welfare state' or, as Clarke (1996: 31) suggests, a '...'rolling out' of state power but in new, dispersed forms...forms [having] the objective of promoting integrative relationships which both cross and reorganise the conventional boundaries of public and private (state and non-state)'. In either event, the volunteering option is being used as a powerful ideological affirmation of civic responsibility owed by DSS recipients to the 'community' in return for their welfare benefit and indicates the state's need to legitimise the new bargain — a bargain which begins to redefine the nature of social citizenship itself.

References

ACOSS 1996, A Future that Works for All of Us: goals and strategies for Australia, ACOSS Paper No. 78, May, Australian Council of Social Service, Darlinghurst.

Beilharz, Considine and Watts 1992, Arguing About The Welfare State, Allen & Unwin, Australia.

Bell, S. and Head, B., eds. 1994, State, Economy and Public Policy in Australia, Oxford University Press, Melbourne.

Castles, F. 1985, The Working Class and Welfare, Allen & Unwin, Australia.

Clarke, J. 1996, The Problem of the State after the Welfare State, in Social Policy Review 8, eds. M. May, E. Brunsden, and G. Craig, Public Policy Association, London, pp13–39.

Emy, H.V. 1993, Remaking Australia: The State, the market and Australia's future, Allen & Unwin, Australia.

Emy, H. and Hughes, O. 1991, Australian Politics: Realities in Conflict, MacMillan Education, Melbourne.

Ewer, P., Hampson, I., Lloyd, C., Rainford, J., Rix, S. and Smith, M. 1991, Politics and the Accord, Pluto Press Australia Ltd., New South Wales.

Gregory, B. and Hunter, B. 1996, Increasing Regional Inequality and the Decline of Manufacturing in Dialogues on Australia's Future, eds. P. Sheehan, B. Grewal, and M. Kimnick, Centre for Strategic Economic Studies, Victoria University, Melbourne, pp 307–324.

Grewal, B. 1996, 'Infrastructure for National Development: In Defence of Public

Investment' in *Dialogues on Australia's Future*, eds. P. Sheehan, B. Grewal, and M. Kimnick, Centre for Strategic Economic Studies, Victoria University, Melbourne, pp 163–184.

Healey, K. 1994, *Changes at Work: Issues for the nineties*, Spinney Press, Australia.

Jones, M.A. 1990, *The Australian Welfare State*, 3rd. edition, Allen & Unwin, Sydney.

Langmore, J.and Quiggin, J. 1994, *Work for All: Full Employment in the Nineties*, Melbourne University Press, Victoria.

Newman, J. 1996, 'Voluntary Work Made Easier. Unemployment Payments. A New Era In Customer Service', News Releases, August & September 1996, by Senator Jocelyn Newman, Minister for Social Security, AGPS, Canberra.

Pixley, J. 1994, 'After the White Paper — Where?' *Just Policy*, N 1, Nov, pp20–26.

Rees, S., Rodley, G. and Stilwell, F. eds. 1993, *Beyond the Market: Alternatives to Economic Rationalism*, Pluto Press, Australia.

Rogers, L. 1992, *Volunteering and Young Unemployed People*, The Volunteer Centre of South Australia Inc., Adelaide.

Vanstone, A. 1996, *Reforming Employment Assistance*, Ministerial Statement by Senator the Honourable Amanda Vanstone, Minister for Employment, Education Training and Youth Affairs, August, AGPS, Canberra.

Watts, R. 1990, ''Reviewing the Review': The Social Security Review and Social Policy in Fin De Siecle Australia' in SPRC *Reports and Proceedings*, N 81, April, pp 99–110.

A Comparison Between Burnout Levels of Case Management Staff and Non-case Management Staff Working Directly with the Unemployed

Richard Goddard and Wendy Patton

This study sampled levels of burnout and employee perceptions of their working environment in federal government employees working directly with the unemployed in a sample of Commonwealth Employment Service (CES) offices located across Southern Queensland and Northern New South Wales. In all, 104 administrative service officers from 15 CES offices completed the Maslach Burnout Inventory, the Work Environment Scale and the Eysenck Personality Questionnaire (Revised short-form) between December 1995 and December 1996. Comparisons between the responses made by staff who were currently working in a case management role and staff who had never undertaken case management duties were made on these measures. Consistent with the expectation that the case management role would be more demanding than the non-case management role, case managers endorsed responses which indicated higher burnout levels, and perceptions of lower role clarity, poorer physical comfort, and greater work pressure, than their non-case manager co-workers.

The Burnout Construct

It is now widely accepted that burnout is a syndrome of emotional exhaustion, depersonalisation, and reduced personal accomplishment that occurs among individuals who work with people in some helping capacity (Byrne 1993; Glass, McKnight & Valdimarsdottir 1993; Lee & Ashforth 1990 1996; Maslach, Jackson & Leiter 1996; Schaufeli & Dierendonck 1993). The construct is thought to be a unique response to job stress resulting from frequent and usually intense interactions between staff and their clients (Cordes & Dougherty 1993; Lee & Ashforth 1996; Maslach 1982).

Throughout the 1980's burnout was extensively researched in the helping professions (see Cordes & Dougherty 1993; Maslach, Jackson & Leiter 1996 for recent reviews). While much of this research has been criticised for being conducted in an atheoretical manner (Glass, McKnight & Valdimarsdottir 1993) the conservation of resources theory of stress (Hobfoll 1989; Hobfoll & Freedy 1993) has emerged as a robust theoretical framework in which job demands and resource predictors have been associated with the three burnout dimensions, namely Emotional Exhaustion, Depersonalisation and Personal Accomplishment (Hobfoll & Freedy 1993; Lee & Ashforth 1993 1996; Maslach, Jackson & Leiter 1996). To summarise Hobfoll and Freedy (1993), job demands are thought to directly trigger strain reactions manifesting as emotional and physical exhaustion whereas the presence or absence of adequate job resources primarily influence the need to use internal defensive coping mechanisms to cope with stress and to enhance one's self-efficacy.

In a refinement of Hobfoll and Freedy's model, Maslach, Jackson and Leiter (1996) distinguish distinct predictors for each of the three subscales of the MBI. These researchers have proposed that the emotional demands of providing services to others, coupled with the demands of maintaining interpersonal relationships with both co-workers and supervisors, are predictors of Emotional Exhaustion.

Resource demands such as social support, autonomy, and involvement in decision making are proposed as predictors of Depersonalisation and Personal Accomplishment. Clearly then a range of work climate variables are particularly germane to this model of burnout and need to be included in studies seeking to advance the knowledge base in this area.

The effect that differing personality traits might have on the explanatory power of this model has not yet been systematically investigated despite strong warnings that stress assessments may be influenced by the personality disposition of the respondents (Costa & McCrae 1987; Funk 1992; McCrae 1990; Payne 1988). In particular, Payne (1988), in a longitudinal study of the unemployed that included a measure of neuroticism along with several survey instruments measuring psychological well-being and environmental influences, found that neuroticism accounted for so much of the variance in the other variables that it totally swamped the multiple regression analysis.

Burnout in Employment Service Personnel

To date there has been very little published work on the topic of burnout in staff working with the unemployed. A recent search of the burnout literature yielded only one study that tangentially referred to burnout in employment service personnel (Banka 1993) and a concurrent search of the literature in the field on unemployment yielded no references to this type of research. This result stands in stark contrast to the copious literature on burnout generally (see Cordes & Dougherty 1993; Maslach, Jackson & Leiter 1996 for recent reviews), and a large volume of research into unemployment conducted both in Australia (for a recent review of the Australian literature see Maher 1993) and overseas (see Allatt & Yeandle 1992; Leana & Feldman 1992). The paucity of studies examining the psychological impact of working with the unemployed was acknowledged by Kelvin and Jarrett (1985) more than a decade ago. Their observation that Psychological work on unemployment has so concentrated on the unemployed individual himself that it has virtually ignored the partners to his situation (p. 77) is still relevant today.

Rationale for the Research

A clear understanding of the impact that working with the unemployed has on the staff undertaking this task is particularly important for Australian society for several reasons.

Firstly the research is of importance as a direct result of the size and ongoing cost of addressing the problem of unemployment in this country. At the time this research was initiated (1995), Australia's official unemployment rate had been in excess of 8% for the past decade (Senate Employment, Education and Training References Committee 1995) and direct government spending on programs designed to assist the unemployed into employment was cost more than two billion dollars annually (Department of Employment, Education, Training and Youth Affairs 1996). Clearly research that has the potential to significantly impact on the service delivered to the unemployed will have great importance to any authority or organisation administering social welfare in this country, especially given the above economic and social dimensions of the problem in Australia at this time. While the assumption has always been that burnout does have a detrimental impact on the quality of service delivered (Cherniss 1980; Maslach 1982 1983), Maslach, Jackson and Leiter (1996) suggest that research confirmation of this relationship is still required before it can be relied upon absolutely.

While there may still be some questions about the extent that burnout in staff detrimentally influences the quality of service that staff can deliver, there are no such questions about the effects of burnout on the well-being of service delivery staff themselves. Research in this area has documented and replicated findings of deleterious physical, emotional, interpersonal, attitudinal and behavioural consequences of burnout across a range of occupations (see Cordes & Dougherty 1993; Kahill 1988; for comprehensive reviews of this material). Clearly then, research into burnout of employment services personnel, not having been conducted previously, is particularly germane to effective personnel management in this area. The need for this research in the Australian context has been further emphasised with the recent changes to how employment services are being delivered to the unemployed in this country (these will not be reviewed here; see Commonwealth of Australia 1994; 1995).

Method

Subjects

All subjects were Australian Commonwealth Government employees of the Department of Employment Education Training and Youth Affairs

(DEETYA). A total of 104 subjects participated in this study. Experimental subjects were case managers, Employment Assistance Australia (EAA) personnel, physically located within offices of the Commonwealth Employment Service (CES). Control subjects were CES staff working in the same CES offices as the experimental subjects. The criterion for selecting control subjects was that they were CES staff who were in some way working directly with unemployed clients but who had never undertaken work as a case manager. Seventy percent of participants approached participated in the survey, a proportion consistent between the experimental and control groups. In all, 55 case managers and 49 non-case managers completed the set of questionnaires described below.

Table 1 summarises general demographic information for both groups. One way ANOVAs indicated no significant differences between the case manager (experimental) and the non-case manager (control) groups on the biographical measures of age and number of years employed with DEETYA. Chi-square tests indicated no significant sex differences between the composition of the case manager and non-case manager groups.

Instruments

Burnout was measured using the Maslach Burnout Inventory (MBI) (Maslach & Jackson 1986), a 22 item self report instrument described in the literature as the most widely used operationalization of burnout (Lee & Ashforth 1996). The MBI describes burnout in terms of 3 dimensions, Emotional Exhaustion (EE), Depersonalisation of clients (DP) and diminished Personal Accomplishment (PA). In this study subjects responded to each MBI item by selecting the frequency, ranging from *never* (0) to *every day* (6), that they experienced particular feelings or behaviours characteristic of burnout. High scores on the EE and DP subscales and low scores on

TABLE 1

Demographic Variables for Case Manager and Non-case Manager Groups

		Case Managers (n = 55)	Control Group (n = 49)
Age (Years)	M	39.69	39.71
	SD	8.15	10.76
	Range	24–64	22–60
Years Employed in DEETYA	M	8.52	7.21
	SD	6.19	5.59
	Range	1–26	0.5–25
Sex	Male	19	20
	Female	34	23
	Unknown	2	6

the PA subscale are characteristic of burnout. Good reliability and validity data are reported in Maslach, Jackson and Leiter 1996.

This study used the Eysenck Personality Questionnaire (Revised short-form edition or EPQ-R short) (Eysenck & Eysenck 1991) to measure the principle personality dimensions for each respondent. This is a 48 item instrument that asks respondents to make yes/no decisions on items describing behaviours or responses typical of one of the four major dimensions of personality.

The EPQ-R short-form contains 12 items chosen from each of the 4 personality subscales of the 100 item EPQ-R. The personality subscales measured by the EPQ-R short-form are Psychoticism (P), Extraversion (E), Neuroticism (N), and a Lie Scale/Social Desirability dimension (L). Reliability and data reported in Eysenck and Eysenck (1991) reflecting forty years of development and thousands of psychometric and experimental studies is more than satisfactory.

The Work Environment Scale (WES) is a 90 item self-report questionnaire which asks respondents about their working environment using a true/false forced choice format. The scale yields summary scores with respect to 10 subscales described by Moos (1994) as distinct though somewhat related aspects of work environments . The present study used the Real Form (Form R) of this instrument to obtain perceptions of actual current working environment. Acceptable reliability and validity data are reported in Moos (1993 1994).

Procedure

EAA case managers and CES staff who had never worked as case managers were approached in 15 offices of the Commonwealth Employment Service (CES) to participate in a survey into perceptions of their work. CES offices were located in Southern Queensland and Northern New South Wales.

Experimental subjects were recruited at case manager meetings which were held regularly in each CES office. Psychologists employed by DEETYA were recruited to administer the survey. They explained the survey to prospective subjects as an investigation into case managers' perceptions of their work. Control subjects, CES staff who had never participated in case management, were recruited by being approached individually by DEETYA psychologists in the same offices from which the case managers had been recruited.

All subjects were provided with the set of questionnaires described below along with a reply paid envelope so that subjects who chose to participate could complete the survey in their own time and return the survey anonymously. Participation was voluntary, and no incentives were offered to participants.

Subjects completed the three psychological measures. Additionally, all subjects provided biographical data covering sex, age, and length of employment with DEETYA. Case managers were also asked to provide details about the length of time they had worked as case manager, their preparatory training, size of their current case load and the number of successful outcomes achieved in the previous month.

Results

Gender Differences

Of the 104 respondents to the survey, 39 or 37% were male, 57 or 55% were female and 8 respondents (8%) did not indicate gender. Statistical analyses indicated that there were no gender differences in the way case managers, non-case managers and the total study sample responded.

Workload, Performance and Training

Case managers indicated that, on average, they had been undertaking case management for 15.1 (SD = 7.4) months, had an average case load of 122 (SD = 38) clients and were actively working with an average of 79 (SD = 28) clients.

In the month preceding the survey, case managers indicated that they had achieved an average of 13.5 (SD = 9.75) outcomes in respect of the clients they case managed. An outcome was defined as any event causing a case managed client to cease being eligible for the unemployment relief allowance called Newstart , usually by commencing employment or full-time education, or by otherwise changing their circumstances.

In excess of two thirds of case managers surveyed (ie. 69%) indicated they had commenced case management duties without preparatory training. Twenty-nine percent of respondents indicated that they had undertaken relevant preparatory training. Only one respondent failed to answer this question. All case managers were asked if they had undertaken stress management training at any time prior to the survey. Thirty six percent indicated that they had undertaken some type of stress management training, and 60% percent indicated that they had not. Two failed to respond to this question.

Comparison Between Experimental and Control Subjects

This section will determine if there were differences between the case manager (experimental) and the non-case manager (control) groups' mean scores across all major dependent variables used in this study. Comparisons were undertaken using a series of one way ANOVAs. As noted above, no significant differences were found between the case manager and the non-case manager groups on the biographical measures of age, sex, or length of employment with DEETYA. Table 2 presents summary statistics detailing the comparisons between these two groups on dependent variables.

Personality. No significant differences between the experimental and control groups were found across any of the four personality variables measured.

Burnout. In contrast to the personality variables, the two groups differed significantly on the Burnout dimension of Personal Accomplishment, $F(1, 102) = 4.89$, $p = .03$. Case manager responses on this dimension were, on average, lower, corresponding to a higher burnout level, than the mean response of the non-case manager group. Additionally, on the Emotional Exhaustion dimension, there is a strong trend toward higher burnout levels in the case manager group, $F(1, 102) = 3.55$, $p = .06$.

Work Climate. Across the 10 subscales of the Work Environment Scale, significant differences between the experimental and control groups were found on 2 subscales. Most notably was the difference in perception of Work Pressure between the two groups, case managers indicating that as a group they perceived themselves to be under greater work demands and time pressure than their non-case manager colleagues.

TABLE 2

Summary Statistics for Dependent Variables

Variable	Experimental Group (n = 55)		Control Group (n = 49)		Differences between experimental/ control groups	
	M	SD	M	SD	F	p
MBI Subscales						
Emotional Exhaust	23.42	9.77	19.57	11.04	3.55	. 06
Depersonalisation	9.58	5.63	8.08	4.91	2.07	.15
Pers. Accomplish.	33.65	5.57	36.61	7.98	4.89	.03 *
Personality						
Extraversion	7.63	3.49	7.19	3.94	0.36	.55
Psychoticism	2.26	1.73	1.96	1.53	0.86	.36
Neuroticism	5.69	2.91	5.21	3.47	0.57	.45
Lie Scale	4.56	2.29	5.08	2.64	1.17	.28
Work Environment						
Involvement	5.60	2.12	5.04	2.61	1.45	.23
Cohesion	5.36	2.41	5.76	2.14	0.76	.38
Support	4.67	2.34	5.39	2.06	2.70	.10
Autonomy	5.62	2.11	5.49	1.88	0.11	.75
Task Orientation	5.56	2.29	5.37	2.39	0.18	.67
Work Pressure	6.15	2.38	4.61	2.36	10.82	.000 ***
Clarity	3.44	1.97	4.22	2.14	3.82	.05
Control	5.00	1.55	5.33	1.85	0.96	.33
Innovation	4.11	2.31	4.14	2.08	0.01	.94
Physical Comfort	4.82	2.76	6.31	2.53	8.17	.005 **

Note. * $p < .05$. ** $p < .01$. *** $p < .001$.

On the WES dimension Physical Comfort, a dimension which assessed the extent to which physical surroundings were perceived to contribute to a pleasant work environment, the study found that case managers scored significantly lower than the non-case manager group. Case managers were therefore placing less value on the impact that their physical surroundings were having in contributing to a pleasant environment, or, stated another way, case managers perceived their physical surroundings to be a greater detraction to a pleasant work environment than non-case managers who worked in the same offices.

Staff Training and Burnout

To assess the impact of staff training on the three dimensions of burnout a series of one way ANOVAs were undertaken to compare case managers who had undertaken (a) stress training and (b) case management skills training with those case managers who had not undertaken such training.

Only on the dimension of Personal Accomplishment was prior training associated with significant reductions in reported burnout. The group of staff who indicated that they had undertaken preparatory case management training (n = 16) scored significantly higher on the Personal Accomplishment subscale, corresponding to lower burnout, than staff who had not participated in such training, $F(1, 52)$ = 7.34, p = .009.

Stress management training appeared to have a similar effect. The group of staff who indicated that they had undertaken stress management training (n = 20) also scored significantly higher on the dimension of Personal Accomplishment, $F(1, 51)$ = 7.33, p = .009.

Discussion

As predicted, case managers, as a group, endorsed responses indicative of greater work pressure and higher burnout levels than their non-case manager colleagues. Furthermore, this study identified that case managers were less clear about both their role and the rules and policies of the new case management organisation they were working in, that is Employment Assistance Australia, than their colleagues who had remained working in their traditional Commonwealth Employment Service roles.

These results are not surprising given (a) the large case loads reported and (b) the fact that more than two thirds of the case managers surveyed had commenced their duties as case managers without the advantage of preparatory training directly pertaining to the new role. Burnout has consistently been linked with both work demands and role clarity in studies seeking identify causes of this phenomenon (Cordes & Dougherty 1993) and the results presented here can be interpreted as further support of these links. The strong impact that preparatory training appeared to have on the burnout dimension of Personal Accomplishment is particularly interesting in view of the support it gives Maslach, Jackson, and Leiter's (1996) structural model of burnout. The model postulates that lack of resources, such as training support, directly contributes to diminished accomplishment and efficiency.

The implications of this research are wide. The results address a primary objective of the study, that is to provide an estimate of burnout in public sector case managers working with the unemployed at this time. In doing so it publishes data of particular relevance to human resource managers responsible for the well-being of employment service personnel undertaking intensive case management duties with the unemployed. Future studies will be needed to replicate these findings and to extend the domain of the research into the private sector where, different organisational parameters could be expected to operate.

References

Allatt, P. and Yeandle, S. 1992, *Youth unemployment and the family: Voices of disordered times*, Routledge, London.

Banka, A. 1993, 'Unemployment stress as perceived by officers working with the unemployed', *Polish Psychological Bulletin*, V24: 41–50.

Byrne, B. M. 1993, 'The Maslach Burnout Inventory: Testing for factorial validity and invariance across elementary, intermediate and secondary teacher, *Journal of Occupational and Organizational Psychology*, V66: 197–212.

Cherniss, C. 1980, *Professional Burnout in Human Service Organizations*, Praeger Publishers, New York.

Commonwealth of Australia 1994 *Working Nation: Policies and Programs*, Australian Government Publishing Service, Canberra.

Commonwealth of Australia 1995, *Working Nation: The first year 1994–95*, Australian Government Publishing Service, Canberra.

Cordes, C. L. and Dougherty, T. W. 1993, 'A review and integration of research on job burnout', *Academy of Management Review*, V16: 621–658.

Costa, P. T., Jr., and McCrae, R. R. 1987, 'Neuroticism, somatic complaints, and disease: Is the bark worse than the bite?' *Journal of Personality*, V55: 299–316.

Department of Employment, Education and Training. 1996, *Annual Report 1995–96*. Australian Government Publishing Service, Canberra.

Eysenck, H. J. and Eysenck, S. B. G. 1991, *Manual of the Eysenck Personality Scales (EPS Adult).*, Hodder and Stoughton, London.

Funk, S. C. 1992, 'Hardiness: A review of theory and research', *Health Psychology*, V11: 335–345.

Glass, D. C., McKnight, J. D., and Valdimarsdottir, H. 1993, 'Depression, burnout, and perceptions of control in hospital nurses', *Journal of Consulting and Clinical Psychology*, V61: 147–155.

Hobfoll, S. E. 1989, 'Conservation of resources: A new attempt at conceptualizing stress', *American Psychologist*, V44: 513–524.

Hobfoll, S. E., and Freedy, J. 1993, 'Conservation of resources: A general stress theory applied to burnout', in *Professional burnout: Recent developments in theory and* research , eds. W.B. Schaufeli, C. Maslach, and T. Marek, Taylor and Francis Washington, DC, pp 115–129.

Kahill, S. 1988, 'Symptoms of professional burnout: A review of the empirical evidence', *Canadian Psychology*, V29: 284–297.

Kelvin, P., and Jarrett, J. E. 1985, *Unemployment: Its social psychological effects*, Cambridge University Press, Cambridge, England.

Lee, R. T. and Ashforth, B. E. 1990, 'On the meaning of Maslach's three dimensions of burnout', *Journal of Applied Psychology*, V75: 743–747.

Lee, R. T. and Ashforth, B. E. 1996, 'A meta-analytic examination of the correlates of the three dimensions of job burnout', *Journal of Applied Psychology*, V81: 123–133.

Leanna, C. R., and Feldman, D. C. 1992, *Coping with job loss: How individuals, organizations, and communities respond to layoffs*, Lexington Books, Lexington.

Maher, R. J. 1993, 'Unemployment: Australian research 1983 to 1993 reviewed', Unpublished manuscript, University of Southern Queensland, Toowoomba, Australia.

Maslach, C. 1982, *Burnout, the cost of caring*, Prentice-Hall, Englewood Cliffs, N.J..

Maslach, C., and Jackson, S. E. 1986, *Manual of Maslach Burnout Inventory*, Consulting Psychologists Press, Palo Alto, California.

Maslach, C., Jackson, S. E., and Leiter, M. P. 1996, *Maslach Burnout Inventory Manual*, Consulting Psychologists Press, Palo Alto, California.

McCrae, R. R. 1990, 'Controlling neuroticism in the measurement of stress', *Stress Medicine*, V6: 237–241.

Moos, R. H. 1993, *Work Environment Scale: An annotated bibliography*, Department of Veterans Affairs and Stanford University Medical Centres, Centre for Health Care Evaluation, Palo Alto, California.

Moos, R. H. 1994, *Work Environment Scale Manual*, Consulting Psychologists Press, Palo Alto, California.

Payne, R. 1988, 'A longitudinal study of the psychological well-being of unemployed men and the mediating effect of neuroticism', *Human Relations*, V41: 119–138.

Schaufeli, W. B., and Van Dierendonck, D. 1993, 'The construct validity of two burnout measures', *Journal of Organizational Behavior*, V14: 631–647.

Senate Employment, Education and Training References Committee 1995, *Report on the inquiry into long term unemployment*, Australian Government Publishing Service, Canberra.

Effect on Self-Esteem of Participation in Training Courses and the Possible Moderating Effect of Willingness-to-Participate

Brian Drury, Peter Creed, and Anthony Winefield

This paper reports on the continuing investigation into the effects of willingness-to-participate in training courses for the unemployed. The study examined the effects of (a) the willingness-to-participate, and (b) self-esteem outcomes for a group of long-term unemployed people who attended training courses. Willingness-to-participate was measured by a specially devised Influence on Participation Scale (IPS) (Drury, 1995), and self-esteem was measured using the Rosenberg Self-Esteem Scale (RSE) (Rosenberg, 1965). It was hypothesized that attendance at the training would improve self-esteem, and that high willing participants would improve more than low willing participants. Contrary to expectation self-esteem was unaffected by either participation or by willingness-to-participate and did not change over time.

Effects of Training on Well-being

Many unemployed people have found the experience of being without a job to be a negative one (Winefield, Tiggemann, Winefield & Goldney, 1993; Winefield, 1995). A great deal of research has been directed at identifying the negative effects of unemployment on individuals and their families, but less work has been done to examine ways to reduce these widely reported negative effects (Caplan, Vinokur, Price & van Ryn, 1989; Drury, Creed & Hicks, 1995). A recent study of the effects on well-being of attending a training course revealed there was a significant improvement in mental health in the short term for participants (Creed, Machin, & Hicks, 1996). Individuals who completed the training did so with significantly lowered levels of psychological distress than they exhibited before the course, and when compared with the control group. This finding was consistent with previous studies reported in the literature, and it reinforced the findings reported by Drury, Creed and Hicks (1995). The findings also suggested that occupational training courses for the unemployed may contribute to improvements in other areas of psychological functioning. This was important because it implies that there is a value to training that goes beyond the acquisition of knowledge and skills.

Self-esteem

Although it has been extensively researched, self-esteem has not been demonstrated to show a clear relationship with unemployment status. While some studies have found differences between employed and unemployed samples (Donovan & Oddy, 1982; Feather, 1982; Muller, Hicks & Winocur, 1993; Patton & Noller, 1984), others have not (Hartley, 1980; Shamir, 1986). Still other studies have revealed differential effects for different groups. For example, low self-esteem was observed with unemployed skilled workers (Perfetti & Bingham, 1983), but not for school leavers (Winefield, Tiggemann & Winefield, 1992).

Many researchers have noted the lack of studies that have evaluated the self-esteem outcomes of training based interventions for the unemployed (Caplan, et al., 1989; Creed, Hicks, & Machin, in press; Drury, et al., 1995; Eden & Aviram, 1993). In some of these reports mental health benefits were identified for participants in training courses for the unemployed (Creed, Machin, & Hicks, 1996; Harry & Tiggemann, 1992). In other reports, however, positive changes in mental health as a result of training have not been found (e.g., Branthwaite & Garcia, 1985; Caplan et al., 1989; Drury, Creed & Hicks, 1995), and in some reports, negative mental health consequences for participants have been identified (Donovan, Oddy, Pardoe & Ades, 1986; Kristensen, 1991; Oddy, Donovan, & Pardoe 1984).

Willingness-to-Participate

Willingness-to-participate in training has been identified as an important issue for both employed and unemployed people (Banks, 1990; Noe & Wilk, 1993). For meaningful skills acquisition, attitude change and personal benefits, the individual must clearly want to engage in development activities (Noe & Wilk, 1993). The recent, and ongoing, changes to the delivery of services to the unemployed in Australia, together with the more focused targeting of labour market programs, has made it more important than ever to ensure that positive outcomes for the unemployed individual in training are optimized. Logically it would also be important to the unemployed individuals participating in training courses that they achieve some sort of positive outcome, such as skills acquisition and improved self-esteem, and a subsequent increased capacity to seek and maintain work. Therefore it makes sense to identify those unemployed individuals who are willing to attend training courses, as these are the people who are most likely to benefit from the intervention. Thought can also be given to ways of influencing the willingness of unemployed individuals so as to increase their chances of benefiting from training interventions

One of the prime objectives of training for the unemployed is to provide skills, but it can also be seen to fulfill some of the "latent functions" of employment that Jahoda (1982) has suggested are vital to psychological well-being. The relevant latent functions include the imposition of a time structure, regular shared experiences and contact outside the nuclear family, the linking of individuals to transcending goals and purposes, the definition of personal status and identity, and enforced activity.

In this study it is hypothesized that;

- self-esteem will improve as a result of attending the course, and
- improvements in self-esteem will be greater for those who are willing to participate.

This paper reports on a continuing investigation into the effects of the willingness of unemployed people to participate in training interventions. The main issues to be reported are: (a) the short-term effects on the self-esteem of unemployed people who attended a training course; and (b) the relationship between willingness-to-participate and self-esteem outcomes for participants.

Method

Subjects

Subjects were 184 unemployed people. Participants were 114 unemployed people (69% female; average age 31 years) who attended suburban Skillshare training centres in Brisbane, Australia. Eligibility criteria for the training courses were that participants be unemployed for six months or more, (or be classified by the Commonwealth Employment Service (CES) as being especially disadvantaged), be registered with the CES, and possess sufficient literacy skills to be able to read the materials used in the course. Control subjects (47% female; average age 28 years) were 70 waiting list unemployed people who met the same eligibility criteria for attending the training course as did the participant group. They were drawn from the same CES geographic area as the experimental group. Control subjects were continuously unemployed during the period that the experimental subjects were attending the training courses. Although there was a significantly greater proportion of females in the participant group than in the control group, c^2 (1) = 8.94, $p < .01$, the groups did not differ significantly on the basis of age, length of unemployment, relationship status, or education level.

Training Courses

The training courses were Federally funded Skillshare programs which were designed to provide participants with skills to assist them with their job search and to improve their well-being so that they might cope better with the task of looking for work. They were occupational skills based (office skills, tea and tidy, security, work options, and bar skills), and included personal development components (self-esteem building and vocational guidance). The courses also routinely provided participants with a number of other elements that included social contact, an imposed routine, some individual attention, and an opportunity for a work assessment. The courses were conducted at outer suburban training centres. They were full time, and ran between four and six weeks.

Instruments

The Influence on Participation Scale (IPS) (Drury, 1995) is a seven item scale specifically designed to measure a person's "willingness" to attend a training program. It was designed to measure the extent to which subjects volunteered for, or were willing to participate in, a training course. For control subjects, the wording of the IPS was slightly modified to reflect the subject's willingness-to-participate in a course if one was offered. Drury (1995) reported an alpha reliability coefficient for the IPS when used with a similar group of unemployed people of .77.

The Rosenberg Self-esteem Scale (RSE) (Rosenberg, 1965) was used to obtain a measure of the global self-esteem of subjects. The scale comprises ten items (e.g., "I feel that I have a number of good qualities"). Subjects rated the extent to which they agreed or disagreed with each. Responses were scored from 1–4 in the direction of increasing self-esteem. The RSE has been used extensively in occupational studies (Feather, 1982; Feather & Barber, 1983; Feather & Bond, 1983; Rowley & Feather, 1987). Feather and Barber (1983) reported an internal reliability of 0.83 for a group of unemployed subjects. In the present study an internal reliability of .70 was calculated from total scores across time.

Procedure

All subjects were administered questionnaires at the beginning and end of the training program. All questionnaires were administered in person to participants. Time 1 questionnaires were administered in person to the control group, with Time 2 being sent through the mail. For participants, 73 (64%) completed Time 2 questionnaires. The comparable number for the control group was 48 (69%) at Time 2.

Results

Initial analyses indicated no Time 1 differences between the participant and control groups on the measure of self-esteem (RSE), participant group M = 21.90, control group M = 21.14, F < 1.00.

Attrition Bias

Analysis was carried out to determine whether those who dropped out of the study differed on Time 1 scores from those who completed it. Analysis of variance revealed no significant difference between dropouts and non-dropouts on age, willingness, or length of unemployment. See Table 1.

The Moderating Effect of Willingness-to-participate

In this section, participants who scored higher on the willingness-to-participate (IPS scores) at Time 1 were compared with those who scored at a lower level at Time 1. This was to determine if those high on willingness-to-participate in the training (higher on IPS) responded differently to training than those who were low on willingness-to-participate (lower on IPS).

For this analysis, all subjects were allocated to a high willingness or a low willingness group, based on a median split of Time 1 IPS scores. To investigate whether the high willing subjects in the participant group improved in their level of self-esteem (RSE) over the period of the course differently to low willing subjects, RSE data were analyzed using a repeated measures ANOVA, with a between group factor (participant group x control group), an across time factor (Time 1 x Time 2), and a dichotomous split factor (high versus low willingness). There were no significant main effects for group, $F < 1.00$; for willingness, $F < 1.00$, or time, $F(1, 115) = 1.31, p > .05$. There were no significant interactions for group x time, $F < 1.00$; willingness x time , $F < 1.00$; or group x willingness , $F < 1.00$. To be able to attribute any differential effects on the high and low willing participants, what was required was a significant three way interaction (group x time x

TABLE 1

Means, Standard Deviations, and *F* ratios Between Dropouts and Nondropouts on Age, Willingness, or Length of Unemployment

Measure	Group	Mean	Standard deviation	*F* ratio
Age	Dropout	29.32	10.49	$F < 1.00$
	Nondropout	29.79	11.46	$F < 1.00$
Willingness	Dropout	26.36	5.10	$F < 1.00$
	Nondropout	26.83	5.50	$F < 1.00$
Unemployment length	Dropout	19.20	15.56	$F < 1.00$
	Nondropout	22.91	17.76	$F < 1.00$

TABLE 2

Mean RSE Scores for Participant and Control Groups, High Willingness and Low Willingness Subgroups at Time 1 and Time 2, Based on a Median Split of IPS Scores at Time 1

Group	Time 1	Time 2
Participant — High	19.70	19.87
Participant — Low	22.36	20.29
Control — High	20.73	22.06
Control — Low	21.39	20.07

willingness), irrespective of the significance of any main effects. No three way interaction was found, $F < 1.00$. The means are reported in Table 2.

Discussion

Effects of Training on Self-esteem

The finding in relation to self-esteem was that there was no significant change across the training period, for participants, controls, or when both groups were combined. These findings lend support to the notion that occupational training courses for the unemployed may not contribute to improvements in psychological functioning, defined here as self-esteem. This is important because it suggests that improvements in self-esteem, which will influence the job search and return to work process, may need to be pursued through specific interventions, either stand alone self-esteem courses or specific self esteem enhancing courses that can be attached to occupational skills training programs. The evidence here is that courses aimed at providing occupational skills, even when they include personal development components, may not at the same time enhance self-esteem.

Willingness-to-Participate

The findings in relation to willingness to participate and self-esteem were that lower-willing participants did not respond significantly differently to the course than higher-willing participants. These results are in conflict with those from a previous study (Drury, Creed & Winefield, 1996) which reported that higher-willing participants had significantly lowered psychological distress, as measured by the General Health Questionnaire (GHQ) (Goldberg, 1978), than lower-willing participants following attending occupational training programs. The evidence from the Drury et al. study was that higher-willing participants attending occupational skills training programs had significantly better outcomes in relation to psychological distress than lower-willing participants. Psychological distress as measured by the GHQ can be characterized as the individual's perception of immediate/very recent well-being. The result from the present study in relation to the more stable construct of self-esteem was that there were no differences between lower-and higher-willing participants. Occupational skills training programs then have been shown to reduce immediate perceptions of distress, with higher-willing participants doing better. However, they have not been shown to have impacted on more global, stable views of the self, regardless of whether the participant is a volunteer or not.

References

Banks, M. H. (1990). A policy to motivate employment training? *Bulletin of the British Psychological Society, 6,* 3–5

Branthwaite, A. & Garcia, S. (1985). Depression in the young unemployed and those on youth opportunities schemes. *British Journal of Medical Psychology*, *58*, 67–74.

Caplan, R., Vinokur, A. D., Price, R. H., & van Ryn, M. (1989). Jobseeking, reemployment and mental health: A randomised field experiment in coping with job loss. *Journal of Applied Psychology*, *74*, 759–769.

Creed, P. A., Hicks, R., & Machin, M.A. (1998). Behavioural plasticity and mental health outcomes for long-term unemployed attending occupational training programs. *Journal of Organisational and Occupational Psychology* (In press).

Creed, P. A., Machin, M. A., & Hicks, R. (1996). Neuroticism and mental health outcomes for long-term unemployed youth attending occupational skills training programs. *Personality and Individual Differences*, *21*, 537–544.

Donovan, A., & Oddy, M. (1982). Psychological aspects of unemployment: An investigation into the emotional and social adjustment of schol leavers. *Journal of Adolescence*, *5*, 15–30.

Donovan, A., Oddy, M., Pardoe, R., & Ades, A. (1986). Employment status and psychological well-being: A longitudinal study of 16 year old school leavers. *Journal of Child Psychology and Psychiatry*, *27*, 65–76

Drury. B., (1995). Impact of willingness-to-participate on well-being outcomes for unemployed people who attend occupational training courses. Master's thesis. Queensland University of Technology

Drury, B., Creed, P. & Hicks, R. (1995). Unemployed people's willingness-to-participate in occupational skills training, in Proceedings of 2nd National Conference on Unemployment Queensland University of Technology.

Drury, B., Creed, P. & Winefield, A. H. (1996). Unemployed people's willingness-to-participate in occupational skills training, in Proceedings of International Congress on Stress and Health. Sydney

Eden, D., & Aviram, A. (1993). Self-efficacy training to speed re-employment: Helping people to help themselves. *Journal of Applied Psychology*, *78*, 352–360.

Feather, N. (1982). Unemployment and its psychological correlates: A study of depressive symptoms, self-esteem, Protestant ethic values, attributional style, and apathy. *Australian Journal of Psychology*, *34*, 309–323.

Feather, N., & Barber, J. G. (1983). Depressive reactions and unemployment. *Journal of Abnormal Psychology*, *92*, 185–195.

Feather, N., & Bond, M.J. (1983). Time structure and purposeful activity among employed and unemployed university graduates. *Journal of Occupational Psychology*, *56*, 241–254.

Harry, J. M., & Tiggemann, M. (1992). The psychological impact of work re-entry training for female unemployed sole parents. *Australian Journal of Social Issues*, *27*, 75–91.

Hartley, J. F. (1980). The impact of unemployment on the self-esteem of managers. *Journal of Occupational Psychology*, *53*, 147–155.

Jahoda, M. (1982). *Employment and unemployment: A social-psychological analysis*. London: Cambridge University Press.

Kristensen, O. S., (1991). The unemployed and adult education: a longitudinal study of unemployed persons in adult education. *Scandinavian Journal of Educational Research*, *35*, 145–159.

Muller, J., Hicks, R., & Winocur, S. (1993). The effects of employment and unemployment on psychological well-being in Australian clerical workers: Gender differences. *Australian Journal of Psychology, 45,* 103–108.

Noe, R. A. & Wilk, S. L. (1993). Investigation of the factors that influence employees' participation in development activities. *Journal of Applied Psychology, 78,* 291–302.

Oddy, M., Donovan, A., & Pardoe, R. (1984). Do government training schemes for unemployed school leavers achieve their objectives? A psychological perspective. *Journal of Adolescence, 7,* 377–385.

Patton, W. & Noller, P. (1984). Unemployment and youth: A longitudinal study. *Australian Journal of Psychology, 36,* 399–413.

Perfetti, L. J., & Bingham, W. C. (1983). Unemployment and self-esteem in metal refinery workers. *Vocational Guidance Quarterly, 31,* 195–202.

Rosenberg, M. (1965). *Society and the adolescent self-image.* Princeton, N.J.: Princeton University Press.

Rowley, K., & Feather, N. (1987). The impact of unemployment in relation to age and length of unemployment. *Journal of Occupational Psychology, 60,* 323–332.

Shamir, B. (1986). Protestant work ethic, work involvement and the psychological impact of unemployment. *Journal of Occupational Behaviour, 7,* 25–38.

Winefield, A. H., Tiggemann, M. & Winefield, H. R. (1992). Unemployment distress, reasons for job loss and causal attributions for unemployment in young people. *Journal of Occupational and Organisational Psychology, 65,* 213–218.

Winefield, A. H., Tiggemann, M., Winefield, H. R. & Goldney, R. D. (1993). *Growing up with unemployment: a longitudinal study of its psychological impact.* London: Routledge.

Winefield, A. H. (1995). Unemployment: Its Psychological Costs. In C. L. Cooper & I. T. Robertson (Eds.). *International Review of Industrial and Organisational Psychology.* Chichester: Wiley.

POLITICAL WILL

Too Much Work or Too Little …
Unemployment, Working Time
and The Australian Labour Market

Jennie George

The number one issue facing Australia is unemployment. This should be the focus of the Government, employers, unions and the community in 1997. This paper addresses the 1997–8 Federal Budget, the Living Wage case and Working time reform in the context of unemployment and the Australian Labour Market. Changes in working arrangements and the distribution of working time are discussed in terms of employment and related industrial issues.

This is a timely conference about Australia's number one economic and social problem — *unemployment*. It is symbolic that the conference is in South Australia — a state with its fair share of employment problems but a state that has had a strong tradition of innovative solutions to social and economic problems.

I think it is important that historically South Australia has not believed in leaving all our problems to the forces of the free market. This is the state that first created the arbitration system, first gave women the vote, built up innovative economic policies under Tom Playford, and socially progressive policies under Don Dunstan. This is not a place where the level-playing field philosophy of the Productivity Commission remains unchallenged. This is a place where people think more carefully about complex problems — and this conference is an example of that environment.

I wish to tackle three themes. Firstly, the Howard Government's 'invisible' employment strategy, secondly, the Living Wage Case and the role of the Reserve Bank in wages and employment issues, and finally, the important issue of the distribution of working time.

Jobs and the Budget

The Treasurer Peter Costello brought down the second budget of the Howard Government in May 1997. It was clear that all that mattered in the budget was that the bottom line pleased the financial markets and that Peter Costello could be seen to have 'filled in the black hole'. In fact most of the damage, in terms of expenditure cuts, had been done in the first budget which, in turn, slowed the economy down. The change in the bottom line was due to the revenue increase from asset sales — such as Telstra, Federal Airports, and National Rail.

The budget bottom line may have pleased the financial markets but it is not an end in itself. It is not the true test of any budget. The budget should provide vision and a national strategy to solve the problems of the Australian community. In my view the number one problem facing the Australian community is unemployment. The budget shows that the Howard Government has in fact admitted defeat on unemployment. Its economic growth forecast from the Treasury of 3.75% is insufficient to make significant inroads into unemployment.

Further, it has not proposed any industry policies or labour market initiatives to arrest the unemployment problem. Insufficient growth, insufficient policies. This comes in the wake of the scrapping of trade and industry programs and the Working Nation program in the first Costello budget which had adverse effects on the economy and led to criticism even from the Coalition's own allies in the business community. It is clear that much needs to be done on employment and job creation, particularly in regional Australia.

Simple solutions are often offered on the issue of unemployment. One so called solution is the call for wage reductions and labour market 'deregulation'. This solution was offered recently by the Reserve Bank Governor, Mr MacFarlane and many 'dry' economic commentators. This was a major issue in the Living Wage case, taken by the ACTU before the Australian Industrial Relations Commission (AIRC) which I now wish to comment on.

The Living Wage and the Role of the Reserve Bank

The Living Wage decision was of course a disappointment — especially to lower paid workers and their families. The Commission, with the exception of Vice President Ross, failed to grasp the social implications of inequality in a 'two-tiered' labour market. If workers on award rates continue to see their living standards decline, and fall further behind those on EBAs (and even further behind those on executive salaries) then I think that Australia's social cohesion will be threatened. The AIRC majority decision failed to adequately address the needs of the low paid and has allowed inequality in the labour market to continue.

An unfortunate aspect of the Living Wage Case was the uninvited interference from the Reserve Bank Governor in the case. In my view the AIRC was unduly influenced by RBA threats of a monetary policy reaction if the ACTU claim was granted (see the decision Safety Net Review — Wages, decision Print P1997: 18).

Unfortunately the RBA sees itself as the 'wages police' in the post Accord world and uses monetary policy threats whenever there is an opportunity for workers to get wage increases. Even though the AIRC could have granted more than the $10 (even on the analysis of Bankers Trust) and remained within the RBA wages 'comfort zone', the AIRC chose not to do so.

The RBA followed up their Living Wage Case intervention with an attack on the Transport Workers Union award application. A recent RBA argument is to say that US-style labour market deregulation is necessary to reduce unemployment. Governor MacFarlane's recent comments to the House of Representatives Standing Committee on Financial Institutions and Public Administration reflect this. He says:

> I do think there has been a tendency, particularly for the European countries, and I think in some respects we are a bit more like Europe in this than we are like the United States, to have an institutional framework which promotes job security essentially. The first priority is job security and to impose lots of conditions and minimum wage conditions and other conditions and usually provides reasonably accessible sickness and unemployment benefits and usually involves a high degree of trade union involvement and decision making. I am just describing a sort of a classic European type economy, and that sort of economy usually also tends to have centralised decision making on wages, which we had which we have moved away from under both governments. So rigid sorts of arrangements rather than flexibility are the sort of things that tend to characterise that sort of economy. At the other extreme, the US type you have highly a deregulated system.
>
> That has some disadvantages and people are often conscious of the disadvantages that go with a highly deregulated system, but the evidence does seem to be there that the deregulated systems do produce better results in terms of lower unemployment.
> (Governor MacFarlane's evidence, FIP A31, Thursday 8 May 1997)

The Governor's comments reflect the views of several right wing economic commentators. They say it is simply a matter of getting rid of awards, the IRC etc. and having a (low) minimum wage and all our unemployment will 'disappear'.

The ACTU rejects this labour market deregulation approach to unemployment because it has been shown to be flawed according to some of the economic analysis. Minimum wage laws and other labour market 'regulations' do not have the adverse effects that some critics claim. For example, in the Living Wage Case the evidence of eminent labour economists Professor John Nevile of UNSW and Professor Bob Gregory of ANU was noted on the subject.

On minimum wage laws, Professor Nevile surveyed the international statistical evidence and noted that:

> ...at least within the range of difference studied, high minimum wage rates have little or no effect on the employment of unskilled workers.
> (quoted in the decision, Print P1997: 148)

On the question of the Australian labour market being more 'deregulated' along US lines, Professor Gregory compared the two country's respective labour market institutions and concluded that

> ...it seems unlikely that greater relative wage flexibility will significantly reduce Australia's unemployment problem [and that] restoration of full employment will lie in a direction other than reducing the wages of the low paid. (Print P1997: 149)

Significantly, the Reserve Banks *own* economic research showed that Australia's labour market was a high performer compared to other countries. RBA research says:

> Our cross-country analysis of relative wage data suggests that the Australian labour market may have been relatively more flexible over the 1970s and 1980s than popular perception holds. Insofar as cross-country comparisons of wage flexibility (as measured by wage dispersion across ten sectors) can be made, we observe that Australian wage flexibility was on the scale of that in the United States — a country which is considered to have a flexible labour market. (RBA, RDP Discussion Paper, Coelli, Fahrer and Lindsay, cited in ACTU Submission to Living Wage, Section, p.5)

In short, it is clear that unemployment will not be solved by attacking wages, unions, awards and collective agreements.

Working Time Reform

Another solution offered to unemployment is the idea of 'job sharing'. Whilst this could be an attractive option for certain workers in white collar industries, the international evidence shows it is no solution to high national unemployment levels. Sydney University's ACIRRT has noted that the employment effects of work sharing initiatives have been modest '...usually generating or maintaining jobs for fewer than 0.5% of the labour force.' (Brotherhood/ACIRRT 1996: 1).

However, the issue of job sharing does raise the broader issue of working time. The distribution of working time and working time reform is one of the key priorities of the union movement and any policy dealing with employment and equity must deal with working time.

The report by the Brotherhood of St Laurence and ACIRRT (1996), presented in the context of the Living Wage Case, provided some important facts about working time arrangements in the contemporary Australian labour market. It is clear that the labour market has changed quite dramatically in the last 20 to 30 years and there is now a diversity of working time arrangements in Australia. The full-time, 38–40 hour week of 9 to 5 Monday to Friday working days is no longer 'typical' of how Australian's work. Some of the labour market trends in the Brotherhood/ACIRRT report bear this out.

The trends show that:

- Male, full-time, permanent work is declining...whilst female, part-time and casual work is growing.

- Australia is experiencing one of the highest levels of part-time and casual work in the OECD — indeed the high level of precarious employment faced by many workers in Australia (in terms of casualisation and temporary work) is *not* shared by the majority of industrialised countries.

- Many Australians are working too many (unpaid) hours....whilst others are not getting enough work.

- An increasing number of part-time and casual workers are wanting more work whilst existing full-time employees are working excessive hours.

- There is an increase in workplace stress due to excessive hours in terms of work intensification, heavier workloads, and a difficulty, particularly for women workers in balancing work and family responsibilities.

The main issue is how hours of work can be distributed more equally between those in work working excessive hours, those seeking more hours, and those who are without any paid employment.

Some have argued that if we took the hours worked by full-time workers (current average 42.2 hours per week) and reduced it to 38, then 26 million hours (approximately) could be made available, which is equivalent to 689,084 full-time jobs — almost 85% of our unemployment pool. (See Bob McMullan's speech to John Curtin Memorial Breakfast, p.7).

Unfortunately it is not as simple as that. All workers are different so it is not possible to do a straight hours/people swap. Much of the overtime is in trades and managerial areas. The long term unemployed may not necessarily have the skills required.

We must remember too that many workers work extra hours for regular income. The Brotherhood/ACIRRT Study showed that trades, plant and machine operators are occupations that rely heavily on overtime. We must be aware of differences across industry and occupations as well as the different preferences from employees about working time (by age, gender, income and industry).

For example, a recent ACIRRT/Newspoll survey (1996) found that 27% of workers would like to work *fewer* hours. However, employee preference differed depending on age, income and occupation.

- 22% of blue collar workers wished to work fewer hours compared to 35% of managerial/professional workers — (blue collar workers are more likely to rely on paid overtime);
- those on larger incomes overall (eg. over $50,000) preferred to work fewer hours.

The ACTU intends to pursue this issue further through membership surveys conducted by individual unions. It is important that this issue be driven by workplace representatives in terms of the specific needs and circumstances of their particular workplace. There is no, one overall magical solution.

Unions will be conducting membership surveys in the lead up to the September 1997 Congress on:

- current working time arrangements;
- the effects of working time arrangements on income and employment security;
- employee preferences.

This approach recognises the needs of different workers in different industries and workplaces.

The ACTU is also concerned about the 'flexibility' agenda. It should not mean, as it too often does, 'flexibility' for the employer alone. The ACTU wants to ensure that flexible working arrangements can be provided without:

- loss of income and conditions of employment;
- jeopardising workers' ability to balance work and family responsibilities;
- causing increased health and safety hazards and undue stress.

The ACTU sees that 'safeguards' for part-time work determined by the IRC in the Personal Carer's Leave Test Case should be adopted as a minimum.

The limitations applied by s.89A in the current Act in respect of part-time work also need to be carefully examined. There should be scope for inclusion of protections to ensure that there is consistency of income, and job security for part-time workers and casuals.

The Workplace Relations Act limits the ability of the AIRC to provide these protections for part-time workers in terms of minimum and maximum hours per week, stable hours, regular starting and finishing times and reasonable notification of changes to rosters. There is the danger that part-time work will become 'quasi-casual' and that all the benefits important to workers who wish to be permanent part-time rather than casual will be eroded. This will adversely affect women workers who make up the majority of those workers who have a preference for part-time work.

Unions will also be focussing on regulating part-time and casual employment through enterprise agreements. Guidelines will be developed for negotiating enterprise agreements, based on the outcome of membership surveys, specific to particular industries.

In terms of policy solutions, a number of options based on overseas and Australian experience are worth further consideration. These include:

- *Premium for precarious employment*: There may be scope to apply a monetary premium to compensate for the financial insecurity associated with precarious employment. The focus would be on improving income security through the provision of regular and consistent hours of work. Any monetary premium would need to be carefully examined so as to avoid inequitable outcomes.

- *Annualised salaries*: In considering annualised salaries, unions need to explore the relationship between working time arrangements and income, and weigh up the advantages and disadvantages of annualised salaries. Annualised salaries should not be a precursor to the loss of wages and conditions.

- *The adoption of 48/52 schemes*, to average payments over an entire year. This has been applied in some state public sector workplaces. The employee is paid for 48 weeks averaged over the whole year. This allows them to 'purchase' an additional four weeks annual leave so a total of eight weeks annual leave is taken per year.

- *Reductions in standard working hours*: Research shows that attempts to reduce standard working hours have not had a significant impact on unemployment. The international evidence on Germany, France and Belgium for example shows this has not been effective in reducing national unemployment. President Mitterand reduced the standard working week in France from 40 to 35 hours with very minimal impact on France's unemployment. Belgium, Germany and Holland also attempted shorter hours initiatives. In Holland's case it was accompanied by wage cuts. In the case of the German manufacturing industry there was scope in a highly skilled industry with a *mainly full-time workforce* with high productivity levels for shorter hours. I.G. Metall maintains that *in manufacturing* the reduced hours initiative did have an impact on job creation and retention. However, this is industry-specific and may not be appropriate elsewhere. (See ACIRRT/Brotherhood of St Laurence 1996: 55–65)

- *Overtime restrictions* or *caps on maximum hours* (weekly, monthly or annually) could be considered. However, given the heavy reliance on paid overtime in some industries, the specific needs of workers must be taken into account.

- *New leave options* could be considered by unions. For example, career breaks are a form of unpaid leave which can contribute to quality of life.

However, the effect of such schemes on employment generation needs to be further considered. For example, in education a teacher taking a years sabbatical may allow a newly trained teacher to get some experience. This option will only generate jobs if a replacement person is given a job (assuming they have the appropriate skills).

- *Retirement options:* The relationship between retirement, social security, superannuation and taxation should be examined in respect of the income security and retirement options of older workers. Part-time work instead of retirement could be an option if the social security/retirement income measures are conducive and if the opportunity for trainees or young employees are taken up.

ACTU's Response

Any strategies considered in relation to working time arrangements must be based on the needs of workers and industry. However, I add a warning: appropriate economic and industry policies are the *main* instruments needed to promote employment. Working time initiatives *will not work* in the absence of a growing economy and a willingness by employers to invest in, and create jobs. There must be higher levels of economic growth and continued investment if working time measures are to have some impact. The ACTU does not support purely 'supply-side' solutions where workers make sacrifices but employers do not invest or create employment opportunities, and governments absolve themselves of responsibility.

Further, the ACTU believes there are some positive measures that can be undertaken by governments, unions and industry to promote employment.

In brief, we would advocate an employment promotion package that includes:

1. *Active Industry Policy Measures:* Australia's industry policy should reflect the realities of world competition and Australian industry, not some textbook economic model. Unilaterally disarming our tariffs while the rest of the world keeps up its trade barriers is not the answer. A sector-based industry policy based on world class, highly skilled, high quality, innovative industries will assist employment and international competitiveness and in turn reduce Australia's balance of payments constraint.

2. A *Regional Development Strategy* to boost jobs and infrastructure in Australia's regional labour markets.

3. Active *labour market programs* such as traineeships. An estimated 90,000 traineeships have been instituted since the creation of NETTFORCE in 1994. It is estimated that 90% of those who complete traineeships go on to paid employment (usually with the same employer). This compares favourably with the 10,000 places in the 'Work for the Dole' pilot projects, none of which lead on to assured jobs.

4. An assessment of the role of the *public sector* in job creation. There is a place for the public sector in areas of social infrastructure (aged care etc.) and related industry policies such as government purchasing.

5. Integration between *education* and training in the labour market. A well educated, highly skilled labour force is important to Australia's international competitiveness. We should continue our development of education and training to continue Australia's investment in 'human capital'.

These measures are just part of a package, which together with appropriate macroeconomic policies based on growth and working time reform should go some way to addressing Australia's unemployment problems.

The Howard Government's 'hands off' approach and their belief in the virtues of the market forces are increasingly seen by the community as totally inadequate responses, especially in the areas of job creation and reducing unemployment.

In recent research reported in the Sydney Morning Herald on 7th June 1997, ANOP's Rod Cameron points to 'a major sleeping issue that is about to break through and become a dominant new theme in Australian community and public life : namely industry policy.'

His research, confined initially to a wide cross section of people of varying ages and occupations in Sydney and Melbourne, identified five triggers giving rise to this growing concern:

- The 'seemingly intractable' problem of unemployment and people's 'genuine fears' of job security.

- BHP's planned closure of its Newcastle Steelworks and the accompanying 'it is inevitable, nothing can be done' imagery of the Howard Government's response. Perhaps no single announcement by a company in recent years has had a greater unsettling impact on ordinary Australians.

- The absence of jobs for apprentices when they finish their time and what is seen as the general decline in the manufacturing industry.

- A nostalgia for an Australia that was seen as making things. 'Combined with a worry about an over reliance on imported products, this is leading to an ever emerging popular consensus that 'enough is enough' when it comes to tariff cuts.'

- The growing absence of Australian made goods and produce. 'That concern is heightened every time an icon of Australian manufacturing is bought by a foreign-owned company. And when even governments join the sell out by privatising basic utilities like power and water into the hands of non-Australians, then confusion really grows.'

Cameron concludes that:

> these individual triggers are combining to create a state of mind in Australia that is far from relaxed and comfortable. Instead

there is an insecure and vulnerable society in which there is:

- a genuine concern about the future of the country;
- a real fear of the permanence of growing youth unemployment;
- an emerging frustration that government cannot see the sense of supporting and encouraging Australian industry.

Australians are demanding that their leaders produce a plan — a plan for industry — that shows them how jobs will be created where they want them.

This is the *real* challenge for the Howard Government.

Conclusion

In conclusion, can I summarise the key themes of my address:

First, much more needs to be done on the employment front — the Federal Government's do nothing/let the market work policy is not providing the leadership and results that this country needs and deserves.

Second, the Reserve Bank's approach of attacking wages and promoting labour market 'deregulation' is shown by a number of economists in the economic literature to be flawed. Further, it will create inequities which will jeopardise Australia's hard fought-for social cohesion and sense of fairness.

Finally, any approach to employment policy must include working time issues — the fairer distribution of working time is a priority issue for the union movement in Australia.

References

ACIRRT 1996, 'Reforming Working Time: Alternatives to Unemployment, Casualisation and Excessive Hours', ACIRRT/Brotherhood of St Laurence, July.

ACTU 1996, *Living Wage Submissions*, ACTU, Melbourne.

ACTU 1997, *Discussion Paper on Working Time*, D No. 39/1997, ACTU, Melbourne.

AIRC 1997, *Safety Net Review — Wages*, April 1997 (Print P1997).

Coelli, Fahrer and Lindsay 1994, 'Wage Dispersion and Labour Market Institutions — A Cross-Country Study', RDP9404, Reserve Bank of Australia, Sydney.

Harcourt T 1997, 'The Economics of the Living Wage', ACTU D No. 84/1996, *Australian Economic Review* (forthcoming).

House of Representatives 1997, — Evidence of Standing Committee on Financial Institutions and Public Administration, I.J. MacFarlane, Governor of the Reserve Bank of Australia, Sydney, 8 May.

The Great Australian Challenge: Reducing Unemployment

Robert Fitzgerald

This paper provides an overview of the unemployment situation in Australia as it is today, its impact on people, how the government proposes to address the problem, and the strategy which ACOSS advocates pursuing. Issues such as the poverty and stigma attached to unemployment are addressed, as well as the proposed "work for the dole" scheme, and the risks and opportunities of the new competitive market for employment services which the government intends establishing.

Unemployment in Australia Today

There is no doubt that reducing unemployment is the greatest single challenge facing Australia today. The government states that this is its top priority and that its goal is to return Australia to the path of full employment. And most people in the community would endorse this goal. Unfortunately, there is also no doubt that we are further away from achieving it than we were fifteen months ago when the Coalition took office. The facts show that we are moving backwards, not forwards, on the employment front.

The preliminary figures for May (released by the Australian Bureau of Statistics on 12 June 1997) provide some critical information, namely:

* We now have 809,800 unemployed people — 39,000 more than when the Coalition took office.

* Of these, almost 240,000 (29.6%) have been without work for longer than a year. Again, this is 33,100 more long-term unemployed people than a year ago.

If we look behind the nationwide average of 8.8% unemployment, we see that some regions of Australia are being hit much harder than others — and have unemployment which is up to twice this national rate. The outlook is not promising because other figures show that only 20,000 new jobs were created in the first quarter of this year — not nearly enough to meet the estimates set by the government in the last Budget for jobs growth this year. Worse still, most of these new jobs are part-time jobs. Full time jobs continue to disappear. Around two-thirds of the jobs which jobseekers are getting are casual or part-time. In May 1997, there was a fall of 40,300 jobs — 23,100 of them full-time.

It would seem that unemployment, and particularly long term unemployment, is unfortunately now deeply entrenched in the Australian labour market and the Australian society — and will remain so unless the government changes tack and implements more directly interventionist and effective policies. Yet there is little indication that it will do so.

Despite establishing a Cabinet Employment Committee in January charged with focusing on this task, the only new policy which has emerged is the 'work for the dole' proposal — a most unwelcome policy shift which is not only unnecessary and wasteful of public monies but also takes a 'blame the victim' approach.

The end result of all this inertia or wrong-headed action is that poverty is increasing in Australia because of one inescapable fact — unemployment is the most savage determiner of poverty and disadvantage in our community. There are now 700,000 children being raised in families in which no one has a job. One in every nine Australians live in poverty — 1.8 million people. From the late 1970s to the early 1990s, the gap between the wealthiest one-fifth of our population and the poorest one-fifth increased by almost 50%.

We are losing the fight against poverty because we are losing the fight against unemployment.

The consequences of unemployment can be devastating. The longer people are out of paid work, the harder it is for them to get a job; they lose contact with the labour market and there is less opportunity to find out about job vacancies. Over time, skills deteriorate, confidence wanes and morale is sapped. Moreover, employers come to believe, rightly or wrongly, that the longer a person has been out of work, the less employable they are. Together, these factors put people who have been out of work for long periods at the back of the jobs queue. This is little comfort to Australia's 239,500 long-term unemployed people.

On top of this, the social stigma attached to unemployment is crushing. Increasingly, people in government, business and the community generally are inclined to turn their backs on unemployed people and even to blame them. The media has also added fuel to the flames in order to boost their ratings. In recent months we have seen the return of 'dole bludger' and 'allowance rorts' headlines; the introduction of a 'dole diary' among other proposals for tougher activity testing (despite their existing toughness); and the current legislation before the Senate to introduce 'work for the dole'.

It is as though both government and many in the public are wilfully blind to the fact that the vast majority of unemployed people are *desperate* for a job, and that the real problem is that there are around 13 unemployed people for every one job vacancy. They also refuse to acknowledge the high degree of compulsion that has long been part of our social security system. There are already enough 'sticks' to make sure that unemployed people do all in their power to improve their employment prospects and take up any job opportunities.

ACOSS fully supports the notion of 'reciprocal obligation' or 'co-responsibility' whereby the government guarantees ongoing intensive job search assistance in return for the commitment of the job seeker to maximising their chances of gaining long term employment. We also support the principle whereby the payment of income support to unemployed people is linked closely with active employment assistance measures — but *only* where active employment assistance is being provided.

The work for the dole scheme which guarantees no training, no job search assistance, and no skills or qualifications, is a far cry from anything that can be described as active employment assistance. The proposed new structure of employment assistance as outlined in Senator Vanstone's Ministerial Statement 'Reforming Employment Assistance' will exclude significant numbers of job seekers from obtaining any form of employment assistance at all.

The huge cut of $1.8 billion to labour market programs over four years in the last federal Budget, combined with the tighter eligibility rules for assistance, will see many people miss out altogether, long waiting lists and a decreasing number of services. The failure of this package to provide guarantees of access to employment assistance, even for *eligible* people, raises doubts as to the continuing validity of the co-responsibility principle.

The effect of the government's proposals and the debate they have stirred is both divisive and destructive to society. We are creating a divided nation with an underclass of unemployed people, particularly young unemployed people, made to feel inferior and entirely personally responsible for their situation. I don't believe that this is really what Australians want for our communities. It certainly offers no hope for the type of society and environment we want for our future generations.

Finger pointing, blame and guilt have no place in debates on unemployment. The simple fact is that we have more people than jobs and this means that not all people who want a job will get one. What we need to do now is to implement a policy which ensures that, as the economy grows and jobs become available, those without jobs are ready and able to take them up if given the opportunity to do so.

The Changing Focus of Employment Services

ACOSS believes that the government has an obligation to assist all job seekers to gain employment, and that the most disadvantaged jobseekers should have individually tailored assistance. This means adequate funding for quality employment assistance services and no excessive waiting queues.

We argue that employment assistance is not a 'cost' to government; it is an obligation and an investment in the kind of society we want in Australia. ACOSS is deeply perturbed by the extremely large reduction in employment assistance expenditure introduced in the 1996–97 Budget and is disappointed that the trend was not reversed in this year's Budget.

We estimate that, as a result of the government's massive withdrawal of resources, only one in four long-term unemployed people will receive substantial employment assistance at any one point in time in a year. Such rationing of assistance is a national shame and completely unacceptable. The more government rations employment assistance, the more people are slipping over the line into long-term unemployment, and the harder it is for them to reattach to the workforce.

The government's *Reforming Employment Assistance* package (which should perhaps more accurately be called *rationing* employment assistance!) creates a radical new structure, based on a 'competitive market' for employment services.

The package places the responsibility for assisting unemployed people on the shoulders of 'employment placement enterprises' (referred to as EPEs). I doubt that the government will take responsibility if their new system doesn't work — it will be put down to 'market failure', not government policy failure.

This is a very risky experiment for both jobseekers and employment service providers. Both parties are entering unchartered territory and, largely, will be risking their futures. For unemployed people, the labour market has rarely delivered a fair outcome. There is an inherent power imbalance stacked against them in their search for work and assistance to find employment. For employment service providers, the financial risks of entering this market are enormous. The very idea of setting up a business that relies on placing jobseekers in scarce jobs is daunting to say the least. But for both parties, the potential to benefit — and, more importantly, the lack of an alternative — demands their participation in the experiment.

Contracting Out and the Community Sector

ACOSS supports the government's new focus on outcomes — provided that it is based on an understanding of the short and long-term labour market needs of each individual.

If the new system operates as intended, there will be benefits for both jobseekers and EPEs. In the case of relatively job-ready jobseekers, EPEs will be able to snap them up and place them in a job quite quickly and easily. A win-win situation for both parties. For those less job-ready jobseekers, EPEs will be offered larger 'outcome payments' and be given a free rein to adopt flexible and innovative assistance measures tailored to the needs of individual jobseekers. Again, a potentially win-win situation.

However, we have doubts that the system will actually work this way. It is more likely that the pressures inherent in the payment system for EPEs to achieve outcomes as quickly as possible will lead to what is commonly known as 'creaming' — that is, EPEs opting to assist only the most job-ready people in order to achieve fast outcomes, and avoiding those requiring more intensive and longer-term assistance.

Such quick-fix solutions will do little to reduce long-term unemployment or to achieve sustainable, quality outcomes for jobseekers. I cannot stress enough the importance of maintaining the focus on high quality, sustainable outcomes.

Under the new arrangements, jobseekers will have only one chance of assistance before they go to the back of a very long queue. That chance needs to be the best chance possible. They will need high quality and appropriate training, skills development and work experience to be able to achieve sustainable employment.

Unfortunately the proposed system contains few checks and balances or incentives to encourage EPEs to provide the quality skills training and other support which most disadvantaged jobseekers need to improve their medium to long-term employment prospects. Rather, I think it has been quite widely acknowledged by both the government and most commentators that, to balance the effects of creaming by commercial EPEs, community and not-for-profit EPEs will be required in this new marketplace to provide assistance to the most disadvantaged.

I believe the government is relying upon the community sector and its willingness and expertise to help disadvantaged jobseekers in order to make its new system work. The government is also relying on the community sector to implement its work for the dole scheme.

Work for the Dole

The compulsory work-for-the-dole proposal represents a major policy shift in the basic principles underpinning public assistance for unemployed people. It turns the clock back to the great depression years of the 1930s, prior to the introduction of unemployment benefits. During this time, when approximately one third of the Australian labour force was unemployed any assistance in cash or in kind for unemployed people with no means of support (the 'dole') was only provided in return for work on public projects. This work was almost entirely unskilled and rarely led to secure employment.

From its inception in 1944, the unemployment benefit in Australia has always been based on a reciprocal obligation: on the part of the government, to make a sustained effort to generate full employment and to pay unemployment benefits to those still unable to find work; on the part of the unemployed person, to make a sustained effort to seek employment and take advantage of any job opportunities that became available.

By the late 1980s, high and entrenched levels of unemployment forced a re-think of the Australian system of employment assistance. By this stage, there was a sizeable structural component to unemployment which was evidenced by high levels of long-term unemployment. In response to this problem, Australia (together with most OECD countries) introduced active labour market strategies during the 1980s and early 1990s. Long-term and other severely disadvantaged unemployed people were individually counselled and referred to labour market programs to improve their employability.

ACOSS is not suggesting that policy has returned full circle to that of the 1930s. However, there has been a definite and worrying shift of emphasis which is symbolised by the scheme currently under consideration. The title of the Bill includes the words 'work-for-the-dole', which, of itself is graphically symbolic of the changed approach. Unemployment benefits have not been officially described as 'the dole' since the 1930s. The current term is Newstart Allowance — a change which was introduced to reinforce the new approach of an active employment strategy in the early 1990s.

As far as ACOSS can ascertain, this policy shift is not based on hard evidence of a generalised weakening of the work ethic among unemployed people. No such evidence has so far been presented by the government. Moreover, the present unemployment benefit system is extremely stringent — more than enough to both encourage and require people to actively seek employment and participate in labour market programs. Penalties for breaches of the 'activity test' are already excessively harsh, and can result in people being left with no payment for weeks or months on end. Further there is strong evidence that the Department of Social Security's strategy has been very effective in addressing fraud and non-compliance with activity tests. Indeed many countries look to Australia as a model in these matters.

Rather than presenting factual evidence of a weakening of the work ethic among unemployed people, the government justifies a compulsory work-for-the-dole scheme as a response to 'community views'. ACOSS recognises that community views should be taken into account in formulating policy. However, sound public policy cannot be constructed on this basis alone, especially with regard to disadvantaged groups whose situation is not well understood by the community at large.

We are not against unemployed people having the opportunity to contribute to their communities — but we are against them being *forced* to do so at the threat of losing their income. All unemployed people already have the opportunity to undertake voluntary work as part of their activity requirements to look for a job. We do not need this punitive legislation to give them that opportunity.

The $21.6 million which the government has set aside for its work for the dole proposal would be much better spent on increasing the pool of resources for proper employment assistance for long-term unemployed people — to assistance which is directly aimed at improving their employment prospects and directing them into 'real jobs' and training.

There is no doubt that the current system needs improvement. The present labour market program structure and delivery arrangements would be enhanced by greater flexibility to provide personally appropriate assistance to each unemployed person. There is also a need for a greater focus on outcomes as well as processes. The key 'positives' in the government's proposed reform package are a continued emphasis on individual case management and the introduction of more flexible program structures to enable providers to put together the best package of assistance for each person. ACOSS also supports a greater emphasis on employment outcomes, *provided* this is based on an understanding of the short and long-term labour market needs of each individual.

Nonetheless we are of the strong view that there is insufficient evidence to show that the radical restructuring of employment assistance which the government proposes to introduce from December 1997 onwards is warranted.[1] Unemployed people are afforded no personal security under the new system — there is no guarantee of assistance for long term unemployed persons, and the introduction of need and 'capacity to benefit' tests adds to the uncertainty job seekers face.

We need to turn around the direction of public policy and attitudes towards unemployment and unemployed people. The government must take responsibility for unemployment, they must create an environment for jobs growth, and they must provide unemployed people with the assistance they need to get their fair share of jobs. Rather than pointing the finger and conjuring up schemes to punish the unemployed, the government should be concentrating their efforts and resources on creating a positive environment for jobs growth and reducing unemployment.

A Strategy for Full Employment

We should never lose sight of the need to keep the goal of full employment as the focus of all our efforts. Distractions such as the proposed work for the dole scheme are unhelpful to this goal and wasteful of precious time and public monies. ACOSS has spent much time and effort developing a workable strategy for full employment. We believe it is a realistic and pragmatic approach to resolving our country's unemployment problem, based on a comprehensive and integrated raft of public policies.

In a nutshell, the strategy involves six key elements:

- effective macro-economic management;
- effective industry development policies;
- targeted regional development;
- taxation reform;
- effective and adequate employment assistance for unemployed people; and
- an adequate social safety net.

The first element, well balanced and effective macro-economic management, is crucial to reducing unemployment. While a rigid approach to inflation targets and a reliance on high rates of interest must be avoided, the current account deficit must be kept under control. This requires new mechanisms to ensure equitable and effective wage restraint, and to dampen asset speculation, at times when the economy is growing strongly.

The second element of the ACOSS strategy involves policies to revive and broaden the industrial base and to improve the international competitiveness of industry. Australia relies excessively on trade in primary resources, and has made too little progress in modernising its manufacturing base and expanding the service industries which will form a growing part of international trade in the coming century. As a result, whenever the economy grows strongly enough to substantially reduce unemployment, the current account deficit increases to unsustainable levels.

The scope of micro-economic reform should be broadened from the current emphasis on harnessing competitive pressures to one which incorporates active long-term industry development and export facilitation policies with a long range focus. By comparison with many of our trading partners in East Asia, this aspect of policy is poorly developed in Australia and was unduly weakened by 1996 Budget decisions.

Industry development must be complemented by regional development — the third element of an effective full employment strategy. This is necessary to ensure that the fruits of economic growth are shared by those regions which have borne the brunt of economic restructuring and long-term unemployment. Public investment in physical and social infrastructure has a crucial role to play in reviving regional Australia. ACOSS advocates the introduction of a Regional Employment and Social Development program for non-metropolitan regions to encourage a more balanced pattern of regional development throughout Australia.

Such a program would:

- improve coordination of government and private sector activity;
- promote public and private sector investment to encourage employment growth and new commercial initiatives;
- introduce employment-related training targeted to the specific needs of individual non-metropolitan regions;
- improve access to essential services in non-metropolitan regions.

Rather than channelling public funds into a single regional development program, this new program would be designed to stimulate and improve coordination among all levels of government across a range of programs, especially those in employment and training, industry development, and community services.

The fourth element of the strategy is reform of the taxation system to reduce distortions that presently encourage over-investment in property rather than more productive activity, and reward debt rather than saving. The main problem is the inefficiency of savings and investment in

Australia, rather than an overall deficiency in saving and investment levels (although the latter is also of concern). This should be addressed by streamlining and broadening the tax base and the tax treatment of different forms of long-term saving. There is, however, no convincing evidence that overall tax rates for income derived from savings or investments are too high.

The fifth element is a set of well crafted labour market initiatives designed to ensure that long-term unemployed people and other deeply disadvantaged jobseekers have a fair chance of benefiting from employment growth. Without good quality and timely assistance, their chances of regaining employment are almost negligible. They will be left behind as the economy grows and employment opportunities are expanded. The use of public and community sector job creation programmes should also be considered in parts of the economic and business cycle when the private sector is incapable of providing enough jobs for all people.

The sixth element is an adequate and secure income support for unemployed people. The importance of this element is often down-played by those who argue that it weakens work incentives. However, the Australian social security system is very stringent. On average, unemployed people can expect their household disposable incomes to double if they obtain full-time employment, and the level of benefits paid in Australia is very low by international standards (especially for single people and youth).

Together, these six key elements provide a sound strategy for full employment, achievable within a reasonable period of time. All public policies, and all of our efforts in the community services sector, should be directed towards this goal.

Endnotes

1   The commencement date was subsequently delayed to May 1998

'Ask Not What You Can Do For Your Country. Ask What Your Country Can Do For You.'

John Tomlinson

The Federal Government has the capacity to reduce unemployment to 1% within a year if it decided that it wanted to abolish joblessness. This paper examines the stark choice between dramatically expanding employment, and allowing it to remain at 8% until the end of the century. I argue that the first step in the process of moving to full employment is to recognize that we as a nation presently provide massive subsidies for many existing jobs, and then to extend this subsidised employment creation to other jobs which need to be done. I argue that unless we introduce a guaranteed minimum income and create jobs for those most marginal to capitalistic production then we will never become a socially productive country.

Fudging the Figures

Unemployment can be explained away by individualising the reasons of joblessness. 'Joe Bloggs is a workshy dole bludger', 'Mary Smith lacks skills'. Such explanations may have elements of reality but they in no way account for the fact that from 1945 to 1972 unemployment seldom reached 3%, and since 1980 has seldom been below 6%, and has averaged close to 8%. Explaining unemployment in terms of industry and government policy paints a national picture but tells us very little about an individual's reasons for being out of work. It is however closer to an explanation of unemployment than would be achieved if we collected the totality of individual explanations for being out of the paid workforce enunciated by expert psychologists. If we could collect the totality of self explanations for being out of work then we still would have very little idea as to why unemployment fluctuates from year to year or how to reduce its incidence. Even if we added together the experts' summation with the collected individuals' insight into their unemployment we would not have an explanation of unemployment because the explanation would simply compound the limitations of individualised explanations.

Should we wish to abolish unemployment, would the best approach be to assign a therapist or a skiller or some other expert to every unemployed person to case manage them, cure them, get them job ready, and so forth; or would we be better off to expand the job vacancies by 2 million? I am not suggesting that every case manager is a waste of space, that all therapy is useless, that all training regimes fail to skill or that there are not some people who would benefit by remedial programs. Hopefully many of the job vacancies would be assigned to human service, educational and health personnel in order that those who might benefit from voluntary remedial or support programs did so (Langmore & Quiggan 1994).

Solutions

At one level I am saying that the solution to unemployment is beyond the scope of any one individual, organisation, company, or even state government. I say this not to reinforce feelings of powerlessness but simply to recognize the breadth and scope of the problem. Having said that, it is equally important to note that 'If you don't fight you lose' [Redgum].

> The fight for the liberty of a people cannot be waged alone.
> And so they took Ned Kelly and hanged him in the jail,
> For he had fought single-handed although in iron-mail;
> And no man single-handed can hope to break the bars,
> It's a thousand like Ned Kelly who'll hoist the flag of stars.
> [John Manifold].

No-one should underestimate the importance of groups such as the unemployed workers movements of the 1970s and 1980s nor the Reworking Australia Movement in the 1990s. Unemployment will not be solved without the active involvement of all humanitarians because the political pressure necessary to force the Federal Government to alter course will not be generated.

There have been many proposals about jobs (currently not done) which need to be done. Langmore and Quiggan (1994), setting out a blueprint to reduce unemployment to 3%, suggested a massive expansion of the human service industry. Other proposals have included the revegetation of much of Australia, the desalination of the Murray — Darling River system, massive investment in the social and technological infrastructure and the rehabilitation of toxic dumps and worked-out mine sites. In 1995 I proposed a considerable expansion of research into areas of concern to Third World countries (Tomlinson 1995). Many have proposed expansion of research into alternative technology whilst others want to see a huge investment in general scientific work backed up with a real commitment to develop the ideas which flow from the research. If we did this then we might manufacture and export technologically sophisticated products and services.

We don't need to chose between these compatible proposals; we can afford to undertake all of them. All these proposals have one thing in common if they were implemented we would be a richer country. We would be richer socially — just making child care universally available, providing accessible education to all who wanted it and guaranteeing people with disabilities and the frail aged appropriate services would enhance our humanity by removing the pressure (placed primarily on women) to be unpaid carers. We would be better educated and therefore more likely to solve complex issues which confront us. As well, a better basic education would enhance our capacity to learn required job skills. We would be utilising the human resources of this country in an effective manner. We would increase the environment sustainability of our food producing areas, we would start to put a halt our appalling record on species extinction and might as a result massively expand our eco-tourism.

Aboriginal and Torres Strait Islander Employment

On Australia Day 1997 Prime Minister Howard claimed that Australia has become 'a magnet of tolerance' (ABC TV, News 1997). Responding to the Wik High Court judgement relating to native title on pastoral leases his Deputy, whilst acting Prime Minister 11 days previously, had declared 'hunting and fishing rights with a boomerang and an arrow might be the traditional way, but Aborigines in some areas hunted and fished using fleets of 4WDs and 'every legal weapon known to man'.' (O'Malley, Lehmann & Johnstone 1996). The fact that the acting Prime Minister was happy to reveal his lack of knowledge of Aboriginal traditional hunting technology is one thing but to choose Winton in the heart of Queensland's pastoral country as the place to trot out the pastoralists racist cliches is quite another. It is probably no surprise to indigenous Australians that Tim Fischer believes that Aborigines' entitlements under native title should be restricted to 18th century technology.

There is an alternative future that non-racist Australia would wish for this country: working alongside our indigenous brothers and sisters to ensure meaningful, culturally appropriate employment, at award rates in the places where Aborigines and Torres Strait Islanders live would do much to provide the basis which indigenous communities could use to escape fourth world conditions in which many just survive. This is not a new idea; it has been around in various forms since Aborigines have been confined to missions and reserves, but always Aborigines were paid at less than award rates (Tomlinson & Davey 1982).

If a government were prepared to provide this style of employment at award rates, it would have to relinquish the attraction that white governments have for the Community Development Employment Program (CDEP) — a work for the dole scheme on indigenous communities not unlike the 1930s' 'susso schemes' for whites. The CDEP does ensure that indigenous people work, but because it is paid at a rate equivalent to the unemployment payment it is a system of welfare coupled with compelled labour. It is in breach of international covenants and conventions Australia has signed and ratified (eg Article 8(3) International Covenant on Civil and Political Rights). At the end of the day many CDEP workers do jobs which their communities require to be done, they may willingly do this work in preference to enduring enforced idleness. But the rates at which they are paid leave them and their families in poverty. This ensures their communities do not generate sufficient income to create award rate jobs. Aboriginal and Torres Strait Islanders work but they are excluded from what Castles (1994) called the 'workers welfare state' (Tomlinson 1996).

The new culturally appropriate employment programs, proposed here to replace the CDEP would need to be paid at a rate commensurate with wages in the broader community if the intention were to create employment, promote economically viable communities and start to handle the appalling health, housing and poverty difficulties to which white Australian governments subject indigenous Australians (ABS & AIHW 1997).

Some might argue that the creation of decent paying culturally appropriate jobs in areas where indigenous Australians live will be expensive. However, the failure to do so will be more expensive. Australia cannot afford to continue to treat indigenous Australians as if they are non-citizens, suitable only for confinement in fourth world conditions and a source of stolen children. Nor can white Australia ignore the international response to issues like the institutionalisation rates and the associated deaths in custody, shameful mortality / morbidity figures and the failure to come to a reconciliation with the original owners of this land (ABS & AIHW 1997).

White Australia's affluence has always depended on international trade. Globalisation has increased this effect simply because federal governments in recent years have slashed tariffs, deregulated the financial market and promoted the sale of Australian assets to foreign investors. Trade, tourism and international reputation are intimately linked — they can only flourish in a stable peaceful environment. The run-up to the Sydney Olympics will provide white Australia an incentive to establish a just basis for reconciliation. If white Australia gets bogged down on petty legal instruments designed to provide certainty to pastoralists and miners rather than negotiating a just accommodation with the indigenous owners of this land, then the opportunities for increased trade and tourism will evaporate and with them the employment opportunities of us all.

Poor, White and Out of Sight

Rural white Australians have been a receptive target for racist and particularly anti-Aboriginal campaigns run by organisations like the Katherine Rights for Whites, the League of Rights and the La Rouch Foundation. In order for the indigenous employment program to become politically acceptable two things would need to be done. Firstly there would need to be a commitment by the Federal Government to create enough employment in rural and remote Australia to abolish unemployment in these areas, and, secondly, there would need to be a concerted campaign initiated to explain the subsidies which are currently provided for existing jobs. In the USA, like here, governments provide massive subsidies to industries and comparatively little to citizens (Nader cited in Ritchie 1997).

We might start by pointing to the estimate of $43,000 a year subsidy to every production worker in the automobile industry (Industry Commission 1996, pp. 221–222). Forestry workers are subsidised by the various state governments who grant clearing concessions to timber companies for a minuscule amount compared with the real cost of replacing the timber. Farmers and graziers have their incomes bolstered by subsidies, drought assistance, flood mitigation works, dam construction, preferential lease deals, subsidies on export trade promotion and by governments turning a blind eye to the farmers' repeated failure to meet lease conditions. These subsidies pale into insignificance when compared with the National Party's post Wik suggestion that all pastoral leases should be converted into freehold title in order to extinguish native title.

Similar subsidies occur in the mining industry where the resource is provided for a pittance, the electrical power to refine the extracted ore is subsidised, tax transfer pricing arrangements are given a wink and a nod, tax on gold mining profits are forgone, and preferential arrangements entered into such as the West Australian Government's guaranteed annual purchase of a set volume of North West Gas irrespective of usage. Governments provide massive subsidies to some types of mining: frequently the requirement to install expensive equipment which miners promised to use to protect the environment is waived after the mine is given the go ahead. Uranium miners were provided with the entire backing of the State to crush the anti-uranium movement. Uranium and coal mining is promoted ahead of alternative energy production. Jobs in the Tasmanian Hydro Electricity Commission were ensured by jacking up the price of electricity in order to promote the expansion of the 'hydro' — the cost of destroying the Tasmanian wilderness was seldom considered by governments. The consumers and the wilderness subsidise the jobs of workers in many of the examples provided above.

Whilst many of the subsidies, tax breaks, allowances and assistance provided to increase employment or profits in these industries are acknowledged, some, like transfer pricing, are denied. There is another order of subsidy which is seldom acknowledged. The best example of this is the superannuation industry. The overwhelming majority of the Australian working class have been conscripted into paying a compulsory superannuation levy. The working class is subsidising the employment of workers in the superannuation industry as well as boosting the profits of the owners of these insurance companies. These changes to the income support system in this country were imposed upon us all by Federal politicians whose well paid salaries and lucrative perks are provided to them by way of a 100% taxpayer subsidy.

Once Australians come to understand that many jobs in this nation are subsidised either directly or indirectly then the idea of subsidising jobs to create work, where workers choose to live, will not be seen as divisive. We subsidise jobs in the armed forces and jobs in the health and welfare industry, and in education and in the CSIRO and frequently as a nation we receive a return. As part of the process of developing a nation-wide understanding of the complexities of social policy each of us has a duty to demolish the convenient myths such as the unemployed enjoy being a drain on the productive people in the work force and the old in the 21th. century will be unaffordable (contra McCallum & Geiselhart 1996). We have to consistently re-emphasize the insight of the Government's Green Paper on full employment that 'The loss of production through unemployment is the single greatest source of inefficiency in our economy' (Committee on Employment Opportunities 1993: 1).

One Last Piece to the Jig Saw

The existing targeted social security system generates divisions amongst the recipients and separates those who receive benefits from those who don't. This creates a major obstacle to the introduction of progressive social policies in employment, housing, education, community service and health.

Because the social security system in this country is inordinately complex, few, if any, Australians working in the Department of Social Security or academe are able to simultaneously understand the eligibility conditions and the totality of schemes it encompasses (Raper 1995). Because many poor whites don't get social security, or if they do then it is insufficient to keep them in dignity, they assume that the stories about Aborigines or migrants getting more than them must be right. For this reason alone the social security system should be greatly simplified (Perry 1995, Baldwin 1995) or, more preferably, changed to one of guaranteed minimum or basic income (Watts 1995, McDonald 1997, Tomlinson 1997). For the suggested proposal to work in a way which was truly liberating and socially cohesive there would need to be put in place an income guarantee for every permanent resident of this country which did not presume any 'contribution' (Goodin 1992) but simply relied on people's desire to reciprocate voluntarily (Bleasdale &Tomlinson 1996).

> If we create work for all who want it and put in place a universal non-presumptuous income guarantee then 'we will build a country fit for heroes and you and me as well' [Eric Bogle].

References

ABS & AIHW 1997, 'The Health and Welfare of Australia's Aboriginal and Torres Strait Islander People', ABS Cat. 4704.0, ABS &AIHW, Canberra.

ABC 1997, TV News 26 January.

Baldwin, P. 1995, 'Beyond the Safety Net', Department of Social Security, Canberra.

Bleasdale, M. & Tomlinson J. 1996, 'Holding the State Accountable — The Quest for a Bill of Rights.' Paper given at the Justice for Everyone, Intellectual disability and the Law Conference, 28–29 Nov., University of Woollongong.

Castles, F. 1994, 'The Wage Earners Welfare State Revisited: Refurbishing the

Established Model of Australian Protection, 1983–93', *Australian Journal of Social Issues* V29 (2).

Committee on Employment Opportunities 1993, *Restoring Full Employment*, AGPS, Canberra.

Goodin, R. 1992, 'Towards a Minimally Presumptuous Social Welfare Policy.' in *Arguing for Basic Income*, ed. P. van Parijs, Verso, London.

Hancock, K 1976, *A National Superannuation Scheme for Australia*, AGPS, Canberra.

Langmore, J. and Quiggan, J. 1994, *Work for All*, Melbourne University, Carlton.

McCallum, J. and Geiselhart, K 1996, *Australia's new aged: issues for young and old*, Allen &Unwin, St. Leonards.

McDonald, A. 1997, 'Universal Income Support and Work for All.' in *Unemployment: Policy and Practice*, eds. J. Tomlinson, W. Patton, P. Creed, and R. Hicks, Australian Academic Press, Brisbane.

O'Malley, B., Lehmann, J. and Johnstone, C. 1997, 'Short cuts on title possible: Pearson.' *The Courier Mail*, 16 January, p. 6.

Perry, J. 1995, *A Common Payment? Simplifying Income Support for People of Working Age*, AGPS, Canberra.

Raper, M. 1995, 'Wrestling the Octopus — Complexity and Confusion in the Social Security System.' in VCOSS & The Good Shepherd *Income Support in an Open Economy: Basic Income Revisited*, VCOSS & The Good Shepherd, Melbourne.

Ritchie, I. 1997, 'The Need for a New Approach to our Society which includes a Universal Basic Income.' in *Unemployment: Policy and Practice*, eds. J. Tomlinson, W. Patton, P. Creed, and R. Hicks, Australian Academic Press, Brisbane.

Tomlinson, J. and Davey, S. 1982, 'Economic and Social Development in Aboriginal Communities in Northern Australia.' in *Social Work: Community Work / Betrayed by Bureaucracy*, ed. J. Tomlinson, Wobbly, Darwin.

Tomlinson, J. 1995, 'There are Solutions.' in *Unemployment: Developments and Transitions*, eds. R. Hicks, P. Creed, W. Patton and J. Tomlinson, Australian Academic Press, Brisbane.

Tomlinson, J. 1996, 'Partnerships can only work once Income Guarantees are in Place.' in *Partnerships that Work?* eds. D. McDonald and L. Cleave, Social Work, University of Canterbury, Christchurch.

Tomlinson, J. 1997, 'There but for the grace of wealth go I.' Paper given at the Beyond Poverty — Citizenship, Welfare and Well-being in the 21 st Century Conference, Massey University, 14–16 March, Auckland.

Watts, R. 1995, 'Unemployment and Citizenship: Reconstruction Social Policy in the Twenty First Century' in *Unemployment: Developments and Transitions*, eds. R. Hicks, P. Creed, W. Patton and J. Tomlinson, Australian Academic Press, Brisbane.

The Old and the New Politics of Unemployment

Stewart Sweeney

This paper will review the politics of unemployment in the context of the shift of global capitalism from New York and the USA to Shanghai and China. After 700 years of growth and expansion through Genoa, Amsterdam, London, New York it will be argued that capitalism is entering a new and unprecedented phase in terms of both the scope of global capitalist production and it location.

It is this qualitative change in capitalism along with developments in technology, the rise and fall of the male breadwinner and ecological constraints that render much of the old politics of unemployment redundant.

The recent literature on capitalism and employment will be reviewed along with the current policies of leading international organisations and some governments (including the USA and the UK)

Three future scenarios will be outlined:

- reactionary reforms involving an intensification of existing policies
- reformist reforms based on changing the policy agenda in important aspects but failing to make a real difference to employment and unemployment
- breakthrough reforms based on comprehensive changes to the policy agenda that makes a real difference to unemployment.

Some strategies and tactics for developing and implementing breakthrough reforms in Australia and South Australia will be outlined.

There is no shortage of proposals for delivering the economic promise of full employment. However there are few proposals that deal with the challenges of developing and sustaining the political and democratic will to deal with unemployment and create full employment (ILO 1996; Compston 1997). In this brief paper much of the focus is on fundamental medium and long term issues. However, the key argument is on the need to connect short, medium and long term thinking and action to an unswerving commitment to full employment. Thinking the unthinkable takes courage and imagination; developing a shared vision takes organisation and time. It is politics as the art of the impossible (Cockett 1993; Havel 1997).

So Near Yet So Far

In *Work for All: Full Employment in the Nineties*, John Langmore and John Quiggin provided one of the most comprehensive efforts to date to address the issues relating to full employment and political will (Langmore and

Quiggin 1994). The approach detailed in *Work for All* provides both an illustration of detailed alternative thinking and a useful benchmark for assessing other proposals. Five strengths of this book are firstly, the identification of the crucial issue in the struggle to achieve full employment (defined as three per cent) as being the weight given to the employment objective compared to others; secondly, the consideration of political will including community attitudes, influences for and against work for all, including the role of the Labor Party; thirdly, the consideration of the need to refocus both public policy and enterprise practice; fourthly, the consideration of 'green jobs'; finally, the consideration of national and international issues. Areas reviewed in relation to political will are the role of business, the union movement, the churches, other non-government organisations, media, satirists and scholars. Finally some ideas on developing a coalition for full employment are reviewed.

However, despite these strengths it will be argued here that *Work for All* did not effectively place Australian developments and challenges in the context of developments in capitalism in an era of globalisation and did not fully consider some key aspects of the old politics of unemployment and the new politics of full employment in Australia. These failures are reflected even more clearly in other recent proposals (ACTU 1993; BCA 1993; Blair 1996; OECD 1996).

In summary, the old politics featured a simple conception of class; a focus on the male bread winner; a blindness to race and ethnicity; a simple model of growth and progress and a primarily national focus. The new politics features at best a confused understanding of class; a more gendered conception of work; a consideration of race and ethnicity; a focus on young and older workers; a more critical model of growth and progress; a local, national and developing international focus.

Langmore and Quiggin successfully straddled aspects of the old and the new politics of full employment but remained mired in the old politics in relation to their understanding of capitalism, work, class and above all the fundamentally antisystemic nature of an effective struggle to achieve full employment. The approach outlined overly relies on the markets and the Labor Party to deliver an approximation to full employment.

This is clearly reflected in the apparently ambivalent commitment to the full employment objective. The book's title and much of the proposed economic policy program imply a strong commitment to achieving full employment. However, they also appear to walk away from the full employment objective when they say of their own proposals, 'although the future cannot be forecast with precision, these policies could, under favourable conditions, lead to restoration of something approaching full employment' (Langmore and Quiggin 1994). In the end the book does not make the clean and decisive break that is required from current policies and processes. Such caution is easy to understand. The combination of the dominant ideology in economics and the poverty of political pragmatism is daunting. However, it is the contention of this paper that there is no escaping the reality that an effective commitment to full employment requires in part a leap of imagination and an act of faith. It is individual belief and individual will that provides the basis for developing and organising political and democratic will. The science of economics may be necessary but it is not sufficient to achieve full employment (Heilbroner 1995). It is hard to imagine that capitalism can deliver full employment any more than it can eliminate poverty. New imagination, new believers and true believers are more than ever the basis for action to achieve full employment. The animal spirits of capitalism need to be replaced by the social spirits of class and community (Cox 1995; Wood 1995).

Capitalism in an Era of Globalisation

The differences between the old and the new politics of employment and unemployment are primarily a result of changes in capitalism in an era of globalisation (Shannon 1996).

The reality now being faced makes achieving full employment harder, not easier. We are it seems faced with two fundamental and related changes in the capitalist world system of accumulation. Firstly, the capitalist system of accumulation and production is becoming truly global in its reach. In broad terms the other half to two-thirds of the planet's population is being brought into the capitalist production system (Arrighi 1994). In terms of sheer scale it is as though the industrial revolution in 19th century Britain is being repeated year after year after year. Secondly, the global centre of the capitalist system of accumulation is in transition from the USA to China and from New York to Shanghai (Arrighi 1994). It is these two changes that distinguish today and tomorrow from all previous periods.

Finally, globalisation is producing an ever greater concentration of economic, financial and political power in a handful of corporations and financial institutions, separating their interests from the human interest and exposing the market system's blindness to all but its own short term interests. A continuation of existing trends in capitalism and political responses is likely to widen the gap between what is needed to achieve full employment and the reality of high unemployment over the next ten to twenty years (Korten 1995).

These developments imply that a political response to unemployment requires an even greater leap of imagination and act of political and democratic will and organisation than was required in the past. In the past the focus was primarily on action within nations; now the focus requires action within regions, within nations, and globally, and action that simultaneously addresses issues of class, gender, race and ecology. Thinking the unthinkable has just got harder.

Class in an Era of Globalisation

Class and class conflict remain central to an understanding of what is going on. However, the old basic three class categories of capitalists, workers and petty bourgeois, based as it is on relations to the means of production, can now hinder as much as help analysis and action. In particular they do not deal with the problem of the 'middle class' among employees nor the unemployed. The reality of such contradictory class locations requires a more complex and effective conception of class to underpin organisation, campaigning and the struggle for change.

The recent publication of *Class Counts* (Wright 1997) provides a breakthrough in our understanding of class and class consciousness and a new elaborated class typology that identifies twelve class locations among employees. The three basic class locations, capitalists, petty bourgeoisie and workers, are considered in the context of their relationship to authority, scarce skills and number of employees to provide a new map of class. This new map provides a basis for a deeper understanding of class structure, class consciousness, class formation and above all class organisation. It provides a benchmark study and new insights into the relationship between class, gender and race.

Finally it provides a powerful tool for rethinking future developments within unions and labour parties as well as between the labour movement and other social movements. This study re-establishes the centrality of class as a fundamental source of opportunity and constraint in efforts at political organisation and change to achieve full employment.

Work in an Era of Globalisation

Work and the structure of occupations and jobs are undergoing profound changes. The conceptual and practical value of the traditional categories of work and occupations (ABS 1994) was challenged a few years ago by Reich in *The Work of Nations*. Reich argued that there were three jobs of the future: the routine producers; the in-person service providers and the symbolic analysts or knowledge workers (Reich 1991). Reich concluded that maintaining a high living standard was best achieved through increasing the proportion of knowledge workers in a nation's workforce.

Reich's perspective raises a number of issues that cannot be ignored. In particular a key feature of knowledge workers is that they are footloose. These workers are increasingly linked to the global economy and less and less to their national economy. In sum, the difficulties of dealing with footloose capital are being compounded by the emergence of nationally and globally footloose labour. In response to this Reich proposes a positive economic nationalism in which each nation's citizens take primary responsibility for enhancing the capacities of their fellow citizens for full and productive lives but who also work with other nations to ensure that these improvements do not come at other's expense (Holland 1983; Reich 1991).

The fundamental implication of these changes in work is to reinforce the need for nations to develop both socially inclusive policies that retain a linkage between the interests of footloose knowledge workers and their fellow citizens; and to develop supra-national coordination in relation to labour as well as finance, the ecology and taxation.

Antisystemic Movements in an Era of Globalisation

In sum these developments in capitalism, class and work require a comprehensive and above all antisystemic response to capitalism (Arrighi, Hopkins et al. 1989). The struggle to achieve full employment requires an unprecedentedly effective and radical antisystemic response. In essence it is antisystemic movements that are both the product of and the carriers of political and democratic will (Wood 1995).

The concept of antisystemic movements builds on the idea of a world-system of historical capitalism. The initial ad hoc and spontaneous responses to historical capitalism developed in time a more permanent and effective form. Riots and rebellions were replaced by parties, unions and mass organisations. The antagonism of craftworkers towards de-skilling innovations was probably the single most important factor sustaining and shaping the development of the European labour movement at the turn of the century. It could be argued that in the period 1945–1965 these antisystemic agencies achieved a large number of their intermediate objectives: organisation of the industrial working class and a significant rise in their living standards, plus accession into a place in the state political structure.

However, the unions and political parties found themselves to a significant degree locked into reflecting this traditional central core of the working class whose numbers were no longer growing. They found it more difficult to appeal to the three growing segments of the wage labourforce: the salaried professionals, the feminised service sector employees, and the ethicised unskilled or semi-skilled labour force.

It seems therefore no accident that the three major varieties of 'new' social movements have their social bases in these groups: the peace/ecology/alternative lifestyle movements; the women's movements; the 'minority' rights/Third World movements. In different ways each of these movements was expressing its discomfort not merely with the socio-economic structures of capitalism that governed their lives but with the historical political strategy of the political parties, unions and mass organisations in pursuing their conception of the need for change.

The relationship between the two sets of movements has gone through two main phases so far. The first phase from 1960 to 1975 featured deteriorating relations between the old and the new movements, with serious explosions in 1968. The period since 1975 has been a period of continuing uncertainty between the old and the new antisystemic movements. Both parties are constantly debating their relations with each other, able neither to move closer together nor to move further apart.

The central question now is how the old antisystemic movements, framed as they are by their current forms and immediate concerns, can recompose themselves into agencies, not only of national change but also for world historical transformation of capitalism. This recomposition would mean that they become in the future as subversive of the nation state system and capitalism per se as they have in the past been its products and proponents. The immediate and in part contradictory question is how to develop support for the full employment objective nation by nation and region by region. The challenge now is to think and act both locally and globally. The challenge is to think and act for the short, medium and long term.

The Swedish Model in an Era of Globalisation

It is the contention of this paper that the Swedish model represented in important respects a highpoint of the old antisystemic movements based on unions, parties and mass organisation with a national focus. In a number of respects the Swedish model arguably still provides the best basis for developing full employment within and beyond particular nations. The Swedish model sustained full employment through the 1970s, 1980s and even in 1990 the unemployment rate was 2 per cent. Today Sweden has unemployment of eight per cent, a large deficit and has been trimming its welfare state. Nevertheless Sweden's eight per cent unemployment still compares relatively well with the average of eleven per cent in Europe.

The essence of the Swedish model was a sustained exercise of political and democratic will that produced an institutionalised commitment to full employment. Over a forty year period the Swedish model became increasingly effective in its results and more radical in its approach. The core model was developed in a number of areas, including active labour market programs, industrial democracy and, above all, the social control of investment. Success bred success.

In a comparative and empirical analysis of explanations for full employment, Therborn concluded that the existence or non-existence of an institutionalised commitment to full employment is the basic explanation for a better track record in maintaining full employment (Therborn 1986). The full employment goal permeated all parts of the economic policy — illustrated by then Prime Minister Olof Palme when he at one point rejected a union proposal to appoint a special minister with responsibility for employment by saying, 'each member of my cabinet is a warrior for full employment'

Therborn's analysis revealed that in each of the five countries with the best track record in sustaining low unemployment the full employment commitment had been institutionalised and had been embodied in a wide-ranging set of politico-economic institutions and had become part of the 'common sense' of politicians, voters, trade unionists and businessmen.

Therborn summarised the justification for full employment policies as being based on either one, or a combination of, two major concerns: the wish of strong labour movements for full employment as a class interest and the concern of capital for social stability.

Recently, Rudolf Meidner, who along with Gosta Rehn was the author of the Swedish model, has reflected on its success in an era of mass unemployment (Meidner 1997). Meidner considers that the relative success of the model depended on three factors: the vast majority of the Swedish people were in agreement with the twin goals of the model —full employment and equality; the congruence of society's and union's interests, executed by a powerful a labour movement and centralised union movement; the means of the model were consistent and mutually supporting

Critically, it was recognised from the beginning that the two high priority goals of full employment and equality had to be fitted with restrictions to avoid conflict with other important goals. Specifically it became clear that full employment was difficult to combine with price stability. Thus employment policy had to be anti-inflationary. The distinctive feature of the Swedish post-war policy was that the wage policy was integrated in the policy for a stable economy and full employment. Consequently, it is correct to label the Swedish wage policy a 'national wage policy' that means a policy carried out by responsible unions with an eye on the national economy.

The Swedish model has faltered in recent years and much has been made of its demise (Hermele 1993). However, its track record remains so superior to others that thinking the unthinkable must surely start with a reconsideration of the Swedish model (Layard 1997). It continues to provide a foundation for both national action and international collaboration and coordination to produce short, medium and long term results.

The Old Accord and the Old Politics

The old ALP/ACTU Accord was a relatively narrow product of the old politics (Singleton 1990; Ewer, Hampson et al. 1992; Foundation 1995). While the Accord drew some inspiration from Sweden neither its economics nor its politics matched that of the Swedish model. Its economics merely replaced the previous policy of fighting inflation with the objective of simultaneously fighting inflation and unemployment. It failed to make an unequivocal commitment to fighting unemployment first. In essence the old Accord operated to take pressure off capital by increasing profits and profits' share of the gross domestic product through cuts to wages and public sector expenditure. The theory being that capital would then invest to produce growth and jobs. In contrast, the real Swedish model aimed to put capital under pressure and to support innovation and restructuring through a mix of policies including improved wages, increased public expenditure and an active labour market policy.

The old Accord's politics was limited at best to the peak union body, the

ACTU, and the Labour Party, and subsequently the Labour government. It quickly became the property of a handful of individuals.

However the scope of the Accord was broader than the traditional conception of industrial issues as indicated by its concern with both the money wage and the social wage. In time even this potential strength was undermined by its use as a device to increase profits by facilitating cuts in the money wage.

Much of the impetus for the Accord came from the then Amalgamated Metal (now Manufacturers) Workers Union (AMWU) in an effort to develop a manufacturing industry policy as the basis of restructuring the overall economy. In a version of the trickle down theory it was assumed that developing manufacturing would provide the basis for benefits to flow to other workers and sectors of the economy including the unemployed. It was assumed that capital would invest to produce jobs.

Imagining a New Accord

It is essential to start imagining new ways in which full employment can be achieved. Firstly, some working assumptions:

- achieving full employment is harder than ever and will take decades rather than terms of governments to achieve
- capitalism cannot deliver full employment
- the version of the mixed economy developed since 1945 cannot deliver full employment
- class and organisation based on class remain central to change
- the Swedish model provides the most effective effort so far to deliver full employment

In imagining the possibility of full employment in a future Australia the following ideas are suggested for debate:

- the need for a new Accord
- an unequivocal commitment to full employment as the prime objective of all areas of policy. No ifs; no buts; no backsliding
- detailed short, medium and long term programs linked to an unswerving commitment to full employment.
- a regional, national and international focus
- a balanced commitment to issues of class, gender, ethnicity, race and ecology
- inclusive, both of the parties involved and in its content
- comprehensive short term national and regional initiatives including improvements to community services and expansion of active labour market programs, particularly for the long-term unemployed

- development by the unions and other social movements and community organisations
- A useful beginning would see increased cooperation between the unions covering manufacturing, education, finance, retailing, construction, the public sector and the regional trades and labour councils in conjunction with the social movements and community organisations
- involvement of sectors of capital from the above areas particularly those with a focus on
- competing on innovation and quality rather than cost
- competing on medium and long term rather than simply the short term
- responding to the positive role and pressure of regulations
- developing democratic and high trust enterprises
- a balanced and new scorecard of economic and social indicators

All underpinned by campaigning and activism both within the parliamentary electoral process and beyond.

In the Meanwhile ...

Ideas, organising, networking and campaigning for the best of the short-term measures needs to continue unabated.

References

ABS 1994, 'Australian Standard Occupational Classifications', Australian Bureau of Statistics.

ACTU 1993, A Program Towards Full Employment, Australian Council of Trade Unions, Melbourne.

Arrighi, G. 1994, The Long Twentieth Century: Money, Power and the Origins of Our Times., Verso, London.

BCA 1993, Australia 2010, Business Council of Australia.

Blair, T. 1996, New Britain: My Vision for a Young Country, Fourth Estate, London.

Cockett, R. 1993, Thinking the Unthinkable: Thinktanks and the Economic Counter—Revolution, 1931–1983, HarperCollins, London.

Compston, H., Ed. 1997, The New Politics of Unemployment: Radical Policy Initiatives in Western Europe, Routledge, London.

Cox, E. 1995, A Truly Civil Society. Australian Broadcasting Commission, Sydney.

Ewer, P., I. Hampson et al. 1992, Politics and the Accord, Allen & Unwin, Sydney.

Foundation, E. 1995, 'Strategic Unionism — The National Policy Track Record 1983–1995', Unions 2001, Evatt Foundation, Sydney, pp 165–183.

Havel, V. 1997, Politics: The Art of the Impossible, Cambridge University Press, Cambridge.

Heilbroner, R. 1995, The Crisis of Vision in Modern Economic Thought, Cambridge, University Press Cambridge.

Hermele, K. 1993, 'The End of the Middle Road: What Happened to the Swedish

Model', *Monthly Review* March pp 14–24.

Holland, S., ed. 1983, *Out of Crisis: A Project for European Recovery*, Spokesman, Nottingham.

Hopkins, T. K., Arrighi, G. et al. 1989, *Antisystemic Movements*, Verso, London.

ILO 1996, *Employment Policies in a Global Context*, ILO, Geneva.

Korten, D. C. 1995, *When Corporations Rule the World*, Bettett-Koehler, San Francisco.

Langmore, J. and J. Quiggin 1994, *Work for All: Full Employment in the Nineties*, Melbourne University Press, Melbourne.

Layard, R. 1997, 'Sweden's Road Back to Full Employment', *Economic and Industrial Democracy* , V18 (1): 99–118.

Meidner, R. 1997, 'The Swedish Model in an Era of Mass Unemployment', *Economic and Industrial Democracy* , V18(1): 87–97.

OECD 1996, *The OECD Jobs Strategy: Pushing Ahead With the Strategy*, OECD.

Reich, R. B. 1991, *The Work of Nations: Preparing Ourselves for 21st-Century Capitalism*, Simon and Schuster, London.

Shannon, T.R. 1996, *An Introduction to the World-System Perspective*, Westview Press, Boulder, Colorado.

Singleton, G. 1990, *The Accord and the Australian Labour Movement*, Melbourne University Press, Melbourne.

Therborn, G. 1986, *Why Some Peoples are More Unemployed Than Others: The Strange Paradox of Growth and Unemployment*, Verso, London.

Wood, E. M. 1995, *Democracy Against Capitalism*, Cambridge University Press, Cambridge.

Wright, E. O. 1997, *Class Counts*, University of Cambridge, Cambridge.

Jobs and Environment: Modernising The Debate

Kate Crowley

The future development of post industrial economies is said by ecological modernists to depend upon an ability to produce high value, high quality products with stringent enforcement standards. In these terms, environmental amenity becomes a superior good, and environmental protection not an economic burden, but an opportunity for enhanced growth and job creation (Weale 1992). But what is the employment impact of such claims? Could ecologically modernist, integrative environmental policy alleviate unemployment in the Australian context? This paper firstly examines the place of ecological modernisation within the Australian green employment spectrum. It then considers the employment potential of the pragmatic, ecologically modernist project to 'ecologise' the growth economy. It finds that ecological modernisation may be a stepping stone to sustainability, but that it offers no guaranteed environmental or employment outcomes.

There is a growing body of literature on ecological modernisation as an emergent concept in environmental policy theory. This paper reviews ecological modernisation with a view to establishing its utility in the employment creation context. In an uncritical sense, ecological modernisation does seem both economically promising, and with the potential to alleviate unemployment. But whether this is in fact the case, and whether the political will is there to pursue ecologically modernist employment opportunities is less certain.

In earlier work (Crowley 1996a), I identified three waves of official environmental employment initiatives in Australia (ecological restoration; green jobs in industry; and green employment brokering). These I found to be couched in rhetoric that asserted both natural resource dependency and economic growth, i.e. with no pretence of ecological authenticity. If the state is indeed an institutional actor capable of social learning, as Weale (1992) suggests, then ecological modernisation may hold promise as a pragmatic middle pathway to greener employment and enhanced ecological outcomes (Table 1). However, employment uncertainty and environmental risk are curiously linked as distinctive features of late modernity, and symptomatic of reactive, economically constrained policy. The obstacles to their resolution are so deeply embedded in productivist logic that they are cause to reflect, as Hajer (1996: 266) suggests, upon the need to reinvent democracy by 'bringing society back in'.

Creating Green Jobs in Australia

The term 'green job' is broadly applied, most commonly to those jobs that rehabilitate or clean up the mess that we have made of the environment, but increasingly to those jobs that would result from the pursuit of ecologically sustainable development. Jobs in the waste management, pollution control and ecological restoration industries are created after the fact of ecological decline, whereas jobs in the waste minimisation, clean technology, and environmental protection industries are created proactively, with the avoidance of ecological damage in mind. Employment in green industries such as energy efficiency, eco-tourism, waste management, land management and clean production, 'represents one of the fastest areas of job growth in Australia'. In 1994, these industries were said to have turned over $3 billion annually in Australia and were recognised by the then Labor Ministers for Employment and Environment to be poised for growth rates of 4.5% each year (Bita, 1994; Bita & Cant, 1994). However, from Jacobs's (1994) green economic perspective, a green job is also the employment outcome of the implementation of environmental policy, principally in regulatory measures, green public spending, eco-tax reform and environmental research and development. In general, green economists agree that industrial restructuring and development is an inexorable process, with employment levels shrinking in mature industries and rising in emergent ones. However, given the ecological concerns and risks facing industrial societies today, they add that restructuring should achieve not only economic objectives, but also greener economies, greener employment and a reduced impact upon dwindling natural resources.

Jacobs (1994) acknowledges that pursuit of sustainable development which seeks to harness social and economic change, redirecting it toward environmental efficiency and greener consumer lifestyles, is sometimes described as ecological modernisation. Indeed this is increasingly the case, as discussed below. However, ecological modernisation does not necessarily promise greener employment in the proactive sense identified above. An 'ecologically authentic' green jobs agenda seeks more than ecologised growth. It seeks the arrest of ecological decline by asserting both the value of ecological capital and the employment potential of a bone fide societal shift towards ecological sustainability rather than towards more sustainable development (Crowley 1996b:6). Milne, for example, defines green jobs in the deep green sense as 'ecologically responsible, socially desirable, culturally feasible and ethically defensible'. They are achievable, therefore, only when society transforms itself, redefining its relationship to the marketplace by challenging resource depletion, species extinction and economic rationalism (Milne 1995). Similarly, when Renner (1992) talks of sustainable jobs in industrialised societies, he is talking about minimising waste, maximising reuse and recycling, avoiding the use of hazardous materials and preserving biodiversity. Ecological modernisation, on the other hand, applies as much to the greening of existing industries, even ecologically unsustainable ones, as it does to industry based upon minimal impact technology. In short, there are at least three readily identifiable means of achieving a more ecologically sustainable employment culture, from the deepest to the lightest of green, with ecological modernisation a pragmatic middle pathway (see Table 1).

Conservationists in Australia have long sought greener employment alternatives to the exploitation of dwindling natural resources, in particular old growth native forests. Indeed it is largely from their critiques of the declining employment base of primary and secondary industries that the green employment agenda has evolved. Local employment initiatives advocated by the Tasmanian Greens and implemented during the short-lived Labor-Green 'Accord' government, have already proven the value of environmentally benign local solutions to regional unemployment problems. However, whilst conservationists talk in a 'deep green' sense of redefining normative employment concepts to include human and ecological issues, official environmental employment programs are generally couched in light green rhetoric of rehabilitation, resource dependency, and enhanced growth. Nevertheless, in a comparative sense, the green employment agenda appears relatively advanced in this country. Until the recent change of federal government, a broad range of green employment opportunities was available, predominantly 'landcare and environmental action programs' in ecological restoration. Greening Australia estimated that the 1994 White Paper on Employment and Growth would have delivered 100,000 green jobs in regional environmental repair, revegetation and green industrial labour market exercises. Limited green job opportunities have also been created by combining labour market exercises with 'green jobs in industry' and 'cut waste and energy' programs piloted by the Australian Conservation Foundation and the Australian Council of Trade Unions (Crowley 1996a; Lowe, 1991: 13; Green Independents, 1991; ACF-ACTU 1994, 1995; Weekend Australian, 4 May, 1994: 17).

The rhetorical embrace of environmental employment opportunities by the Liberal-National Coalition government has to be seen as green in the

TABLE 1

Deep Green, Ecologically Modernist and Light Green Pathways to Green Employment

	Deep Green	Ecologically Modernist	Light Green
mode	proactive	integrative	reactive
scope	long term	intermediate term	short term
nature	transforming	reforming	conforming
objective	redefine growth	'ecologise' growth	enhance growth
operation	rejectionist	reinventionist	accommodationist
aim	ecological sustainability	ecological modernity	sustainable development
jobs	preserving nature	greening industry	remedying ecological decline

lightest, least ecologically authentic sense. Green jobs were first advocated by the current Prime Minister in his role as coalition opposition leader when he spoke of creating a 'green corps' of young volunteers to work in regional and remote Australia. Since his election, Prime Minister Howard has cut labour market funded employment opportunities which have underpinned landcare jobs in Australia by $1.7 billion over four years, dedicating $42 million instead to establishing a Green Corps of 3,500 jobs created over three years to replace the LEAP[1] program (Gordon 1996). Although LEAP has achieved invaluable restoration and revegetation of degraded landscapes, it has been criticised by Greening Australia for not creating 'real jobs' in environment industries, and for failing to achieve the most basic ecological objectives (Bita, 1995: 8). The ACF-ACTU (1994) argue that green jobs have a much wider application than ecological restoration, and that labour market programs need to make synergistic links with the private sector to realise green employment potential. Green employment potential in Australia has also been the subject of a recent federal inquiry which made a broad range of recommendations including inter-agency mechanisms to coordinate environmental policies and programs with job creation potential. Also supported was a doubling of the landcare program; enhanced pollution control and waste management measures; the establishment of a national renewable energy strategy; and investigation of the employment implications of nature conservation and biodiversity programs (CWLTH 1994; Appendix One).

Ecologically Modernist Employment Solutions?

Although not ecologically authentic in the deep green sense discussed above, ecologically modernist employment opportunities are worth exploring as practical policy tools for moving toward more sustainable jobs in Australia. However, in doing so it should be recognised that a broad range of theoretical claims are made as to the meaning of ecological modernisation, ranging from the most to the least pragmatic in an employment creation sense. Ecological modernisation is essentially a reconceptualisation of environmental policy discourse away from the language of 'balancing impacts' that dominated policy making in the 1970s, and beyond the language of 'sustaining development' that dominated policy making in the 1980s. To embrace ecological modernisation is to appreciate the resilience of the ecological challenge, to see this not as a crisis but as opportunity, to embark on a program of full internalisation of environmental degradation in the production process, and thus to 'ecologise' the growth economy (Boland 1994; Blowers 1996; Hajer 1996). But as Christoff (1996) explains, there is no consensus on the definition of this emergent concept, which he argues is being used in the various contexts of: technological adjustment; policy discourse; belief systems; and deeply embedded, ecologically self-conscious forms of cultural transformation. In terms of greener employment, ecological modernisation could be described, after Simonis (1989), as industrial restructuring for sustainable development. In this limited sense, ecological modernisation seeks not to jettison the industrial basis of the ecological crisis, but as Hajer (1996) suggests, to remedy its ecological deficiencies with another round of industrial innovation.

How then could an ecologically modernist, integrative approach to environmental policy formation alleviate unemployment in the Australian context, even if only in Hajer's narrow sense of industrial restructuring? As Spaargaren and Mol (1992) explain, ecological modernisation, as a theory of industrial society, seeks to write ecological value and the sustenance of ecological resources into the production process. But would this 'ecologising' of industry create jobs? 'Yes' Jacobs (1994) argues, because environmental regulation would stimulate investment and therefore employment. 'Yes' Repetto (1995) argues because a clean environment will require new industries and new jobs. 'Yes' Renner (1992) argues because there are more jobs in environmental sustainability than in resource depletion. According to such authors, ecological modernisation offers an employment antidote to the pervasive structural unemployment that characterises advanced industrialised economies the world over (Renner 1992). There are, however, 'two crucial caveats' to the positive employment dynamic of environmental policy formation which Jacobs (1994) identifies. Firstly, he argues that green jobs don't happen by themselves, but require proactive environmental policy; and, secondly, that measures should be in place to mitigate the loss of any jobs in the transition to ecological sustainability. Jobs will inevitably be lost in the quest for ecological sustainability, Beaumont (1992) concedes, but even the International Labor Organisation has found that environmental regulation alone rarely accelerates plant closures. Indeed, Repetto (1995) argues that aggregate employment levels need not necessarily be affected, if, for instance, the transition to sustainable production is eased by public policy adjustment measures (see Jacobs 1994: 18).

Langmore and Quiggan (1994) cite i) the controlling of pollution and the managing of waste; ii) the greening of technology; and iii) the conserving of nature, as examples of ecologically sustainable development objectives that deliver green jobs in Australia. These are also, respectively, examples of i) light green jobs created by remedying ecological decline; ii) ecologically modernist jobs created by technological innovation; and iii) deep green jobs created by preserving ecological integrity (see Table 1). The burgeoning 'light green' employment opportunities in Australia are in its pollution control and waste management industry, which is worth billions of dollars and expanding rapidly, but which ironically thrives on ecological decline. In this narrowly defined sector, job growth between 1988–1993 in Australia was 'a startling 107%, with a further 26% growth expected' in the few years after that (Kell 1995: 22). Japan, Germany and Denmark, on the other hand, provide paradigmatic examples of the ecologically modernist employment opportunities that arise from pollution prevention regimes.

Ecologically modernist jobs there have been created as technology has 'greened' to meet increasingly stringent, regulatory measures designed to move pollution control, for example, from the 'end-of-the-pipe' to prevention at its source (CWLTH 1994:15; Hajer 1996:249). Such government regulation is crucial to job growth in the environment industry. Indeed, despite the innovative response of many individual firms to environmental pressures, it is widely recognised, Kell (1995:23) argues, that 'most of this activity would not take place without regulatory requirements'.

In summary then, even in its narrowest sense as the next phase of industrial innovation, ecological modernisation has enormous employment creation potential. This is reflected both in the rapidly expanding environment industry, and the phenomenal growth rate of the pollution control and waste management labour market. In 1994, ACF-ACTU Green Jobs in Industry research findings predicted employment growth of 30% in the water industry; 20% in waste management and clean production; and 11% in recycling over the following two years to 1996. Growth over the five years to 1994 of 20% was found to have been achieved by the energy industry, and of 130% by eco-tourism enterprises that rely on the management and preservation of natural areas. The 'core environment industry'[2] in Australia was even then conservatively estimated by this research to comprise 2.5 to 5% of the paid labour force, representing 200,00 to 400,00 jobs in environment industries in 1992. Potential growth in Australia's pollution industry alone is estimated to be at least 20,000 jobs by the end of the decade, while Australia's capture of only 2% of the world market by the year 2000 would generate $8 billion of business and could generate 150,000 jobs (ACF-ACTU 1994; Kell 1995; CWLTH 1994). Meanwhile, an ecologically modernist shift to cleaner production is recognised to have huge employment potential even by the current federal government, not least for its export potential into the Asian market (Hill 1996).

Conclusions

In terms of relieving unemployment, probably the easiest, quickest, cheapest and yet the least 'green' job solution would be to expand the federal government's 'green corps' approach. Easier, quicker and cheaper still, however, is the federal government's masterstroke of rhetorical veenerism in declaring its $1.25 billion National Heritage Trust environmental funding package to be a job creation bonanza. This package now combines environmental and employment objectives to propose 'thousands of jobs' in rural and regional Australia over the next five years in vegetation, rivers, biodiversity, land, coast and clean seas programs (Hogarth 1997). The more difficult road, however, is the road to ecologically sustainable development, and with it the redirecting of social and economic change toward environmental efficiency and greener consumer lifestyles (Jacobs 1994). This ecologically modernist notion is essentially all about restructuring — about 'establishing and expanding energy efficient, waste minimising, low-polluting industries, and allowing the environmentally offensive processes to decline' (Langmore & Quiggan 1994:198). Raising the efficiency with which the economy uses environmental resources, and hence raising productivity and competitiveness in the economy generally (Jacobs 1994), is at least a pragmatic first step towards sustainability. Even a nation as wedded to natural resource exploitation as ours, will eventually realise that the more actively we preserve nature, green industry and remedy ecological decline, the more jobs we will create.

Appendix

Implementing Environmental Policies to Stimulate Employment Growth[3]

Contrary to federal policy and practice that has confirmed State custody of environmental issues in Australia, the House of Representatives Standing Committee Inquiry [HRSCI] into 'Environmental Policies which Stimulate Employment Growth', mentioned above, finds environmental degradation to be a national problem that needs to be addressed on a national scale. It supports the establishment of a National Environmental Protection Council, and recommends that all federal industry, economic and employment measures include sustainable development and environmental protection statements. A high level federal inter-agency co-ordinating group is recommended to secure interdepartmental cooperation and consultation on environmental policies and programs with job creation potential. Such a group, including the environment, industries and treasury portfolios, is also recommended to develop options for using fiscal measures to stimulate both cleaner production in industry, and the development of an Australian environment industry.

The HRSCI further recommends environmentally sound purchasing policies; national environmental standards; and environmental management certification. Recommendations on waste management and minimisation include landfill charges, recycled content requirements, tax reduction or exemption for recycled products, and the rationalisation of energy efficiency and renewable energy promotion programs. A National Pollution Inventory is recommended as a community 'right-to-know' measure, with mandatory reporting requirements to provide the public with sufficient information to be able to assess the environmental performance of particular sources of pollution. Other energy measures include the examination of carbon taxation and its implications for industrial activity and employment creation, and the establishment of a National Renewable Energy Strategy to incorporate a previously developed renewable energy sources and systems research strategy.

Quite a few of the Inquiry's recommendations address the national 'landcare' program, including the suggestions that funding be at least doubled to

$A200 million per year, and that funding to State agencies be subject to the appointment of dedicated landcare officers and regular reporting of their numbers. Other concerns are that landcare participants receive structured training, that landcare based labour market programs be regularly and closely monitored and evaluated, and that priority funding be available for landcare groups in drought affected regions. Priority labour market funding is also recommended for rural areas with high unemployment, and for Regional Environmental Employment Programs should these begin to deliver significant employment and environmental benefits. The Inquiry is aware of the potential for labour market trainees to displace employed environmental professionals and suggests this be investigated, as should the employment implications of national biodiversity measures, feral pest eradication, Aboriginal lands restoration and maintenance, and ecotourism industry development and standardisation (CWLTH 1994).

Endnotes

1 Landcare and Environmental Action Program.

2 There is no precise or agreed definition of this industry. It is commonly described as diversified, and comprising those industries whose activities make a positive contribution to ecologically sustainable development. More narrow descriptions employed for example by the OECD focus on pollution control, waste management (CWLTH 1994: 13). Activities undertaken within the more narrowly defined environment industry typically include air pollution control; water and wastewater treatment; waste management; contaminated land remediation; energy management; environmental monitoring and instrumentation; environmental services; noise and vibration control; and marine pollution control (Jacobs 1994:20).

3 Summary of recommendations in Crowley (1996b:624–625).

References

ACF-ACTU 1995, *Cut Waste & Energy Initiative: Create Green Jobs*, Australian Conservation Foundation & the Australian Council of Trade Unions, Melbourne.

ACF-ACTU 1994, *Green Jobs in Industry: Key Findings*, Australian Conservation Foundation & the Australian Council of Trade Unions, Melbourne.

Beaumont, R. 1992, 'Jobs versus the Environment: Dispelling the Myth', *Habitat Australia*, V20 (1): 26–31.

Bita, N. 1994, 'Faulkner Heralds Green Jobs Growth', *The Australian*, 21 July: 5.

Bita, N and Cant, S. 1994, 'Crean Links Jobs to Green Industries', *The Australian*, 22 July, p.2.

Bita, N. 1995, '$1.8bn Green Jobs Scheme Inefficient', *The Australian*, 4 April, p.8.

Christoff, P. 1996, 'Ecological Modernisation, Ecological Modernities', *Environmental Politics* V5 (3): 476–500.

Blowers, A. 1996, 'Environmental Policy: Ecological Modernisation or the Risk Society', forthcoming in *Urban Studies*.

Boland, J. 1994, 'Ecological Modernisation', *Capitalism, Nature & Socialism*, V5 (3): 135–141.

CWLTH 1994, *Working with the Environment: Opportunities for Job Growth*, Commonwealth House of Representatives Standing Committee on Environment, Recreation & the Arts, AGPS, Canberra.

Crowley, K. 1996a, 'Environmental Employment Opportunities: How Green Are Australia's Green Job Credentials?', *Environmental Politics*, V5 (4): 607–631.

Crowley, K. 1996b, 'Ecology & Social Change: Is Greener Employment Possible?', *Just Policy*, V8 Nov: 3–10.

Gordon, M. 1996, 'Jobs: Howard's Great Gamble', *W'end Australian*, 31 August: 17.

Green Independents 1991, *Green, Dynamic & Prosperous: the Green Independents Business & Industry Strategy*, Parliament House, Office of the Green Independents, Hobart.

Hajer, M. 1996, 'Ecological Modernisation as Cultural Politics', in *Risk, Environment & Modernity: Towards a New Ecology* eds. S. Lash, B. Szerszynski & B. Wynne, Sage, London, pp. 246–268.

Hill, Sen. R. 1996, 'Exporting Environmental Expertise to Asia', media release 70/96, 13 June.

Hogarth, M. 1997, 'Howard Hails New $1.25bn Era for the Environment', *SMH*, 23 May.

Jacobs, M. 1994, *Green Jobs: the Employment Implications of Environmental Policy*, World Wild Life Fund for Nature, Brussels.

Kell, P. 1995, 'Government & the Environment Industry: Constraints into Opportunities', *Current Affairs Bulletin*, April/May: 20–28.

Langmore, J. and Quiggan, J. 1994, *Work for All: Full Employment in the Nineties*, Melbourne University Press, Carlton, Victoria.

Lowe, I. 1991, 'Towards a Green Tasmania: Developing the Greenprint', *Habitat Australia*, Aug: 12–13.

Milne, C. MHA., 1995, 'The Green Employment Vision', keynote address, *The Green Employment Vision: Policy, Politics & Practice*, 8 April 1995, Department of Political Science, University of Tasmania, Hobart.

Renner, M. 1992, 'Creating Sustainable Jobs in Industrial Countries', in *State of the World 1992*, eds. L. Brown et al., Earthscan Publications, London, pp. 138–154.

Repetto, R. 1995, *Jobs, Competitiveness, & Environmental Regulation: What are the Real Issues?*, World Resources Institute, Washington.

Simonis, U. 1989, 'Ecological Modernisation of Industrial Society: Three Strategic Elements', *International Journal of Social Science*, V121: 347–361.

Spaargaren, G. & Mol, A. 1992, 'Society, Environment and Modernity: Ecological Modernisation as a Theory of Social Change', *Society and Natural Resources*, V5: 323–344.

Weale, A. 1992, *The New Politics of Pollution*, Manchester University Press, Manchester.

Wilks, L. 1993, 'Green Jobs: New Alliances — New Solutions', *Habitat*, V21 (3): 6–7.

Economic Promise and Political Will

Don Dunstan

The present policies of privatising and downsizing government enterprises has not and will not lead to an improvement but to a worsening of our job situation. The reason that we are facing unemployment at the present time is no different from what Keynes identified in the time of the depression of the thirties - there is a lack of economic demand for what can be produced.

This paper argues that in any modern society there must be community intervention to stop the excesses of the market manipulators and to maximise the use of resources to provide gainful employment.

Australia, like other developed economies, is caught in a bind which stems from the failure of the post-war vision of world economic co-operation and regulation put forward by Lord Keynes at the Bretton Woods conference. The regulation of International commodity prices, of exchange rates, of development strategies, has not only not occurred, but economic ordered development to achieve the objects of the so called Atlantic Charter have been subverted. The so-called Bretton-Woods institutions have been taken over by the so-called economic rationalists whose policies are affecting us internationally and domestically and producing the economic and social malaise from which we are now suffering.

Under the IMF and the World Bank — neither fulfilling the roles originally designed for international financial institutions by Keynes' Bretton Woods proposals - developing countries have been caught in a bind of debt, which has been used by those institutions to force on them policies which did not reduce but compounded poverty, maldistribution of income, and lack of development of markets.

While Australia reduces its aid to developing countries to a tiny fraction of the UN target, fails to pursue a policy internationally to co-operate in debt cancellation, avoids insisting that Australian companies internationally operate with standards both in the environment and in the workplace at the level set by international agreements and consistently with those insisted on domestically in Australia, it is being foolish. For the reason that we are facing unemployment at the present time is no different from what Keynes identified in the time of the depression of the thirties - there is a lack of economic demand for what can be produced. There is little point in constantly looking at the efficiencies of the supply of goods and services (though that should never be neglected) when, however, no matter how efficient you are in supply (and in many cases Australia has some of the best efficiencies in the world) the people who need our product do not have the money to buy it. By saying that we have poverty here and therefore we have no obligation to help the impoverished nations of the world to develop to the state where they can pay for our product, we are pursuing the same course internationally which I shall deal with domestically — not providing jobs but preventing them.

Economic Rationalism and Privatisation of Government Services

Any study of economic history shows that while a market economy is necessary to provide the necessary indicator of demand by the populace, an unregulated market place does not necessarily produce an optimum pattern of production, provide the services or products needed, nor produce any kind of fair distribution of income. Unregulated capitalism produced the ghastly results chronicled by Marx from official records in "Das Kapital" and gave rise to movements such as Communism as a reaction. The lesson is that in any modern society there must be community intervention to stop the excesses of the market manipulators, to provide services and products needed but not arising from market operations or where those services are socially necessary but considered uneconomic by private investors, and to maximise the use of resources to provide gainful employment.

But the attachment of the present State and Federal Governments to the theories of the so-called "economic rationalists" means that they constantly pursue the reduction of publicly provided services and the employment that provides, and the "privatising" of government services. Of course this means that there is less money in the market place to buy the goods and services provided by existing employment, and any small business will tell you that economic demand has declined.

Let me digress for a moment to deal with the nonsense that appears to underlie the push to 'privatise' government services. The assumption of the disciples of this policy is that private sector economic activity is inevitably more efficient than public sector activity. That is untrue. There can be inefficiency in the private sector — and in the public sector. Efficiency is a matter of effective hands-on management, and because there have been some failures of such management in the public sector does not lead one to conclude that things would necessarily be better in the private sector. Australia in the late eighties saw the spectacular failures of the Bonds, Connells, Skases and Spalvins of this nation — those held up previously as the icons of private enterprise, but overlooked now when arguments are advanced that everything would be better off in the private sector.

Let me give some examples from the history of this State.

Forestry

South Australia at the time of white settlement was fairly sparsely wooded and much of that wood was felled early in the settlement period. Lacking adequate native forest, the forestry officers of government conducted experiments and it was here that it was established that pinus radiata would grow more quickly here than in its native habitat. Government forests were then established and have been the basis of the industry - without public initiative we would have no forestry industry here. It has been the major foundation of the economy of the South-East of South Australia and of South West Victoria.

Electricity

Sir Thomas Playford was determined to establish an adequate electricity supply as a foundation for his industrialisation policy. The private owners of the existing electricity enterprise refused to extend their activities accordingly, and so he accomplished the nationalisation of the Adelaide Electric Supply Co and extended its activities throughout the State, with its own publicly owned soft-coal mine at Leigh Creek. With this he was able to offer good deals to industry to establish, and provide electricity to all including the poor and the remote. It could not have been done and was not done by the private sector.

Water and Sewerage

This is the driest state in the driest continent. South Australia, unlike most other states, undertook the supply of water and waste water management centrally, using governmental loan funds rather than the higher-priced semi-governmental loan funds. It was an extremely efficient operation. Not only was water widely provided throughout the State, we have not had to have water restrictions even in drought since 1957, and Adelaide was provided with a sewerage service comprehensively by the early 1950s — well ahead of other States. Indeed in 1972 Gough Whitlam was elected Federally with a policy of sewering Australia's major cities and offered money to the States for it — but he said to me there is no money for you because you've already got efficient sewerage of Adelaide. I had to fight like hell to get a share of the money by saying — yes but we need money for water filtration because when we pump water from the Murray the quality is not good. But we had a very efficient administration, and as is always necessary in any human institution it was examined and revised from time to time to make sure that its efficiency was kept up and its social objectives maintained.

The present State Government (without any mandate to do so) has sold off the management of our water and sewerage system to foreign interests. The assurances that were given by Government that this would not lead to an increase in water prices above inflation, that the company would within a limited period be 60% Australian owned, that this would lead to a great water industry supplying developments in Asia because the parent companies were bound contractually to source their supplies here, have all been dishonoured. Water prices have increased more than inflation, employment has been reduced by down-sizing of staff and has not been compensated for by increased employment in companies contracting to supply undertakings overseas, — indeed the parent companies are not bound to source their materials here. The most that the Premier (who was responsible for this extraordinary deal) can say is that local suppliers "have the ear" of these foreign companies in developments in Asia since they involved in South Australia. Their involvement was supposed to have brought greater efficiency. We have the most noisome demonstration that it has not. The sewerage plant was so badly managed that raw sewage escaped into the holding ponds for a period (it is not established for how long, clearly it was not being monitored) and destroyed the bio-mass responsible for the treatment in the holding ponds. The result is a dreadful smell overhanging much of Adelaide. Greater efficiency can hardly be said to be evident.

Housing

South Australia by the operation of the largest proportionate State housing undertaking in Australia, and through associated land management programs publicly operated, has been able to maintain the lowest housing costs to the public of any major city as well as in major country towns. The SA Housing Trust was building 23% of total housing in this State, and a further 13% was provided through funding by the State Bank. The present Government is ceasing construction through the Housing Trust and selling of its stock or rental housing, and of course the State Bank has been sold off. The rate of house building has disastrously declined, though there is an enormous waiting list. Since economic demand has been depressed by the sacking of people in the public sector, few investors are building houses to rent, and rents and housing costs will inevitably increase. This situation will be compounded by the Federal Government's reduction in immigration figures. Immigration contributes to the demand for houses and the white goods furniture and fittings to go in them- all supply industries heavily concentrated in this State. The Housing Trust was an extremely efficient operation, and there is no way that private sector investment is going adequately to substitute for it.

Market Failure and Political Will

The assumption that private investors are full of originality and ingenuity so that the market place will inevitably operate to call forth the goods and services the public want and are prepared to buy is not justified by any examination of history and is absurdly naive. As Keynes said in the 1920s in his secure on "The End Of Laissez Faire":

> The world is *not* so governed from above that private and social interest always coincide. It is *not* so managed here below that in practice they coincide, It is *not* a correct deduction from the

Principles of Economics that enlightened self-interest always operates in the public interest. Nor is it true that self-interest generally is enlightened; more often individuals acting separately to promote their own ends are too ignorant or too weak to attain even these. Experience does *not* show that individuals when they make up a social unit are always less clear-sighted than when they act separately.

Let me give just two examples currently in the news. The South Australian Film Corporation has been closely involved with the making of the film "Shine" which has won enormous acclaim and is very successful in the market place. But if the private sector had been left to its own devices there would not only be no South Australian Film Corporation, there would be no film industry in South Australia, and the employment generated by the presence of the film industry would never have occurred. The winning of the award in New York for the sets of the "King and I" and the commercial success of that production stemmed from the fact that the Adelaide Festival centre Trust was provided by me with an entrepreneurial fund, and the sets were made in its workshops. The private sector before that had sold down any business it had in theatre in South Australia.

Is there economic promise, given the fact that present policies prevent jobs instead of creating them? Yes there is — but it will take political will of a different kind from that presently being demonstrated.

Despite the international constraints — and I have already dealt briefly on some of the policies we should be reversing there — it is possible to build on Australia's resources to provide production and employment in the long term. This requires governments to take a pro-active part in the development of the industries concerned, acting with the private sector in a co-operative effort that involves both public and private investment.

Again let me give examples. The developing nations to our north have very large populations which require feeding. Australia has shown that it is capable of being at the cutting edge of efficient food production, and we have a long way to go yet to develop the variety of food production for which we can find markets. Our existing resources in fishing are strained to the limit, as are the world's. The days when rock lobster and even yabbies were affordable to the average family in Australia are passed. Those goodies disappear overseas where high prices are paid. We have the beginnings of aquaculture here and ideal conditions for it have already been shown. But we have so far only scratched the surface. The economic demand is certainly there but the industry has faced the problem that its development takes time and money is not privately available readily for long term investment. As a community we should be making commitment to the development. Food types not currently being produced but certainly economically demanded are there to pursue. Australia has the great opportunity in agriculture, horticulture and aquaculture to becoming a major supplier of food to our neighbours.

We are now under great pressure to reduce emissions from the burning of fossil fuels. We have every reason to invest as a community in solar and wind power technology. It is clearly the way the world will go, and Australia has shown in the past that it is able to be technically advanced - we have the example of one successful industry now in South Australia particularly, the wine industry - it is only having the success it now has because we are technically better than most of our competitors.

As unemployment started to rise in the mid 1970s it was clear that there would be problems in the long term and I set up a unit to identify alternative production which could be marketed and which could be set up with government backing and accounting guidance using public land and for co-operative organisations of young people. We were well on with developing that program when I resigned, and unfortunately it was then discarded. We need the involvement of the community not only on the large scale but the small in order to find every means of employment creation. I had the same sort of operation going on Aboriginal lands in South Australia when the Commonwealth took responsibility for them. Unfortunately many of these were discontinued.

Conclusion

There are always risks, of course attached to any public enterprise or investment. But, to use a phrase beloved of the economic rationalists, "there is no alternative." The present policies of downsizing, reducing government employment and the services those employees provide, privatising and downsizing government enterprises has not and will not lead to an improvement but to a worsening of our job situation. It is singularly useless for Senator Vanstone to ape Mr. Micawber and to assure us that something will turn up. The present policies on employment are not inspired by any vision or light on the hill. The light can be lit, but we must bury the policies of cutting everything in sight and with political will we can make a positive future.

Re-thinking the Politics
of Full Employment

Belinda Probert

There are many different ways in which the problem of unemployment is defined for policy purposes, and as the problem appears to become more intractable, so the interest in new frameworks intensifies — as manifested in the current interest in worksharing. A further feature of contemporary debates is the framing of particular social groups as constituting problems requiring targeted assistance — young people, or people in depressed regions, for example. What has proved far more difficult to sustain is a strong political commitment to the general goal of full employment. This paper will look at these different political constructions of the problem, and the gap between popular attitudes and policy.

> The creation and building of new traditions, or new versions of old traditions, must be taken seriously as a requirement of social policy itself.
>
> Nathan Glazer, *The Limits of Social Policy*, Harvard University Press, Cambridge, 1988, p. 122.

Much of the debate about unemployment in Australia occurs in a political vacuum. A wide range of policy measures are put forward, ranging from the promotion of lower wages to Keynesian public sector job creation, and their technical merits are fiercely argued. Far less attention is paid to the political circumstances that would be necessary if any of them were to be seriously implemented. It has been suggested that the politics of unemployment are a politics of impotence — that the most well argued case for policy intervention founders on the absence of political will.

It is hard to disagree with the argument that the politics of unemployment are the politics of impotence in Australia. Yet, if this is so, it is essential that we confront this obstacle rather than continue to recycle our policy platforms from one conference to the next. This paper tries to identify some of the barriers to political mobilisation around full employment, and it begins by arguing that we do not face insuperable opposition. This impotence is not the result of the overwhelming influence of groups standing in opposition to a politics of full employment.[1] Rather, we are confronted with the constant fragmentation of the problem — and the search for new angles — all of which, in different ways, keeps us very busy while at the same time immobilising us politically. And when I say 'us' I do not simply mean those of us who attend conferences on unemployment, but the very large numbers of Australian citizens who, I believe, recognise unemployment as one of the most serious and damaging social facts of our times.

The sense of political impotence is the result of several factors, not the least of which has been the absence of significant difference in the discourse about unemployment deployed by the major parties over the last two decades.[2] While the Prime Minister, John Howard's "Work for the Dole" scheme attracted so much critical comment, it should be remembered that in 1986 Bob Hawke proposed a 'dole-work scheme', on exactly the same grounds, namely that 'the unemployed, particularly young people, had "a responsibility to undertake some community work" in return for the dole' (quoted in Pixley 1993, p. 212). Soon after, the Australian Council of Trade Unions (ACTU) put forward its own proposal to link all income support for young people to their involvement in school, a job or training program. This was the prelude to a range of measures all of which undermined the concept of unemployment benefits as a right.[3] Ten years later, both major parties pin their unemployment strategies on private sector driven economic growth, with the Secretary of the ACTU recently claiming that unemployment can be solved by unleashing the potential for economic growth in Australia and standing back.[4] (This is not to deny the existence of significant differences between the parties, most of which relate to the size and quality of labour market programs to be supported.[5])

The continuities between recent Labor and Coalition governments in relation to unemployment seem to me to far outweigh their differences. I do not believe, however, that these continuities are the product of popular or electoral constraints on policy making in this area. On the contrary, it might be argued that there is some paradox between the 'conservatism' of recent policy and the extent of public concern with unemployment. This is a tension that the American theorist of public policy, Theda Skocpol (1990), explored in relation to the failure of every attempt since the end of the Second World War to get U.S. national governments to coordinate the range of available policy instruments to achieve 'employment assurance'. The first thesis Skocpol examines is the argument that basic American values (and hence public opinion) are so deeply embedded in an ethic of self-reliance and individualism that large scale sustained state intervention on behalf of the unemployed is doomed. It could be argued that in Australia the 'wage-earner's welfare state' and the residual conception of state support which accompanied its historical development, have created similar difficulties.

Skocpol argues that American hostility to 'welfare handouts' was, in fact, tied to the widely held belief that 'while people are helping themselves, government should also help the unemployed to acquire jobs through which they can then get ahead through hard work.' And 'public authorities had a special responsibility to help able-bodied people get jobs' (1990, p.198). The theme of 'government ensuring work or training rather than providing relief has echoed through American politics' (p. 201). The plea was really not

'Brother can you spare a dime?', but 'Brother can you spare a job?'. The active society approach has a long history in the U.S. Looking at the evidence about Australian attitudes to unemployment, Rodney Smith comes to somewhat similar conclusions (1993).

The second thesis Skocpol addresses is that the failure of employment assurance in the U.S. can be explained by that country's distinctive political class formation, and in particular by the relative weakness of unions and the absence of a labour based political party (a version of the working class mobilisation thesis). This, in turn, has allowed the capitalist class undue influence over public policy. Her argument against this is that, in fact, there have been moments of strong cross class support for government policy on unemployment which have still failed to produce enduring policy, and that opposition has been stronger from other kinds of social forces such as agricultural interests in the south and west, and from Democratic representatives in racially segregated areas.

Skocpol's explanation for the failure of employment assurance policies in the U.S. focuses instead on the peculiarities of the American political system and the role Congress plays in transforming what are national objectives into mechanisms for spreading federal subsidies to as many congressional districts as possible. In other words there has been lots of public spending on job creation, but it is delivered as pork barreling — hence preventing the emergence of any discourse around nationally coordinated public works. Congressional brokering ensures a lot of national resources are spent on job creation for the middle classes and construction and defense workers across many localities. But people in especially depressed regions and localities (in other words, inner cities) were left without help. And these people came to feel, eventually, that they were not entitled to ask for political help, unlike the more militant unemployed workers of New York City back in the 1850s (Skocpol 1990, p. 206). In this way, Johnson's War on Poverty began as a universalistic social alliance, but was implemented as a series of new programs for 'poor and black groups', added on to established or locally based interests (1990, p. 211).

I do not wish to suggest that the national state structure has played a similar role in Australia. But Skocpol's account of the way America's preference for work over welfare has failed to translate into a sustained focus on employment creation resonates against recent Australian policy history. Under the last Labor government, Australia also saw a significant movement to 'restore full employment' translate into a multiplicity of different new programs aimed at dealing with a range of problems which stem from persistently high levels of unemployment. These programs did not, however, coalesce around what might be called an 'employment assurance' policy, or even an 'employment policy'.[6]

There are two major categories of policy making at work in recent Australian developments. The first involves the recognition of certain groups as being particularly hard hit by unemployment, and the development of specific measures designed to counteract what comes to be seen as the nature of their 'disadvantage'. The second concerns the need for measures to actively reintegrate those with a significant experience of unemployment into the labour market. In recent years the categories of young people, older men with blue-collar work histories, and relatively recent migrants from non-English speaking backgrounds have been singled out as being particularly disadvantaged (categories which, it is important to note, generally manage to render unemployed women relatively invisible).

The point I wish to make here is not that particular population groups do not bear the brunt of unemployment, but that there is a real danger in the way this approach starts to constitute being young or being old or being male or being from a non-English speaking background as the problem. I am also well aware that this point is not new — but what is extraordinary is how often one has to make it. The evidence, as I understand it, clearly suggests that the young or the old are not particularly unsuited for much of the available employment, but that educational credentials remain one of the most accepted sorting devices to deal with the underlying problem — which is, of course, that there are not enough jobs.[7]

It might perhaps be argued that the constant redefinition of the problem in terms of the characteristics of different groups is more damaging to the development of a coherent and broadly supported employment policy than the relatively muted focus on dole bludgers which surfaces from time to time. It is striking that in the promotion of both the Labor and Coalition versions of work for the dole schemes, there has been almost no reference to dole bludging as such, but rather an emphasis on 'reciprocal obligations' and the socially integrative functions of work.

The fragmentation of the problem of unemployment in terms of its uneven geographical impact similarly serves to detract from a coherent employment policy. It is interesting that some of the most innovative recent measures to combat unemployment have been targeted to regional or rural areas which are seen to face particular hardships. The New Work Opportunities program, for example, through which 'substantial paid employment will be provided in projects which are of demonstrated value both to the worker and the community' (*Working Nation*, 1994, p. 123), was defined as appropriate for rural and remote areas. The justification for this exceptional acceptance of public sector job creation is that there are indeed some areas 'where employment opportunities are limited' (p. 122). Out of this selective definition of the problem, it becomes possible for key public figures on all political sides to tour the 'regions' in support of 'regional initiatives' while studiously ignoring those metropolitan 'regions' (or ghettos) which constitute the centrepiece of this country's difficulties (Gregory and Hunter 1995).

The second major area of recent policy development concerns training and labour market programs, which vary along a spectrum from humanitarian and sympathetic to authoritarian. These differences matter, but again,

the key issue is less the degree of compulsion than the place of such programs within an overall policy on unemployment. Far more attention has
been given to policies designed to reintegrate the unemployed (and especially the long-term unemployed) into the workforce than to the ways in
which unemployment is created. For example, a comparative report prepared for the United Nations analyses the particularly detrimental impact of
industrial job loss, and concludes that 'when there is a major decline in
industrial employment this results in large-scale geographically concentrated redundancies which flood local labour markets with less educated labour'
(Glyn and Gregg 1994). Similarly, a comparison of unemployment across
OECD countries found it was closely correlated with the loss of industrial
jobs (Glyn and Rowthorn 1988). We know a great deal about what causes
long-term unemployment, but have no policies to prevent it.[8] BHP's plans
for Newcastle are the most striking case in point.[9] As, Giddens, puts it, 'most
welfare measures in fact are designed to cope with events once they have
happened, rather than at origin — a major source of "state failure"' (1994,
153).

I do not at this stage intend simply to announce what we of course know
to be true — that a full employment strategy must bring together industry
policy, social security policy and labour market policies. Nor do I intend to
now wheel in the power of 'neoliberal ideology' to explain our impotence —
important though those ideas have been. Nor have I very much to say on
the role of technological change and global economic integration as causes
of our employment difficulties. My view is that these factors are more important for the way they have transformed the environment in which we must
think policy, rather than that they are critical problems in and of themselves. I intend rather to pursue further the possible reasons why broad popular support for full employment fails to translate into consistent policy, and
what role political ideologies from the left have played in this failure.

The Politics of the Welfare State

Little that is now written about responding to unemployment in the English
speaking advanced economies carries with it any kind of radical impulse[10].
Anthony Giddens, in his book *Beyond Left and Right: The Future of Radical
Politics* argues that it is the right which now lays claim to radicalism, while
the left has retreated to the defense of the welfare state. In Europe, by contrast, concerns about the quality of life and ecology have been integrated
into re-thinking employment, producing serious debate about the question
of working hours, as well as proposals to break the work/income nexus
through some form of Guaranteed Minimum Income or Basic Income (Van
Parijs 1992; Lipietz 1992; see also Probert 1993). Within Australia, it is certainly the 'idea' of the welfare state which has provided so much of the intellectual underpinnings to recent thinking on employment policy.

There are some aspects of the welfare state which are general and others specific to Australia which need to be discussed here. The first point is that the welfare states of the post-war period have been critical in shaping the social institutions of 'working life, employment, and the labour market' (Esping-Anderson 1990, p. 141). They have done this in significantly different ways, of course. In Esping-Anderson's typology, for example, this has ranged from the minimalist welfare state (the 'liberal' welfare state') in which 'means-tested assistance, modest universal transfers, or modest social-insurance plans predominate', to the 'social-democratic' welfare state promoting an 'equality of the highest standards' (pp. 26–27). Despite the very different character of these welfare regimes, and extremely uneven commitment to the goal of full employment, they all now face a fundamentally similar problem in the shape of rising unemployment levels in the 1990s. As Esping-Anderson argues, 'despite fundamental differences in institutional accommodation and policy choices...advanced capitalist democracies appear to converge in one respect; namely, in their incapability of ensuring both full employment and balanced economic growth' (1990, 164).

It is not possible here to engage fully with the debate on the causes of this 'incapability'. For Esping-Anderson the 'principal reason has to do with the limited means available (within any kind of institutional framework that has, so far, been tried in capitalism) to channel zero-sum conflicts into workable bargains. Within the range of limited means, the welfare state came to play a dominant (and problematic) role' (1990, p. 164). To this focus on the structural conflict between capital and labour, I would add the issue of 'increased demand for work rather than reduced availability' (Glyn and Gregg 1994; Freeland 1995).

In the face of these common difficulties it is the right or neo-liberalism which has become a radical ideology, arguing forcefully for the necessity to role back the state, cut back regulation, and radically shift the balance between state and market in favour of the latter. At the same time, the socialist underpinnings to extending or moving beyond welfare state capitalism have collapsed, together with the belief that a system, the economy, 'can best be organized by being subordinated to a directive intelligence (the state, understood in one form or another)...[W]hile this set-up might work reasonably effectively for more coherent systems — in this case a society of low reflexivity, with fairly fixed life-style habits — it doesn't do so for highly complex ones' (Giddens 1994, p. 8). For Giddens the problem is not simply economic globalization, but 'the social revolutions of our time' (1994, Chapter 3), and the arrival of the first 'thoroughly post-traditional society', with new forms of polarization, new politics of identity and reflexivity.

In Australia, left radicalism has been driven back into the position of fighting a rear-guard action to try and defend key institutions of the welfare state, in opposition to successive Labor governments. Here the hollowing out of intellectual support for welfare state radicalism has been exacerbated by particular interpretations of Australian welfarism and its ability to respond to the new economic order. These interpretations hinge on several key arguments. The first is the familiar one that the Australian welfare state was always weak since it relied for economic security on the wage system to a far greater extent than in Western Europe, for example (Castles 1986). In Esping-Anderson's typology, Australia has been an archetypal example of the 'liberal' welfare state. The historical success of this regime relied on a) tariff protection, b) controlled immigration, c) wage arbitration and d), as feminist scholars have more recently asserted, the male-breadwinner family norm . Castles' 'wage earners welfare state' has become part of the dominant orthodoxy in explaining the crises of the 1980s and in narrowing the visible range of policy responses.

If the distinctive feature of Australian social welfare policy was its reliance on tariff protection, what is to be done when it becomes widely accepted that protection is a major barrier to economic growth? As Paul Smyth has pointed out, Paul Kelly's book *The End of Certainty* has been a powerful voice in shaping this perspective. In Smyth's words, the core of the Australian settlement on which post-war affluence and welfare was built, 'was protection...until it finally unwound in the 1980s under what [Kelly] sees as the imperative of deregulation and integration of the national economy with the forces of economic globalisation' (Smyth, p. 7). Smyth argues that this 'post-protection' scenario

> can be seen to have forged a rather unholy alliance between the economic fundamentalists and segments of the left. Having virtually identified past government economic intervention with tariff protection both now unite in acceptance of the logic of the market as far as job creation is concerned and differ only in their views on the levels of compensation which should be afforded those made unemployed in the newly opened economy (1996, p.11).

Within this 'post-protection' framework policy on unemployment retreats to the terrain of compensation — to the range of measures which can be used to assist those who suffer most. Debate focuses on social transfers: the level of benefits and terms on which they are to be available; the scale of training and retraining programs for the unemployed; the provision of targeted measures to assist the most politically visible groups. [11] This is the reactive and fragmented response which dominates the political agenda today across the major parties.

What has been lost in this account of the strengths and weaknesses of the Australian welfare state is the role that the Keynesian 'revolution' played in shaping Australian economic and social policy. The significance of this obliteration of the role of Keynesianism in Australian public policy is that it eliminates one of the key elements of a more radical revitalisation of the welfare state — namely the recognition that the market (on whatever scale) and private enterprise are not enough to achieve full employment 'without positive and continuing action by government' (Smyth 1996, p. 12). [12] From the post-protection viewpoint, full employment was in a sense a lucky break, overdetermined by Australia's peculiar economic circumstances which for a while, at least, created a virtuous circle between protection, profits and wages. Now that lucky break is history. New economic circumstances have undermined that coalition of interests. But, what is lost in this account is the recognition that full employment in the postwar years was a significantly 'political' achievement. This is not to suggest that Australia was unique in this respect, for almost all comparative studies of the employment records of different welfare state regimes conclude that the differences are essentially the result of political factors (for example, Therborn 1986, Esping-Anderson 1990; Glyn and Rowthorn 1988). (The role of politics cannot, however, be reduced to something called working class mobilisation, or the political colour of the government, for in many cases success depended on support from a range of social groups.)

The points to be emphasised here concern the political lessons to be learned from different interpretations of the Australian welfare state. As Watts has argued, the effect of Castles' legacy is 'to play down any interest in looking in any systematic way at the actual social protection system Australian social policy makers produced in the twentieth century, and at the respective roles played by a number of different political and social collective actors' (1997, 10). As Esping-Anderson has insisted, in explaining the emergence of different welfare-state logics, 'politics not only matters, but is decisive' (1990 p. 4). 'It is a historical fact that welfare-state construction has depended on coalition-building. The structure of class coalitions is much more decisive than are the power resources of any single class' (1990, p. 30). As Paul Smyth has argued in the Australian context, 'a full employment policy without a supportive coalition of major economic interest groups is unimaginable' (1996, p. 18). Not only are the political actors lost from sight, but so also is the recognition that full employment necessarily requires government intervention not simply in the sphere of distribution, but in the management of the economic environment more broadly. As Therborn concludes in his review of sixteen countries' employment records during the 1970s and 1980s, in none of the most successful was the institutionalisation of the commitment [to full employment] limited to an endorsement of Keynesian demand-management. All have developed a range of specific state interventionist policies' (1986, p. 111). These have included import licensing, credit direction, comprehensive incomes policies, public investment and employment policies, direct intervention into supply of and demand for labour, and extensive subsidies to peripheral private enterprise.

The speed with which Australian social democracy (or laborism) accepted the marginalisation of politics in the face of the rising unemployment of the 1980s and 1990s is captured in Paul Keating's famous comments about the threat of the 'Banana Republic' and later, 'the recession we had to have'. (Paul Kelly considers the Banana Republic warning in May 1986 to have 'facilitated the demise of the old order and the advance towards a new one...It lifted community consciousness about Australia's economic predica-

ment to an unprecedented level and it changed the limits of political tolerance' (1992, p. 196).)

The White Paper on unemployment which finally appeared in 1994 was
the captive of this particular interpretation of the limited role of the welfare
state. As the Introduction to *Working Nation* claims, 'Economic growth is
the best way of generating new and worthwhile jobs to meet the needs of an
expanding workforce and to make inroads into unemployment'.
Government intervention focused heavily on the question of labour market
programs, extra assistance for 'special groups', regional measures, and incentives to keep as many people as possible 'work ready'. This is in no sense to
disparage the significance of many of these proposals, but rather to focus
attention on what has been excluded from the discourse on unemployment.

Reinventing Full Employment

The purpose of questioning the dominant wisdom on the distinctive
basis of the Australian welfare state is not to suggest that we can in some
way return to the Keynesian settlement of the post-war period. Rather it is
to highlight the extent to which the left's contemporary defense of welfare
has been deprived of the kind of substance needed to respond to the problem of unemployment. More positively it is to insist that the problems
remain as much political as economic, and that Australia's distinctive welfare history does not necessarily leave it deprived of any experience of a
more interventionist government strategy.

While recognising the economic difficulties faced by national governments in a post-Fordist and increasing global system of production and markets, the focus of the last part of this paper is on the political questions
which are central to new solutions. The shared difficulties of all welfare
states in the 1990s are as much political as economic. The social contract
which underpinned the welfare state (in its broadest sense) of the post-war
years was built on inevitable class and distributional tensions. They were
never eliminated, but rather managed. Full employment brings with it political difficulties — as Kalecki predicted — enhancing labour's power, and
constantly threatening to destabilise any capital-labour pact. The creation
of more jobs, whether through private sector expansion or public sector
employment comes at a cost (in the first case, in the form of lower wages, in
the second case in the form of higher taxes). It is also something which (in
either case) requires some new form of political coalition. Such a debate will
require the reintegration of economic and social policy. As Esping-
Anderson concludes, 'there has been little effort devoted to studying the
interconnections between many of the powerful structural changes that
took place over the past 40 or so years. This seems to be...particularly the
case with the relationship between full employment economic-stabilization
policies, and the welfare state. Our intellectual forebears saw these as intimately linked in their scenarios of a new and more democratic capitalism.

Contemporary scholarship has gone its own specialized ways' (1990, 186).

The mobilisation of popular support and political commitment to full employment may drive the construction of a political coalition, but political commitment remains only the first step[13]. In the recent past the achievement of full employment has required a 'commitment that had been *institutionalized*; had been embodied in a wide-ranging set of politico-economic institutions and had become part of the "common-sense" of politicians, voters, trade unionists, and businessmen' (Therborn 1986, p. 112). With the demise of the Accord (and its recognised failure to ensure adequate quid pro quos from employers) there is an urgent need for new kinds of institutional creativity around the issue of wage restraint and an incomes policy. As John Buchanan has argued in relation to the value of employment plans and multi-employer training and employment pools: 'In the past this country has shown it has the ability to develop novel solutions to complex problems. It is equally capable of doing so again now' (1993, p. 83).

Many analysts of the 'crisis' of the welfare state have identified the tensions caused by an increasingly international economic system and 'the resolutely national character of "modes of regulation" which, in the golden era of Fordism, gave clear-cut solutions relevant to that era' (Lipietz 1992, p. 26). Some have also recognised the tensions arising from the transformation of gender relations during the same period. Esping-Anderson for example sees these as the 'two crucial conditions that fundamentally alter the original conception of how to deliver full employment'. In his conception, it is the 'radically altered meaning that full employment has been given by the inclusion of women as normal participants in the labor market. Statistically, this might entail a revolutionary augmentation of the full-employment clientele' (1990, pp. 164–5).[14] The scale of women's increased workforce participation varies widely within advanced industrial economies, as does the underlying 'gender contract' and the institutional mechanisms by which it has been achieved.[15] But in all cases, the employment patterns of women are inseparable from the development of the welfare state, either as an employer, a provider of the necessary institutional support (such as maternity leave and child care), or in the form of a range of incentives to either stay at home or enter the workforce.

As many feminist scholars have pointed out, the definition of full employment needs to be revisited in the light of the gendered interests of men and women. In Australia the 'gender contract' has been transformed in some social strata by new labour force participation patterns, while in others it remains committed to the family breadwinner model of an earlier period (Probert 1997). In fact as Ilene Wolcott has suggested:

> as a community Australia appears to take an ambivalent stance on the household-equal status gender contract continuum. Women are encouraged to enter the labour force and be economically independent and men are exhorted to become more involved in family caring, yet there are not the community

resources such as child and elder care to enable families to accommodate such joint responsibilities. Neither is the organisation of work time structured to incorporate the everyday requirements of family life nor do taxation and income support arrangements favour such sharing (1996. p. 16).

The White Paper *Working Nation* provided a significant lead here with its radical proposal to make individual men and women, rather than couples, the fundamental unit in the social security system, but at the same time it reflected the profound ambivalence described above. The re-invention of full-employment for the 21st century presupposes what Giddens has called 'the creation of a range of social pacts, including that between affluent and poor but also especially between the sexes' (1994, p. 248). The nature of a new gender contract (or contracts) will not only affect the degree to which women are integrated into the new commitment to full employment, but the relationship between work and income and work and income security. At present, in Australia, government is playing less and less of a role in shaping this relationship, with private enterprise moving to play a determining role in whether women with families work or not. The new head of the Office of the Status of Women has argued that women must look to enterprise bargaining for assistance in the area of work and family, and only as far as it can be seen to be demonstrably good for profits. For Ms Goward, it is not to be seen as a question of women's 'rights'.

This retreat from the conception of women's right to transcend the barrier between work and family raises, in one particular form, the broader question of to what extent a reinvented welfare state might erode the boundaries between work and welfare. To the extent that the low wage and high 'flexibility' path to maximising market employment is adopted, issues of income security spread out from the 'margins' into the mainstream of the labour market. In the Scandinavian welfare states numerous rights to income support from the state permit significant numbers of people to be absent from work at any one time, but in so doing allow far greater percentages of the adult population to remain attached to the labour market. Indeed the right to be absent is dependent on the reciprocal requirement to be present at other times.

In Australia a quite different philosophy is visible in the campaign to ensure a range of legitimate ways to claim income support which are independent of work history (such as the parenting allowance, and pressure for the recognition of other kinds of socially useful participation as grounds for income support). While debate about the value of a Guaranteed Minimum Income, or Basic Income approach has been limited in Australia, it undoubtedly constitutes a radical extension of programs intended to weaken the link between work and welfare rights. However, at this point, as Rodney Smith has argued (1993) it seems likely that popular political support is insufficient — which is where this paper began.

Whatever the constraints imposed by our continuing belief in the value of work, it is clear that a radical reinvention of the full employment welfare state would also require a renewed vision of the 'good life'. For Giddens, for example, the problems of the welfare state cannot be defined in fiscal terms and the need for renewed social contracts to define who should pay. It is not so much the problem of rising costs and declining revenues and the absence of institutional mechanisms for resolving social conflict which is at issue, but rather 'resources being organized in ways which are more and more inappropriate to the problems they were set up to meet. Welfare systems designed for emancipatory ends become strained or ineffective where life-political issues loom increasingly large and where generative political programmes are needed to cope with them' (1994, p.153)

For Giddens globalisation poses not only a set of economic policy difficulties, but is also the central force behind a 'thoroughgoing detraditionalization'. 'Life politics, and the disputes and struggles connected with it, are about how we should live in a world where everything that used to be natural (or traditional) now has in some sense to be chosen, or decided about (1994, pp. 90–1). 'Life politics is about the challenges that face collective humanity, not just about how individuals should take decisions when confronted with many more options than they had before' (p. 92). For both Giddens and the French economist Alain Lipietz, a central challenge, which any renewal of the welfare state must face, is 'the ecological crisis' and the 'impasse of productivism'. This perhaps is the potential for transformative politics, but one that still lies far beyond the current politics of unemployment.

Endnotes

1   At the release of the latest appalling unemployment figures the most appropriate response seemed to come from the Managing Director of Daimaru (the Japanese Department Store in Melbourne) who asked, with some passion, "When are we going to make unemployment public enemy number one?"

2   At the same time this constitutes a genuine opportunity for the Labor Party now in opposition to construct a new policy framework. Conferences such as these take on a particular significance at such moments.

3   See Pixley (1993, especially Chapter 7) for a full discussion of this period.

4   Bill Kelty, speaking at The Australia Institute Seminar on Redistributing Work: Innovative Solutions to Unemployment and Overwork, Parliament House, Canberra, 24 March 1997. For a further analysis of the Labor Government's recent approach to unemployment see Probert (1995).

5   The introduction of individual case management under *Working Nation*, represented a significant new departure for Labor, for example.

6   The significance of the Green Paper's programmatic title, *Restoring Full Employment*, in contrast to the White Paper's ambiguous title *Working Nation*, was noted by many.

7   Given this bi-partisan definition of the unemployment problem it is perhaps rather surprising that there has not been a greater backlash around the charac-

teristics of one or more of these identified 'problem' groups, or a greater tendency to prioritise their rights. Pauline Hanson's attack on Asian immigrants and handouts for Aborigines is the significant exception. Women's rights to work seem to be rather better established than they were in the 1970s.

8   An ARC funded research project following the fate of a large cohort of retrenched clothing, textile and footwear employees has found that the majority have failed to find employment three years after the event, despite the best intentioned retraining program (Weller 1997).

9   In the case of passenger motor vehicles, and clothing, textiles and footwear, we clearly see a powerful cross class alliance at work in defense of employment in these industries. Yet, it would be hard to be sanguine about future outcomes. See the section below on arguments for a new 'post-Protection' settlement.

10 For a review of some recent European developments, see Hugh Compston (ed.), *The New Politics of Unemployment: Radical Policy Initiatives in Western Europe*, Routledge, London and New York, 1997.

11 Responding to the Howard government's backdown on tariff cuts for the motor vehicle industry, Padraic McGuinness insisted that tariff cuts are the key to increasing Australia's welfare. 'This is by now an incontrovertible conclusion, although of course, there are valid arguments about the adjustment costs, the welfare costs and the human costs' (*The Age*, 16 July 1997)

12 For scholarly accounts of the significance of Keynesianism in Australia see Smyth (1994); Whitwell (1994).

13 An analysis of the nature of middle class and capitalist class support for full employment would be of assistance here. This might include looking at the way Area Consultative Committee's have functioned, the role of high profile individuals and groups such as Lindsay Fox, or the Body Shop, as well as the support for employment protecting industry planning in areas such as clothing, textiles and footwear and the motor industry.

14 Glyn and Gregg (1994) conclude that 'the immediate cause of the upward trend in joblessness has been increased demand for work rather than reduced availability', with women creating the increased demand (p. 5).

15 See Pfau-Effinger (1992) for a discussion of the concept of a gender contract and a comparison of Finland and Germany.

References

Buchanan, John (1997), *Reforming Working Time*, Brotherhood of St Laurence, Melbourne, Victoria.

Buchanan, John (1993), 'The importance of employers and coordination arrangements' in Paul Smyth (ed.), *The Employment White Paper: A New Social Charter*, Discussion Papers No 1. UNIYA, Sydney.

Castles, Francis G (1985), *The Working Class and Welfare: Reflections on the Political Development of the Welfare State in Australia and New Zealand*, Allen and Unwin, Sydney.

Committee on Employment Opportunities (1993), *Restoring Full Employment: A Discussion Paper*, Australian Government Publishing Service, Canberra.

Esping-Anderson, Gosta (1990), *The Three Worlds of Welfare Capitalism*, Polity Press, Cambridge

Freeland, John (1995), 'Reconceptualising work, full employment and incomes policies', *The Future of Work*, ed. Australian Council of Social Service, Pluto Press, Sydney.

Giddens, Anthony (1994), *Beyond Left and Right: The Future of Radical Politics*, Cambridge, Polity Press

Glyn, A. and B. Rowthorn (1988), 'European Unemployment, Corporatism and Structural Change', *American Economic Review*, May.

Glyn, Andrew and Paul Gregg (1994), 'Employment in the Developed Market Economies', Paper prepared for the United Nations World Economic Report.

Gregory, R. G. and B. Hunter (1995), 'The macro economy and the growth of ghettos and urban poverty in Australia', Centre for Economic Policy Research, ANU. Discussion Paper No 325.

Kelly, Paul (1992), *The End of Certainty*, Allen and Unwin, Sydney.

Langmore, John and John Quiggin (1994), *Work For All: Full Employment in the Nineties*, Melbourne University Press, Melbourne

Lipietz, Alain (1992), *Towards a New Economic Order*, Polity Press, Cambridge.

Pfau-Effinger, B. (1992), 'Modernisation, culture and part-time employment: the example of Finland and West Germany', *Work Employment and Society*, 7, 3, pp. 383–410.

Pixley, Jocelyn (1993), *Citizenship and Employment: Investigating Post-Industrial Options*, Cambridge University Press, Melbourne.

Probert, Belinda (1997), 'Gender and choice: the structure of opportunity', in Paul James, Walter Veit and Steve Wright (eds), *Work of the Future: Global Perspectives*, Allen and Unwin, Sydney.

Probert, Belinda (1994), 'Thinking about the White Paper: Problems for a Working Nation', *Australian Geographer*, 25, 2, November

Probert, Belinda (1994), 'The Employment White Paper: Proposals for New Directions', in Paul Smyth (ed.), *The Employment White Paper: A New Social Charter?*, Discussion Papers No. 3, UNIYA.

Skocpol, Theda (1990), 'Brother, can you spare a job? Work and Welfare in the United States', in *The Nature of Work: Sociological Perspectives*, eds Kai Erikson and Steven Peter Vallas, Yale University Press.

Smith, Rodney (1993), 'Australian attitudes to employment and unemployment', in *The Employment White Paper: A New Social Charter*, ed. Paul Smyth, UNIYA, Sydney.

Smyth, Paul (1996), 'Reinventing full employment: Work for All in retrospect', paper presented to the Academy of Social Sciences Workshop on Employment, Equality and Inequality in Australia, Canberra.

Smyth, Paul (1994), *Australian Social Policy: The Keynesian Chapter*, University of New South Wales Press, Sydney.

Therborn, Goran (1986), *Why Some People Are More Unemployed Than Others*, Verso, London.

Van Parijs, P. (1992), 'Competing Justifications of Basic Income', in Van Parijs (ed.), *Arguments for Basic Income*, Verso, London.

Watts, Robert (1997), 'Ten years on: Francis G. Castles and the Australian 'wage-earners' welfare state', *Australian and New Zealand Journal of Sociology*, 33, 1, March.

Whitwell, Greg (1994), 'The power of economic ideas? Keynesian economic policies in post-war Australia', in Stephen Bell and Brian Head (eds), *State, Economy and Public Policy in Australia*, Oxford University Press, Melbourne

Wolcott, Ilene (1996), 'Work and Family in Australia: Reality and Rhetoric', paper presented the Families and Work Seminar, Family Policy Studies Centre, London, January.

Working Nation: Policies and Programs (1994), AGPS, Canberra.